D1567577

Plant and Maintenance Manager's Desk Book

Plant and Maintenance Manager's Desk Book

W. H. Weiss

AMACOM
American Management Association
New York • Atlanta • Boston • Chicago • Kansas City • San Francisco • Washington, D. C.
Brussels • Mexico City • Tokyo • Toronto

This publication is designed to provide accurate and authoritative information in regard to the subject matter covered. It is sold with the understanding that the publisher is not engaged in rendering legal, accounting, or other professional service. If legal advice or other expert assistance is required, the services of a competent professional person should be sought.

Library of Congress Cataloging-in-Publication Data

Weiss, W. H.
    Plant and maintenance manager's desk book / W. H. Weiss.
        p.   cm.
    Includes index.
    ISBN 0-8144-0329-8
    1. Factory management. 2. Plant maintenance—Management.
3. Plant engineering.   I. Title.
    TS155.W447   1997
    658.2—dc21   97–16067
                                                        CIP

Printing number

10 9 8 7 6 5 4 3 2 1

Contents

List of Exhibits

Preface

This book is written for plant and facility managers, including maintenance managers who are involved with manufacturing, processing, and other industrial operations. In this book you'll find sound and practical advice for setting up the plant organization, for decision making, directing employees, performing operations, and providing the services needed to enable the plant to run efficiently and profitably.

Plant & Maintenance Manager's Desk Book is designed to furnish information and explanations of how the basic principles of management and operation of a plant are carried out. The book was written to aid you in handling your major problems and to answer your questions on the subject of managing a plant. Since it covers the full range of the plant manager's responsibilities and provides practical solutions to everyday plant problems, you should have it handy to refer to daily.

The book was written also because of the widespread need of managers to know about the many regulations of governmental agencies, ways to train and motivate employees, and how to make the most of outside resources. Although a plant manager's major responsibility is to safely and profitably operate a facility, the job is much simpler and easier if you understand plant operations, production and maintenance functions, and the many systems and tools used in the plant to achieve the company's objectives.

Plant & Maintenance Manager's Desk Book covers these subjects in a clear, descriptive, and comprehensive fashion. The first five chapters deal with the organizational structure of the plant, company policy, management techniques, communications, and the use of computers. This is followed by techniques for helping plant and maintenance managers in their relations with employees. These chapters cover safety, compliance with federal regulations, training, and working with the union. Other chapters discuss the technical aspects of plant management including layout and design, equipment, material handling, and cost control.

Later chapters are concerned with improving plant and employee performance, the benefits and advantages of ergonomic applications, dealing with contractors and service groups, and the need for environmental control.

The information and data in this book are arranged so that you can locate them quickly. Thus, the material is given not only in the usual manner by subject and main heading but also by subheadings and sub-subheadings. With a very expansive index that is extensively cross-referenced, you can easily find information and data you're looking for.

Much effort has been made to fill this book with the latest successful procedures covering most of the troublesome situations or problems a plant manager encounters. With information and subject coverage like this, *Plant & Maintenance Manager's Desk Book* will prove to be a big help to you in your management job.

W. H. Weiss

Organization and Principles

A plant doesn't run by itself. You need able and efficient employees, effective leadership from all levels of management, teamwork, and cooperation of the plant's departments to carry out the operations and processes.

The objective of organization is to set up relationships and procedures in which employees can obtain the best results from their combined efforts. This is to be accomplished by minimizing and overcoming the negative factors of conflict, confusion, and frustration. The stronger the structure of the organization, the more efficient and smooth-running the plant will be.

Because the organizational structure is based on what the plant is to accomplish in the quantity, quality, and cost of its output, there must be specific objectives in mind when it is established. In addition, policies must be instituted to guide various company functions and decisions. Leadership and management responsibilities must be practiced full-time if the plant is to operate successfully.

FORMAL AND INFORMAL ORGANIZATIONS

A formal organization dictates the relationships among people and resources. These are organized in an optimal way to facilitate the accomplishment of the work of the organization. The strategy that exercises the most influence or control of a company leads to its structure. A company puts in place a formal organization to maximize its human and other resources; this formal organization depends greatly on what the company wants to accomplish.

Typically, the formal organization is a system of reporting, responsibility, and authority that reflects the power of the organization members. An informal system of interpersonal relationships, known as the informal organization, springs up around the formal one. For a company to be most effective, the formal and informal organizations have to support each other.

The informal organization is a complex network in that the relationships between its members cannot be diagrammed like the formal organization, yet they are just as important to the smooth operation of a company. By their nature, they are different for every company and are continually changing. This organization is made up of ad hoc work groups and friendships among employees that cross functional lines. Noted for its spirit of cooperation and service, the informal organization is seen as the human side of the formal organization. The intangible nature or culture of the organization distinguishes one company from another.

CENTRALIZATION AND DECENTRALIZATION

When businesses develop their optimal organization, they frequently arrange for some parts of the company to be centralized and others decentralized. If a plant is in a highly competitive industry such as the manufacture of computer hardware or software, for example, its organizational structure must supply various types of communication equipment and service for the consumer. This type of plant needs to be supported by a decentralized network of service- and customer-oriented retail dealers.

LINE AND STAFF

Regardless of the level of centralization that a company is structured for, each position on the organizational chart has either a line or a staff relationship with the other positions. Line positions such as production, maintenance, and subsidiary processing groups are directly involved in making the output of the organization profitable. They accomplish the major objectives of the organization. These line positions constitute the functions, processes, or departments around which the company is organized.

Staff positions furnish line departments with advice and assistance, usually of a technical nature. Departments like human resources, safety, accounting, and research and development are common to most of the larger manufacturing plants. Staff managers support the line managers and line workers at all levels in the organization. Efficiently operated plants develop staff departments only to the size required to adequately service the needs of the line departments.

ORGANIZATIONAL PROCEDURES

Organization is a procedure that involves planning. We build a plant and start manufacturing something—not to have an organization, but for a purpose; basically, to satisfy a consumer need or want. We then come up with a plan to achieve that purpose, followed by the creation of an organization to implement that plan.

Analyzing, identifying, and defining the work to be performed or the job to be done to meet the plant's purpose are the basics of organizing.[1] If you do this properly and in an encompassing manner, you will arrange for a grouping of work and a means for individuals (plant employees) to cooperate effectively and efficiently in achieving objectives.

Effective organizing requires that management take several steps:

1. *Unity of purpose.* Determine what work is to be performed.
2. *Division of labor.* Decide what has to be done to achieve that purpose: what functions must be carried out, who will carry them out, and what authority they will have to accomplish the work.
3. *Staffing.* Determine the type, number, and experience of individuals who will implement the work.
4. *Structure or organizational framework.* Develop the chain of command and flow of information to provide for teamwork in terms of reporting relationships.
5. *Managing.* Make a commitment to get things done effectively through others. The organizational structure is the vehicle to make this happen.

If management does not adopt sound management principles, the employees will find ways to bypass the structure. This may result in the organization not being as effective as it might be. The performance of management usually determines whether a plant operation is profitable or not. Exhibit 1-1 shows a typical organization chart for a small plant engaged in manufacturing one or more products. This plant operates twenty-four hours a day with three shifts. The horizontal line across the chart separates hourly from salary employees.

The managerial structure may differ as the company expands, down-

Exhibit 1-1. Organization chart for a small manufacturing plant.

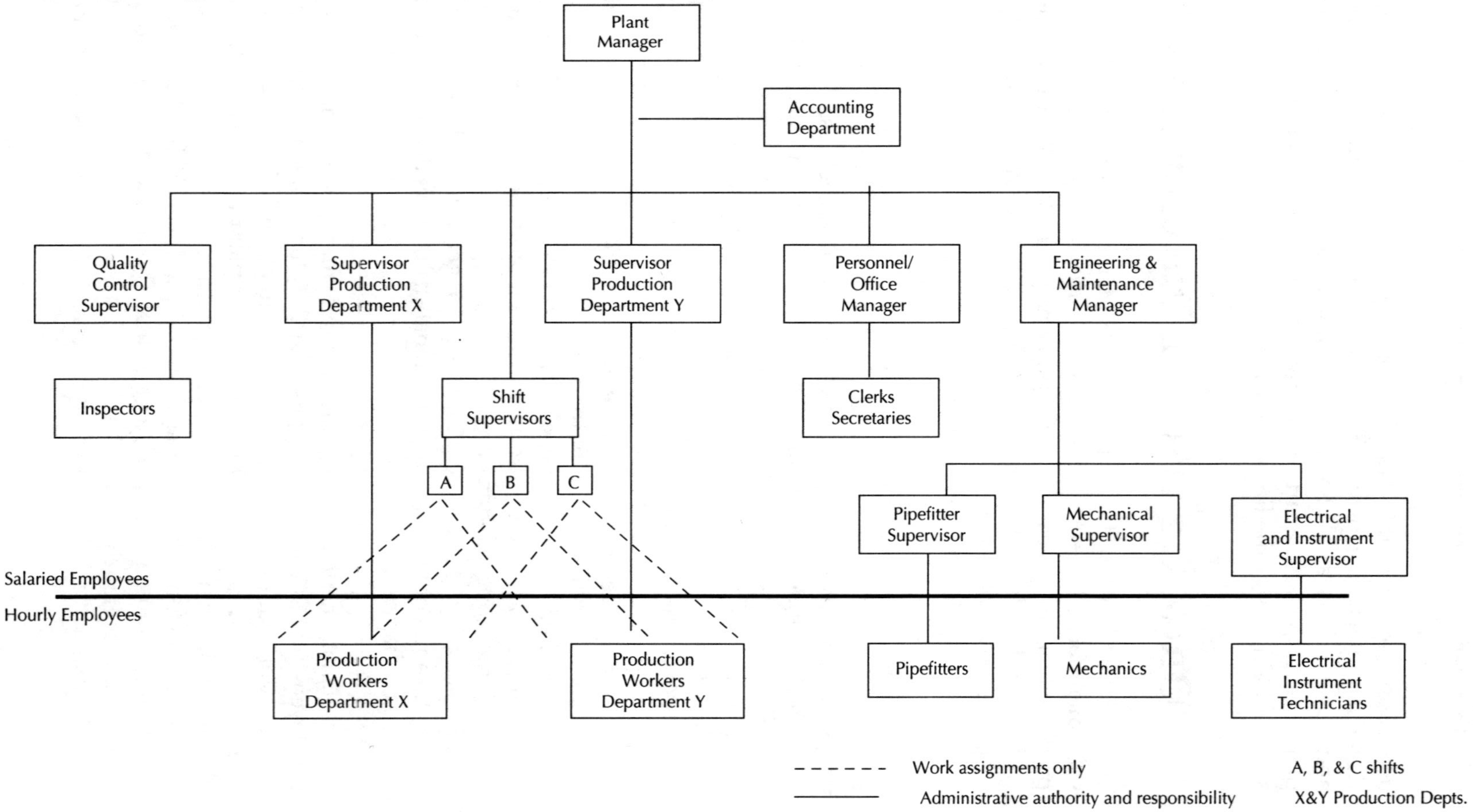

Salaried Employees

Hourly Employees

- - - - - Work assignments only

————— Administrative authority and responsibility

A, B, & C shifts

X&Y Production Depts.

sizes, or changes its product line. However, the point at which the structure needs to be revised because of one or more of these activities cannot be determined by rules; it must be determined by the plant circumstances. For example, a plant might need a technical superintendent and a staff of chemical engineers if it starts producing chemicals or engages in chemical processes. Regardless of the size of the plant or the extent of its development, management must initiate and implement the following principles when creating the managerial structure:

1. *Set up a chain of command.* Every plant employee reports to and takes orders from one supervisor only. Although employees are usually hired by the human resources department, they are trained, promoted, and receive their primary work instructions from their department supervisors. When on shift, however, they get instructions and assignments from the shift supervisors. Exhibit 1-1 shows this by dotted lines.[2] When dotted-line situations exist, the point where the authority of one manager ends and another begins should be clearly defined.

2. *Decide on the span of control.* Most authorities agree that the optimum number of employees one manager can supervise is eight to twelve, but this number is best determined by the conditions of the job. When employees are spread out over a large area, or are performing complex operations, a smaller number may be better. When they are all in the same room, or doing relatively simple jobs, a supervisor may be able to handle thirty employees or more.

3. *Minimize the number of employees.* If more help is needed later, it is easier to add people than to face the problem of eliminating some if there is no work to do. Innocent people should not be made to suffer because of a management error.

4. *Adopt the principle of definition.* This is accomplished by writing out job descriptions. Job descriptions are critical to the operation of the plant because they cover the areas of responsibilities for each member of management and staff. They should include:

- Job title
- Minimum requirements for eligibility, including education, skills, and work experience
- List of specific duties and responsibilities, starting with the most important elements of the job
- Extent of authority that goes with the job
- Job location in the chain of command

5. *Assign employee responsibilities.* Management should never rely on verbal assignments on matters of this importance; they are too confusing,

may be easily misinterpreted, and sometimes overlap. The most reliable document for determining the responsibilities of employees is a Company Operations Manual or a compilation of Standard Practice sheets. Usually consisting of forms and notices, and distributed in a looseleaf binder, a manual contains the responsibilities of both departments and individuals. Often it also includes the procedures to be followed in operating the plant as well as running the processes.

Management should revise and update responsibilities as personnel are reassigned and as process methods, equipment, and operational procedures change. The updates and revisions should be as clear and organized as the documents they replace. It's critical that they be made prior to or at the same time as the changes requiring them.

STRUCTURED ORGANIZATION

Although the principles of structured organization run counter to all of the work-team/empowered employee philosophy currently popular, it has long been felt that to assure high productivity, emphasis must be placed on the management functions that promote efficiency and job accomplishment. Building a structured organization of employees and group leaders is the way it is achieved.

You need to determine what work needs to be done, who will do it, and what will be required to do it. The procedure involves several steps, which must be followed in sequence. Avoid making a list of jobs to be done; instead establish the basic tasks that must be accomplished, and proceed from there.

Start by listing the tasks that must be done by the employees. But make no decisions about job content until your list of what you expect the employees to accomplish is complete. Working from this list, combine the tasks in different ways into jobs. This gives you a way to find the best combinations of tasks and jobs for your company—those that will result in the greatest output at the lowest operating cost.

Next, group the employees into sections and departments. To achieve the best efficiency at the lowest cost, whether you are reworking an old system or building a new one, choose between process and product orientation. Adopt the system that requires the least number of people. Verify your decision by acknowledging offsetting cost factors. You may have to make a cost analysis to clarify the question.

Then provide the amount of supervision and/or group leaders you anticipate will be needed. When developing the management structure, keep it lean, ensure unity of command, determine the span of control, and specify the line-staff relationship.

Make sure that all departments are assigned responsibilities. Put them in writing and match the responsibilities assigned to a group with its numbers, skills, and physical facilities. Responsibilities must be re-assigned as process methods, equipment, and available labor skills change.

To keep the organization running smoothly, coordinate the activities of the sections and departments. Do this by arranging the use of facilities, machines, and equipment to avoid conflicts. Also, specify the condition in which materials completed by one department are to be passed on to the next. Last, require cooperation among departments and help them in their lateral communications.

COMPANY POLICY

Company policy[3] is an understanding among members of a company that makes the actions of each member in a given set of circumstances more predictable to other members. Yet it is one of the most impersonal elements in any company.

Policy statements are usually limited in distribution to those people with an established need, but all employees should be able to locate any particular policy quickly. You should have a complete and current set of policy statements directly affecting your and other managers' functions.

Although company policies usually originate with top management and arise from a need of middle or lower management, they also may be inferred, from the actions of managers; in addition, they may be required to comply with trade associations or government agencies. Policies may apply to all departments of a company or only one, yet they are generally considered to be the company's most important decisions.

Policies may have limitations as well as faults. Lack of understanding of a policy is the greatest limitation on its effective use faced by a company and its management people. A given policy may be unsound in concept or incorrectly stated, thus hindering achievement of company objectives. The climate and environment of business operations may change, calling for a policy change that is not made; left as it is, the original policy will be misleading and will inhibit effective planning and action.

If you get into the habit of referring to a company policy as the only reason for your action, you are using the policy as a crutch, and defeating its intent. Although policies support and provide direction to the actions of all management people, if a policy remains in existence long after conditions have changed, it can impede progress. If policies are stated in broad and clear terms, they may tend to encourage managers to avoid responsibility for their own decisions.

Rigid adherence to policies often leads to unforeseen and unwanted consequences. People are different, one from another, and the situations they get into are seldom exactly alike. However, the person who originated the policy or made the rule had to assume that all the situations covered by that rule in the future would almost exactly duplicate the specific one he or she had in mind when framing it. This is why the rules found in policy manuals may sometimes seem unrealistic or impractical to the persons who are asked to follow them. A first-line manager coming across such a rule might be heard to say, "I can see that whoever made that rule never worked as a first-line manager."

Policy manuals can be of great help to you if the statements and guidelines are presented in terms of goals and objectives. Manuals should simply outline the ways and means that users should consider in managing. In this form, a policy manual would be looked upon as standard practice instructions designed to ensure consistency and uniformity in handling most standardizable work.

Guidelines for Critical Company Policy

Status in the community and the well-being of a company are closely related to a plant's ability to provide products that are not only useful, but durable, reliable, and dependable. There may even be a number of public laws that define a plant's obligations.

Product quality and safety are so important to customer relations and to a company's reputation that the company may create a department in the plant whose sole responsibility is to oversee those functions. One of its responsibilities is to monitor the company's performance and ensure that it is always in compliance with the law and the company's quality standards.

In carrying out this responsibility, the department may periodically issue letters to officers and employees of the company stating the company's policy in specific areas. Typically, a letter may read as follows:

> No matter what your job is—salesperson or secretary, repairman or researcher, production worker or trainee—you share the responsibility of immediately reporting to your superior whenever you know, or even suspect, that a company product is unsafe or inferior.
>
> The rule of thumb is this: If you have only the slightest doubt, report it to your superior, who, in turn, has the responsibility of reporting the information to the Quality Control Manager having direct responsibility for the product in question. A safety-related defect is admittedly difficult to define. A generally accepted rule is that a product defect that creates a risk of injury to anyone is considered a safety-related defect.

In all our relationships, we strive to act as responsible corporate citizens in matters of product quality and safety. You are directed to give complete dedication to this policy.

Evaluating and Promoting Company Policy

Since other managers and employees may not tell you directly what they think about company policies, you must read and interpret various sources of information to gain this knowledge. Here are a few matters you can attend to in this respect:

- Study performance appraisals to learn what other managers are saying about subordinates.
- Analyze grievance complaints to identify areas where policies and procedures are being tested.
- Review reports of training programs to tell you where there are weaknesses or deficiencies.
- Critique the feedback that the company received from outside consultants.

All of this feedback will help you evaluate existing policies and procedures and pinpoint areas which some day may become problems or at least require revision.

The ability to "sell" company policy is critical. By being an advocate of the policies, and showing employees precisely what they can do to improve the company, you contribute to the plant's success. Whether it is improved productivity, better quality, more job satisfaction, reduced stress, or smoother operations, all help the company's image in the community and enable it to grow.

LEADERSHIP AND MANAGEMENT

Now, as perhaps never before, there is a growing awareness that the success and profitability of plant organizations are directly dependent on the effective use of human resources. The real test of your ability as a leader and manager is how skilled you are in establishing and maintaining human organizations.

Leadership and management are responsibilities that must be practiced full-time. Each minute must be spent wisely, and this is not easy. Because they involve the complexities and eccentricities of people, leadership and management almost defy description and understanding. Along the same line, it is still virtually impossible to identify with certainty, the specific causal factors that determine managerial success at a specific time and place. This is because real-life situations are in a constant state of change, with many factors or variables in place at the same time.

Distinction Between Leadership and Management

While these two concepts are often thought of as one and the same, there is an important distinction between them. Leadership is a broader, more encompassing, process than management. Management is a special kind of leadership in which the achievement of organizational goals is of most importance. The primary difference between the two concepts originates with the word *organization*. Leadership manifests itself anytime you try to influence the behavior of an individual or group, regardless of the reason. It may be for your own goals or for those of others, and the goals may or may not agree with organizational goals.

LEADERSHIP SKILLS

To lead effectively and dynamically, you must possess three competencies:

1. The skill of diagnosing—being able to understand the situation you are trying to influence
2. The skill of adapting—being able to adjust or fit your behavior and your other resources to meet the contingencies of the situation
3. The skill of communicating clearly—being able to communicate in a way that people can easily understand and accept

COMPONENTS OF EFFECTIVE LEADERSHIP

It's a good idea to be familiar with the latest information and advice concerning motivation and leadership. You will find much coverage of these subjects in subsequent chapters of this book. To benefit the most, you should place emphasis on those procedures that best fit your situation and the conditions in the plant. Here are the most significant ones:

■ *Concentrate on the most important parts of your job.* One of these concerns how you respond to forces and events outside your control: unexpected equipment breakdowns, labor problems, governmental regulations, and the like. Although your attention to these matters is necessary, handling them successfully gains you only a reputation for competence.

The more critical part of your job consists of the work you, as a manager and leader, should do. It involves the opportunities for the plant to outdistance the competition, increase safety, improve product quality, cut costs, and operate the plant more effectively and efficiently. Whatever the area, this effort sets you apart from all other managers, and establishes you as a true leader.

- *Set high standards for yourself.* If you set a good example by the amount of energy you put into your work and your determination to reach objectives, you will challenge your organization to match your performance. The only way you can expect high standards of performance from subordinates is to set even higher standards for yourself.

- *Assure that the needs of employees are satisfied.* The lowest needs of people are food, clothing, and shelter. Higher needs are recognition, security, belonging, and self-fulfillment. Plant employees can get the lowest needs by working almost anywhere, and sometimes by not working at all. Therefore, their willingness to stay and to work hard at the plant depends on the degree to which the needs for recognition, belonging, and feeling that they are involved in something worthwhile are filled.

You should be aware, however, that sometimes the needs of the employees and those of the company are in conflict. Also, not all psychological needs can be provided by working in the plant. You must identify those areas where the needs of each coincide, for example, in safety, and use this fact to the greatest advantage of both. When you have identified the areas of conflict, as in absenteeism, you can face up to them so that employees know where they stand.

- *Develop strong and efficient subordinates.* If employees are to feel that they are growing and increasing their knowledge, they need to be given challenging assignments; as they successfully complete such projects, their self-confidence and sense of participation increase. Managers who develop their subordinates not only have a stronger team working in the plant, but they create additional time in which to be productive on their own jobs.

- *Perfect your managerial style.* There are three concerns to keep in mind as you work at becoming known for your distinctive style of managing:

1. Study your own personality and adopt those management techniques that suit you best.
2. Alter and modify any personality traits that conflict with your job objectives or the company's philosophy.

3. Avoid trying to imitate someone else's style of managing; you'd be unconvincing and appear to be insincere.

LEADERSHIP QUALITIES MOTIVATE EMPLOYEES

The Menniger Letter[4] recently discussed transformational leadership as a factor in motivating employees. With today's trend of layoffs, early retirements, and reengineering, the question of how best to manage and motivate employees is a significant one. Researchers are increasingly finding that employees are more motivated, productive, and satisfied in an atmosphere of transformational leadership.

Transformational leaders move employees beyond self-interest to concern for the overall organization by encouraging the questioning of basic assumptions and problem-solving from new perspectives. They unite them with a common purpose or mission, and they encourage them to view challenges as opportunities.

Employees identify with and emulate transformational leaders who motivate them to work toward mutually desirable goals. Many of these employees also feel supported in thinking for themselves, in addressing challenges, and in considering creative ways to develop personally.

It should be noted that this leadership style is not new but rather has garnered attention in recent years because of its effective use by the growing number of female managers. Researchers Bernard Bass and Bruce Avolio of the Center for Leadership Studies in Binghamton, New York, say that female leaders, in particular, tend to structure organizations with fewer positions of authority at the top. This flatter hierarchy encourages employees to work toward achieving their own highest potential.

TEAM LEADERSHIP

One of the toughest managerial jobs is to lead work teams to the point at which they perform at their greatest potential. With the use of teams on the rise in the automotive industry and elsewhere, managers need to learn to become effective team leaders.

A self-directed work team is a good example of where astute leadership is required if the team is going to be successful. Employees on such a team are responsible for identifying and solving problems, setting goals, and, in some cases, even arranging their own work hours. Although it may seem that there's not much left for a team leader to do, his or her job actually involves several activities of a leadership nature. These include identifying training needs, deciding which team members to train, providing overall support, and others. Of most concern, the leader must ensure that the members possess the right skills and abilities.

A team leader must also serve as the liaison between the team and other employees within the plant. This activity could involve representing the team in negotiations, promoting the team's accomplishments, or gathering information on matters that affect the team. Because a team environment is often stressful, managing conflict is one of the major challenges that a leader faces. No matter how much a leader tries to divide the work fairly, some members may inevitably feel that they did more than others. Additionally, a few members may feel a sense of injustice when a coworker gets a raise or promotion.

Good team leaders try to eliminate the sources of conflict among team members. They do this by creating a sense of personal accountability and achievement among team members and by motivating individuals.

MAINTENANCE LEADERSHIP

To improve their performance in maintenance, today's plants require new forms of leadership at various levels in the organization.[5] Competent leaders are challenged by the traditional management establishment and the old saw that "these are the ways things are supposed to get done in our company."

Although these leaders work with plant employees to achieve remarkable results, it is difficult for some to become leaders without support from their superiors. Nurturing works both up and down the company. In addition to needing security, effective leaders must know that their superiors are effective leaders too. Leadership beliefs, values, and behaviors start at the top of the organization and "rub off" on individuals on the plant floor and on crew leaders. Leadership skills to improve a company's effectiveness are not limited to management. There usually are a few able leaders among the hourly employees.

Leadership flexibility is one of the requisites of effective maintenance managers. They must constantly shift between being a manager, leader, or team member to fit the current situation. The combination is essential for high performance leadership. Most traditional managers stay with one role, one style. Typically, one role is all they learned and all that was expected of them.

Maintenance managers should pay close attention to the needs of their work group and the requirements of the jobs they perform in the plant. They can then decide what would be the best leadership style to use under particular circumstances. For example, when the work group obviously needs direction, they can provide detailed instructions while also closely supervising the work. Leadership of this type is essential if the work group is relatively young and inexperienced or the levels of overall job competence are fairly low.

If the work group needs coaching, the manager explains why the job is important and must be performed in a certain manner. The manager should also ask the group for ideas and suggestions on how to do certain jobs more efficiently. Coaching is appropriate when workers are gaining experience and learning how to work together with a leader.

Occasionally, the work group may need support. If the members understand the job enough and their skills are sufficient, the manager may be able to make an assignment without giving detailed instructions. He or she then shares the decision-making responsibility with the work group. The manager may supply additional support by securing essential data from other engineering or maintenance work groups. When work groups begin working well together and have reached progressively higher levels of job competence, the manager should commend them for their efforts.

Use of the leadership style that is most suitable to the project or job being performed often determines the time it takes to complete it. Workers get satisfaction from their jobs only when they know they've done their best and they feel they've pleased management. By recognizing that effective leadership means changing your style to suit the needs of the work group and the job, you will have taken a major step in demonstrating your competence as a manager. Learning, refining, and consistently practicing a wide variety of leadership behaviors is the next step, followed by facilitating teamwork and learning within the work group.

MANAGERIAL FUNCTIONS

The managerial functions of planning, organizing, motivating, and controlling make up the management process. This is a step-by-step way of doing something, regardless of the type of organization or level of management with which you are concerned.

Planning involves setting goals and objectives for the organization and indicating how these are to be accomplished. The procedure of organizing includes specifying how capital, machines and equipment, and people are to most effectively be used. Organizing thus is the integration of resources.

Along with planning and organizing, motivating is a factor in determining the performance level of employees which, in turn, influences how effectively and efficiently the goals will be met. Motivating, of course, plays a large part in communicating with and leading employees.

In controlling, you evaluate the progress of the organization toward its goal. You do this by measuring how operations and activities are proceeding at appropriate times, and you check to see if efforts are correctly focused. If you find a misdirection or malfunction, you take action to bring efforts back on target.

Even though these managerial functions may appear to be separate entities and as discussed seem to have a specific sequence, they are closely related. At any one time, one or more may be of primary importance.

MANAGERIAL AUTHORITY

Before you exercise your authority in the plant, you should understand what it consists of and how it should be used.[6] Some managers mistakenly believe that it comes with the job, but there are other sources.

Authority is the right to command, use resources, and influence behavior. Certain managers in a plant wield much more authority than others, although they may be shown on the organizational chart at the same job level. In addition, there are supervisors and foremen who make decisions and provide input on a variety of high-level issues. In some cases, they have more clout than other managers.

Varying degrees of authority can be best explained by examining the sources. To a great extent, the amount of authority depends on function, responsibilities, performance, expertise, behavior, and trust, Explanations of the relation and extent of authority with these sources follow:

■ *Function.* One or more functions in an organization may gradually become more important that others. Thus, managers of those functions come to have more inherent authority. For example, in recent years departments involved in technology and quality assurance have become more important, especially in manufacturing plants.

These changes in organizational authority by function will continue to occur. Managers involved in those functions will have more authority than others since they will have the ability to influence others significantly.

■ *Responsibilities.* Much of your authority arises from your job responsibilities; actually, they are the only legal authority you have. Responsibilities represent the decision-making limits inherent in the job and the control that you exercise over the subordinates who report to you.

■ *Performance.* Managers have authority based on their individual performance. Top performers command respect and are able to influence others. They have the ability to get things done and make things happen.

Other managers will seek their guidance and direction. They may ask for help in solving organizational problems that may be outside their normal scope of responsibilities. This type of authority is developed over time through consistently high levels of performance.

- *Expertise.* Some managers acquire authority by demonstrating and being known for their skills, knowledge, and ability. First-line managers, in particular, with high levels of competence are valuable to a plant, especially if they share their knowledge and skills with others. They are usually labeled technical experts and may have such credentials as advanced degrees or professional certifications. It has been common practice in recent years to place chemical engineers in first-line managerial positions in chemical manufacturing and chemical process plants. Since they have the technical know-how and know what to do at a given time, they exert much influence over others.

- *Behavior.* Managers also have authority based on their personal behavior and actions toward others in the plant. They look, feel, think, act, and react to events and other employees in a positive manner. Consequently, they attract others as well as influence their behavior.

- *Trust.* Authority based on trust refers to the quality of relationships with other managers and those others with whom they have regular contact. Managers with high degrees of this kind of authority work with people in an open and honest way. They have no ulterior motives or hidden agendas. Other individuals know where they stand and will trust these managers and their actions because they have the best interests of others in mind, as well as those of the plant.

Being a Leader Rather Than a Driver

How well do you get along with your subordinates? Do they respect and admire you? If there is a question in your mind about this relationship, maybe you are more a driver than a leader. A driver demands things be done rather than requesting something in a normal way. A driver doesn't really look for respect or cooperation, relying mostly on authority to move subordinates.

If you are a driver, you are probably weak in handling the human relations aspect of your job as well. Nevertheless, you should be aware that pressure tactics simply don't pay off in dealing with people in the plant. Here are some of the most common taboos when it comes to treating others, along with why they are considered poor managerial techniques.

- *Don't set impossible goals.* If you allow subordinates to plan their own work and set their own goals, you avoid setting impossible goals for them.

Few activities provide as much potential for increasing one's motivation as the determining of one's own schedule. When you demand increased productivity, you gain only stressed and frustrated employees.

■ *Don't find fault.* Avoid finding fault with the work or performance of anyone. Everyone needs to feel that they're doing a good job, even though you may occasionally point out where they can make improvements. Since most jobs are done well rather than poorly, show that you are as skilled at recognizing good work as you are at recognizing bad.

■ *Don't instill fear.* Realize that you can't get more work or better performance out of people by threatening them. Punishment has only a minimal, if any, effect on productivity. What you most likely get from threats are poor morale, high absenteeism, and dissatisfied employees.

■ *Don't oversupervise.* When you hand out assignments, move out of subordinates' way and let them handle the project the way they see fit. Show confidence in their abilities by not oversupervising them. If you furnish too much direction, you deprive them of being creative, and they will not be able to demonstrate their competence.

■ *Don't argue.* There is never a need for you to argue with anyone in the plant; people know that you are in charge. If a first-line manager handles an assignment poorly, or is wrong in his or her thinking, say so. But if you make an argumentive remark, you are in trouble. Although you may win an argument, you lose something much more valuable—the cooperation and respect that you need to be a successful manager.

■ *Don't overrule.* Always have a very good reason to reverse or overturn one of your subordinate's decisions. Never blame someone for a bad decision. Instead, take the opportunity to improve your communications with the individual, and commend initiative. If you don't have a face-saving reason for overruling someone, look for one. You don't want to destroy a person's ego and self-confidence.

Giving Orders

To give an order is a comparatively easy thing to do. But to give an order and get results is something different. The results you get usually are directly proportional to how much thought and planning you did before giving the order. By analyzing what you want done and then giving the order clearly and completely, you have a much better chance of getting good results.

Recognize that orders given too briefly may not be carried out properly. Consider all the information required, and then state each item in as few words as possible. With this procedure, you are not likely to confuse the person receiving the order.

SOCIALLY RESPONSIBLE MANAGERS

Should business and industry be bound only by civil laws or should they also comply with moral laws? Social responsibility has become an issue in management circles. After all, business and industry have the resources, the skills, and the opportunities. And it can be argued that developing a healthy society will serve corporate self-interest.

If industry takes on a bigger share of the job of improving society than government, the matter of cost must be considered. In the case of industry, it must be passed on to the consumer; in the case of the government, it is borne by the taxpayer. As to what has already been done, industry has expended large sums in environmental efforts by paying the bills for cleaning up air and water. Government has contributed through various agencies and regulatory bodies that have been created.

However, ethics, reliability, and professionalism are of more concern to society than money in searching for answers to who should contribute what. More and more people are losing confidence in their government and looking to the corporations to solve public problems and provide society with better living conditions. The public looks for help from business and industry to solve major social problems including crime, discrimination, poverty, health, and education, among others.

Opposing Viewpoints

Not all experts and influential persons agree that moral issues should be the businessman's concern. Economist Milton Friedman frequently stated that business can serve society best by concentrating on what it does best; that is, doing business. Robert V. Horton, assistant professor of economics at Purdue University, Lafayette, Indiana, and a former general partner at Goldman, Sachs & Company, said, "Business has no public responsibilities beyond conducting itself within legal restraints. Its sole purpose is to make a profit for its stockholders or owners. That's how it can best serve the public."

Frederick W. Dow, professor of marketing at the University of Notre Dame's College of Business Administration, said, "Business must go beyond the pure economics of any issue, but we have no right to ask it to solve the social ills of the world. I believe there's a great deal of misunderstanding of the role private enterprise plays in our society. People argue that if business only had proper ethics we'd solve all our problems. This simply isn't so."

Social Responsibility

What is it going to require on the part of the industrial plant manager and the corporation leader if the trend to expect help from business on the problems of society continues to grow? Business leaders and plant managers will be faced with some great challenges. To meet them, they will have to change some of their thinking, go beyond the profit goal for their organization, and think more of the needs and wants of the public. The public does not really object to profit-making per se, but it expects the profits to be used for the public good. The public more and more is expecting corporations to show response to its needs.

Consumers think they should get better service and longer life from the products they buy. They sense that many items have built-in obsolescence, and this concerns them. In their alarm with environmental problems, they frequently point at industry as being responsible, if not directly such as by pollution, then indirectly by being the manufacturer of an offensive product.

The realization is emerging that managers will have to humanize their thinking and decision making. They must concentrate more on what is good for the community and relate it to what they know will be good for their companies. They are going to have to show more professionalism in what they say and do.

To be professional is to be "engaged in, or worthy of, the high standards of a profession," according to Webster. Professionalism is a base of ethical behavior that manifests itself in honesty and integrity. Professionals operate under a standard of values that they will not violate. They have empathy and sympathy toward people and they accomplish their objectives without using or hurting them.

Industrial managers feel they should be considered professional; they say they have no less morals and consciences than other professionals. They want to be recognized as good and responsible citizens. But also, they are aware and may even revel in their position—to do what is best for their company and yet be able to present their action and deed as a "social responsibility."

To demonstrate professionalism, the people in the top echelon of business organizations must do more than the minimum necessary to enable them to hold their jobs. By their actions they need to show that they are equally interested in serving society and in making a profit for their companies.

To live up to the hopes of the public is not going to be easy since a negative attitude toward business exists in the minds of some people. Business has often been criticized in that it does not have the public interest in mind, in that the goals and objectives of business are not compatible with those of society.

Unfortunately, business periodically has been guilty of promoting this negative image through corrupt and illegal doings. In addition, business sometimes fails to do a good job through false advertising, by putting out inferior products, and by overcharging for them. In order for business to gain the confidence of the public, it's going to need to clean up its house and, above all, get its story across to the public on what it is truly doing.

Stewart S. Cort, chairman of the board of Bethlehem Steel Corporation, stated, "Although advertising and speeches are one way for management to improve the public image of business, personal contact with workers and students is the best way to create a better understanding of the American economic and business system." Cort made a point that the reason the business image suffers is because groups criticize out of lack of knowledge about business.

The growth of doubt and skepticism that government will solve problems that arise is leading to more reliance on business and its leaders to aid society and to improve the welfare of the public. The socially responsible manager, it would seem, holds the answer to improvement in our standard of living and to the continual growth of American enterprise. What this manager does and how he or she does it therefore is of much concern. Conscientious individuals operate under a standard of values and a high level of professionalism. The socially responsible manager must act, make decisions, and be an example of the highest level of professional performance.

Environmental Compliance

Many aspects of the Environmental Protection Agency's (EPA's) laws and guidelines deal with a range of maintenance controls and recordkeeping. This includes preventive maintenance of environmental equipment and various work-order logs that track repairs and contain a wealth of information on problems and their solutions. With publicizing of these laws, along with reports of fines and jail sentences for violators, you would expect that all individuals and plants affected by the laws to keep accurate maintenance records.

But such is not the case in some plants.[7] Because of the insufficient number of EPA inspectors, most violations go undetected until incidents or losses occur. Then the plants try to remedy situations and catch up with their paperwork. As for why the plants ignore these laws and regulations, it is often a lack of awareness on the part of management. But the primary reason at many plants is the obsession that companies have with "downsizing" or "rightsizing." These activities are undertaken without any (or little) consideration for the technical functions within the plant. The engineering and maintenance management functions are viewed as optional or unnecessary.

With less engineering and maintenance expertise left in the plant, the maintenance department is reduced to firefighting and situational reacting. Under such conditions, it is only a matter of time until a failure occurs in one of the systems that is key to environmental compliance. The EPA investigates and finds records showing the plant *used* to keep the necessary records and *used* to give the equipment the proper attention. However, the plant quit doing so when it eliminated jobs. Since the records show the company once had employees who knew the law, the violation appears deliberate. Thus, the EPA imposes heavier penalties, all because of socially irresponsible and unprofessional management.

NOTES

1. Patrick Montana and Bruce H. Charnov, *Management* (New York: Barron's Educational Series, Inc., 1987), pp. 148–149.
2. W. H. Weiss, *Plant Supervisor's Complete Desk Book* (Englewood Cliffs, N.J.: Prentice Hall, Inc., 1992), pp. 2–3.
3. Ibid., pp. 46–48.
4. Reprinted with permission from *The Menniger Letter* 3(8)(August 1995): 1,6. Copyright by The Menniger Foundation, Topeka, Kans.
5. Robert M. Williamson, Strategic Work Systems, Mill Spring, N.C. "The Secrets of Maintenance Leadership," *Maintenance Technology,* Applied Technology Publications, Inc., April 1993, pp. 49–50.
6. Weiss, pp. 5–7.
7. Terry Wireman, "The EPA and Maintenance Management," *Engineer's Digest,* July 1993: 10.

2

Management Strategies and Techniques

While the dictionary defines management as the act, manner, or practice of managing, handling, supervising, and controlling, management is simultaneously an art and a science. The scientific aspects of the management discipline are fairly straightforward, and anyone with average intelligence and the desire to accomplish something can learn the mechanics.

But you can't be successful as a manager if you are familiar only with the rules and procedures of managing. You need to be adept at the art of managing. This means understanding what it is you are responsible for doing, determining the best way to do it, recruiting and training the right people, and motivating these people to realize their full potential. When you adopt appropriate management strategies and advanced managerial techniques, you have the makings of an effective and efficient manager.

Like other disciplines, management involves procedures and operations such as planning, organizing, controlling, and decision making, among others. Since these topics involve skills that can be taught and learned, they can be called the objective sciences of management. Another set of topics that includes motivation, communication, training, and feedback can be called the social sciences or art of management because more subjective approaches and direct contact with other people are involved.

No activity or procedure requiring management can be successfully completed without considering and applying three functions: planning, organizing, and controlling. These functions always are carried out, to a greater or lesser degree, in every organization or company. They constitute the management cycle, a term that appropriately implies that the work done in any of the three functions is never complete in itself, but must be periodically modified to reflect changes in each of the other two.

MANAGEMENT BY OBJECTIVES

The concepts of management by objectives (MBO) were introduced by Peter Drucker in the early 1950s and have become popularized throughout the world, particularly through the efforts of George Odiore and John Humble. Since that beginning, managers in all kinds of organizational settings, whether they be industrial, educational, governmental, or military, have attempted to run their organizations by MBO procedures. Management by objectives is basically:

> A process whereby the superior and the subordinate managers of an enterprise jointly identify its common goals, define each individual's major areas of responsibility in terms of the results expected of him, and use these measures as guides for operating the unit and assessing the contribution of each of its members.[1]

Generally, medium-size and large plants today are reasonably well managed. Despite the ups and downs of the business, the complaints of a few employees, and the changes in managers and executives with time, these plants make the most of their managerial talent. While some managers are more effective than others, comparatively few fail to survive periods of austerity.

It follows that managers at all levels in such plants are usually satisfied with their performance. They adapt well to the changes and problems of conducting their plant's operations. However, a few managers have been unwilling to settle for reasonably effective organizational performance. They have looked for better methods of managing.

Management by objectives has evolved as one of the methods, and it is practiced by first-line as well as upper-level managers. An assertive attitude is an essential ingredient for the managing by objectives style. The assertive manager focuses on objectives as a natural way of getting things done.

When you manage by giving detailed step-by-step instructions to employees, the employees depend on your presence to know what they must do. Further, when they finish an assigned job, they must solicit the next assignment from you.

This procedure does not require that the employees know or agree with the purpose of the work. You simply tell them what to do and imply that they are not to do anything else. Basically, you are managing by control.

However, when you go to the trouble of explaining to employees the reason for the work they are doing, and how it fits into what other employees are doing, then employees can quite readily show an interest and desire to do a good job. In addition, when they understand the purpose behind the work and the objectives of the company, they can go ahead with further work.

Employees can proceed toward the objectives to some degree even without your presence. By explaining the overall objectives to them, you free yourself from the need to provide continual direction and guidance, and liberate the employees as well. This is management by objectives.

The successful use of management by objectives depends on two assumptions:

1. Employees do better on the job if their work has meaning to them; if they can see the reason for doing it.
2. Employees generally will work to achieve objectives if they know what those objectives are and they can expect to be rewarded for helping to reach them.

You manage by objectives when you look ahead, determine where you want to go, set a means of measuring your progress, and communicate with your people in terms of the total project.

Yet there is more to the concept. As in all goal-directed efforts, follow-up is essential to evaluating accomplishments. Such an assessment is also valuable as a precedent when setting future goals and performance levels. An assessment of performance is beneficial to both you and subordinates because it provides a totaling of accomplishments, a forum for airing problems, and an opportunity to refuel motivational drive.

Setting Objectives

Whenever you set objectives, whether it's for yourself, subordinates, or the company, you should ensure that they have the following characteristics. They should be:

■ *Specific and measurable.* An objective to reduce waste in the plant, for example, should be "To reduce waste by 25 percent by December 31," not just "To reduce waste."

■ *Inclusive of those who are responsible for achieving the objective.* People are more committed to the successful attainment of goals they helped create. Managers who participated in setting objectives for the company will work harder to achieve them.

- *Challenging but attainable.* When objectives appear impossible to reach, they are demotivating to those people involved. However, goals that require employees to "stretch" but are attainable can be very motivating. People get satisfaction from reaching goals; consequently, they are much more motivated to go after the next one.

- *Reviewed and updated regularly.* Nobody is truly interested in working hard to achieve something that has lost its value over time. Similarly, as employees gain experience and technological advances occur, goals set earlier may be reached easier and faster.

- *Ranked on their relative importance.* Recognize that at any given time, you and others in the plant will be pursuing several objectives. Obviously, some will be more important than others. You should make sure everyone is aware of the relative importance of the objectives so they can allocate their time and resources accordingly.

Advantages of Management By Objectives (MBO)

There are several advantages and benefits to be realized from the implementation of MBO in a plant:

- By establishing a system of coordinated goals at several levels of management, the goals of everyone are combined into one common objective.
- With the commitment to stated goals, management works toward better productivity, higher quality, and lower costs, rather than just "operating the plant."
- The MBO system supplies purpose and substance to the company's performance appraisal program. Managers have measurable standards to apply which they helped to create and develop.
- The system creates opportunities for employees, releases their potential, removes obstacles, encourages growth, and provides guidance.

MANAGEMENT BY EXCEPTION

Although management by exception is not a complete system of management, it is a strategy that limits its scope and defines how you will manage.[2] You simply make it clear that you will not put any time and effort on procedures, projects, and processes that are going well; only those problems that cannot be handled at a lower management level are to be brought to your attention. Adoption of this management principle requires that you meet two requisites:

1. You must have established reliable operating procedures that allow the normal daily activities to proceed smoothly without your attention.
2. You must be willing to delegate authority and to ensure that problems are handled at the lowest possible management level.

There are several benefits to be realized from managing by exception:

- You or any manager can do this, whether or not any other manager does.

- You gain additional time to concentrate on more important matters as well as to work on problems that require your special attention.

- This style of managing develops subordinates by requiring them to make decisions on matters that are within their abilities and competence.

- The concept is a simple, practical method of managing readily understood by both subordinates and superiors.

Managing by exception, however, does have a disadvantage—you do not hear about a problem until it is beyond the control of someone else; the opportunity to take preventive action is lost. Since management by exception is a method that many managers adopt intuitively, it seldom is given the publicity accorded to other methods. Thus, it doesn't receive the attention that more elaborate methods receive.

PLANNING AND SCHEDULING

To have high productivity, emphasis must be placed on the management functions that promote efficiency and job accomplishment. Planning and scheduling the work of your department is the way to go about it.

Planning determines what work needs to be done, when it should be done, and what will be required to do it. Scheduling assigns people to jobs at a specified time. The procedure involves coordinating people, materials, tools, and equipment to ensure that all are available at the time to start the work. Among the many benefits you gain from planning and scheduling are:

- *Attention and action based on priorities.* You can make sure first things come first. When you consider customer orders, conditions in the plant, availability of labor and material, and the other factors that affect service and production, you can make decisions to get the optimum from your resources within the time available.

- *Better procedures for getting work done.* Planning and scheduling prompts study of the job, which results in finding the best method. If you give an employee a job without instructions, the individual may do it in an inefficient manner as well as waste material. He or she may also run into a problem on the job and wait for you to come along to ask for help. When a job or project is well-planned, such waste of time and material is avoided.

- *Better coordination of labor and materials.* Planning enables you to decide what materials and tools are required. You can then see that they are on hand before starting a job. An employee shouldn't have to wait for material or be unable to complete a job because of the lack of it.

- *More efficient utilization of people.* When planning a job, you consider its scope and size. This prepares you to assign the optimum number of people and time to get it done. Estimating the time to do a job helps with scheduling people, thus improving their efficiency. It also enables you to avoid or minimize working people overtime.

- *Better credibility.* Planning and scheduling enables you to be more accurate with job completion promises. This enhances credibility and reputation along with confidence in ability to get the job done.

Techniques for Recognizing People

Good planning is not the result of technical analysis alone, but of a greater emphasis on human resources. Effective planning depends on a tie-in between programs and people, between procedures on paper and actual operations, and between planned goals and the proven abilities and desires of people. Unless you make these tie-ins realistically, all your projections, simulations, and schedules are of little value.

In the plant, planning is closely related to scheduling in that it usually involves work to be done within a time frame. If a manager is dealing with employees who will be directly involved in doing a job, both the manager and the employees should know specifically what is going to be accomplished.

There are five steps to formulating a plan that correlates procedures, resources, time, and employees:

1. *Define the job.* Make sure everyone understands it and there is agreement on the time frame.

2. *Assure that resources are available.* Check on materials, machines, and equipment.
3. *Consider alternatives.* Flexibility is necessary if you are to succeed under unexpected conditions. Be ready to change your plan.
4. *Select the course to follow.* Whether the decision is made by a majority or by group consensus, you are responsible for the decision.
5. *Review all the details of the final plan with each person involved.* Get each person to describe his or her responsibility and how that responsibility fits with others.

Good planning is always worth the effort. You and all the employees will gain satisfaction with a job well done. Planning is a key management skill that will ensure coordination and teamwork, resulting in getting work done in the most efficient manner.

Scenario Planning

Many organizations today cannot withstand a future they did not foresee or prepare for.[3] Common sense tells management to accept uncertainty and prepare for it. Organizations must come up with some way to contend with it.

Scenario planning, first developed at Royal Dutch/Shell Group, is a way to prepare for uncertainty by realizing that you can never predict the future with certainty. An excellent approach to the problem is to creatively and logically determine a range of possible futures and assign corresponding decisions for each one. Additionally, you must determine the signs or indications that will allow you to recognize each prospective future.

This type of planning prompts managers to use their imaginations to create situations and conditions that might prevail in the future, realizing that there is no correct or incorrect one. Strength and power derive from understanding the assumptions and estimations inherent in each scenario and determining how plausible they are.

To implement scenario planning, select four or more futures that are logical, persuasive, and easily understood and communicated. Give each a metaphor or description that immediately conveys the idea. Then select the one that you want to work toward, and decide what you can do to try to make that one happen.

Planning in the Plant

The manager with a plan almost always accomplishes more than one who is less organized. Moreover, he or she usually makes fewer mistakes and carries out his or her duties with less stress. Many managers have demonstrated to themselves and to their company that planning helps get more jobs done with better results and in less time. Planning pays off in several ways:

1. It enables you to set a course of action to achieve goals and reach objectives.
2. It helps you to solve your problems faster and more easily.
3. It prepares you for what you should do in case certain things happen, what you should do under particular circumstances, and how you should react to future events.

When you plan, you keep in control of people and events because planning involves getting information, facts, and data that enable you to make good decisions. The more knowledge and know-how you have, the better equipped you are to handle your job. To illustrate what planning is all about, let's say you are a production manager. The plant manager expects you to get the product out and has given you people, material, and machines to work with.

You decide which people you are going to assign to which jobs. You determine the material that will be needed and you make arrangements to have it available. You think about the machines and equipment that will be operated and the tools that will be used. You consider the time factor such as when the work will start, how long it will take, and when it will be finished. You think about quality and quantity of the product and how you will ensure them. During all this thinking and deciding, you keep in mind safety, costs, and human relations, all factors in the production process.

To get the most from your planning, you must be careful how you do it. Here are some recommendations:

- *Be specific rather than general.* The more explicit and clear your plan is, the less chance there is for it to be misunderstood or misapplied.
- *Distinguish between the known and the unknown.* Estimate the probable effects of the unknown.
- *Make a plan as logical and practical as possible.* The more facts it is based on, the better it is.
- *Introduce flexibility and looseness so that the plan may readily be modified if circumstances require it.* Recognize that no plan is infallible nor can it cover all possible contingencies.
- *Be sure the plan is consistent with the aims and goals of the company and the way the company conducts its business.* Formulate the plan to be acceptable to the people who will implement it and to those who will be affected.

FORMAL SCHEDULING

Scheduling is a basic procedure required in all manufacturing plants. Whether it answers questions on material handling, production, engineering, maintenance, or shipping, the order in which these activities should occur defines the formal schedule. But in many plants, it is simply a charade that looks good on paper and works badly on the plant floor; when foremen and managers don't believe in schedules, they won't use them. Informal systems take their place.

Although an informal scheduling system may seem better than none at all, it can be the reason for high costs, excessive inventories, production bottlenecks, and poor customer service. In contrast, a formal system produces order and discipline, knowledge of where you're going and what you're doing, and most important of all, doing first what needs to be done first.

When reliable data and information are available for decision making, formal scheduling systems give you worthwhile benefits, but only if they have credibility with users. To ensure that everyone from upper management to the people on the plant floor have faith in the formal schedule, here are some "rules" that must be adopted.

■ Responsibilities and duties must be clearly defined and understood. The schedulers are held accountable for the quality of their plans, and the users are evaluated by their compliance.

■ Priorities in schedules must be faithfully honored. If expediting is necessary, it is subject to the tenets of the formal planning system.

■ Plans are aggressive but achievable. There is commitment on everyone's part to meet the plans.

■ Management processes are integrated in that all plans are tied together starting with strategic plans and including operating plans.

■ Continuous improvement is practiced throughout the company to simplify scheduling further.

Gantt Charts

A Gantt chart provides a quick and easy way of scheduling small projects, as well as partly or ill-defined projects of any size.[4] The chart graphs time on the horizontal x-axis and activities on the vertical y-axis. See Exhibit 2-1 as an illustration of the steps to be followed for the installation of a large, heavy machine in a plant production line.

When planning and scheduling this job, the project manager estab-

Exhibit 2-1. Gantt chart for a machine installation.

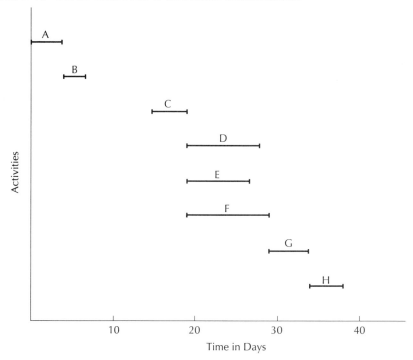

lished the following activities as being required before the machine would be ready to operate productively:

- *Activity A:* Preparation of site where machine is to be installed, including dismantling of structures and equipment presently in that area.
- *Activity B:* Pouring of concrete foundations for the machine.
- *Activity C:* Setting the machine on the foundations.
- *Activity D:* Installing mechanical components and auxiliary equipment on the machine.
- *Activity E:* Installing piping and controls.
- *Activity F:* Installing electrical systems and controls.
- *Activity G:* Painting, lubricating, oiling, and other preparations for use of the machine.
- *Activity H:* Start-up and testing of operation and controls.

The first activity for the project, Activity A, is scheduled to begin at time zero and be completed three days later. Activity B may begin when Activity A is completed, and Activity C may begin ten days after B is completed.

Activities D, E, and F can all start when Activity C is finished, although some shop work and prefabrication of material may start a day or two earlier. Activity G follows when all other activities are completed, and the project is completed when Activity H ends.

Note that the Gantt method starts activities as soon as possible—as soon as their predecessor activities end. The duration of each activity is scaled along the horizontal axis. The project manager, or a planner, must periodically check the chart to ensure that an activity is not started early; the chart shows which activities occur each day.

The Program Evaluation and Review Technique

A network plan is one of the best planning tools available to a project manager. With this technique, all the activities and events in a project are pictured graphically. The method makes it easy to visualize the events in a project that are interdependent. The plan also is of value in recognizing that some activities must occur in ordered sequence, while others can take place simultaneously.

The name for the network plan is *Program Evaluation and Review Technique* (PERT). With this plan, you can determine how a project is progressing; if it is on schedule; and if costs are in line. The system is also called the *Critical Path Method* (CPM). Although a few different terms are sometimes used, the basic concepts are identical.

UNDERSTANDING THE BASIC CONCEPTS OF PERT

Use of the PERT system involves preparation of the network plan. It shows in graphic form what must be accomplished to complete the project. The chart provides information on two elements: activities and events.

Activities are time-consuming actions that must be carried out to complete a project. The PERT chart represents these activities by lines with arrowheads pointing in the direction of passing time (conventionally to the right). In the network plan, the activity arrows are not vectors; their length is not related to their duration, and their direction has no specific meaning.

Events are points in time, usually exact dates, that indicate the planned start or completion of activities. The PERT chart represents events by circles, which can be defined as either the beginning or end of one or more activities. The chart needs only one event circle between the two activities to indicate the end of one and the beginning of the other.

Exhibits 2-2a and b depict the relation among multiple events. The lines in Exhibit 2-2a signify that Activities B, C, and D cannot begin until Activity A is completed. The event circle that represents the finish point of Activity A is the beginning for Activities B, C, and D. Although the circle could be for either the beginning or end of an activity, it usually indicates the finish.

Exhibit 2-2b shows activity lines where one event depends on the completion of three prior activities; Activity H cannot begin until E, F, and G are finished. If E takes longer than either F or G, the beginning of Activity H must still await the completion of E. This relationship can occur often during the life of a project.

The time required for the longest concurrent activity in Exhibit 2-2b is the quickest the following event can be expected to occur. No matter how quickly Activities F and G are completed, the duration of Activity E

Exhibit 2-2. PERT network charts.

(a)

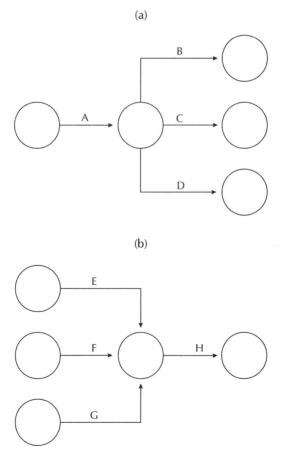

(b)

is the critical time—the time that must be used in establishing a schedule for the event.

Whenever there are multiple dependencies, such as those shown in Exhibits 2-2a and b, a critical path can be identified in the network along the lines representing the longest-time activities. Thus, the "least possible" time to complete the project can be determined from the event dates along the critical path.

DELEGATION

Managing begins with the setting of objectives, followed by considering the functions that must be accomplished. Then the work to be performed or the responsibilities to be assigned are determined. After the functions, personnel, and physical resources are put into an organizational structure, managers are ready to delegate.

Delegation is an integral part of managing, and no manager can succeed without being able to delegate effectively. But managers are judged and evaluated by different criteria than employees. While employees are evaluated on the quality of their individual work, managers are evaluated on their department's performance. Managers who try to do most of the work themselves are bound to fail. By not delegating or by delegating poorly, they limit their department's output to what they can personally accomplish. Managers with this weakness cannot take on additional responsibilities or develop others in their department.

Delegating Effectively

You can become an effective delegator by adopting a simple five-step procedure.[5] This procedure is shown in Exhibit 2-3 and explained as follows:

1. *Identify all tasks.* As a manager, you are responsible for everything your department does or fails to do. The best way to meet this responsibility is to keep a list and frequently update it. You may be surprised at the number of activities and tasks your department handles; the list will confirm that there are far more jobs than you can do yourself.

2. *Delegate each task appropriately.* Determine from the list which tasks you should do and which you can delegate to your subordinates. Those that can be delegated (probably most of the list) should now be assigned to particular subordinates. To do this, decide what skills each task requires, and who in your department is best qualified to handle the job. You may be constrained by the subordinates' areas of job specialization in some cases, but even if you are, you may want to make the assignment

Exhibit 2-3. The five-step process of effective delegation.

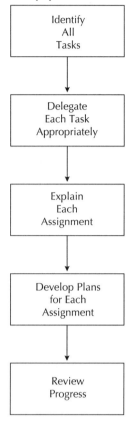

anyway. You'll find that what may appear to be constraints imposed by requirements for specialized skills are often opportunities to develop subordinates' abilities in new areas.

3. *Explain each assignment.* Understanding and properly communicating assignments is critical to effective delegating. You have to decide what you want the subordinate to do. But this doesn't mean what you want the outcome to be, and it may not mean how you want the subordinate to do the job.

The degree of initiative you expect the subordinate to take is a factor. In one case, you might require the subordinate to keep you constantly advised and come to you for all decisions. On the other hand, you may want the subordinate to solve the problem without involving you. The decision should be based on the urgency of the problem and the subordinate's capabilities. Regardless of what you decide, make sure the subordinate understands what is expected.

When delegating, you should also explain why doing a job or carrying out an assignment is necessary. Most people are more motivated and make better decisions when they understand how their work fits into the big picture. For example, if you ask a secretary to work overtime to finish a report, the individual will probably feel better about doing the work if he or she understands why the overtime is required (perhaps the report is needed to close an important sale). In the plant, you might ask the employees to clean their work area at the end of each shift. You would explain that good housekeeping promotes safety, and that the next shift has a right to enter a clean work area. You'll find that whatever the reason, subordinates to whom tasks have been delegated generally do a better job if they understand why the tasks are necessary.

4. *Develop plans for each assignment.* Most projects will either fail or be carried out inefficiently if they are not planned. A plan should state how the project will be approached, the steps involved, and the date by which each step should be completed.

Depending on the subordinate's experience, you may make the plan, the subordinate may do it, or you may do it together. If you let subordinates take the lead in developing a plan, and you act as a reviewer or coach, they will generally do a better job of following it.

5. *Review progress.* Even though you delegate jobs and other work, you are still responsible for their outcome. This means you should review progress periodically to ensure the right direction is maintained. The amount of supervision you impose during these reviews, and how often you do it, depends largely on the subordinate's experience. If you check too often, your actions will be seen as overconcern on your part or distrust of the subordinate. Either of these will probably discourage the subordinate.

To get around this problem, include progress reviews as part of the plan for accomplishing the task. The subordinate will then know how frequently you intend to review progress and this will dispel any fear of why you are doing it.

Delegation Risks

Although the large number of management responsibilities necessitates delegation, this situation presents a problem to managers—delegation involves taking risks.[6] Among the risks are loss of control, reverse delegation, and even loss of a job. Explanation of those risks follows:

1. *Loss of control.* A manager who has lived by the adage "If you want it done right, do it yourself" may find it difficult to delegate tasks for which he or she will ultimately be held accountable.

The key to successful delegation is assigning the right responsibilities to the right person. Of course, you never know who the right persons are until you meet and work with them. But you must assume that someone in your department is competent, willing, and responsible. This assumption does not address itself to the fact that it is nearly impossible today for a manager to be technically superior to all employees. A staff that is not used effectively because of a manager's failure to delegate is a major loss to a company; a waste of human resources.

2. *Reverse delegation.* Managers usually spend more time with their employees than they realize, especially when a problem is brought to the manager's attention. In encounters with employees, a manager's use of simple phrases, such as "Send me a memo on that," or "Let me think about that and I'll let you know," causes the problem to come back to the manager.

The manager assumes the responsibility for handling the task that was delegated to the employee in the first place, and when the employee reaches an impasse, the manager is required to take the next step. This is reverse delegation, and many employees are adept at it. Naturally, there will be situations in which the next step is justified, but unless the manager wants numerous visits from employees, he or she should avoid the casual and repeated use of those phrases that permit employee problems to ride on the manager's back. In fact, this principle of delegation is that accountability to a superior cannot be delegated.

A solution to this problem is to encourage initiative in employees. Employees should not have to wait until they are told to do something, nor should they have to ask. They should practice the completion of assigned tasks. By keeping the responsibility where it belongs, the manager will increase discretionary time to manage, and still handle system-imposed tasks. To develop initiative in employees early is one of the ways to develop a new generation of capable managers.

3. *Loss of job.* What if a subordinate develops so much initiative that he or she becomes superior to the boss? This is a threatening problem for the manager. The employee would be very happy if his or her development resulted in promotion, but there is still the problem if the promotion means the manager's job.

Consensus among theorists suggests that the employee should be given the opportunity to perform to as high a level of responsibility as possible if this improves the group's performance. The manager should then endeavor to reward that person accordingly, even if it means helping that person to get a better job outside the organization. To neglect and waste the talents of any individual is as criminal as the misuse of company funds or equipment.

You undoubtedly at one time or another have heard stories from individuals who feel more competent than their managers. It would seem that the best safeguard a manager has in preserving his or her position is to be a good manager and to prepare for his or her own advancement.

CREDIBILITY

If you've got personal credibility, you have just about the most important business asset you could get. When you gain the confidence, trust, and respect of those with whom you work and communicate, your ideas and opinions will get fair consideration. What you say and do will have an impact on others.

Credibility, however, has a fragile nature. Anybody may be damaging their credibility without even knowing it. What puts a stop to credibility? Here are the likely answers:

- *Positiveness in assertion of opinion.* This is deadly, especially when it is unwarranted or arrogant. Of course, there are times when personal conviction is appropriate. But it's usually a better idea to listen to others' perspectives. What would happen to your plant if every single employee refused to compromise?

- *Failure to keep promises.* Since this causes others to mistrust your word, a commitment from you means nothing. Others will justifiably feel that they can't count on you. If something comes up that prevents you from keeping a promise, inform the people involved immediately.

- *Betraying confidences.* This is bound to instill distrust and earn disrespect from colleagues and subordinates. Whether it's highly classified company information or a personal revelation, divulging it to others can destroy friendships and productive work relationships.

- *Incapability of controlling emotions.* When your actions or words show you are unstable and unable to hold your temper in check, you adversely affect your credibility. You must be steady and constant in your efforts at all times.

You cannot force people to rate you as credible. You have to earn credibility. And the only way to do that is through your words and actions. Once you lose credibility, it's very difficult to regain it.

RISKS

Many people tend to be extreme in the way they handle risks, either favoring wild speculative gambling or minimizing their exposure to losses.

With managers, setting moderately difficult but potentially achievable goals may be translated into an attitude toward risks.

Gamblers seem to choose the big risk because the outcome is beyond their power and, therefore, they can easily rationalize away their personal responsibility if they lose. The conservative individual chooses tiny risks where the gain is small but secure, perhaps because there is little danger of anything going wrong for which that person might be blamed.

Achievement-motivated people take the middle ground, preferring a moderate degree of risk because they feel their efforts and abilities will probably influence the outcome. In business and industry, this aggressiveness is the mark of the successful manager.

Of all the definitions of risk, the most simple is exposure to loss or harm. Risk is also defined as the probability of loss multiplied by the magnitude of the loss. Yet another definition of risk calls it uncertainty, and in particular, the uncertainty associated with meeting all requirements. For plant and maintenance managers, all of these definitions may apply at one time or another in the operation of plants.

MANAGING RISKS

The risks associated with operating a plant are numerous and diverse. You may be up against risks such as financial and legal problems, safety, product quality, labor unrest, the reputation of your company, and many other issues. If you are introducing a new product in the marketplace, you may be faced with the effectiveness of your advertising, performance or testing of the product, and acceptance by customers. Whatever problems you anticipate encountering, what should you be doing today to minimize or prevent these problems from developing? This is essentially what risk management is all about. It is really nothing more than a practical approach to understanding what is needed to accomplish the objective, identifying the problems involved in meeting these obligations, and doing what needs to be done to eliminate or minimize the risks.[7] This process is depicted in Exhibit 2-4. An explanation of the steps in the chart follows:

1. *Define requirements.* Defining all the requirements should be the first step of any venture involving risk, whether it's the introduction of a new product, or the implementation of a new manufacturing process. These requirements may come from several sources: governmental laws and regulations, customers, company policy and/or standards, and public image. Pursuing these sources involves three efforts on your part:

- Study and review every document and publication associated with the project. Some of these documents may contain requirements that should not be overlooked.
- Ask experts in other departments of your company to identify requirements that may affect your project. Managers and staff personnel in legal, safety, environmental, and public relations are valuable sources of information.
- Keep a list and file of all requirements and check to see that everyone complies with them. The list and file will ensure that you won't forget any.

Exhibit 2-4. The managing risks process.

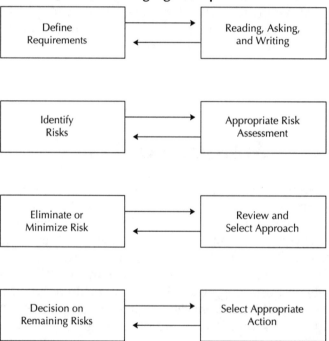

2. *Identify risks.* You can identify risks in three areas: projects, procedures, and products. When assessing the risks in these areas, it's also advisable to consider the risk of not changing. The greatest risk of all may be to do nothing. The techniques for identifying risks in the above areas are as follows:

- An accepted technique for identifying project risk is a yes–no analysis.[8] With this technique, you use block diagrams to identify all the project elements, and decide if each can be accomplished. How this analysis is carried out is shown in Exhibit 2-5.

Exhibit 2-5. Yes–no analysis for obtaining and implementing a software package.

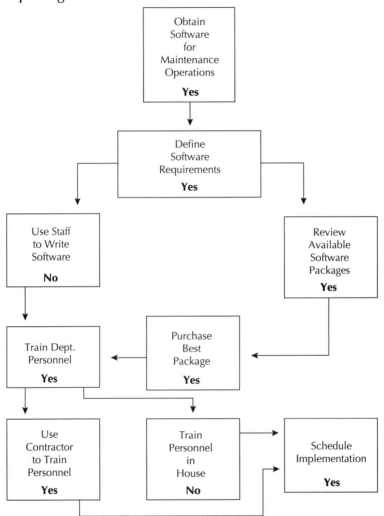

As manager of the Maintenance Department, you are responsible for obtaining and implementing a software package that will meet the needs of your department. The yes–no analysis starts by identifying the project as shown in the top block of Exhibit 2-5. Since you are confident you will have no problem in obtaining software to be used with the plant's computer because you've purchased other software programs, a "yes" is put in the top block.

A "no" in a block doesn't necessarily mean you should abandon that step. You need to identify what makes the block a "no." The jobs in those blocks labeled "yes" are ones you are sure you can accomplish. You are not certain, though, about the blocks labeled "no." If you decide to go ahead with the steps in blocks labeled "no," you should schedule them as early as possible.

People naturally tend to delay starting difficult jobs. A "yes–no" analysis prevents this by identifying the high-risk tasks. Knowing this, a manager must make sure the high risks can be handled early in the project, to avoid wasting the company's money. The idea is that if you can't accomplish the "no" blocks, you won't be able to complete the project. If that's going to be the case, you want to switch to a "yes" block before you've spent most of your money and also delayed the project's completion.

- Procedure risk assessment techniques are designed to identify the risks with operations such as manufacturing sequences, administrative work-flows, or use of a product. Perhaps the best way to uncover and identify procedures that entail risks is to make detailed flowcharts and assess the consequences of missed steps, out-of-sequence steps, or improperly performed steps.

For example, in the manufacture of some chemical products, a series of operations must be carried out under closely controlled conditions. Not only are pressure and temperature critical to a successful chemical reaction, but often the raw materials must be purified before use. In addition, modifiers and catalysts must also be charged. If any one of these steps is omitted or not handled correctly, the product probably will not meet the customer's specifications, resulting in a loss of several thousands of dollars.

- When you determine if a new product can meet all the requirements of the consumer, you are making a product risk analysis. The requirements include such matters as safety, performance, reliability, quality, cost, or appearance. But to make such analyses, you must be skilled in characteristics, testing, and measuring techniques. Although product risk assessments are complex, they are important both to manufacturers and consumers. It only takes a few failures or malfunction incidents to bring a product into disfavor with the public.

3. *Eliminate or minimize risks.* Project risks usually cannot be adjusted or altered to eliminate or minimize risk. The best you can do is to change the requirements or modify the schedule to do the least certain jobs first.

Procedure risk involves only two choices. You can either change the procedure or provide special reminders. The former is usually preferred.

When you are faced with a product risk, you have three options:

- Warn users of the risk.
- Train users to avoid injury.
- Redesign the product to eliminate the hazard.

To eliminate the risk entirely, you should adopt the third. The other two are less desirable because they depend on people to follow instructions, which is much less certain.

4. *Decisions on remaining risks.* After you have defined the requirements, identified the risks, and eliminated or minimized as much risk as possible, the next step is to study the remaining risk and decide what to do about it. Remember, the greater the risk, the more detailed your study should be. Now you have to decide what to do about the remaining risks. Here are your options:

- *Accept the risk.* If it has a low probability of occurrence or the consequences are not severe, this isn't a bad decision.
- *Share the risk.* For example, appliance manufacturers share repair-cost risk with their customers by imposing time limitations on their warranties.
- *Transfer the risk.* The usual way to do this is with insurance, especially if the probability of occurrence is low but the consequences are disastrous. Fire and flood insurance are good examples.
- *Refuse the risk.* Remember that risk is defined as the probability of loss multiplied by the magnitude of the loss. If you find that a remaining risk is too likely or severe, and it cannot be shared or transferred, giving up on the venture is the best move you can make.

Risk Analysis

A useful technique for analyzing problems is available to help managers in making decisions. This technique—risk analysis—involves the risk associated with the act. The decisions that a manager must make in planning and carrying out a project are based on the relationships between several variables, many of which contain some uncertainty coupled with a fairly high degree of probability. Thus, the wisdom of undertaking a project might depend on the individual costs of labor, equipment, and material. A best estimate of the total cost might thus be made.

But suppose that further study of each of the three variables shows that the labor cost has an 80 percent probability of being accurate, the equipment cost estimate a 90 percent chance of being correct, and the material cost estimate a 70 percent probability of being correct. In this case, the calculated probability of the total cost estimate for the entire project's being right would almost certainly be less than 85 percent; exactly how much less would depend upon the values of each variable. However, the probability of all the estimates of the three variables being correct is only 50.4 percent (.80 × .90 × .70).

The risk-analysis technique involves the preparation of a probability distribution curve for each variable. This is done by gauging the range and probability of each variable. No matter how judgmental the preparer of these estimates may be, a range of values and probabilities is better than a single best estimate. Given such information as this, a manager is better able to determine the probability of completing a project within a specified maximum cost.

BENCHMARKING

As a management tool, benchmarking is a means to improve operations by measuring your company against the most successful companies, both in and out of your industry. In the past, companies could easily set future goals simply by exceeding past performance. This is no longer adequate or sufficient in today's competitive marketplace. Now you must learn what tactics and procedures make successful companies superb. Considering your own needs, you can then develop a model to strive to equal or excel. In this sense, benchmarking has become a formal, continuous procedure that companies are increasingly practicing.

Benchmarking has enabled plants to learn how to operate at their potential, as well as to improve on what their managements thought possible. Success has been achieved because benchmarking uses a logical method for developing winning policies and plans. While the procedure is relatively simple, it does require strategic thinking. Here are the steps to staying focused, keeping the proper perspective, and maintaining your beneficial direction:

1. *Decide what to benchmark.* Determine the critical processes that have the most significant effect on the company business.
2. *Identify the best companies in the critical processes.* Recognize that a competitor may be the best in some areas but not others. Become involved only when the method optimizes processes within your environment.
3. *Measure the performance of the best companies and yours.* For the critical processes, gauge your performance against the best.
4. *Quantitate the difference in performance.* Measure it precisely, so you can place most of your efforts in the areas where they are most needed.

5. *Plan how to overcome differences.* Decide and schedule what your company needs to do to become the best.
6. *Act immediately.* Implement your plan to reach your objectives. Follow up continually to track your progress.

Benchmarking not only helps plants to continually improve their operations, it tells managers whether they are already performing to the best of their abilities. But you must be wary of losing sight of company budgets, and getting carried away with "being the best" in a particular discipline that may not be important to overall company operations.

NOTES

1. Paul Hersey and Kenneth H. Blanchard, *Management of Organizational Behavior* (Englewood Cliffs, N.J.: Prentice Hall, Inc., 1993), p. 140.
2. Charles H. Becker, *Plant Manager's Manual and Guide* (Englewood Cliffs, N.J.: Prentice Hall, Inc., 1987), p. 7.
3. Paul T. Hertz, "Using Scenario Planning for Uncertainty," *Chemical Processing,* January 1995: 97.
4. W. H. Weiss, *Plant Supervisor's Complete Desk Book* (Englewood Cliffs, N.J.: Prentice Hall, Inc., 1992), pp. 291–292.
5. Used with permission of Sterling Publishing Co., Inc., from *Managing Effectively,* by Joseph and Susan Berk, Copyright 1991 by Joseph and Susan Berk.
6. Patrick Montana and Bruce H. Charnov, *Management* (New York: Barron's Educational Series, Inc., 1987), pp. 157–159.
7. Joseph and Susan Berk, *Managing Effectively* (New York: Sterling Publishing Co., Inc., 1991), p. 177.
8. Ibid., pp. 179–182.

3

Decision Making and Problem Solving

The ability to make sensible decisions calmly and with reasonable speed is helpful in any position in life. It is especially so for managers because they are so closely involved with people. One sure way to differentiate between a better-than-average manager and a mediocre one is to judge them on their decision-making ability. Those who are decisive and effective gain the respect of both their subordinates and their superiors.

Understanding the whys and hows of decision making is an asset to people because the knowledge tends to lessen the tension and pressure they feel when they are required to reason, analyze, and act on a problem. By learning the process of how decisions are made and by recognizing the factors involved, people improve their managerial ability.

Initially, managers may look to their own qualifications and the training they've received to perfect their decision-making skill. How their knowledge is influenced by the many external factors that affect decisions then needs to be resolved. Although a manager's orders or instructions invariably bring action, they are just the culmination of a procedure that may have involved consideration of people, conditions, and the circumstances of the particular situation.

The experienced manager has an advantage over the neophyte when a decision must be made. This is not to say, however, that experience is a prime requisite for effective decision making, because then only the older, been-around-a-long-time person could be expected to make good ones. Experience is a valuable aid primarily when snap decisions must be made. The experienced person remembers similar problems and situations and draws upon this memory to solve the current problem. The value of experience should not be taken lightly. High-level executives attain their positions through a series of upward managerial steps, with each higher position demanding more skill and ability in making decisions and requiring that they call more and more on their training and experience.

BEING TECHNICALLY AWARE

When you are called upon to make a decision that is innovative or that will result in a basic change in an existing procedure, you must be fully informed about the technical details of the undertaking. New and original ideas are developed and promulgated best by informed and knowledgeable individuals who have a good understanding of the basics and have studied the subject extensively.

For example, if you are required to make a decision about buying a word processor or a computer, you must be familiar with the capabilities and features of various systems available to you. Otherwise, you could not make a sound decision as to which system would be best for your organization. Similarly, if you are faced with a decision concerning a work procedure, you should be aware of the present procedure in its entirety, including the principles that govern it. Having such knowledge, you could decide what effect a change would have. To make a sound decision relating to the behavior of people, you will stand a better chance if you know them individually, how they think and why they behave as they do. Being cognizant of such matters will enable you to properly and effectively employ the stimuli that will cause them to perform more efficiently.

DECISION-MAKING STRATEGY

Everyone on the job makes decisions that are related to his or her position and the environment.[1] First-line and higher-level managers have the added responsibility for decisions that affect others. The environment of the decision maker and the position he or she assumes affect the decision-making process, but basically, a decision maker selects a course of action from available alternatives in order to achieve a desired result.

First, a choice must be made; if there is only one way to go, no decision is necessary. Second, making decisions requires use of mental faculties at the conscious level; logic is essential, yet emotion will also play a part. Third, a purpose is behind each decision; the decision is made to achieve or reach some objective.

The process of making a decision evolves in five phases in the mind of an individual:

1. The manager understands the situation and is aware of the factors that should be considered. His or her education and experience may tend to complicate matters, in that the factors may appear innumerable.
2. The manager recognizes the true problem. This is so important that when a person is sure that the problem is correctly defined, it is already partially solved.
3. The search for and analysis of available alternatives begins. Logic plays a part in working out the consequences of various alternatives.
4. The manager selects the best alternative. It may be only slightly better than a number of other options.
5. The decision is accepted by the organization. The person or persons responsible for implementing it do so.

These five phases form the strategy of the decision-making process. The techniques vary, depending on the type of decision to be made. Two types are most common: the initiation type and the approval type. In the initiation type, the decision maker originates the process; in the approval type, the decision maker receives recommendations and approves their implementation.

The Art of Decision Making

Managing and making decisions go together. All managers must make decisions, and many decisions must be made when conditions are uncertain. Thus, managers must be able to handle uncertainty if they are to carry out their responsibilities.

As for who will make good decisions, look to the enthusiastic person, the one who shows innovation and imagination when expressing himself or herself. Such an individual demonstrates both creativity and versatility. He or she is not satisfied with handling today's problems the same as yesterday's. Decision making involves treading a path between two extremes—procrastination or impulsive action. Yet when a call for action is urgent, even a poor decision may be better than none. Since making a clear, decisive judgment is sometimes difficult, managerial decisions often turn out to be compromises, even though such solutions are appalling to the strong, committed-to-the-job executive.

Dealing With Uncertainty

Uncertainty, as noted, is part of the game of making decisions. In order to deal with uncertainty, managers must recognize the problem. There is no uncertainty about the various courses of action available to them. Such alternatives either exist or they don't. The uncertainty lies with the consequences of the courses. Making decisions is difficult because there can be several consequences to each alternative. For example, when a manager makes an assignment, the individual receiving it could: (1) do a good job, (2) do a poor job, or (3) not do the job at all. To make matters worse, whether the assignment brings about a favorable or unfavorable result sometimes depends on other factors beyond the knowledge or control of the manager. The individual could be ill, tired, in a bad frame of mind, or not paying attention. These factors, uncontrollable at the moment, are responsible for the uncertainty surrounding the manager's decision. If the manager knew that the individual was well, rested, in a receptive mood, and paying attention, the results of the decision to make the assignment would be more certain. Even then, a manager can never be absolutely certain, because people change their minds, give misleading impressions, and are often simply unpredictable. Nevertheless, the manager must deal with this uncertainty in some manner. Mathematicians and statisticians have developed various techniques for dealing with uncertainty. Although many of these are impractical or not applicable to the decisions facing managers, some are simple and relatively easy to use.

When faced with making a decision when they are uncertain, insecure managers will attempt to dodge the issue or try to share the responsibility with other people. They may solicit the advice of others, including their superiors, when they unquestionably should make the decision themselves. Secure managers recognize that they cannot sidestep taking some risks; they simply use their best judgment and hope for the best.

Even the most capable managers are not infallible. Like the average person, they are occasionally guilty of mistakes, including errors in judgment. Everyone has a bad day now and then despite all efforts to avoid it. Although infallibility cannot be assured in making decisions, there are certain steps that can be taken to minimize the possibility of making bad decisions. Good decision makers take their time. They consult with knowledgeable persons, and they are very thorough in searching through the records for historical information. In addition, they may laboriously list the advantages and disadvantages of all the alternatives. So when they finally make their decisions, they know in their own minds that they have done their best.

Responsible Decision Making

One of the most difficult lessons for a manager to learn is that making decisions demands toughness and tenacity. It's possible to become so emotionally involved with one of your people that you can't make the decision you should make concerning him or her. You eventually learn that every problem and every personality calls for a specific approach. When you alone are affected by the outcome of a decision you make, you have more leeway because you're answerable only to yourself. Decisions you make on the job deserve more of your consideration, since they affect other people and the company you work for. You tread dangerous ground when you make decisions unsupported by logic or reasoning. It's better if you gain the trust and respect of your people by knowing exactly what you're doing and why you're doing it.

As you learn to carry out all the responsibilities of a manager, you become aware of the steps you must follow in order to make good decisions. You see that when you have a problem, you must first define it. Then you must get facts and data relative to it, search for alternative answers, consider the probable outcome of each alternative, and finally select the best one.

You can use this analytical technique with just about every decision you make. If you feel that many of your decisions are too minor to justify going through the steps, you should do it anyway to get into the habit. The more frequently you do, the more effective you'll become in making decisions. To carry the process further, you might want to make a record of how you reached certain decisions. Then, when you learn how your decision fared, you can refer to your notes to determine why the decision proved to be sound or unsound.

When you must make a quick decision, you can do nothing more than call upon whatever knowledge and information you have at the moment. But it would be foolhardy to follow this procedure with decisions where you have more time. Making snap decisions when you don't have to causes resentment and a loss of respect. One of the basic rules for responsible decision making is to allow time and patience to prevail. Listen to and consider the suggestions people offer you. It's smart to assume that you don't have all the pertinent information. Why not consult with other individuals who may be able to contribute something critical?

When a manager makes a decision that should logically be made by someone who works for him or her, the manager is denying that person the experience of studying a problem, reaching a conclusion, and taking action. Remember that everyone gets satisfaction from an accomplishment and feels good about it, especially if that accomplishment is important work and contributes to the department's objectives.

The Stress of Decision Making

Making decisions is stressful to people who are very much aware of the risk of suffering serious losses from whatever course of action they take.

Additional stress is experienced if they worry about the difficulty of reversing their decisions, should that be necessary. With these uncertainties to worry about, it is understandable why decision makers are reluctant to make irrevocable choices.

The most common expressions of stress are revealed in feeling uncertain, being inclined to hesitate, and tending to vacillate. Many executives in business and industry report sleepless nights, loss of interest in eating, and almost unbearable tensions. Other symptoms of stress that are experienced at the time of making a difficult decision include feelings of apprehensiveness, a wish to escape having to make a choice, and self-blame for having allowed oneself to get into a situation where all available alternatives seem unsatisfactory.

At one time or another, all decision makers are likely to face situations that cause extreme stress. However, with day-to-day decisions where risks are minimal and losses would be inconsequential, correspondingly less stress is felt. Yet even these decisions may have an effect on the quality of fact-finding and evaluation that decision makers employ. If a decision seems trivial, you may not spend much time thinking about it before acting. But when you must make a decision that will affect your future welfare, you may find it painful to commit yourself, particularly when you know there are some risks and costs no matter which course of action you follow. The obvious way to cope with this situation is, of course, to avoid making the decision. We all are inclined to procrastinate to some degree whether or not we are aware of it. Furthermore, if we refuse to be guilty of procrastinating, we can substitute a rationalization for ignoring a worrying doubt. There is no question that procrastinating and rationalizing are means of avoid decision making and a way of coping with its stress. In reality, though, they can be just as detrimental to making good decisions as acting impulsively.

Decision makers who have a high batting average are careful to avoid making decisions when they are under stress. They've learned from experience that it's better to delay a decision than to make it when they are angry or upset. Decisions made with emotion as a basis are never as good as those made through reasoning and logical thinking. But most decisions made in business and industry are based on much more than just logic and reason. All of us are influenced by emotion. It plays a large part in our lives. We must learn to handle it if we are to get along with people and have a successful career.

People who have a decision to make think and act in two ways. They either reason the problem out, or they decide what to do through emotion. While reasoning involves dealing with logic and facts, emotion concerns one's feelings. Most people consider themselves experts on logic and reason. They honestly believe that the statements they make and the acts they perform are logically and reasonably thought out beforehand. Yet studies have shown that 20 percent of their decisions are based on reason and 80 percent on emotion.

Making decisions under stress is not easy. Sometimes your decision may be clearly right but difficult to carry out. Other times, you may need exceptional wisdom or inspiration to come up with the best thing to do. Whatever problem you face, be sure you take time to focus on <u>what</u> needs to be decided and what the objectives are. If you have an interpersonal decision to make, you must plan when you and where you will discuss the problem with the person involved. If the person is emotional when the subject is brought up, allow some time for cooling off before you again get together. Choose a time when neither of you will feel stress or tension and the atmosphere is relaxed. You will find yourself better able to reason out a decision that is satisfactory to both of you.

Confidence in Making Decisions

Competent managers do not like to have decisions made for them. They feel that they would be abdicating their responsibilities if they permitted this to happen. You should not entrust important decisions to others. To pass them off is to give up your personal obligations—literally, how you are going to live your life. Avoiding decisions that are rightfully yours in reality puts you out of the game. Making your own decisions shows maturity and personal responsibility.

Some people believe that many decisions will be made for them if they just wait long enough. Other people believe that many decisions are unnecessary because "what is going to happen, will happen." In some situations, decisions cannot be postponed. Letting time and the natural course of events make your decisions for you means that you are resigned to accept whatever happens; that you'll get by somehow if the worst happens. The truth of the matter is that people are better off and happier when they have more control over their destiny.

You may decide something simply in order to get rid of a problem, thereby getting out from under a situation that bothers you. Although you may succeed at the time with this approach, you will often be sorry later. Such decisions are usually made without a lot of thought and consideration; thus, there's a strong likelihood that you will make more bad decisions than good ones.

If you feel that looking at both the pros and cons of a situation on which you must act is usually a waste of time, you are probably impulsive. You'd be better off if you got in the habit of considering the advantages and disadvantages of all the alternatives. Although weighing consequences takes time, by doing so you get a broader perspective of the art of making decisions. To be able to see a problem from several viewpoints is an aid to the decision-making process because this makes you flexible. Being flexible enables you to change your mind and come up with a better decision.

Checking decisions to see how they worked out is commendable because it indicates not only that you are curious about the outcome of a decision for its own sake but also that you want to discover the outcome in order to make better decisions in the future.

Your confidence that you will make a good decision may suffer if you feel confused when you have to make an important one. Your confusion may be caused by asking the wrong questions or asking too many questions. But you may also be confused because you don't have a good way to arrive at a decision. Whatever the cause, you give up hope and guess. Perhaps you are not confused, but headstrong instead. Then you may confuse opinion with fact and feel that your decisions are always right; you don't want to be bothered with facts because you have already made up your mind. Even if you aren't confused, you may frequently oversimplify a problem and are then just as likely to make a bad decision as a person who is confused.

Do you lack confidence when making decisions because you have second thoughts about whether they are right? You shouldn't let this bother you. Most decision makers are unsure of themselves a good bit of the time. They wonder whether they considered all the facts, overlooked something, or used faulty reasoning. People normally ask themselves such questions. If they review and analyze their decisions, they learn how to improve them. However, if they subject themselves to useless postmortem questioning, they may easily lose their self-confidence and even succumb to deceiving themselves in trying to justify their decisions.

Making a Poor Decision

It's tough to have to admit you made a poor decision. It's also a blow to your self-confidence. Yet if you stick with your decision after you realize that it is wrong, all you do is make matters worse. Very few decisions should be thought of as absolute. Decisions are only as good as the facts and information they were based on. Any decision could prove to be bad, regardless of who made it. Decision makers must be prepared to change their decisions should that become necessary.

If you feel that your decisions are usually poor no matter how hard you try, your self-confidence will certainly be affected adversely. In all likelihood, you make decisions in a reckless manner. To compound the problem, your bad decisions are probably remembered, thus refueling your defeatist attitude. You may eventually reach the point where you will take no responsibility for any decision you make.

To make no decision is usually preferable to making a bad decision. Taking action does not guarantee that a problem is handled or that benefits will be realized. You should be aware that no decision is the best course to follow with some problems, especially when you know that you lack information.

Your self-confidence that you can make good decisions is strong if you believe that consulting with others about those decisions can only confuse the issue. Yet such thinking is probably based on whose help you have been seeking. Many people are ready to give you advice, but not all are qualified to assist you with your particular problem. The right people, those who can help you make a better decision, are those who have previously made decisions on matter similar to yours. Of course, if you have already made up your mind about a problem, talking to other people may be disconcerting because a new slant or more information might come out of your discussions. Be aware, too, that if you have higher status than the people you consult, they may not be of much help simply because they may be afraid to speak up or disagree with you.

How do you feel about helping other people with their decisions? If you feel competent at this, it says much for your self-confidence. Yet you may want to consider what this means. People who feel confident in making decisions for others are not necessarily confident in making decisions for themselves. Then again, just the opposite may also be true. Regardless, if your advice is asked for, take a good look at yourself. You probably are a better decision maker than you think.

Technique and Procedure

Every manager early in his or her career learns that the job entails continually making decisions. Although making a decision isn't a new experience, differences in the type of decisions to be made are apparent, and the consequences of those decisions have become important. A good manager soon realizes that he or she should formulate a procedure for making decisions that will ensure that all alternatives are considered and that each decision made is the best one possible under the circumstances. In doing this, the manager should keep in mind that:

1. There is no one best way to make all decisions.
2. The steps of making a decision invariably overlap.

3. Conscious as well as unconscious factors influence many decisions.
4. Decisions made on the basis of logic alone may be faulty.

A manager doesn't have to be on the job very long before he or she realizes that making decisions is not a separate responsibility of the job but is included in nearly everything he or she says or does; also, that decision making is so akin to problem solving that managers are faced with more problem decisions than opportunity decisions. While most industrial managers today are proficient in making good decisions, some are novices in learning the best procedure to follow to perfect their decision-making skill. Although there is no surefire way to be a success, here are some guidelines to get you started on the right path:

1. Concentrate on the objective of a decision you must make. Know what you want to achieve. Hold off making any decision until you are sure you know all that is involved.

2. Constantly reconsider the objective and be ready to change your approach if you sense that you should. Be flexible to the extent that you can readily adjust to new information. Changing circumstances may require you to make a new decision. To reverse or modify a decision does not mean you're inept as a decision maker.

3. Accept the advice and recommendations of others but rely on your own judgment and experience when it comes to making the decision. Don't automatically follow an expert's advice.

4. Give your hunch or intuition considerable weight. Hunches emanate from more than just facts and information; they should be considered along with the other bases of your decisions.

5. Be fearless and aggressive when making a decision. Meekness does not convey assuredness. Major changes can be made more easily than minor ones. But be sure your attack has been planned and well thought out.

6. See that your decision fits the particular circumstances and that you're not making it because such a decision worked before. It is risky to assume that two situations are identical and can therefore be handled the same way. Priorities, directions, and people change. You must judge each situation as separate and distinct from all others.

7. Consider the preferences of other people, including corporate management. It is sheer folly to make a decision that conflicts with their thinking unless you have a very convincing argument to back it up.

8. Take your time, especially with important decisions. The more impact the decisions will have, the more time you should devote to them.

9. Be wary of selecting your first choice of alternatives. Experienced decision makers say that you can almost always find a better one. Consider as many alternatives as possible.

10. Be prepared to change course once you act. Decisions often trigger new problems, and the reactions to a decision can alter a situation greatly.

Developing Skill at Making Decisions

When you make the right decision, no one notices. When you make the wrong one, everyone does. Knowing how to deal professionally with people relationships and make more competent decisions will help you to become a more effective manager.

You might think that the more decisions you make, the more skilled you'd become at it. But decision making is not like making a speech or driving a car. The number of decisions you make has nothing to do with your skill at making them or how they turn out. The art of decision making does not receive a lot of attention from educators and personnel training groups. We take lessons to learn how to drive or to become good at golf, but rely on our own instincts to learn how to make decisions. If it is believed that making decisions is easy, that is simply not true.

In order to make good decisions, you have to understand values and be able to weigh one thing against another. If a decision or series of decisions is to help you reach your goal, you must first decide what your goal is—that becomes your basic decision. For most people, it's a difficult one because they work at a job and go through life without having any clear objectives.

How do you learn to make good decisions? Some people say that you can learn only from experience. If you pursued the subject further and asked how you could get experience, these people would say that making bad decisions will provide you the experience. But that's not the total answer. To learn to make good decisions, you must possess knowledge about the problems you face and develop your analytical skills. You also need to acquire confidence in your abilities. Last but not least, you must be willing to take risks.

Managers are paid to make decisions, many of which involve risks. Invariably, you will make some poor decisions, but that is how you learn. When you learn how to deal with a bad decision, you will have less fear of the consequences of making a mistake. If you make a bad decision, you should review how you reached it and determine where you went wrong. Now you're ready to modify your decision or make a new one.

Another facet of decision making that deserves consideration is the motivation behind making one. Some people are directed mainly by their minds, others mainly by their emotions. The decisions that derive from the mind are the conscious and logical ones; those from the emotions are the subconscious and intuitive ones. Even the most logical people make some decisions emotionally, and the most emotional make some logically. Which are the better decisions, the ones that arise from feelings or the ones that arise from reason?

The great majority of decisions affect people. Since people by their very nature feel as well as think, a logical decision may fail if those on whom its success depends reject it for emotional reasons. A decision you make about yourself, no matter how logical, may not be right if it doesn't feel right. The most lasting and sound decisions contain both reason and emotion. It is the balance or proportion that is crucial to whether or not a particular decision is good or bad.

When making a decision concerning someone, you have a much better chance of winning the person's acceptance and support if you consider his or her feelings. A major reason for much of the discontent in business and industry today stems from the exclusion of people from participation in the decisions that affect them. If management asked employees to become involved in these decisions, many demonstrations, sit-downs, and strikes might be prevented.

In developing your skill at decision making, vary your style to fit the situation. No single style works in all cases. Make some decisions by consulting with your subordinates and superiors. Make other decisions alone. When you talk to people about a problem, ask only for information sometimes and ask for their recommendations at other times.

Being sure you understand the problem is the most difficult step in making a decision. It is the most important step as well. It is important for a manager to make good decisions. But in order to make a good decision, it is first necessary to correctly identify the problem at hand.

DECISIVENESS

Probably no question bothers a manager more than the simple "Should I or shouldn't I?" Yet managers must choose between the two courses of action many times each day. Reluctance to make a decision is a common human weakness, but what holds you back, more often than not, isn't lack of wisdom but timidity. Many people in leadership positions lack enough self-confidence and assertiveness to take action when they face a problem where a decision should be made. This unwillingness to act results in nothing being done or in permitting those who are willing to act to take over.

What is meant by being decisive? When you are decisive, you do more than merely give an opinion—you act on that opinion. Decisiveness is a willingness to commit yourself and to follow up on your conviction. The person who takes a firm stand on an issue and starts the ball rolling toward resolving it is said to be decisive.

How do you acquire the skill of being decisive? Gain insight and develop determination if you want to be decisive. Welcome problems and have the confidence to solve them. Be willing to decide something. Reluctance to make a decision can handicap you because people on the job expect managers to be decisive and in control. Workers become fearful, uneasy, and even unwilling to go ahead with a job when they sense that their first-line manager is unsure of himself or herself. A decisive manager commands respect and gets action.

Being decisive in handling your responsibilities requires that you make minor decisions promptly. By disposing of them as quickly as possible, you will have more time to spend on problems that are really important. Be solid and firm when you make a decision. Don't be half-sure or leave any doubt about your intentions. Put aside any thoughts that you might make a mistake. Such thinking weakens your resolution to be decisive. Also, forget the alternative once you make a decision. There is no sense in wasting time thinking about what you could or should have done.

To be decisive, you should approach a problem in a definite way. Your course of action should involve several steps to enable you to make the best decision possible under the circumstances. To start with, you must study and analyze the problem thoroughly. Recognize that any decision you make depends on how much you know about it. You may make a poor decision if you know too little, so learn about the situation, how it developed, the issue involved, and what you need to accomplish with your decision.

Consider the possible decisions that could be made. Is your usual answer to this type of problem the best, or must you look for a different approach? Evaluate all possible alternatives. Narrow your choices to the best one by weighing the outcome you could expect from each. Will your decision solve the problem or accomplish your objective? Is the solution fair to all concerned? Is your answer partial or temporary? Will it handle the entire problem now?

Take action on your decision and plan to follow up after a reasonable period of time. You've been decisive if you've not procrastinated along the way.

NETWORKS

Networks are groups of personal contacts you can use to achieve business objectives and get advice on plant operating problems.[2] Networking has become quite popular in recent years and has resulted in the creation of many different kinds of networks. Some are internal to the organization, such as other managers and staff with whom you might discuss current managerial problems and recent technological advances in your industry.

You may benefit even more from networks outside the company. Examples include business acquaintances you have developed over the years, consultants and contractors you have worked with, and people who have left the company. These individuals often can help secure new business. Professional societies also form important networks from which you can learn the latest technologies.

Mentoring

Another special kind of internal network involves the concept of mentoring. A mentor is a senior manager who provides career and business guidance, usually to a more junior person. Only two people are involved in mentor networks—the mentor and the person receiving guidance and direction from the mentor.

A mentor is basically a coach, although the individual may also be considered a career consultant with pertinent insight due to his or her position and familiarity with the organization. The best mentors are those who are not in the chain of command of those they are mentoring. In other words, if you are a maintenance manager, a mentor from the sales department is preferable to having the manager of engineering as a mentor. This arrangement is desirable for two reasons:

1. You get advice and suggestions from a broader perspective (i.e., outside the range and limit of your own department).
2. It eliminates the inherent unfairness of a senior manager supplying a preferential subordinate guidance (i.e., helping the career of one subordinate instead of all subordinates).

Establishing a relationship with a mentor requires delicacy and diplomacy on your part. You cannot approach an upper level manager and simply ask for help in getting ahead. Your best course of action is to select someone outside your chain of command whom you know and who knows you (someone, perhaps, you have contacted for data or information or did some work for in the past). An excellent way to begin a conversation that you hope will lead to the individual becoming your mentor is to ask the individual how he or she advanced in the company. If you do this with courtesy and respect in a relaxed private setting, most successful people are surprisingly willing to talk about themselves. Once such a conversation has started, the prospective mentor will probably ask you about your career aspirations. When you finish the conversation, ask if you can return occasionally for additional guidance.

Working With Mentors

If you are looking for someone to help you rise higher in the plant organization or its corporate offices, here are a few tips on working with mentors:[3]

- Ask someone who has complimented you on your performance and has clout with the people who can help you move up in the company. Don't consider talking to a lame duck.
- Try to make the mentor feel comfortable with you by starting a conversation after a meeting. Ask for advice on something simple. Later, ask for guidance on one of your departmental concerns or a major problem you face.
- After you've established a friendly relationship, ask your mentor to help you get a promotion, a larger staff, or whatever else might be your career aspirations.

Ethics of Networking

Many of today's young employees and some individuals who have just become managers consider networking as "playing politics." Whether you agree or not depends on how you define politics. If you define it as knowing and being able to influence the right people in order to reach objectives, then networking should be seen in a positive light.

If a group of predominately middle-aged managers who hold the real decision-making power in an organization band together in a network, the move can benefit both themselves and the organization. The benefits accrue when the members support each other to develop new sales, recruit new employees, and generally help the company run smoothly and profitably.

PROBLEM SOLVING

You can view your problems on the job in several ways, but basically you have a problem when something stands in the way of reaching your objective.[4] You also have a problem when what you expect to happen doesn't happen. For instance, many things can prevent the plant from reaching its daily or monthly quota. A shortage of raw material, labor, or equipment can become a problem if you haven't planned for it.

Problem solving and decision making are managerial functions that go together. In fact, problem solving can be said to be decision making. Anything that you do in planning, organizing, scheduling, directing, and controlling that requires you to choose a course of action from among several alternatives is decision making. Managers must continually decide whether to do something or not to do it, to say something or remain silent, to correct something or let it continue as it is. They should be aware, however, that even if they do none of these things, they are nevertheless making a choice—it is a decision not to make a change.

Problems are best solved through a systematic procedure, although you may not be conscious that you are following it with minor or routine matters. Yet decision making need not always be systematic. Sometimes you make a decision based on your intuition or hunch. When you are pressed for time, a snap judgment may be your only recourse.

Basic Understanding of the Problem

A manager's decision can be no better than the information it's based upon. If you can't ask people to look up relevant information about a problem you face, you can gather all the data that you know about and that is available to you. How much information you go after and collect depends on the complexity of the problem and how much time you have to spend on it. You may make a poor decision if you know too little about a problem, but you seldom err because you know too much.

In trying to define a problem, consider how it originated and why it exists. Look at its scope. More than likely, the problem consists of several subproblems that can be worked on separately. To gain a basic understanding of the problem, you must be able to answer a series of questions about it; such questions as:

- What really is the problem? Is it based on opinion or fact? Is the information you have on the problem truthful? Are bias and prejudice factors to be considered?
- Could the problem be only a symptom? Would you attack it differently if that were the case? Has the problem been defined too narrowly?
- How did the problem originate? Has it existed for some time? Is it a common problem or a unique one? What are the chances of it solving itself if you do nothing?

- Is the problem critical? How quickly must an answer be found? Should only part of the problem be tackled now?
- What will be achieved by solving the problem? Is there a goal, objective, or purpose? Are the company's plans or goals involved?

You will probably be able to answer some of these questions when you first learn of the problem. What you need now are some guidelines on how to proceed.

Guidelines for Problem Solving

Managers daily face problems of all sizes and degrees of difficulty. Some are so small and inconsequential that little if any analysis and study are necessary to conclude what should be done. Other problems may be difficult and time-consuming, requiring that you put a lot of time and energy into them. What is the best way to attack what appears to be a complex problem? Here are some guidelines:

1. Avoid treating the symptoms of a problem—work on its causes. In many plants, for example, much engineering and maintenance are often directed at the symptoms of a problem rather than at the problem itself, especially when equipment and machinery are involved. Too many managers tend to analyze symptoms rather than causes in trying to correct such problems.

2. Look beyond the simple statement of the problem. The phrasing may or may not clearly identify it. Determine whether the person giving you the problem understands its scope and what is involved. It's often a good idea to question the objective of solving a problem.

3. Be thorough in your search for facts. Consider your approach and try to avoid overlooking something. Determine whether the scope of the problem is completely defined. Check on assumptions to determine whether they are critical to the solution.

4. Don't hesitate to fully apply yourself to a problem if it will make the difference between a good solution and a mediocre one. A complex problem may require a lot of mental gymnastics plus considerable attention to details. A mechanical problem may require you to get your hands dirty. Physical involvement in a project will provide you maximum learning and experience.

5. Seek the help and advice of other people. Working by yourself on a problem that affects others is not advisable. Besides, the affected people may have opinions, ideas, or information that are pertinent. Develop a good communication style in order that questionable points may be

brought into the open. Good communication fosters involvement and promotes cooperation.

6. Be rational when attacking a problem. Make sure your solution is possible with existing technology and knowledge. Use common sense: You don't want to propose a complex or costly solution to a trivial problem.

7. Pause at some point during a problem-solving session to determine whether you are on the right track. Reconsider your approach. Think about what you are trying to do. This ascertainment of your position is an important step in solving the problem in that it provides you an opportunity to uncover errors and introduce simplifications.

8. Call upon your insight and intuition. Your feelings should be given a lot of weight. Trust yourself. Have confidence that you will solve the problem and that your solution will stand the test of time.

Solving managerial problems is not easy. But some managers who are good at it make it look easy. They are able to do so because they take full advantage of all the resources and tools available to them. They aim for solutions that are realistic and practical. To reach these objectives, they organize their efforts, allocate their time, and fully utilize their knowledge and experience.

ANALYSIS PROCEDURES

Science is becoming more and more important in the development of objective decision-making methods, which can be ranked by how much they involve theory and scientific procedure.[5] The totally objective and scientific approach to decision making is at one end of such a ranking, while the approach involving intuition, experience, and subjective application of knowledge is at the other. A mixture of the two extremes is generally used to solve most problems. Yet the subjective approach has been the basis for much decision making in the past. A manager can seldom explain in depth the basis for his or her hunches but can do remarkably well with them regardless.

Several special information sources help problem solvers and decision makers. Accounting contributes information by way of financial statements and cost and performance reports. If these are understood by managers and reach managers promptly, the principle of exceptions can be applied, resulting in better decisions. The statistician provides certain nonaccounting data, designs sampling studies and interprets their findings, creates operations research tools, and formulates statistical decision rules for management use. Computers provide greatly increased amounts of data much faster than ever before; they thus become optimally useful in helping people make good decisions.

The decision maker's reliance on science varies according to the management level of the decision. Scientific procedures are most applicable to lower-level decision making, although the use of the scientific method encompasses all levels of management. In recent years, it has begun to indirectly affect upper-level decision making. As the validity of using scientific decision methods to solve problems has become apparent, managers have provided support and encouragement for these methods. Still, decision theory is felt to be in its infancy. The new methods not only solve existing problems in new ways but also change the nature of those existing problems.

Quantifiable Factors

One form of mathematical decision making concerns quantifying the factors bearing on the problem. To illustrate this procedure, consider the purchase of new equipment by a plant, not to take care of increased demand for its output, but to save on labor costs. If a machine priced at $20,000 will reduce annual costs for a process or operation by $10,000, it will pay for itself in two years, and if no other factors are involved, it will be a better choice than a machine with a payoff period of four years. Or if the costs of maintaining an old machine are higher than the depreciation on a new one, it will be cheaper to make the purchases.

Of course, there are other factors that may influence calculations of this nature, and even though a manager may not be involved, he or she should be knowledgeable about them. For example, many companies take the time value of money into account in making capital investments. They calculate the return that could be expected if the money were put to other uses. They also weigh the cost of delay and the expense of gathering more information against the risk of proceeding with what they already have, which may well be incomplete.

A few assumptions must be made with this type of reasoning. One is that the market for the product made (the equipment output) will remain constant or grow. If the demand were to drop, the labor need would also drop, and the figures used in the calculations would change. Another assumption is that the product will not change enough in the future to make it possible to eliminate the operation entirely. A third assumption is that the best new machine now on the market is the ultimate, at least for a few years; thus, it will not be replaced by something else within a year or two, in which case it might be better to wait.

Unquantifiable Factors

Managers are sometimes required to make decisions where it is not possible to quantify the pertinent factors. In a few cases, it may not even be possible to judge later whether their choices were the best possible. This means that they must rely heavily on their hunches or intuition.

A hunch is described as a feeling that something is going to happen in a certain way and that, therefore, a certain action would likely be good or bad. The hunch may be completely unsupported, or it may be close to a reasonable judgment. For instance, a manager may be able to predict with some degree of accuracy the reaction of his or her people to an edict that management is going to issue. A hunch of this type may be quite accurate because the person having it senses it as representing a good cross-section of other people's feelings and opinions. The safety sense an experienced and long-time construction manager is said to possess or a good job trainer's hunch about how quickly some workers will learn a new job may be due to this factor. Hunches, of course, may be entirely inaccurate. They may be based on wishful thinking or on subconscious associations that have no relevance to the situation.

Judgment is often difficult to define, in that reasoning can never produce a conclusion that is assuredly the best. The case for one alternative rather than another can never be proved beyond a shadow of a doubt, as can a theorem in geometry. Good judgment may be looked upon as a human quality that is inborn yet can be greatly improved through long experience. It may be said that some managers have naturally good business judgment, but only after they have experienced many different business situations can such judgment reach its full potential.

Many executives who are accustomed to making numerous decisions in the course of a day do not know how they make them. Even company presidents have made such remarks as, "You don't know how you do it—you just do it."

The steps preparatory to making decisions are easier to identify and define than the procedure itself. For managers, these include assessing people's capabilities; the availability of material; and the various contingencies of time, past practice, and cost, among others. In some cases, decisions are a matter of compromise, particularly if a management/union contract is in effect or the company is in an austerity period and managers are under pressure to reduce costs. For example, a decision about whether or not to work people overtime is frequently made by a first-line manager. Top management tends to question his or her judgment only if shipments to customers are delayed or services are not provided on schedule.

Decision-Making Tools

When you are given a particular problem and have several techniques you can use to arrive at a solution, which technique can be expected to produce the best results? To answer this question, you must consider three factors: feasibility, reliability, and cost. Although there are other factors you might consider, they will not influence most supervisory decisions.

The feasibility of a technique is usually easy to determine. If no computer were available to a problem solver, it would not be feasible for him or her to go to the trouble of borrowing or renting one for the sole purpose of solving a particular problem. It would also not be feasible to attempt to solve a complex simulation problem without a computer.

The major factor that must be considered in selecting a decision-making tool is its level of reliability. How much error in a particular solution is tolerable? In arriving at a solution, you would like to know not only the estimated payoff but how reliable that estimate is. Some tools are highly reliable—you can be reasonably certain that the values of the estimated and actual solutions will be almost the same.

When the reliability of a decision tool is known, risk or uncertainty is less. You may be willing to accept a solution with less payoff if it has greater reliability. But when you reach a decision intuitively, reliability can seldom be determined ahead of results because it is very difficult to test a solution that you reached unsystematically. Although a solution may initially seem to have merit, it may produce results that are significantly different from what you expected. The person who makes a decision intuitively cannot be sure within a predictable range that the expected payoff will actually happen.

As with any venture, the cost of the procedure or tool is a determinant of whether you use it or some other method. To determine the total cost of taking a mathematical or analytical approach to a problem, you should consider the time, the cost of staff people, and the cost of use of the computer. The pay rate of programmers and the cost of computer time are not difficult to figure, but the total time for a particular technique could vary considerably, depending on such factors as the availability of data and the number of variables. The cost of data collection can be significant in problem solving.

Decision-making tools generally are operational only when certain conditions exist. Furthermore, various limitations can restrict their use. Several illustrations of these drawbacks can be given. Functions must be linear if linear programming is to be used. The model with which you work in simulation must reasonably reflect the reality you are trying to understand or control. In fact, the use of all models has some drawbacks.

Most models are theoretical and impersonal, and some are very difficult to understand. A mathematical model may require oversimplification in order to be manipulated. Then again, there is no guarantee that the time spent in constructing the model will pay off in good prediction. The symbolic language may also be a problem. Even a mathematician may have difficulty in managing the model so as to obtain useful results. In gambling-game problems, it may be easier to play a large number of games and determine the probabilities directly than to attempt a mathematical analysis of the probabilities.

If a preliminary survey of the problem reveals that the conditions necessary for effective use of special techniques do not exist, these tools should not be considered. You may also have a constraint in that if a solution to a problem is needed in a few days, the techniques that require more time cannot be used. Another serious constraint may be a shortage of trained personnel to assist you. Some techniques are highly sophisticated. If people trained in such techniques are lacking, your method of analysis would have to be restricted to the skills of the available staff. A final constraint may be that you have an excessive number of problems to solve. Your superior may decide that you should turn to procedures that will conserve managerial time.

Statistical Analysis

Statistics can contribute to more effective decision making in a number of ways. First, the statistician provides certain of the quantitative data that management requires but that accounting does not provide. The statistician also designs sampling surveys, market research, and other experiments so that maximum information will be provided from a study and then helps to interpret the findings correctly and logically when the studies are completed. In addition, the statistician helps in formulating useful decision rules and creates new tools for operation research.

Suppose someone hands you a group of figures. The figures could be a record of nearly any activity in the company, such as production tonnage, machine failures, or some other incidents. Of what value are the figures in helping you to make a decision? The figures don't mean much unless they are analyzed, a procedure that is called statistical analysis. By statistical analysis you determine the relationship of each number to all the others. With this knowledge, you are able to make decisions. But that's a very simple explanation. In actuality, statistical analysis takes place in several steps: compiling the figures or data, organizing and analyzing them, evaluating conclusions, searching for cause-and-effect relationships, and detecting trends.

Operations Research

Operations research is defined as the application of mathematical methods to the study and analysis of complex problems. The techniques for solving problems using operations research methods include simulation, queuing, linear programming, and others. Typical problems that can be solved are determining the optimum time for performing preventive maintenance, the optimum number of people who should be employed in a storeroom for minimum cost, and the lowest level of machine parts inventory that should be maintained consistent with management policy. Many problems can be handled by the computer by constructing models simulating actual conditions in the office, plant, warehouse, or storeroom and then studying the effect of altering the variables.

Simulation

The use of a model to simulate a condition or situation is a very effective tool for a manager concerned with planning and control. Today, the technique of simulation through use of mathematical models and the computer enables you to construct a model of a problem and test the results of any number of proposed courses of action. Even with its limitations, the procedure may provide unanticipated information and thus enable you to avoid making a poor decision.

Simulation need not be mathematical, but many of today's business problems are so complex and the important variables so numerous that mathematics and the help of the computer are needed. Some examples of areas of responsibility where simulation is of value are those involving inventory control and the procedures required to operate a new process or production line. Although a manager may feel uncertain about how to proceed, simulation of a course of action can at least give him or her some indication of the size and type of risks involved.

Queues (Waiting Lines)

Another mathematical technique based on operations research theory has been derived for solving waiting-line problems. A user of this technique balances the costs of waiting lines versus the costs of preventing them by providing increased service. The theory is based on the premise that although delays may be expensive in one or more ways, eliminating them may be even more costly.

The people waiting in line at a storeroom window in an industrial plant are a good example of this problem. When a machine breaks down on the production line and can be repaired by use of a part or component in the storeroom, both production time and repair labor time are lost if the mechanic has to wait to be taken care of. But how often does a mechanic have to stand in line? Can adding another storeroom clerk to the payroll be justified?

A similar problem concerns the unloading of tank cars, boxcars, and delivery trucks. Although a company wants to avoid paying demurrage charges and quickly get materials into the warehouse, it may not be able to keep an additional employee busy on such operations. Rather than hire someone who may be idle part of the time, the company should first make a waiting-line study of the existing arrival and delivery situation, along with the time it takes to complete the unloading operations. The study will reveal whether or not an additional person on the payroll would save the company money.

Linear Programming

For one of the most successful applications of operations research in problem solving, look to the technique called linear programming. It is based on the assumption that a linear, or straight-line, relationship exists between variables, and that the limits of variations can be determined.

The production line in a plant is a good candidate for application of the technique by a manager. The major variables in this case are the units produced per machine in a given time, material costs per unit, direct labor costs, and machine operating costs. Most or all of these variables have linear relationships within certain limits; by solving linear equations that express those relationships, you can learn the optimum conditions of costs, machine use, time periods, and other objectives of the production department. This problem-solving procedure is especially useful where input data can be quantified and the progress toward objectives can be measured.

Linear programming is appropriate for solving problems of production planning, use of warehouse and storage areas to permit extended production runs to hold those costs to a minimum, and routing of shipments to take advantage of low shipping rates. The major drawback to the use of the technique today is that it depends on linear relationships between variables. If relationships are not linear, the technique cannot be used.

NOTES

1. W. H. Weiss, *Decision Making for First-Time Managers* (New York: American Management Association, 1985), pp. 2–19.

2. Used with permission of Sterling Publishing Co., Inc., 387 Park Ave. S., New York, N.Y. 10016, from *Managing Effectively,* by Joseph and Susan Berk, Copyright 1991 by Joseph and Susan Berk, pp. 91–92, and 97.
3. "Mentors Make, Break Careers," *Working Together* (Chicago, Ill.: Dartnell, February 28, 1994), p. 3.
4. Reprinted with permission of the publisher, from *Decision Making for First-Time Managers,* by W. H. Weiss, pp. 20–41, Copyright 1985. Published by AMACOM, a division of American Management Association. All rights reserved.
5. Ibid., pp. 134–145.

$$\boxed{\textbf{4}}$$

Communications: Key to Successful Leadership

Today's plants could not operate efficiently or productively without continual communication between management and employees. Both downward and upward communications are required for a smoothly functioning organization to maintain operations and be profitable. It goes without saying that managers must be skilled in communicating with their people.

Verbal communications include information and instructions, meetings, and announcements via the plant's intracommunications system. Written communications are disseminated through operating procedures, specifications, plant regulations, bulletin board notices, safety and other handbooks, and the company newspaper. Employees not only need to get clear instructions from their superiors, they want to know about their future pay and employee benefits; they also want to understand how they can improve their performance,[1] as shown by Exhibit 4-1.

COMMUNICATING WITH SUBORDINATES

To communicate effectively with your subordinates, keep in mind the following criteria:

Exhibit 4-1. What employees want to know.

Surveyed employees said the most important information to them at work concerns:

• Employee benefit program	82%
• Pay policies and procedures	78%
• Company's plans for the future	73%
• How to improve work performance	65%
• How my work fits into the total picture	61%

Source: The Hay Group Research for Management Database, as reported in *The Wall Street Journal,* August 9, 1985, p.19.

1. *Be specific and straightforward.* If an order or instruction isn't meant to be followed, it shouldn't be given. If it is important enough to be issued, it should be enforced.
2. *Be consistent.* You can't vacillate one day and be stubborn the next. If you are easygoing one time and tough another, you cause uncertainty and anxiety among the people who work for you.
3. *Don't give conflicting instructions.* Telling an individual to do something that isn't standard practice or is against plant rules can get you and the individual into real trouble. The same advice applies to telling one person to do a job a certain way and the next person a different way.
4. *Temper your instructions with reason and practicality.* Giving too many instructions or too many details at one time confuses people. Limit your orders and make them short and to the point.
5. *Be complete.* The type, amount, and completeness of information and instructions that you provide employees greatly determines their safety on the job, the quality of their workmanship, and the extent of their productivity.

Promoting Upward Communication

Your job as a manager is much easier if your employees keep you informed. You will have information and data that will help you make decisions, and you will be able to foresee problems that could arise. For these and other reasons, it is to your advantage to promote upward communication from employees at every opportunity. Here are some steps you can take that will achieve it:

- *Be available and receptive to persons who want to talk.* Listen to all your employees' ideas regardless of how illogical or impractical they may sound. If you suspect that passing a worker's good idea up the line will somehow reflect poorly on you for not having thought of it yourself, dispel that notion.

- *Develop informal relations with employees.* As you walk around the plant, make contact with employees, either singly or in small groups. Take these opportunities to find out what individuals are thinking.
- *Recognize all contributions with feedback.* People on the job appreciate their superiors telling them that their ideas were discussed in management meetings. Also, always thank employees for their suggestions, whether or not they are adopted.

Feedback

Providing meaningful feedback to those who frequently communicate with you can be of great help in raising productivity, increasing safety, and improving efficiency in the plant. Believe it or not, your subordinates and other employees want specific feedback about how they do their jobs.

Consider the following ways to improve the feedback you give people:

1. *Give feedback in small doses.* A listener forgets 80 percent of oral communication within ten to fifteen minutes. If you focus attention on just one aspect of a problem, you are unlikely to overwhelm the employee with too much information. Try: "Overall, this is a good job. Why don't you leave a little more white space on the pages of your report for easier reading."

2. *Define, not accuse.* Let's consider how to give feedback on a job that was finished late: Instead of accusing your employee of forgetting deadlines, define the situation, and probe for a reason. Say: "You normally get these shipments out on time. Yesterday an important one was a day late. Let's see what happened so that we can plan better next time."

3. *Specify what you want to change.* Telling an employee "You need to put in more effort" or "You have a bad attitude" is ambiguous. This type of feedback doesn't focus on what to change.

Instead, peg specific behavior, such as: "I think if you organize your work and do urgent things first, you'll find yourself getting more done and pleasing others who depend on you."

4. *Provide feedback with respect.* Talk to the individual alone, take time to listen, and discuss the issues. If you give feedback when you are rushed, harried, or with your mind on other things, you won't be effective. Feedback may actually come out as severe criticism. Cool down if you're angry, choose your words carefully, and demonstrate that you are interested in working with the person to develop sound solutions to the problem.[2]

COMPUTERIZED COMMUNICATIONS SYSTEMS

An excellent way for management to promote downward communication is to install a system for keeping employees informed. When the system is computerized, it can also reduce paperwork and make fuller use of the company's existing computer system by adding terminals in areas easily accessible to employees. To make the computerized system effective and worthwhile, the following steps should be taken:

1. Publicize the service well in advance of its installation.

2. Give clear, easy-to-follow directions for using the system. Some of the employees may not be computer-literate.

3. Train all employees on how to use the system. Appoint someone from each department to help others to understand and use the system.

4. Survey employees on what types of information they would like to have. The most common include:

- Fringe and job benefits
- Company activities and events
- Job openings and transfer opportunities
- Plant organization changes
- New product development
- What company competitors are doing
- Employee comments and suggestions

5. Plan to expand the services available as the system becomes better used.

SUGGESTION SYSTEMS

Every plant should have a suggestion system if for no other reason than to raise the productivity of its employees. The most common system found in plants is one in which employees write their ideas on a printed form and put them into a suggestion box. Each suggestion is reviewed by a committee, and, if it is accepted, the employee is given a cash award or a percentage of the cost savings for a fixed period.

To raise productivity, you've got to promote efficiency and be conscious of the cost of all the operations and services employees perform. The best way to do this is to ask them to think of better ways to do their jobs. Here is what you should do to sell them on submitting suggestions:

- Start by explaining the company's interest in suggestions from employees. Suggestions help to increase safety, reduce costs, and make work easier to perform.
- Point out some of the problem areas where improvements are needed. Talk about the need to reduce waste, eliminate a bottleneck, and simplify some of the process steps.
- Raise enthusiasm by mentioning the awards that are made for good suggestions. Tell employees that they have a lot to gain with nothing to lose by participating.
- Say that you're available to answer questions and to help anyone in writing up suggestions.

You should, however, be aware of a caution concerning suggestions. When you promote them, be sure you make it clear that turning in suggestions is an entirely voluntary matter. Suggestions are not a requirement of the job, nor are you telling people that they should be submitted. Some employees are more likely to participate when you discuss the subject this way. Also you avoid any arguments that may arise concerning pay for time spent developing an idea on nonworking time.

MAKING SURE YOU'RE UNDERSTOOD

One of the requisites of being a good communicator is having your message understood. You might just as well not say anything if your listeners misinterpret your words. Worse, not being understood can result in employees making errors or in their simply not doing a job.

Fortunately, there are a variety of ways in which you can determine if you've communicated well and your instructions have been understood. It pays to use most if not all of them to verify that employees understand you before they start carrying out your orders to start work on a hazardous, major, or complex job. Here are some ways to do that:

- *Ask them if they understand.* Although this is the most frequently used method, it is not the best. Few workers feel comfortable in admitting they do not understand directions given by their boss. As a result, the positive shake-of-the-head response to "Do you understand?" has gotten more managers in trouble than any other response. What has happened is that instructions have been carried out incorrectly or not at all. Except for workers you have directed a long time or in low-risk situations, you are better off with another way.

- *Have them repeat your directions.* Don't be concerned that they will think you don't trust them. This may be true only if you use the method with every little direction you give. It is a good procedure if used sparingly, especially when communication is vital, such as when safety is at stake.

■ *Ask them about key points.* Effective carrying out of instructions often hinges on a key step or point. Rather than have all your instructions repeated, it's more practical as well as effective to ask only about the key point. For example, if you've given a lot of directions to a craftsperson on the completion of a machine repair, ask the individual only to confirm when you said the job should be finished.

■ *Ask a question about a procedure.* How well someone understands how a job is to be done can be demonstrated by what steps the person intends to take to do it. Rather than focusing directly on the decision to get the job done, determine the extent of understanding from his or her plan of action. A side benefit from this method is that the person will feel more "in" on the project.

■ *Have them paraphrase your directions.* By having workers feed back your directions in their words, you can check for accuracy and understanding. In addition, ownership of the job is increased when workers put it in their own words. The only problem with this method is that it is not natural to restate in another form someone else's words. If you have many situations where accurate communications are required, it may be worthwhile to train persons to paraphrase because it is probably the most accurate verification technique.

■ *Have them explain your directions to someone else.* This method of communicating is appropriate when more than one worker is involved in carrying out an instruction. You can listen to the explanation and add encouragement if it is correct. Should the worker doing the explaining leave out something important, you can add it. By having one employee explain to another, both become more involved. Not only that, but the chance to share directions with their words may strengthen commitment to do the job.

You may wonder if employees will become suspicious if you start using one of these methods of communicating, especially if you adopt one or more every time you give directions. The answer to this is to introduce them slowly and in the proper situations. When used cautiously and correctly, few employees will become concerned or disturbed. You may find that as you begin to favor verification methods, workers will begin to use them also. This will improve communications among all the employees in your department.

MANAGEMENT INFORMATION SYSTEMS

Today's management information systems provide a wide source of data to all levels of management. Systems are designed to collect, analyze, store, and furnish data to users for the purpose of control of materials, manpower, machines, and money. Through the use of subsystems, information relating to plant level operations of manufacturing, sales, marketing, warehousing, and distribution is made available to the people concerned with those functions.

Every organization has a lot of information about its operations spread in the memories of its managers, in records, and in files. But, for a management information system to be effective and readily available, the various data, figures, and facts must be organized and put in a form that permits recording, storing, retrieving, and distribution as needed by those requesting it.

With high-speed, time-sharing computers together with inquiry and display systems, you can be in close communication with a central computer system. You can get immediate answers concerning the status of any of a broad range of business activities such as sales, inventories, and costs of a product or service. You can also be informed of plans, schedules, and trends of operations with which you are concerned. Part of the usefulness of systems as management tools derives from their capabilities to produce cost and control reports, information that is needed by decision makers at all management levels.

A system affords its users access to information files so that they may obtain the exact data they need. To do this, it must have the following capabilities:

1. A base file of current data, accessible by remote entry through a terminal designed for two-way communication.
2. Extensive range of detail including source of data if requested.
3. Fast response to the user's request for information.

If a system is very broad and serves all levels of management, it should also have security features to prevent unauthorized users from obtaining confidential information.

The two main reasons for the use of computers in management information systems are the speed and the accuracy with which they process large amounts of data. Information from computers is generally more encompassing and more immediately available than that generated by manual procedures.

MEETINGS

As a manager, you need to periodically hold meetings with employees for a number of reasons. Although most employees are not eager to attend meetings, you can make your meetings more interesting and productive if you conduct them as if you were the manager of a sports team. You make sure that the conditions are appropriate for the game (meeting) to take place, and you see that the players (employees) understand that they are expected to contribute to reaching the meetings' objectives (play their best). In addition, you serve as a facilitator in that you guide the meeting process toward a conclusion, but never take it over or allow yourself to be taken over. You are most effective when you wear the following hats:

■ *Organizer.* Here's how to invite others to talk and express their opinions if they do not become involved in the discussion. Say, "John, what do you think of the two courses of action we could take?" or "Let's hear from the rest of you." Also ask, "Does anyone else have something to offer?" When handled properly, this function is a strong force for making sure that everyone agrees on the steps to be taken and will follow through with the correct action.

■ *Compromiser.* You help the meeting participants to see each other's viewpoints and to reconcile disagreements by finding a common ground on which everyone can agree. To get people to explore differences in a positive way, you might say, "Ed, will you state the objection Tom has to your solution, and then, Tom, will you do the same for Ed's argument? That way, we will know that each of you understands the other's position before continuing the debate."

■ *Supporter.* You enable participants to get what they want from the meeting, not merely what they need. For example, you could say, "I know we came to talk about the booklet on safety issued by the personnel department, but the discussion keeps returning to the rash of eye injuries you people are experiencing. I think we should set another meeting to talk about the booklet, and use this time to deal with the subject of eye safety."

Creative Meetings

A good way to get employees more involved in solving department problems is to periodically hold a creative meeting. It would seem that setting up such a meeting would be simple, but it may require a bit of planning on your part to make it a success. Creative meetings are appropriate when the normal chains of decision making and review have not been able to develop satisfactory answers. The issues may be such subjects as, "How can we eliminate this bottleneck in the process?" or "What can we do to fill customers' orders faster?" and others.

The number of people you invite to a creative meeting should be between four and eight. At least four are needed to get people alert, active, and interested. Meetings with more than eight tend to limit the number of contributions from each member. To maximize the productivity of a meeting, distribute an agenda beforehand. In addition to providing information on meeting objectives, it will encourage both conscious and subconscious preparation among the participants.

Hold the meeting in the morning because most people are mentally freshest then. The room in which the meeting is held should be free from visual distractions and noise. A round table is best in order to maintain eye contact among all participants.

You have to be realistic about a meeting's outcome and what results you will get from it. Any idea presented by the participants, no matter how creative, involves risk, expense, and may require a capital investment; change is inevitable.

The fundamental rule of creative sessions is not to criticize any idea or comment of a session participant. Negative comments and remarks put a damper on creativity. If there are comments about ideas, they should only be positive. Such comments may, in turn, switch on the creativity of a third person.

When session participants bring up a good idea, they tend to want to pursue it, adding embellishments. You, as the leader, must have the skill and discipline to move the group on so that it will generate other, perhaps better, ideas.

Meetings need to be followed by debriefing within a day or two. Even an excellent and apparently fruitful session generates much meaningless information and many ideas. It may take you considerable time and effort to analyze, understand, supplement, or research the session's output.

TEAM COMMUNICATION

An organization's success depends greatly on the ability of team members to interact with each other. The better a manager can mold a team into a group of individuals who recognize each other's capabilities, moods, and temperaments, and make adjustments accordingly, the more likely the team will be successful in their work. Like a well-designed machine, an organization will produce quality products or services only if every part of the organization performs properly. That is where teamwork comes into play.

Here's how healthy, vibrant, and enthusiastic team members respond to each other and work well together. Cooperative team players do the following:

- *Try to be effective communicators.* They are aware that most conflicts come about because they don't understand one another's words—they jump to conclusions and usually guess incorrectly. Every member of a team must speak the same language if the team is to accomplish its goals.
- *Avoid arguments and disputes.* Both are a waste of time and destroy good relationships. If an argument starts and is going nowhere, resolve it immediately or put it aside.
- *Act assertively rather than aggressively.* You can settle conflicts and meet your own needs without dominating others or pounding on them to make a point. Assertiveness is an act that is open and honest; with negotiation, it can help everyone win to some degree. Aggressiveness is a warfare tactic; nobody wins in a battle.
- *Prefer openness to defensiveness.* Recognize that the best way to prevent a situation from becoming a conflict is to be nonthreatening in your approach. Let people know you respect their opinions, even if you don't agree with them.
- *Abstain from a gloomy outlook.* If you are inclined to be pessimistic, cover it up when on the job. People who are consistently pessimistic hold back productivity of both themselves and others. They also negatively affect morale.
- *Never put a damper on others' activities or achievements.* Everyone has something they are proud of; belittling it for no good reason accomplishes nothing. Sincere compliments, however, strengthen a team's cohesion. If you support the people you work with, they will support you.
- *Refuse to be manipulative.* Anyone who tries to shrewdly use others or create discord isn't a true team player and must be persuaded to change his or her ways. Healthy teams provide a challenging opportunity for individual growth and group achievement. But all members must be eager and enthusiastic to ensure the team's success.

COMMUNICATING VIA BULLETIN BOARDS

Although communication with plant employees is one of your primary responsibilities, you don't have to limit it to one-on-one conversations or to group meetings. Don't overlook the benefits and advantages of communicating visually through the plant's bulletin board.

You'll find that when it comes to delivering a consistent message about departmental, team, or individual performance, a picture—the bulletin board—can be invaluable. It can tell a story quickly and with impact.

A bulletin board that maps out a departmental project or other team-oriented work becomes an informative source to other employees. It describes the project or work, explains the process used to get from one stage (the beginning) to the final stage (the end). And it links the department's (or team's) efforts to the overall goal of the company.

Here is how you can use the plant's bulletin board to both motivate and inform employees:

- *Give an account of a successful project.* Explaining the who, what, when, where, why, and how of an employee's project is a good way to give the individual a pat on the back while at the same time showing how one of the company's objectives was reached. A statement of the project's goal should be the central focus of the display. Use large print with plenty of white space when you put the details on the board.

- *Promote interest visually by making the bulletin board bright and eye-catching.* Employees like to look at photos, especially of themselves. Start with a photo of the department or team, and identify each person. When a team begins a project, assign someone to be the "official photographer" to take pictures of each progression step. Post these to show photos of "before," "during," and "after."

Employees like to look at cartoons, too. You may decide to use a cartoon character to put across a particular message, such as a safety tip. Perhaps one of your employees is an amateur artist who can produce drawings of how a plant problem was solved or what your department has accomplished.

- *Tell employees about the plant's achievements.* Facts and figures make dry reading, but graphs and charts portray numbers in a picture. You don't need a computer software graphics package to graph progress. Colored pencils and graph paper produce the same results—a quick-to-read progress report.

To maintain interest, keep the bulletin board up-to-date, and let your imagination go wild on what and how you put the news on the board. Ask for volunteers to help with this goal. Share the pride of authorship with others and let everyone who passes by enjoy a never-ending series of excellent presentations.

COMMUNICATION STYLE

Employees need to know what is expected of them if they are to perform their jobs safely and efficiently. The burden of having them understand instructions and directions is with their manager. This is why it is so important that you be a good communicator.

The words you use in giving orders may be the difference between understanding and not understanding. How you say something and the conditions under which you say it also contribute to your message. In many situations, body language may have more meaning than the words you say.

In both formal and informal communication situations, you run the risk of being misunderstood because of a poor choice of a word or combination of words. Since there are so many words in our language and each one may have several meanings, you cannot hope to master all of them.

What you must do is try to know the common meanings of most of our often-used words. Just about every person has overheard two people, arguing over a point, expressing their ideas in different words while they are really saying the same thing. Because the speakers place different meanings on various words, they feel only disagreement.

Use of Language

The proper use of language is a measure of your training, maturity, and egotism. It's also a measure of your interest in your listener. To be a good communicator, you must:

1. Combine the expectations of the person listening with the requirements of the orders and instructions you give. To achieve this goal, you must be a good observer.
2. Note your listener's reaction to your words. If you get too absorbed in what you're saying, you risk becoming boring. This is true whether you're giving instructions to one of your employees or talking about an on-the-job problem with another.
3. Pause now and then to let your words sink in and to give your listener a chance to comment. Pausing helps to ensure that you are getting through.
4. Maintain your composure regardless of the situation. You'll do a better job of communicating by not being moody, irritable, or easily upset.
5. Recognize that people on the job dislike questioning and will often say they understand when they don't, rather than risk an emotional response.
6. Discount some of what is said by a worker who is clearly angry. To get a better idea of how the angry person really feels, bring up the subject again when he or she has calmed down.

In addition, you should be familiar with the nonverbal ways that people communicate their thoughts and feelings. For example, when a person drums his or her fingers as you talk, he or she is impatient. The person may want to say something, may wish you'd get to the point, or may just wish you'd finish talking and leave. An individual who frowns is either puzzled by what you're saying, expected to hear something else, or doesn't like what he or she is hearing.

You may learn a great deal if you watch people's eyes. Their eyes involuntarily express pleasure, displeasure, inquisitiveness, boredom, understanding, or bewilderment. By being alert to catch these nonverbal ways that people communicate, you can better understand their words. More important, you can tell whether you are getting through with your message.

Nonverbal Communication Techniques

Skill in reading nonverbal cues delivered by employees during a conversation or meeting will help you to be a more successful manager and communicator. Among the benefits gained from learning to read so-called "body language" is the growing sensitivity you gain in understanding the many needs of those you manage.

To understand nonverbal communicating is essentially to recognize and interpret the meaning and significance of body movements, gestures, and facial expression. It's also necessary to see and comprehend the distances people will keep between themselves and others, as well as to know who is sensitive to touch. There are those who want to touch and those who want to stay away.

What some people do with their hands, for example, is considered especially revealing. Aggressive individuals often will wave them about, using this way to show interest and enthusiasm for what they are saying. Reserved, meek, and shy persons seldom do more than raise a hand or point a finger when speaking.

There are those who use their hands to describe something in particular, using cutting and hacking motions when they converse on most any subject. In contrast, others use their hands only to emphasize words.

Nodding is another common way of communicating nonverbally. When you are speaking and your listener nods, you are encouraged to continue talking and to expand on a subject. However, if your listener shakes his or her head, you may lose confidence in what you are saying or be distracted. Thus a nod is usually a sign of agreement. As a manager, you may want to use the nod to encourage employees when they are talking.

The nervous habits of some employees in the plant confirm that they are concerned or worried about something, although they may also be impatient. They show their uneasiness by tapping their fingers, squinting, adjusting their eyeglasses, and pulling on their ears. Other gestures portray various feelings. For example:

- Big smiles and hearty handshakes depict jubilance; you may soon hear some good news if someone greets you in this manner.
- Frowns, downcast eyes, and drooping shoulders tell you that a person is either displeased or discouraged, so prepare yourself to hear a sad story. If you suspect you know the problem, start thinking about how you can perk up or console the person. A kind word or a pat on the back may do it.

Touch plays a big role in nonverbal communications because it tells you if someone is tense or relaxed. You may want to touch one of your employees to show that you appreciate what he or she has done or to reassure the person. A simple clasp of the worker's hand or the placing of your hand on his or her shoulder will do this. Although some managers prefer not to touch someone for fear the person will withdraw or be annoyed, touching, if done gently and casually, carries with it your personal approval.

BARRIERS TO GOOD COMMUNICATIONS

To be a successful manager, you must be an effective communicator, but becoming one is not always easy. Those who have succeeded have overcome the barriers that prevent workers from understanding them and from being fully informed.

Communications within many departments today could be much improved. Not only do employees fail to always understand their first-line managers, they also are sometimes not told everything they need to do their work. Some managers seem unable to get their messages across.

A weakness in human relations skills is one barrier. Others can be traced to bias and prejudice that creep into messages. Some can be attributed to a manager's personal style and manner of communicating. Whatever the reason, you should recognize that such barriers exist and that they prevent you from doing a good job of communicating. The following barriers in particular deserve your attention:

1. *Considering the listener.* Communicating is much easier if you reckon with your listeners. Consider the experience and knowledge of your listener in choosing words to be said. You must also beware of being

indifferent. Persistence and patience may be required to get your message across.

You must realize that people will not always respond to your messages no matter how clear you make them if you disregard their thoughts and feelings. Never use your authority to give orders that are unfair or that infringe on an individual's personal rights.

You should also be aware that the same words may mean different things to different people, and that the same idea can be stated in different words. We express ourselves in our own ways for several reasons. Our backgrounds and education vary. Our training and experience determine the words we use and the meanings we attach to them. Under such circumstances, it's really a wonder that we don't have more misunderstandings.

2. *Giving information.* Managers sometimes withhold information from subordinates, thus hindering them from carrying out their job responsibilities. Right or wrong, they do this on the pretense that subordinates will learn better if they are required to dig out facts for themselves.

But managers may not communicate fully for other reasons. Managers who feel they are going to move up in the company may willingly communicate upward but not so willingly downward. This is often an attempt to gain power and command admiration.

Contrarily, the managers who feel they have reached their peak in the company may freely communicate downward. They realize they must work closely with others in order to remain where they are and not drop lower in position. At the same time, they are not eager to communicate upward because they feel they have nothing to gain by doing so.

Misleading or inadequate communicating can sometimes be attributed to psychological factors. Fear, for example, can be a deterrent—fear of being criticized, disciplined, or denied promotion. Fear of displeasing a superior may be enough to cause information to be presented in an understated form or covered up completely.

3. *Using imprecise language.* You've probably noticed that people sometimes use the expression "you know" in their conversations or adopt vague words (especially those from high-tech fields) without really knowing what they mean. On the other hand, jargon—complex technical language used by a specialist—can also cause misunderstanding.

4. *Believing authorities.* Because of managers' positions of authority, employees tend to believe what higher-level managers say, regardless of whether it is true or not. In addition, the status of the communicator either lends credibility to what is being said or detracts from it. Messages of higher-status people tend to carry greater credibility than those of lower-status people.

5. *Calling on higher authority.* Using the name of a higher authority for leverage is a weak way to request that something be done. If you resort to such tactics, you show that you don't have enough confidence in your own authority, and must use that of a person whose name carries greater weight.

For instance, you should support management decisions on policy when communicating with employees. When you give orders to them, word the orders in a manner as though the policy were yours, even though you may not be fully in agreement with the action to be taken.

Handle your requests for information similarly. Avoid the unauthorative way, "The Boss wants to know. . . . " Obtain the information for the boss without using the boss' words and position as a means.

Other roadblocks to successful communications in plants include: message overload and complexity; personal distortion mechanisms such as inattention, early evaluation, and lack of a common vocabulary; and psychological distortion mechanisms, such as rationalization and denial. Following is a discussion of how these problems prevent effective managerial communication.

■ *Message overload.* With this block, too many competing messages arrive simultaneously with the result that either none have a marked influence on feeling, sense, or mind or that those that do are distorted in the midst of the message competition. Managers should limit the number of messages sent at any one time. The messages should be prioritized, with the most important for the immediate situation sent first. After there has been time to absorb and get the attention of the receiver, then others can be sent according to their lower priority.

Consider, for example, the department manager who wishes to notify members of the department by letter of a new procedure for taking vacation, provide information regarding a change in the health plan, and inform employees of a pay raise. If all three pieces of information are sent in the same letter, they may create an information overload. A better way of presenting this information is to write separate letters on the vacation procedure and the change in the health plan, and put the news of the pay raise in the weekly pay envelopes. The messages, read separately, will be more sequential than simultaneous and reduce the competition for the attention of the receivers.

■ *Message complexity.* There is greater difficulty in understanding a complex message than a simple one. With a complex message, the receiver must try to understand not only the many components of the message, but also the interrelationships of these components. An alert manager tries to reduce message complexity, if possible. This often can be accomplished by breaking a complex message into several smaller and simpler messages.

The most common way of doing this is not by merely inserting periods into a message that contained commas, but by making a complex sentence into many simple sentences. If, for example, the message being simplified contains instructions for sequential actions, the sequence of instruction must be preserved in the order of the simplified messages. To indicate the sequence in which the messages should be read, they may be placed in numbered order or may even contain an overlap section. This is a summary paragraph, or the final section from the previous section—it reminds the reader of what came immediately before.

▪ *Inattention.* Since the brain of a listener can process information at a much faster rate than a message can be delivered by a speaker, inattention is often produced. The process of rapid understanding is further speeded up by the psychological process known as closure. The mind of the receiver completes a message even if it is incomplete and assembles the parts into a whole. In communication, this process operates to fill in the gaps of a partial message so that it can be understood.

▪ *Early evaluation.* Because the receiver completes the message even before receiving it, the receiver may prematurely evaluate the contents of the message. This may lead the receiver to draw false conclusions and assume the message to be something that it is not. This leaping to conclusions can be very destructive to effective communication, and a manager who constantly does this will consistently experience difficulty in understanding what is being said. Some of this early evaluation may arise from a misunderstanding of the words being used.

▪ *Lack of a common vocabulary.* A common vocabulary consists of words that have formally defined meanings that are accepted by a specific group and that facilitate communication by eliminating or greatly limiting the connotative meanings of words. Professional groups, such as engineers and physicians, develop a specific vocabulary, words that have denotative meanings acknowledged by all within the profession. A nonengineer, overhearing a highly technical conversation between two engineers, would probably not understand much of the conversation. The important point is that the two engineers would understand each other exactly, and this is the function of a common vocabulary.

A manager may have to use a different vocabulary when speaking with senior managers than when speaking to the union rank and file. This is not linguistic snobbery but the recognition that effective communication depends upon understanding, and a manager desiring to be understood must use words that are understandable. Managers who use words not understood by employees will have extreme difficulty in communicating accurately with them.

■ *Rationalization.* When an employee justifies behavior and thought that is unconsciously evaluated as unjustified, the individual is rationalizing. This process also creates distortion in communicating with others. Receivers have trouble understanding the nature of the communication and often respond with feedback that points out that the sender is rationalizing. Managers need to become aware when they are rationalizing and realize that it may be a source of difficulty in communicating with others.

■ *Denial.* When someone refuses to acknowledge feelings or opinions when challenged, the individual is expressing denial. For example, a subordinate, having voiced an opinion to a manager, may deny such an opinion if challenged. This will impact upon the communication process when it creates confusion: The manager will have trouble understanding the subordinate's denial. What seems obvious to the manager will not be obvious to the subordinate engaged in the denial reaction.

DEALING WITH UNIONS

Plant employees have the right, by law, to decide whether or not they will be represented by a union. That same law also gives management the right to try to convince the employees that they would be better off by not having a union. If your plant is not unionized, you should want to keep it that way. As shown below, a well-intentioned, professional plant management can do better for its employees and all concerned with the plant without a union.

Keeping your plant nonunion should not be left to chance. All members of management must make a conscious sustained effort to prove to the employees that their needs and expectations can best be met by plant management. Here are the ways you and other managers can do that:

■ *Pay appropriate wages and fringe benefits.* Keep them at least equal to, and preferably above, those of other plants in the area. If the employees believe that they are getting more than unionized plants provide, you are in a good position.

■ *Be aware of the importance of job security.* Employees want continuous employment and fair treatment if layoff becomes necessary. If you see that you might not be able to avoid a layoff, put out a detailed procedure long before the need to use it arises.

■ *Handle all complaints promptly and fairly.* This is best done by establishing a formal, legal, and workable grievance procedure. Publish it, give a copy to every employee, and train all members of management how to use it.

■ *Treat employees courteously and with respect.* They want to feel that their jobs are important and their efforts are appreciated. Many of them also want challenging work and opportunities for advancement.

■ *Be alert and keep in touch.* Nothing can hurt plant management more than to be unaware of the problems and wants on the minds of its employees. You must know exactly where the sensitive and rough spots are in your employee relationships, what employees like and what they dislike. The best way to learn this and keep up-to-date is to visit the plant's work areas frequently and talk with the employees.

Disadvantages of Having a Union

Not only are there few if any benefits to both management and employees of having a union in the plant, there are three major disadvantages:

1. *Waste of managerial time and effort.* Large amounts of managerial time at all levels of the company go into preparing for and handling union negotiations, grievances, and demands. Such time could be better spent in improving operations and conditions in the plant and managing processes for more profits and growth. The security of the plant's employees rests not with the union, but with the efforts of both management and employees to improve the factors that make the plant's products competitive: quality and cost.

2. *Conflict of interest and interference with managerial decisions.* The one-on-one relationship between a company and its employees ends when a union exists in the plant. The union may have no interest in the profitability or growth of the company, yet it must be consulted on every major matter or undertaking affecting the employees. Union officials may order that decisions made by plant management must conform to some regional or national pattern that has no relation to your company's particular situation. In addition, the union may promise benefits to employees that the company has no ability or intention to grant.

3. *Possibility of slowdowns and strikes.* If the union decides to take these economic steps, the plant's output may be cut or it may be shut down. While many of the plant's costs continue, customers are lost and employees become bitter toward the company. Worse, even though such events and incidents are settled eventually, they may have long-lasting effects.

Reasons Employees Join Unions

It's critical that you know why plant employees may want to belong to a union. Such knowledge gives you insight to handling the problem. You also learn what the employees expect from the company. Of the several reasons why employees join unions, four are more common than others:

1. Management typically believes that money and benefits are behind most dissatisfactions, but these issues are often not the real problem. Money becomes a major factor when employees feel they are ignored; this is the primary reason why employees join unions.
2. Some employees believe that membership in a union gives them an opportunity to gain more self-respect. They occasionally would like to "tell the boss off," and they might do so if they had a union to back them up.
3. Other employees feel that unions satisfy their emotional needs so that they no longer need a paternalistic employer. To them, unions tend to take the place of the disinterested employer who serves as the economic father of the employees.
4. Many employees decide they want a union to represent them when they see that management is indifferent to their needs. Plant employees show these feelings in many ways. Absenteeism and turnover increase, productivity is erratic and usually declines, waste and scrap are high, and safety records are poor.

UNION MANAGEMENT CONTRACTS

If plant employees decide they want to be represented by a union, they meet with management to draw up a contract or agreement that covers such subjects as wages, fringe benefits, working conditions, seniority, grievance procedures, and other industrial relations subjects. The contract usually contains a "management rights" clause as well as a statement recognizing the responsibility of both parties to establish and maintain peaceful labor relations and to operate the plant safely and efficiently.

Relations between management and employees do not suddenly change when the plant becomes unionized. Employees continue to want to be treated similarly to nonunion employees; they also expect good leadership from management of the plant. What has changed is the existence of a written contract, the intervention of a third party, and the threat of strikes to enforce employee demands.

The first step that management takes in preparing for contract negotiations is to form a collective bargaining team. Because the results obtained by the bargaining team cannot be expected to surpass the combined capabilities of its members, their selection requires great care. The team is most likely to perform well if the members possess the following attributes and qualities.

- Enthusiasm for and an interest in collective bargaining
- General knowledge of the plant, its operations, and administrative functions
- Ability to work well as part of a team
- Stamina and good health
- Alertness and sensitivity

Renewal of Contracts

Assuming a plant is operating under a union/management contract that will soon expire, here are the specific actions and steps a management team should take to ensure they are adequately prepared for the negotiations. The members should:

1. Study and examine the current contract to determine whether there are areas that need to be modified or changed. Members should also review any arbitration decisions made since the current contract went into effect—such rulings may suggest other contract changes.

2. Analyze past grievances to anticipate situations and conditions where the union will likely make demands. Decide what stand the company will take if any of these become reality.

3. Survey other management people on what changes they feel should be made in the contract. You and other first-line and middle managers are generally a good source of information on employees' opinions, likes, and dislikes of the current contract.

4. Meet with plant union leaders to discuss the current contract, its coverage, and its effectiveness. Talk with the union leaders several months in advance of actual negotiations and ask for information on potential contract issues that will be brought up for negotiation.

5. Keep current with developments on collective bargaining, labor legislation, and industrial relations by reading appropriate labor and management journals. Look particularly for statistics on such subjects as employment, payrolls, and cost of living.

6. Get financial information on the company's status on profits, the costs of doing business, industry conditions, market forecasts, and tax laws and their impact on the company. This information will be needed during negotiations when responding to the union's wage demands.

7. Anticipate and plan how negotiation meetings will be conducted. Consider ways to negotiate and procedures to follow. Plan to:

- Negotiate in private and away from the plant's offices.
- Start with easy issues.
- Agree on the procedure for reporting progress.
- Work at bringing about a "win-win" settlement.

COLLECTIVE BARGAINING

When members of management and the union get together to discuss wages, hours, working conditions in the plant, and fringe benefits for union employees, the procedure is called *collective bargaining*. Various labor laws define what subjects can be included in collective bargaining and what cannot. Generally, however, the term *working conditions* is so broad that just about anything that affects employees on the job or the way they work can be included.

While collective bargaining usually takes place sixty to ninety days prior to the termination of the current union contract, some companies make arrangements to continue the bargaining process throughout the life of the contract. State and federal laws require that unionized plants participate in the collective bargaining procedure. Management or unions that refuse to meet and consider proposals and make counterproposals are liable to charges of unfair labor practices.

Whether or not an issue is an appropriate subject for collective bargaining has no bearing on which party controls the way it is handled. The union can bargain for what it wants, and management has to bargain in good faith on the issues. Both sides have offensive tactics they can use to force the other side into agreement. The union's strength lies in the threat of a strike, and eventually the strike itself. The company can use the lockout, but seldom does so because it wants to keep the plant running. The company's best means of contending are its ability to withstand a strike longer than the union can, and its rights to hire permanent replacements for economic (as opposed to unfair labor practice) strikers.

Interpreting the contract and applying it day after day are what makes collective bargaining work. The contract is rarely changed during its life. But there are many situations and occurrences between you and employees that must be carefully studied to determine how they should be handled in order to carry out the meaning of the contract. It is such interpretation and difference of viewpoint between management and unions that make labor relations a key managerial responsibility.

Unfair Labor Practices

While either the union or management may be guilty of unfair labor practices at any time, most charges are made during organizing campaigns. Whenever either party claims that the other party is acting unfairly, the National Labor Relations Board should be contacted. Representatives of this organization will investigate and rule on the claim. As for what constitutes unfair labor practices, here's how the National Labor Relations Act identifies them:[3]

Unfair Management Practice

1. To interfere with, restrain, or coerce employees in the exercise of their rights to self-organization; to form, join, or assist labor organizations; to bargain collectively through representatives of their own choosing; or to refrain from such activities.

2. To dominate or interfere with any labor organization, or contribute financial or other support to it.

3. To discriminate in regard to hire or tenure or employment, or any condition of employment, in order to encourage or discourage membership in any labor organization (the law specifically exempts a union shop agreement, however).

4. To discharge or otherwise discriminate against an employee because he or she has filed charges or given testimony under the act.

5. To refuse to bargain collectively with representatives of employees.

Unfair Union Practices

1. To restrain or coerce: (a) employees in the exercise of their rights (listed in 1. above); (b) an employer in the selection of his or her representatives for collective bargaining or the adjustment of grievances.

2. To cause, or attempt to cause an employer to discriminate against an employee, or to discriminate itself against an employee whose union membership has been denied or terminated on some ground other than failure to pay regular initiation fees and dues.

3. To refuse to bargain collectively with an employer.

4. To engage in a strike or refusal to handle goods or perform services, or encourage other employed individuals to do so, or to coerce or threaten any person engaged in commerce (including employers) where the object is to: (a) force an employer or self-employed person to join any labor or employer organization, or to enter into a "hot cargo" agreement;[4] (b) force anyone to boycott the goods or business of another, or force an-

other employer to recognize or bargain with a union that is not certified to represent his employees; (c) force an employer to recognize or bargain with a union when a different union has been certified as the representative of his employees; (d) force an employer to assign work to employees in a particular union, trade, or class rather than those in another union, trade, or class.

5. To charge an excessive or discriminatory initiation fee.

6. To cause or attempt to cause an employer to pay for services that are not performed.

7. To picket an employer to force him to recognize or bargain with a union, or force his employees to select that union (unless the union is currently certified as the representative of his employees) if the employer has lawfully recognized another union, a valid election has been held within the past twelve months, or the picketing has continued for thirty days without the union filing a petition for an election. (However, the law exempts truthful informational picketing that does not induce a boycott or a strike.[5])

GRIEVANCE PROCEDURES

Effective grievance handling requires a positive attitude toward employees. You also need to develop the ability to accept and handle complaints promptly in a nonthreatening manner. Another requisite is to make the employee with the grievance feel that he or she has your full attention. If you happen to be busy at the time, it's essential to explain the reason why handling the grievance must wait. In such a situation, set a later time to meet with the employee. Here is a procedure that will get you good results with plant employees:[6]

1. When an employee verbally complains, repeat the person's main points in your own words to make sure you completely understand the problem. You may have to probe a bit to get at the real issue if your summary doesn't accurately reflect the employee's concern.

2. If you see that the grievant is upset or angry, take him or her aside so you can talk in private. This move allows the employee to blow off steam without embarrassment. It also tells the person that you are concerned.

3. Listen carefully and remain calm. Always assume that the complaint is real. But be alert because a grievance may be concealing some other problem that has gone unnoticed.

4. After an employee has finished telling you his or her complaint, assure the person that you will act promptly. Then review all the information you have and investigate to confirm what you have been told.

5. Determine where you can find the answer to the complaint. If it involves a company policy, for example, the employee handbook may contain the information you need. If the complaint concerns interpretation of the contract, study the wording in the applicable section.

6. Be ready to accept the logical conclusion that comes from the facts you uncover. If you find that you have made a mistake, admit it.

7. Give the employee a definite answer. State your decision in such a way that there is no mistake about what you mean. If the company is in the wrong, tell the employee that corrective action will be taken. If the complaint is based on misinterpretation, clarify the matter for the person. By explaining your decision, you will seem to be less of a dictator and more of a communicator.

8. Make a record of the grievance and your answer. If your company has a procedure on grievance handling, follow it to the letter.

NOTES

1. This information was published in *Successful Small Business Management,* Fifth Edition (Plano, Tex.: Business Publications, Inc., 1988), p. 310.
2. Charles Kozoll, "Providing Meaningful Feedback," Dartnell, August 16, 1993, p. 1.
3. A copy of the latest revision of *A Guide to Basic Law and Procedure Under the National Labor Relations Act* (Washington, D.C.: Office of the General Counsel, National Labor Relations Board) is available from the Superintendent of Documents, U.S. Government Printing Office, Washington, D.C. 20402.
4. A *hot cargo agreement* is one in which a union and employer agree to refrain from handling the goods of another employer and from doing business with the company. Hot cargo agreements are forbidden by the act (with certain exceptions in the construction and apparel industries), whether or not they were entered into voluntarily.
5. *A Guide to Basic Law and Procedure Under the National Labor Relations Act.*
6. W. H. Weiss, *Plant Supervisor's Complete Desk Book* (Englewood Cliffs, N.J.: Prentice Hall, Inc., 1987), pp. 402–403.

5

Use of Computers for Operations and Control

Computers are rapidly taking over the jobs of clerks, secretaries, and analysts as computer capabilities expand and the need for information and data is recognized. Through the use of personal computers, minicomputers, and time-sharing on large systems, data can be quickly and accurately received, collected, organized, processed, and reported. Even the smallest plants today must have, or have access to, a computer. As the business expands or diversifies, computers become even more essential.

Computers differ from other office and plant equipment in that programs rather than people direct the processing of the data, and they can store large quantities of information and data. While you have to activate computers and put data and information in them, the computers do everything else. The *hardware,* consisting of machines and related equipment, performs the processing, and the *software,* consisting of instructions and/or programs, tells the computer what to do. Programs designed to carry out functions and operations may be purchased from computer companies and software publishers, or they may be written by an organization's own qualified employees.

Plants use computers for a wide variety of purposes. Some of the more frequent uses include collecting and processing data for planning and scheduling, purchasing, material control, machine and equipment control, and production and maintenance operations. When a change from manual to computer processing is being considered, plant management must decide whether a new accounting or other system should be designed and whether standard or specially designed programs are to be used. You should get help from technically qualified people such as consultants, accountants, and/or sales representatives in revising or initially installing a system for processing data.

THE COMPUTER'S COMMUNICATION CAPABILITIES

The importance of communicating data and information—not only to managers, but to all employees—cannot be overemphasized. Today, a company is successful in proportion to its ability to rapidly and efficiently gather, interpret, and transmit all information describing its activities.[1]

The complexity and amount of data needed to conduct a business have greatly increased over the years. Yet many companies haven't changed their control systems appreciably. Managers frequently are trying to control systems and operations with information that is incomplete as well as out-of-date.

Using the computer's communications capabilities helps managers at all levels with this function. The application is through the use of the computer at the executive decision level to implement management policy, and at the operational level to monitor and control the operations and processing activities.

Documentation on Using the Computer

If you participate in selecting and procuring a computer for your department, make sure the system is supplied with adequate documentation. The degree to which it is supplied is the degree to which you will have confidence in the system and will experience smooth operations. This user's reference manual is the guide to successful productive work.

You will find that one of the first levels of documentation in the manual is referred to as *the system overview*. In this area, how the overall system works is explained. Each part of the system is considered separately and described functionally.

The functional description usually includes information on the module, the input that is expected by the computer at each step, and the output that the computer user can expect to receive at various times during the use of that program. Some description should also be furnished of the file layout and the records in each file.

The most important documentation for a computer system is called *the user documentation.* It is the most critical to the plant because it gives the persons using the computer system a detailed step-by-step procedure that must be followed in order to do each job function.

In addition to the instructions on all job steps in each functional area of a system are the optional responses that can be made by the person at the terminal or workstation. Errors and how to correct them should also be discussed so that an operator can become truly independent after being trained.

Another level of documentation is known as *the programmer's reference.* This is a technical package that is provided for the programmer who is responsible for supporting and maintaining the software. Since it is meant to supply in-depth descriptions of logic flow and coding (programming) that make up the system, it is the documentation least likely to be furnished to users of the computer.

If you find that your responsibilities require you to frequently use the computer, you will probably want to add some special step-by-step procedures to the manual. A few examples are start-of-the-day steps, end-of-the-month jobs, and backup procedures.

Make sure that each routine you wish to include in your manual is complete to the last detail. This will prove to be invaluable to you when you want to delegate a job some day. Anyone picking up your set of instructions should be able to follow your directions without asking you for any extra help.

How the Computer Helps to Cut Costs

Reports generated by the computer greatly aid in cutting costs. Here is an example of how this is done. One of the reports issued for the maintenance department will highlight the most costly equipment in terms of maintenance labor and replacement parts. This report may also rank the equipment by the frequency of corrective work orders issued for its repair.

Such a report enables a manager to determine the cause of excessive breakdown maintenance for critical production equipment, and then correct the cause. When this is done, increased uptime of machines and equipment will result.

Three benefits can be realized by using the report for making decisions:

1. Equipment that is most costly from either downtime or excessive maintenance costs can be given attention first.
2. The causes of the excessive costs are pinpointed.
3. The information could lead to a decision to replace equipment rather than continue to repair it.

PITFALLS TO AVOID WHEN
IMPLEMENTING THE COMPUTER

The successful implementation of the computer in a plant can change the plant from an inefficient, poorly managed facility to a highly organized and profitable one. Computerization, for example, can significantly reduce equipment downtime and make the most productive use of employees.

Don't, however, overlook the possibility of an unsuccessful implementation of a system, with the confusion and frustration that go with it. This can happen if you don't recognize the pitfalls present and take steps to avoid them. If you are given the responsibility of putting in a system, you must contend with these pitfalls:

■ Don't expect that the computer will arrive at the plant completely ready to go and programmed to precisely fit your needs. Realize that your accounting books and maintenance records probably aren't exactly identical to that of any other company. To be more realistic, assume that some modifications will be necessary before the system fits in smoothly.

■ Put aside any notion that you'll be able to anticipate your operating and maintenance needs, and take all necessary actions yourself. Face the fact that even the smallest computer is a very complicated gadget. Since, more likely than not, you have no idea of how it functions, how could you expect to foresee every detail of what's needed to keep it up and running? Find a source of expert advice and rely on it.

■ If you expect that all your employees will like the computer right from the start, you'll be sadly mistaken. Some plant workers may burn at the thought that a heartless piece of metal and plastic can take over and become your new favorite toy. They must be sold on the computer as a tool to make their work easier rather than as a threat to their job security or self-esteem.

■ A serious pitfall is the failure to come up with an effective implementation plan or to use a poor one. A plan is a predefined, mutually agreed-upon set of objectives and responsibilities for the implementation of the computer. There must also be a clearly defined timetable of the procedural steps, including a decision on when sufficient data have been loaded into the system to put it on line.

■ Another problem to contend with is to not conduct training sessions too early. If people are trained on how to use the system in a formal training program, but are not called upon to use that knowledge for weeks afterward, much will be forgotten. Retraining will be necessary and cost overruns are inevitable. You must decide when the system will be started up and plan the training accordingly.

▪ A frustrating pitfall to avoid is to set an unachievable start-up date. Several problems will arise including a lowering of morale if the date is not met. Additionally, the payback period for the computer installation, which was crucial to its justification, might not be realized.

Computer Portability

Advances in technology have resulted in handheld computer terminals that are powerful yet compact. In the process area, at the shipping and receiving dock, and in the warehouse and storeroom areas, portability is now automating jobs that have never been automated before. Moreover, these rugged tools can withstand extreme cold, heat, moisture, shaking, dust, or dirt.

Accompanying this advance—actually part of it—has been the growth of battery power to aid productivity. Although office employees can use two hands and a table top when operating a terminal, plant employees need systems that are truly mobile. The introduction of smaller, lighter, and longer-lasting batteries has enabled people to use terminals in more challenging applications.

A good example of this is the handheld, radio frequency, data collection terminal that a forklift operator uses. This device guides an operator to locations for picking and storing. It also collects data on-line each time material moves. In shipping and receiving areas, the terminal is used to scan bar codes that record changes to inventory. With such applications, ultra high frequency radio waves are used to transmit data to and from a host computer in real time, resulting in up-to-date control over material handling, warehousing, inventory, and similar operations.

Several benefits and advantages can be realized from the use of portable computers in plants:

1. Employees can stay at their workplaces rather than make repeated trips to a stationary computer or record information manually for later data entry into the host computer. Thus, their efficiency improves.
2. Accuracy improves, particularly when handheld data collection is combined with bar coding and scanning, reducing the need for keypunching and the opportunities for human error.
3. Information management and daily decision making also improve. Handheld data computers make current sales and inventory data available much faster than manual data collection methods.

Even though the information and data obtained from portable systems can be quite sophisticated, implementation of the technology by a plant's organization is most often trouble-free. Today's handheld data computers can be programmed in standard programming languages and can run software packages that support specific applications.

SELLING EMPLOYEES ON THE COMPUTER

In many plants, the computer is fast becoming as indispensable as the telephone. Unfortunately, it is in no way as universally understood. This situation exists partly because computer technology has grown at a tremendous rate over only a few years. Yet with the demand for computer services including data processing, software products and turnkey systems are expected to continue to grow at a phenomenal rate for some time. Many companies see the computer as an inevitable investment if a company is to remain competitive much less expand, in its industry. Despite this movement, however, some companies are still concerned with selling the computer to their employees, realizing that if its introduction and use don't get off to a good start, the investment may not pay off.

Complicating the issue, acceptance of the computer must go beyond the line and staff people. Lower, middle, and upper management people are also involved. It's no disgrace to be confused by computer hardware and software. Even the best managers are mystified if they haven't had any training in this area or are unaware of the great value of management information systems.

The Need for Training

Perhaps the best way to sell employees on use of the computer is to see that they are well trained in how to operate it. People lose much of their fear of computers when they know what they can and can't do with them. When employees build the confidence they need to deal successfully with computers and systems, they soon forget their initial fears. Knowing how to run a computer gives a person an ego boost, a sense of power, and a feeling of control.

Training programs that are twofold in nature have proved to work best. The first part should be an awareness presentation that is designed to motivate users to participate in the system's success and to alleviate any apprehension that users who are new to the system may have.

The second part should consist of objective-based instruction on the functions and tasks performed by the employees on the computer. While the first part may be very general in nature and suitable for all employees, the second part must be selective and designed for the employee's specific application area.

Although trainers should be well versed in data processing and computer operation, they should also be good teachers. Trainers who are understanding, easy to get along with, and well liked provide valuable assistance in selling new systems. They usually have the patience to stay on the job until the trainees feel confident they can operate the computer by themselves.

When you are convinced that everyone has been adequately trained and you are ready to make the change from the manual or standard procedure to the computer, do it by operating the department "in parallel" (both ways) for a period of time. This not only gives employees more confidence that they will not make an uncorrectable mistake or error, but also enables everyone to work out problems that might arise. Within a short period, most if not all of the "bugs" will be eliminated and employees will agree that the computer actually does make their jobs easier.

TECHNIQUES FOR USING THE COMPUTER

Starting here and throughout the remaining chapters, you will see how the computer is rapidly becoming the major management tool in the operation and control of the plant. Not only has the computer raised productivity, it has also improved quality, reduced costs, and increased efficiency.

While the completely automated computer-controlled plant is still in the future, computerized information for management is the forefront of this movement. Schedules, production reports, quality records, cost reports, inventory records and other data are playing an important role in the trend to plant computerization. The following techniques are currently being used in the operation and control of plants.

Material Handling and Inventory Control

Plant management has always been concerned with how much inventory the plant should carry. Since it costs money to carry it, the less the better. But too little inventory of raw materials or finished products hinders the plant's ability to serve customers quickly and thus be competitive. With the computer, inventory control has been made considerably easier.

Material handling and inventory operations are greatly speeded up by putting all the data and information in the computer. Calculations of net material available, the economic order quantity, the reorder point, and the value of the inventory can be made instantly. Thus the current status of the inventory is available to managers at any time. Either a mini- or a microcomputer has the capacity to make these calculations for thousands of items.

However, the computer can do much more on material handling and inventory control through a system called Material Resource Planning (MRP). With this system, the computer is preprogrammed to calculate the effects of a production schedule on raw material and parts inventory, and on purchasing. If there are enough parts and material on hand, the computer reserves them for this particular order; if not, purchase orders are issued automatically with delivery dates set to meet the schedule.

By adopting MRP, a plant can greatly reduce the amount of inventory carried. Plants using the system report that inventories can be reduced as much as 50 percent. In addition, inventories are more accurate and customer service is improved.

Manufacturing Operations

The use of computers to control manufacturing operations has been of great benefit to plants in two basic industries:

1. Mechanical fabrication plants in which machine tools modify solid materials, usually metals, into products or components of products
2. Continuous process plants in which solids or fluids go through a series of chemical or physical steps resulting in intermediate or finished products

Mechanical operations such as drilling, turning, grinding, broaching, and threading were automated as early as the 1950s with the development of numerical control (NC). This system involves use of paper tape with punched holes to instruct an electromechanical controller to run a machine through several operations automatically and in sequence.

If the machine is equipped with an automatic tool changer, the taped instructions will also call for tool changes, which are made much more quickly than could be accomplished manually. While NC increases production capacity, improves quality, and reduces labor costs, the computer can be used to further improve the system in two ways:

1. *By simplifying the tape preparation.* Originally, the tape is punched in a special machine operated from a keyboard; typed instructions show up

as punched holes in the tape. The typist follows a set of instructions pre-pared by an engineer who has manually made the calculations required for positioning the machine tool so that it cuts, drills, and grinds in the right locations and to the desired depths. If the machining job is compli-cated, these calculations are long and prone to error.

Simplification of the procedure is accomplished by putting a com-puter ahead of the tape puncher. The engineer, using special software and a high-level language, gives the computer only the basic instructions re-quired to accomplish the machining operations. The computer makes the detailed calculations needed to guide the machine, and instructs the punching machine to produce a properly coded tape.

2. *By replacing the electromechanical controller.* There are two ways of doing this. With the first, the computer is put between the tape reader and the machine tool controls. The tape is used only once; after passing through the reader, its instructions are stored in the computer's memory. This eliminates the need to change tapes every time a new product or part is to be made. The instructions are sent directly to the machine tool from the computer.

The second way of replacing the controller involves using a central computer to control a number of machines. No longer using punched tape, the central computer sends instructions to the machine's tools either through their own computers, or, if they are not so equipped, through a specially designed machine control unit. Instructions for various machin-ing jobs are stored in the central computer's memory and fed to the ma-chine tools as needed.

Each machine may be working on a different product at any one time, or all machines may be working on the same product. With this system, each machine tool tells the central computer when it has completed a job, when it is ready for another job, and the number of types of products it has made. This information enables the central computer to make the most efficient use of the machines available, virtually eliminating idle time waiting for instructions.

Process Control

Automatic control of process equipment is important to a plant for its advantages in upgrading product quality, smoothing production opera-tions, and reducing production costs. Many of the larger installations of the process industries, such as chemical plants and oil refineries, would not be possible without automatic control.

With the computer playing a major role in the automatic control of continuous processes, high levels of accuracy, response speed, and sophis-ticated control are being achieved. Computers are being used at three lev-els of control to accomplish this:

1. *Control of instruments.* Electronic instruments are replacing pneumatic ones in many industrial plants because they provide faster response and more reliable operation. In addition, the electron instruments are more readily converted to computer control. If closer control is wanted than is possible with a standard instrument, a microprocessor can be added.

The microprocessor is a silicon chip that contains in its circuitry all the essential parts of a central processing unit: arithmetic, logic, and control. It has built-in instructions applying to its particular purpose; it also has the ability to perform calculations on data coming from the process to be controlled.

2. *Control of process equipment.* In conventional process control, the variable to be controlled is usually measured after it has passed through the equipment. But this results in over- or undercontrol if input conditions suddenly change.

Installing a computer in the process permits much better control. The sensor of the variable to be controlled is moved to the inlet of the process, and a flow meter is installed with it. Factors affecting the variable are also measured and controlled. All the data are fed into the computer, which is programmed to solve the equation applicable to the system.

The computer calculates what the variable will be if nothing is done. The control mechanism makes the necessary adjustments to the factors before the process system is upset, resulting in much closer control of the variable.

3. *Control of the plant.* Many plants try to optimize profits by adjusting the mix of products they make and the size of their production runs to current business conditions. Raw material availability and cost, sales estimates for each product, and prices that the products are expected to carry are considered. While the product mix and size of runs could be determined from an operations model and calculated manually, a better way is to establish a computerized operations center for this purpose.

With this approach, a plant optimization model is constructed and programmed into the computer. When the costs and other factors are put into the database, the output consists of instructions to management on what products to run and how much of each. By following the instructions, management is able to maximize plant profits.

COMPUTERIZED MAINTENANCE MANAGEMENT SYSTEMS

A major application of the computer involves its use for managing and controlling maintenance functions. While most plants today focus on picking the right computerized maintenance management system (CMMS), successful implementations depend on the readiness of the organization to accept the new computerized environment. All staff members involved in maintenance must be informed and ready to initiate a CMMS. Without adequate preparation, the system installation will be superficial.

Selecting and installing maintenance software can take much time and effort of key maintenance people. The best implementations have the support of the craftspersons, supervisors, and maintenance staff members before the system is activated. After a system is chosen, supervisors and staff should be called upon to do the research and help key in the system's master files.

SELECTING A CMMS

If an organization does not concentrate on a successful CMMS implementation or the cost savings it can generate, the implementation may fail, users are likely to resent the software, and the management team who spent money on the system will be disappointed because it did not yield the savings that were expected.[2]

Two factors are responsible for recent changes in systems on the market today. One change is that the CMMS industry has matured. In the past, when maintenance managers evaluated systems, they looked for core features needed to run their organizations. Most competitive systems now offer a long list of features and strong functions. A second change in CMMS selection criteria is the result of advanced technology within the industry itself. Modern technology has introduced client/server systems in which processing is accomplished on a networked personal computer (PC) located on a desktop rather than on a mainframe computer. Database technology provides faster, more powerful, and more efficient operation. Programming now involves easy-to-use graphical user interfaces such as Microsoft's Windows.

These changes have a direct impact on the power available to modern maintenance departments. Cumbersome menus and highly customized software have been eliminated and replaced with faster, more graphical systems that have the same interface as common word processors and spreadsheets. The power of modern PCs allows CMMS vendors to branch into advanced graphics and report-writing software that works with the powerful database engines.

Today's managers need to know how work is done, how it is executed, and how processes can be improved to reduce costs and improve quality. They expect their CMMSs to provide the answers to these questions. Current technologies allow this type of advanced work process management. But for it to work, the CMMS must be installed successfully. Here is a five-step approach to selecting or replacing a CMMS.

Step 1. Outline and define work processes and flows; make sure that CMMS candidates can work within them. CMMSs often require changes in the work flows of organizations, depending on how the computerized system demands action and how the users actually respond. These areas tend to cause the most friction among users and often contribute to the failure of the CMMS implementation.

The goal is obvious: Reduce the overall impact and strain on the organization by installing a system that supports the way you currently work. Securing the right system will increase the chances for a successful implementation and provide the benefits expected.

Step 2. Determine if the CMMS will meet reporting needs. Definitions of reporting requirements should be broad enough to cover future needs. When upgrading a current system, you must inform the vendor of what new information is expected from the new system, as well as how often you plan to run each report, what time of day, what the expected running time is, etc. These requirements define not only what you want, but also when and how you want it.

Step 3. Determine if the software can interface with existing systems. Define existing systems and decide which ones must integrate with the CMMS. Describe the process and reasoning behind the interfaces and provide practical examples.

Many companies choose not to change existing purchasing or inventory software packages when installing a CMMS. A decade ago, software integration was a difficult and costly process. Today, it is significantly easier and less expensive. A company should never feel forced to install other new software as part of a CMMS implementation unless interfacing is totally impossible.

Step 4. Find out if the vendor assists in CMMS implementation. Many vendors provide onsite training and support during the critical part of CMMS implementation. Find out the depth of vendor services. Some companies customize training to fit specific needs. Find out how much support you can expect to receive.

Step 5. Evaluate software by how it can meet future requirements. Work closely with the staff to determine if current hardware will be used in the future. Often a new CMMS cannot be used on an existing system. Software may be designed to run on a single type of hardware platform. The same rule applies to networking and network communications software.

Tell the vendor what type of equipment the company operates with now and what equipment is expected in the short or long term. How the vendor supports changes in platforms and networks can have a direct financial impact on your system selection.

Departments Involved

Selecting a new computerized maintenance management system (CMMS) is far from easy in companies of any real size. The complexity of these systems is not the issue, but to provide full benefits they must cross departmental lines and boundaries.[3] Most systems need to be used not just by maintenance, but by numerous departments. These packages require support from other organizational elements such as systems departments. Therefore, the selection decision does not fall on one department or functional work group; it covers a wide range.

For example, a maintenance manager knows that installing a CMMS to manage a preventive maintenance program and to allow the staging of parts will save the company a great deal of money. However, the managers of the purchasing operation and inventory/stores report to a different department head. Engineering runs its systems totally independent of the maintenance department.

As a maintenance manager, you can follow two approaches. You can get a new CMMS for the maintenance department alone. It will run work orders and preventive maintenance, but you will not be able to force stores or purchasing personnel to enter information into the new system. Thus cost savings will be substantially lower. Furthermore, additional maintenance personnel will be required to support the system because support will not be available from the information/systems group, further cutting the savings that might be achieved.

The second approach is to involve the various departments as part of the decision-making process for a CMMS. By doing so, you stand a better chance of a successful, cost-saving software implementation.

Some pros and cons exist when involving various organizational elements in purchasing and implementing a CMMS. Each group has vested interests; however, their buy-in, their acceptance, or a work-around to getting the needed functionality is important in the decision-making process.

Furthermore, it is important to determine the weighting that each involved group has in the process. For example, the maintenance department (the department to be most affected by the software) should have more weight than the storeroom manager. Setting these weights is important when determining the final selection of a CMMS; the arrangement must be based on site requirements, data input and uses, group contribution, and other factors. Weighting is not easily qualified generically; it is best determined by the committee or team assembled to review the software.

CMMS Scheduling

Scheduling maintenance from a backlog list is an important part of effectively using a CMMS.[4] However, you must take into consideration the basic concepts of maintenance planning and scheduling. You need to recognize that both are distinct but related functions. It is essential, in this respect, that they be clearly defined as follows:

■ Planning is the allocation of needed resources and the sequence in which they are needed to allow maintenance work to be performed in the shortest time or at the least cost. Planning resources include labor, materials, support services, contracted services, and time available.

Planning of maintenance work identifies all resources required to complete a job. A job cannot proceed without unnecessary delay until the plan is completed. A job is ready for scheduling once planning has been completed.

■ Scheduling is the assignment of many planned jobs into a defined period of time in order to optimize the use of the resources within their constraints. All resources are constrained to some degree; they are not available in unlimited supply. Constraints can include fixed amount of labor, limited or special skills, limited space, physical properties of equipment, rules and regulations, limited money, and limited time.

Scheduling is the way to optimize the use of the resources identified in a planned job. Work is scheduled to make optimum use of machines and equipment, minimize travel time between jobs, and prioritize production operations to meet customer demand.

Scheduling ensures that the most important work is identified and scheduled for any given day or week. The backlog of work filed in a CMMS will grow independent of plant requirements. Each job in the backlog has an implied importance, dictating when the work is performed, or its priority.

Calendar and Resource Files

CMMS programs that provide a scheduling module include calendars and resource files. The calendar file consists of a schedule of workdays and, in some sophisticated programs, provides information identifying the work hours in a workday. The calendar is interactive with the scheduling module; changes within the calendar will immediately be reflected in the schedule.

The resource file keeps track of manpower levels, critical support equipment, or other important constraints to any resources. The resource file is interactive within the scheduling module. Vacations cause fluctuations in manpower levels; these changes adjust the resources available and are in turn reflected in the schedule.

Planning information for a new work order is entered into the CMMS. Resource demands are compared with available resources to determine when the resources will be available. The work order is then scheduled to be carried out on a specific day. Some CMMS programs compare the projected date to the initial priority or requested completion date. If the dates conflict, the work order is flagged for updating by the planner/scheduler. The requested completion date must be changed, or another work order must be dropped from the schedule on that day.

CMMS Scheduling Limitations

Although planners/schedulers agree that CMMS scheduling programs are powerful tools for preparing work schedules, the programs do have some limitations. Often, the projected schedule must be modified to fit within the real needs of the plant. A few of the limitations may be explained as follows:

■ The success of a scheduling system depends on constant adjustments based on changing priorities. These adjustments require good communications with the originators of work, as well as improved knowledge of the plant operation. Failure to update priority data when using a CMMS to schedule is the first step in invalidating the system. Changed priorities on backlog work must be updated continually, or projected schedules will not reflect the most important work to be performed at any given time.

■ Some CMMS scheduling programs overlook the area of optimizing resources. Craftspeople may be traveling from one side of the plant to another and then back again in the course of a workday. Common sense dictates that craftspeople would be better utilized without extensive travel time between jobs. However, to achieve maximum use of resources by relocating them might require last minute negotiations of changed priorities or requested completion dates. These adjustments must be made manually, often in the field.

■ Maintenance backlogs tend to include some invalid work such as duplicate work orders or work that is no longer needed but was never purged from the backlog. CMMS scheduling programs recognize these work orders as valid work and will continue to slot them in the projected schedules. A concerted and ongoing discipline must be in place to keep the backlog clean.

Future CMMS Scheduling

Predictive maintenance databases connected to CMMS programs currently generate inspection work orders only when alarm limits are reached or exceeded within the predictive maintenance effort. As artificial intelligence programs mature, the software will analyze monitored data and determine machinery problems. Mature programs will interact with CMMS and directly generate corrective work orders. When continued monitoring of machinery dictates that the priority of corrective work must be moved up, the CMMS backlog will be automatically updated.

EVALUATING A CMMS

The average life of a computerized maintenance management system (CMMS) is 5 years, a relatively short period considering that the investment may cost from $50,000 to $1 million for software license, maintenance, installation, and training.[5] The short, useful life of the CMMS usually is not caused by faulty software or computers. More often, failure is the result of the user's misunderstanding of maintenance management processes or misconceptions about what a computer system will do. Here are a few examples of what it will not do:

- *A compute will not run itself.* The system often requires more people from within the organization to enter data and support the system.
- *A computer will not always be right.* "Garbage in, garbage out" is the adage commonly referred to when dealing with computers. The output is only as good as the input.
- *A computer will not become obsolete.* A computer system is useful as long as it does not become cumbersome. However, demands on the system may grow to be greater than its design capacity.
- *A computer will not make an organization run right — it can make it worse.* Whatever you do wrong with a manual system will be done wrong faster with a computer.

A CMMS should be reviewed periodically to assure that the plant is getting the most from the program. The reasons the system was purchased must be reevaluated. An excellent approach to evaluation is through an objective analysis.

Objective analysis audits information flow, including the interaction of dependent functions and the service level of these functions. Three information flow paths must be considered when a process using a CMMS is reviewed: data that flow into the system, processing of data within the CMMS, and output from the system. The flow path review should include the following:

■ *Work request and work order systems.* The goal of this study is to establish what happens to work requests and work orders from inception to closure. This information is critical in identifying potential opportunities, as well as problems, in a CMMS.

■ *Stores and material systems.* The information trail required to document material received into the maintenance storeroom, subsequent allocation to a work order by maintenance planning personnel, and potential return to stores if not required, should be studied. The process involved for the purchase and receipt of parts should be documented. Procedures for entering new parts or materials into the stores system also require investigation.

IMPLEMENTING A CMMS

Implementing a CMMS is not a part-time project.[6] While most companies may have capable personnel or staff who could perform such work along with other tasks required to implement a system, those people are usually already involved in other full-time assignments. However, an experienced technical service firm will bring a system up faster (time), do it at less cost, and it will be done right (content) the first time. Established firms provide everything necessary to get your CMMS operational. They are highly qualified in the following disciplines:

1. *Experience and expertise.* Technical service firms deal every day in the development of computerized maintenance management systems. By using one, you eliminate the "trial and error" method of implementation.
2. *Focused plan of attack.* Your own people already wear many hats. A vendor comes in only wearing one hat and focuses only on your project.
3. *Time.* Do you want two of your people experimenting with your system for a couple of years? Or do you want four highly skilled CMMS developers taking four months for the same project?
4. *Reliability and service.* Technical service firms stand by their work. They back it up with strong support teams that work to your

schedule and budget. They are professionals who understand computerized maintenance and are committed to making your system operational.

5. *Education and training.* Let the people who develop and input the information for your CMMS train your employees in using the system. Remember, without an emphasis on education, computerization could do more harm than good.

The startup of your CMMS is probably more important than choosing the software. Do not try to cut corners. A CMMS is only as good as the information that goes into the system. It is estimated that almost 50 percent of all CMMSs fail because of a lack of commitment and funds for the implementation.

LOADING INFORMATION INTO THE DATABASE

In many plants, the purchase of a CMMS is an exciting time. There is new hardware, new software, and new training. But you soon discover that the system can't be used until someone adds to the databases.[7] This means someone must load the following information into the system:

- Equipment numbering schemes
- Equipment nameplate information
- Spare parts numbering schemes
- Spare parts nameplate information
- Preventive maintenance procedures
- Vendor identification information

If, for example, a plant has 1,000 pieces of equipment, 1,500 items in stores, about 1,000 regular preventive maintenance tasks, and 50 vendors, and it takes one hour per item to gather and load this information, then it will take two employees about three months to feed the databases. That must occur before the company can properly use the system.

After this is done, you might think you're ready to use the CMMS. But you're not. In order for anyone to effectively use the CMMS, employees must *daily:*

- Enter work orders.
- Add all employees' time, all material used, all contractor costs, and any equipment rental costs to the work orders.

- Close the work orders to history.
- Plan any new work orders that have been requested.
- Enter and close any emergency orders for the day.
- Reorder any spare parts below the minimum stock quantities.
- Generate the necessary daily reports.

Unfortunately, this scenario plays out in too many plants today. While CMMS vendors have a responsibility to tell customers about the staff time required to keep CMMSs up and running, too often buyers consider only the purchase price. When that happens, the CMMS does not get used to its potential, and the projected savings and benefits used to justify its purchase fail to materialize.

Unless more companies learn or know about the ongoing human resources requirements of CMMS, we will continue to see systems underoptimized. If you are involved in the purchase and implementation of a CMMS, don't fail to recognize the cost of feeding and thereby controlling the system.

Customizing a CMMS

Since the users of CMMS packages have diverse needs, vendors have allowed considerable customization of their products. User customization includes the attachment of graphic report and forms generators, menus, screens and video clips among others. Report generators, in particular, enable users to produce custom documentation more efficiently. In addition, standard reports can be added, revised, or eliminated as users see fit.

Advantages and Disadvantages of Customizing

Customization is often used by companies as a way of gaining a competitive edge. Buying even an excellent off-the-shelf CMMS does not put you ahead of any of your competitors using the same package. Besides, when you customize, you better meet the unique requirements of your operating and maintenance departments.

Another advantage of customization is that the procedure makes you self-sufficient and not dependent on the CMMS vendor to respond to your company's future development requests. In reality, custom programming in-house would give you complete control over the future status of your CMMS.

A disadvantage of a custom CMMS is that it is based on the functions and operations of only one company, thus limiting the opportunity to benefit from advancements in technology. Contrast this with the vendor's CMMS, which is based on the experiences of many companies.

Poor upgrade capabilities are inherent with a customized CMMS. Revisions and upgrades of the CMMS may be slow in being transmitted to the maintenance department, whereas vendor CMMS packages do a better job of keeping up with technological improvements.

USING A CMMS FOR WRITING REPORTS

As a plant becomes familiar with its computerized maintenance management system (CMMS), users will find that more time is spent extracting and analyzing data than entering it. Each user has access to data put in by other users, as well as their own entries. Most systems are seen as tools for organizing and expediting maintenance work. The most important, and sometimes overlooked benefit of a CMMS, however, is its ability to allow users to view work order histories and use the information they contain to prevent failures or to lengthen intervals between failures.

A well-constructed CMMS allows users to enter the condition of each component of a failed piece of equipment into the system. Using codes when entering work order histories forces standardization so that data can be reported and analyzed easily by a computer report writer.[8] The most common use of coded information is to print reports; failures or problems can be analyzed for recurring trends. Instead of simply reporting these codes, however, a simple rule-based report can be written to analyze the codes and automatically print recommendations based on the combinations of codes found at each failure.

CAD/CAE/CAM

Computer-aided design (CAD), computer-aided engineering (CAE), and computer-aided manufacturing (CAM) rank among the more important uses of computers in industry today. As an example of its value, CAD is capable of designing frames and load-bearing members with strong lightweight skeletal structures. Manufacturers of machine tools, storage and handling gear need to make use of that capability because many of their customers need the mobility of lightweight equipment.

Facsimile copiers can send a drawing just about anywhere, and do it very quickly. This capability cuts transit delays and increases flexibility in operations among plants. Both CAD and CAE speed up design by making rough drawings smooth and simplifying drafting. Designers located in different plants may draw from a central CAD database, thus using a company-standard part, when one is available, instead of designing a new one. This provides the benefit of minimizing the number of part numbers in the company.

Computer-aided manufacturing (CAM) takes control when the product design is completed. Its first function is to provide a list of the parts and materials needed to begin production. For each unit to be manufactured, the computer calculates the amount and type of material and the quantities and types of screws and fasteners required to make the product. It then supplies this information to the inventory control or material resource planning system.

By working with the design developed in CAD and using information in the database on the capabilities of the various production and processing machines in the plant, the computer develops a flowchart. This chart routes the product through the plant according to a production schedule also generated by the computer. Once production begins, CAM keeps track of the order as it proceeds through the plant. If the production machines are computer-controlled, CAM issues instructions to them for manufacturing the product.

COMPUTER INTEGRATED MANUFACTURING

Up to this point, you have read how the computer is applied to the different plant functions: product design, engineering, scheduling and monitoring manufacturing operations, control of process machinery, and management of the maintenance function. Each of these functions has an impact on some or all of the others, so it's logical to reason that if the computer improves them separately, it can as well be applied to coordinating them for further upgrading of plant performance. If the information from each of the functions is accumulated and organized into one location, you will have access to the very latest information on the status of production equipment, orders in process, materials available and on order, and even the availability of operating personnel. When you can manage from such a base, you will make better decisions, and be able to make them more quickly.

At the corporate level, managers are concerned with the strategies of new product introduction, marketing campaigns, corporate profitability, addition or reduction of personnel, and the starting up and shutting down of facilities. Just as at the plant level, managers will make better decisions if they have complete, accurate, and up-to-date information on the status of the company's facilities, operations, and market position. Information of that quality can be obtained through a hierarchy of computers sending data from the plants to a central corporate computer. Computer integrated manufacturing also implies a high degree of automation in the plant. Although a completely computer-controlled manufacturing process is not in the immediate future, a step in that direction can be taken with already existing automated systems.

GUARDING AGAINST COMPUTER DISASTER

What do you do to protect your computers from sudden and unforeseen electrical shutdown?[9] How do you contend with power furnished by your local utility that is impaired by spikes, sags, surges, brownouts, and other power line malfunctions?

Computing and telecommunications failures are becoming common events today. A major one occurred in downtown New York City in 1991 when AT&T's switching center went down for seven hours due to a power failure. The crash cut off 5.5 million calls and shut down the city's airports, disrupting more than 1,000 flights.

A few years ago, Commonwealth Edison shut off electrical power to Chicago's "Loop" area to protect its transmission equipment. The event was triggered by the Chicago River flowing through a hole in an old freight tunnel, flooding the basements of numerous office buildings. This power shutdown forced the closing of the Mercantile Exchange and the Chicago Board of Trade. With worldwide stock and commodities trading brought to a halt, business losses were estimated at as much as $50 million per day.

The publicizing of such disasters has resulted in much concern by businesses and industrial organizations across the country. Executives are seriously looking for reliable ways to avoid major power failures. One approach is an uninterruptible power system. For computers, the system comes in sizes that range in capacity from 15 kVa down to 350 Va. These units serve computers and other electronic and electrical devices in two ways:

1. Instant, continuous, computer-grade power in case of blackouts or deep, protracted brownouts
2. Complete line conditioning and filtering that protect against virtually all other line power problems including minor brownouts, sags, spikes, surges, noise, and frequency variation

The system normally powers the critical load through a ferroresonant constant voltage transformer. This results in a clean sine wave output with complete line conditioning and filtering. In the event of a power outage, the inverter/battery section becomes activated. The change to battery/inverter power takes place with no interruption of load functions.

These units also feature microprocessor controls with software interrupt capabilities. The 2 through 15 kVa units have a keyboard to control the microprocessor and information display. Software is available that enables a unit to communicate with computers and also automatically interrupt and shut down a unit without an operator present.

Traditional ways to extend a facility's battery reserve time require the addition of parallel banks of batteries, or the replacement of the existing battery plant with one having a larger ampere-hour capacity. But simply adding batteries to the system requires additional floor space, increases the maintenance required for the system, and often requires additional battery charging equipment. These additions are expensive, add to the complexity of the power system, and reduce the system's overall reliability.

However, equipment is available to supply direct current power to extend battery reserve time. It does this without the problems associated with battery plant additions, or those associated with alternating current phase control and transfer switch operation. The alternating current generator output waveform ceases to be a concern, and frequency stability problems vanish.

To ensure reliability, the microprocessor-controlled equipment has an automatic self-diagnostic test system. It automatically monitors parameters such as fuel, oil, and cranking battery power and sounds an alarm if the unit fails any system check. The equipment also is designed for remote control and monitoring using a password-protected system. A keypad and display permit local monitoring and control. The unit is automatically cycled to run for twenty minutes every two weeks to ensure that it will be ready when needed.

NOTES

1. W. H. Weiss, *Plant Supervisor's Complete Desk Book* (Englewood Cliffs, N.J.: Prentice Hall, Inc., 1987), pp. 125–134.
2. Blaine L. Pardoe, "A New Approach for Selecting a CMMS," *Maintenance Technology,* December, 1994, pp. 21–23.
3. Blaine L. Pardoe, "Who Should Be Involved With CMMS Selection?" *Maintenance Technology,* November 1994, p. 36.
4. Excerpts from the article titled "Maintenance Scheduling and CMMS," *Maintenance Technology,* September 1992, pp. 53–54, 57–58.

5. Michael Bos and Michael Brown, "Evaluating a CMMS," *Maintenance Technology,* March 1995, pp. 12–14.
6. Wally Widelski, "The Implementation of a CMMS," *Engineer's Digest,* February 1994, p. 128.
7. Terry Wireman, "Who Will Feed the Monster?" *Engineer's Digest,* November 1994, pp. 48–49. Copyright, Huebcore Communications, Inc.
8. Paul Smith, "Using a CMMS and Report Writer to Simulate Expert Systems," *Maintenance Technology,* January 1992, p. 53.
9. W. H. Weiss, "How to Guard Against Computer Disaster? Protect It!" *TeleProfessional,* April 1993, pp. 53–54.

6

Safety and Loss Control

All organizations that carry out operations or manufacture a product should be concerned first with employee safety and second with the waste of the organization's assets. While safety procedures are practiced to prevent injuries and accidents, loss control is any activity done to reduce or prevent avoidable waste. The latter, however, also includes control of health and occupational illnesses, property damage, fire, and explosions.

Both safety and loss control are critical parts of every manager's job. Although a manager's responsibility for productivity and profitability is considerable, responsibility for the safety and health of employees is tremendous. Equipment failures and environmental spills can be described with facts and figures, but there is no simple way to explain an employee's accident that resulted in permanent disability or death. A monetary loss is a temporary matter, often regained through better control. But there is no way to regain human losses that result from accidents.

Leadership is important in managing safety and loss control. Top management plays a key role by formulating policy which leads to directives on procedures. These, in turn, result in the best practices for the workplace. A comprehensive loss control system defines what management and employees are to do and how they should go about it. In order to determine the degree of success of the system, you need a way of measuring the system's performance. This accounting procedure should consist of:

- Verifying that documented safety and loss control procedures are being followed

- Interviewing employees to confirm they are aware of and participating in safety, health, and loss control activities
- Assuring that safety and loss control inspections are being made throughout the workplace

In addition, management should adopt the following practices if they are not already doing so: predictive and preventive maintenance; emergency preparedness procedures; engineering and process management controls; and materials, equipment, and contractor controls.

To be effective, safety and loss control systems require the full support of all employees. Whether your organization includes unions, work teams, group leaders, or safety and accident committees, the systems are only as strong as the support they receive.

COMMUNICATING PLANT SAFETY

One of the best ways to sell safe practices in the plant is to continually talk to employees about safety. Work accidents cause injuries and property damage, resulting in medical expenses, increased insurance costs, interrupted production schedules, and decreased employee morale. Unless all injuries are reported, investigated, and analyzed, there is a good probability that accidents and injuries will recur.

Accident and injury records are critical to a successful plant safety and health program. When you study accidents, you identify the cause. This enables you to start control procedures to prevent similar incidents. Even minor injuries should be investigated. An accident's seriousness is often a matter of luck. To learn the cause, investigate as soon as possible after an accident. Prompt investigation usually enables you to get more complete and useful information. With the passing of time, evidence is lost and important details are forgotten.

Insist that employees always report near-misses. The real danger in a "no-injury" accident is that it is too often ignored or too soon forgotten. You may call it a near-miss, but it's still an accident whether or not someone gets hurt or something gets damaged. Near-misses should alert you that something is wrong, either with the way an employee is doing a job or the place the person is doing it.

A major problem facing managers who are concerned with safety is how to motivate employees to report injuries and near-misses. If you can make reporting all incidents as concise and simple as possible, the end result will be an increase in reporting, which would enable you to obtain better statistics and more information.

Most employees today are aware of what is involved with accident reports and the time it takes. Many prefer not to report a minor accident, even though they know it is a protection for them medically, monetarily, and physically. If you can show these people that both accidents and near-misses can be reported without a lot of paperwork and time, you will be able to use their experiences to their and the company's advantage.

We learn to provide safe working conditions and to work safely by talking, listening, and reading about plant safety problems as well as by observing what's going on around us. The more thorough we are in getting and giving information about plant safety, the more we can help ourselves and others to avoid accidents. Operating procedures, specifications, and regulations for working safely must be written, distributed, and discussed. For example, you should see that the following information and similar instructions are provided employees:

- What to do in case of a fire
- Where fire extinguishers and hoses are located
- Whom to notify in case of a major spill
- Where respirators and gas masks are located

In addition, you must plan how you will give your safety talks, the words you will use, and how you will say them. You must know the attitude and experience of your listeners, and tailor what you say accordingly.

But that's only part of the job of talking about plant safety and persuading employees to work safely. You must follow up: first, right after talking about safety to see if what was said was understood, and second, sometime later to see if your employees' attitudes are right and if their work habits are good.

SAFETY INDOCTRINATION

Safety indoctrination[1] is often thought of as putting up posters, posting notices on bulletin boards, holding safety meetings, and passing out safety rule books. It's no wonder that plant safety is sometimes considered apart from getting work done.

Safety indoctrination should include making employees and management alike aware that their personal goals and well-being are closely related to the company's profitability. Safety efforts must pay their way as with any other part of the business.

Relating accidents and injuries to the sales or units of production required to pay for them will convince management as nothing else will that preventing accidents must be a major objective in running the business. Awareness of the extent to which production and sales must be increased to pay for accidents creates a situation in which most companies realize that management must take corrective action.

Although management's concern and awareness may lead to the adoption of an accident reduction and loss control program, more personal reasons must be supplied to employees to make them want to participate in the program. Few employees completely understand the extent to which their own future and that of their families' is tied in with the company's safety program.

Therefore, it is essential that you make employees aware of the extent and nature of the accidents happening in the plant and of how workers are affected. The National Safety Council and several insurance companies have made films on this subject. You should consider showing these to employees as part of your plant safety indoctrination program.

Safety indoctrination should always be directed toward specific employees or departments based on their particular problems. For example, promote the wearing of safety glasses if the frequency or severity of eye injuries in the department is high. Generalizing on safety usually does not get results; besides, it can be costly.

Although more and more companies feel that their workplaces are environmentally safe and the majority of their employees are safe workers, companies have found that most of the accidents occurring in the plant can be attributed to a limited number of employees, a few unsafe practices, and a minimum number of physical facility inadequacies. Knowing who, what, and where the problems are can considerably reduce the cost of safety indoctrination.

You can play a major role in this effort by analyzing machinery and equipment accidents and investigating property damage accidents. By correlating this data with information obtained from first-aid and injury records, those individuals and departments with inefficient and unsafe practices can be brought to light.

The engineering department can help by assigning dollar cost figures to equipment and machine accidents, spills, and fires, among other accidents. Such costs should convince management that control measures are needed and will pay off. With this information, you can inform and advise those individuals and departments of the unsafe practices and conditions that are under their control. You can use costs to make the point that these practices and conditions threaten the company's and their own goals. At the same time, you should solicit suggestions for eliminating or controlling the causes of safety problems.

Of course, problems that only management can handle should be separated from those that the employees can control. For example, employees are unable to eliminate machines, equipment, or tools that are hazardous or inadequate for the operations. What management does to correct these conditions, as well as adopting employee suggestions for eliminating causes, represents an effective form of safety indoctrination.

Training on Safety

Training employees should be a part of every plant safety program. Instructors and trainers have the important responsibility of teaching the safe way to work and do jobs.

One of the best ways to train and instruct workers is with on-the-job training (OJT), a method by which you or a first-line manager does the training, one-on-one. Whether it is called coaching, counseling, or educating, the critical element with this type of training is one individual helping another to work safely.

The method lends itself well to training plant employees on such procedures as:

- How to operate hazardous machines and equipment
- How to handle fire extinguishers and hoses
- How to deal with hazardous materials
- How to handle gas cylinders

A safety training program should include viewing videos and films on head, eye, hands, and feet protection, and on how to work safely in the plant. Be sure you also give employees plant safety manuals and booklets on safe work procedures.

Successful managers of plant safety programs have learned, however, that handing out specifications, safety manuals, and job descriptions is no guarantee that the employees are being trained in plant safety procedures. For one thing, there is no way to be sure that the material is read. For another, if it is read, is it understood? Training is effective only if the sender (manager) gets through to the receiver (employee). If your employees only read or hear the words but don't understand them, then they won't get the message.

The surest way of finding out if your employees understand instructions on how to work safely is through feedback, either by their questions or by the answers to questions you ask them. At some plants, managers use a group of general questions that they ask employees after they have become familiar with the plant and their jobs, and have read the safety rules and regulations. If the employees can't answer the questions, the manager knows that they need more training.

Personalized Safety Training

As part of your effort to convince employees that accidents are caused and don't just happen, you must put a stop to their believing that accidents happen because their number is up; it's the law of averages; it's the price of progress; or they are accident-prone. These are all lame excuses for accidents and far from being logical explanations of why they happen. The accident-prone theory, in particular, has been harmful to plant safety progress. People accepting this idea have been led to believe that there is little that can be done to prevent accidents because accident proneness couldn't be cured.

Fortunately, the accident-prone theory is no longer accepted by most people involved in occupational safety. More and more agree that there is a great deal that can be done to prevent accidents and keep workers free from injury.

Leaders in promoting and implementing safety believe that there is a close relationship between good safety and good supervision. With proper and adequate direction, motivation, instruction, and enforcement of rules, employees can work in environments filled with hazards without having accidents. When safety awareness is lacking, workers find numerous ways of getting hurt.

You can and should develop safety awareness in your employees. You can do this best by talking about safety at every opportunity. But what is needed most is personalized safety training. This type of training includes telling employees specifically what the hazards in the workplace are and how to avoid them. Talking in generalities about the need to be safe is not enough. Each employee must be taught what to do, how to do it, and certainly what not to do.

When you personalize safety training, you, the manager must do the training. You are most familiar with an employee's knowledge, skills, and temperament. You also know the most about the procedures, machines, and equipment that may be involved in the plant operations. While personal training will take more of your time than other training methods, the extra responsibility pays off because of your greater effectiveness.

In addition to personal training, you must enforce plant safety rules. Enforcement is an important element in all safety programs. You must also take corrective action whenever safety rules and regulations are broken. Further, you should carefully watch safety offenders after violations to make sure they are not repeated.

If your employees put on their safety glasses or replace a machine guard when they see a member of the safety department but have no hesitancy about working without eye protection or a guard when you are watching, it is obvious that you have not accepted your safety responsibility and are not enforcing the safety rules.

In developing sound safety programs, you should stress preventive action rather than after-the-fact remedies. Emphasize correcting unsafe acts and eliminating shortcuts in procedures. The same principles and concepts that apply to quality, cost, and production control must be applied to safety. Use posters, contests, and presentations to stimulate safety awareness and motivate employees to work safely.

But these actions won't work unless you take full responsibility for safety. If you set a good example by following all the plant safety rules yourself, and if you are reasonable but firm in handling violations, a safety consciousness should gradually develop among your employees. Under such conditions, the chances for accidents and injuries are considerably reduced.

SAFETY MEETINGS

A safety meeting is defined as one in which a group of employees, not a representative committee, gets together to learn more about, or be reminded of, particular safety issues.[2] Such meetings are a virtual gold mine for putting out safety information and they provide an opportunity to give a group of people the same message at the same time. A plant that doesn't conduct safety meetings won't have a safety program on a par with one that does. Employees' awareness just isn't going to be as sharp.

Learning Meeting Techniques

Meetings are places where many managers, especially first-line ones, are afraid they will fall on their faces, mostly because they simply haven't been trained properly. Learning a few techniques, such as how to get attendees involved and using visual aids, can make the difference between a good and poor presentation.

One way to make safety meetings less intimidating is to call upon others for input. Invite guest speakers to talk to employees. Also, prior to a meeting, ask employees to pinpoint some safety problems and then ask if you can call on them during the meeting to comment, such as talking about a near-miss.

You don't necessarily have to be an expert in all aspects of safety to run an effective safety meeting. If someone asks a question you can't answer, say, "That's a good question, I'll get back to you with the answer later." Or, open the question to the group and ask if anyone knows the answer. This helps take the pressure off you to be an expert on safety.

The enthusiasm you as the meeting leader show is a key to running a successful safety meeting. If you think the meeting is going to be boring, your lack of enthusiasm will rub off on your audience. Try to look at the meeting as something that is interesting and will enable you to help employees to work safely. If you're not enthusiastic or don't have a fairly high energy level, you can't expect people to want to hear what you've got to say.

Promote Involvement

Beware of making a safety meeting too dictatorial with attendees doing nothing but sitting and listening. To get them involved, promote group dynamics, a technique that encourages employee participation. You can do this by bringing up a safety concern or issue pertinent to your department, and calling on individuals to talk about it. Try to get the group to reach a consensus as to what is causing problems; then develop an action plan to combat them.

Another way to involve employees is to ask for suggestions on topics for future meetings. Also, when discussing a hazard in the plant or a safety problem, use workplace-specific examples to illustrate a point. If someone in the plant figured out a solution to a safety problem, ask the person to talk about it during a safety meeting.

Visual Aids

Employees learn to work safely not only by listening but also by seeing and observing. That's what makes visual aids such as videos, slides, overhead transparencies, and flip charts so valuable. A 1986 study by the University of Minnesota and the 3M Company found that employees are 43 percent more likely to be persuaded by presentations using visual aids than by those that don't.

Some companies videotape workers on the job for use in safety meetings. If the meeting's topic is how to lift safely, for example the video segment might show someone who's lifting incorrectly, and someone who's being coached on how to lift safely. Employees enjoy seeing people they know in their videos, and they will pay more attention to the safety message.

If you use a transparency or a flip chart, use color to make it stand out, and don't burden each one with too much information. You will make a better impact if you keep your message short and simple. As to which type of visual aid to use, that depends on your meeting's circumstances such as room size, audience size, and availability of equipment. Overhead transparencies can be used effectively for groups up to one hundred people, but flip charts should be used only for groups of twenty-five or less.

UNSAFE ACTS

According to the Occupational Safety and Health Act (OSHA), plant managers are held responsible for eliminating unsafe conditions and unsafe acts that can cause accidents that injure employees. In addition, OSHA has specified codes for almost every conceivable type of work. These codes list the requirements for eliminating unsafe conditions.

However, even though a plant's management may comply with all the applicable codes, this is not enough. The law states that management must also protect employees against their own actions that can result in injuries. The law thus recognizes that it is possible for employees to injure themselves by an unsafe act, even when working with tools or equipment that meet all code requirements.

With so many unsafe acts that it is almost impossible to codify them, you must determine what unsafe acts are likely to occur in handling the work that you are responsible for. Then you must ensure that your employees do not perform these unsafe acts. At first glance, this might seem to be a formidable task; however, to help you with the job, the American Standards Association has made a list of nine types of unsafe acts:

1. Operating without authority
2. Operating or working at unsafe speed
3. Making safety devices inoperative
4. Using unsafe equipment, using hands instead of equipment, or using equipment unsafely
5. Failing to use personal protective equipment or clothing
6. Unsafe loading, placing, mixing, or a similar act
7. Taking an unsafe position or posture
8. Working on moving or dangerous equipment
9. Distracting, teasing, abusing, or startling other employees

This list is helpful in two ways: It gives you an idea of what to look for, and it enables you to classify those unsafe acts that you find. Thus, by knowing which types of unsafe acts occur most often, you can go to work on the most serious problems.

Of all the various types of unsafe acts that employees might be guilty of, the one they do most often is taking an unsafe position or posture. Statistics confirm that more than half of the accidents in which the prime cause is an unsafe act result when the person involved takes an unsafe position or posture.

The position a person takes relative to the work being done makes the employee vulnerable to an accident. The way to be safe is to place yourself in the clear in the event of failure of the material being worked with, the tool being used, or the machine being operated.

The posture of a person is his or her body alignment relative to the load placed upon it. For instance, the correct lifting posture is to squat and lift the load with the leg muscles. Bending over the load and pulling up with the back muscles gives the mechanical advantage to the load, not to the lifter.

Since every job a person does has its own position or posture requirements, it's up to you to help your employees identify the one best way to handle each job. Then make sure that this way is the one that's used.

Ignoring Unsafe Acts

Failure to correct unsafe practices is a neglect of a manger's safety responsibility and adds to the accident prevention problem instead of helping to solve it.[3] Why do managers sometimes fail to correct employees they see doing their jobs unsafely? Often it's because even though they know that an unsafe act could cause an injury, they also believe that alert and careful employees can avoid accidents. And, of course, that's true for a lot of unsafe acts.

But you can't count on people always being alert and careful. Sometimes they're tired, they may not feel well, or they're distracted at the wrong time. Then an unsafe act can result in an accident. Another thing that lulls managers into being complacent about unsafe practices is that an unsafe act may be repeated hundreds of times without an accident happening. The sobering fact, however, is that when unsafe acts are performed, accidents are possible and will happen sooner or later.

Managers who are complacent about unsafe acts do not solve the problem. They create additional ones: problems in enforcement and credibility. If you ignore some unsafe acts, then you have to decide where you will draw the line—which unsafe practices you will permit and which you will not permit.

What is the solution to complacency about unsafe acts? All managers must exercise their safety responsibility. They must make sure that each employee knows the safety rules and safe job procedures. Then, even more important, they must follow up and correct employees each time they see them deviate from a safety rule or safe job procedure.

HOUSEKEEPING

One of the top contributors to a high frequency of accidents is a lack of adequate housekeeping.[4] You can tell a great deal about the number and type of accidents occurring in a given plant merely by assessing the housekeeping practices and general conditions which are allowed to exist. Indications of less than adequate housekeeping practices include slip/trip/fall-type injuries involving "struck by falling object" and injuries caused by collisions with improperly placed material.

If you suspect that housekeeping may be a factor in accidents, injuries, or property damage occurrences in your plant, consider an evaluation of your housekeeping practices. This can be accomplished by physically inspecting the plant, identifying congestion or problem areas, assessing storage practices, and reviewing accident reports to identify loss causes related to housekeeping problems.

As in every aspect of a loss control program, management support is critical in achieving effectiveness. Your full support of good housekeeping can be helped by the following activities:

- Appoint special cleanup personnel.
- Inform the plant safety committee of its responsibility for housekeeping inspections.
- Clean machinery and equipment after each shift and keep it reasonably clean while in operation.
- Place trash in proper trash bins for easy removal.
- Keep floors, aisles, and working surfaces clean and unobstructed.
- Store materials properly.
- Keep tools in their proper place.
- Clean up spills immediately.
- Empty trash regularly.
- Clean periodically out-of-the-way places such as roofs, overhead beams, shelves, ledges, yards, outbuildings, basements, and boiler rooms.

Along with the reduction of accidents, you can expect to see improved productivity, a better attitude, and greater employee satisfaction as a result of a cleaner and more orderly workplace. An effective housekeeping program is a planned offensive, and is not characterized by an occasional grand cleanup, but rather a planned continual activity. Good housekeeping is good for employees and good for business.

COLOR CODING

Although many managers probably think of on-the-job housekeeping as putting scrap in containers, cleaning up spills, or stacking and storing materials properly, there is another aspect of housekeeping that prevents accidents and injuries by identifying both hazards and equipment or facilities to contend with them. You can identify such hazards by color coding them. Firefighting equipment, dangerous machine parts, physical hazards, and piping systems are some of the objects that should be easily recognized because they are color coded.

Color coding is a safety application that uses seven basic colors—red, orange, yellow, green, blue, purple, and black with white—to highlight specific hazards. These colors, combined with symbols and lettering, provide highly visible signs for employees' and visitors' protection.

Red has long been used to identify fire protection equipment, including alarm boxes, hydrants, extinguishers, sprinkler system piping, and other indicators associated with fire. In addition, use red to mark danger areas, on exit signs, and on emergency stop controls on machines. Danger signals are:

- Warning light at barricades, temporary obstructions, and temporary construction sites
- Stop lights
- Running lights on machines and stop buttons

Use red on safety cans or portable containers of flammable liquids that have flash points at or below 80°F excluding shipping containers. Use yellow with red—either as a band around a red can or to state a container's contents—to furnish additional identification.

Orange indicates dangerous parts of machines and energized equipment that may shock, cut, or somehow injure people. Use orange to call attention to open enclosure doors and open or removed gears, belts, or guards. Use orange also on exposed parts (edges only) of rollers, pulleys, gears, cutting and shearing devices, and power jaws.

Yellow means caution: Use it to mark physical items or material that could cause employees to slip, stumble, fall, trip, strike against, or get caught between something. Yellow and black stripes or checkers, or yellow with a contrasting background draw attention and caution people. Thus, use yellow for steps, guardrails, low beams, pipes, crane hooks, and mobile equipment.

Green denotes first-aid and safety equipment. Use green for stretchers, gas masks, medical kits, respiratory and eye equipment, and safety showers.

Blue should be used for special machines and equipment to indicate that it should not be touched or used except by qualified personnel. Use blue on instrumentation and controls, for informational signs, and to signify temporary repairs.

Purple warns of radiation hazards such as alpha, beta, gamma, neutron, proton, and x-rays. Use yellow with purple on tags, markers, labels, and signs.

Black used with white or yellow specifies traffic routes. Use black to separate process, storage, and housekeeping areas.

You may also want to indicate the contents of piping systems by color. The most common uses are:

- *Red* for sprinkler or other fire extinguishing systems such as carbon dioxide
- *Yellow* and *orange* for materials that are poisonous, toxic, explosive, easily ignited, hot, or otherwise dangerous
- *Green, black, gray, white,* and *aluminum* for safe and nonvaluable products such as water, air, and steam
- *Blue* for protective materials including inert gases (nitrogen) that are used for purging

SAFETY INSPECTIONS

Most plants today have an inspection committee, the members of which are appointed by management. A safety inspection may be done in conjunction with the regular plant inspection and maintenance program, or it may be an inspection where the primary concern is with accident prevention. The latter type of inspection is frequently made by the members of the safety committee.

Safety inspections should focus attention on those items directly concerned with accident prevention. Thus, participating in an inspection affords you an excellent opportunity to check all safety equipment and devices, the condition of machines and other equipment, and the status of the housekeeping program. We have already seen where good housekeeping pays off in accident prevention.

A systematic method of inspection is preferred to ensure that nothing is missed. The inspection should include:

- Buildings and physical equipment
- Machinery, guards, and electrical facilities
- Materials handling and storage facilities
- Special equipment such as pressure vessels, furnaces, dryers, process tanks, conveying systems, elevators, and lifts
- Welding, cutting, and brazing equipment
- Compressed gas and air equipment
- Ventilation and pollution controls for toxic and hazardous substances
- Walking and working surfaces and means of exit
- Hand and portable power tools and other handheld equipment

You should be familiar with the company's safety and health policies as well as the particular laws and regulations that pertain to your plant.

Regulations frequently specify only minimum requirements, thus making it necessary to exceed them to achieve adequate safety. You should also have an analysis of all accidents that have occurred in the plant within the past year.

You should keep careful records of all inspections and the recommendations made in the inspection reports. This is especially important in the event of an accident that results in litigation. Some plants, immediately after an inspection, issue repair or new work orders to repair or correct unsafe machines and equipment uncovered in the inspection. Putting such information in the inspection report accomplishes two objectives: It puts pressure on the maintenance department to get the work done, and it serves as a means of following up on an unsafe condition during future inspections.

SAFETY STATISTICS

Almost all manufacturing plants in the United States are subject to the Occupational Safety and Health Act (OSHA), and most of them use the OSHA methods of reporting occupational injury and illness. To measure how often these events occur, OSHA uses a statistic called "incident rate" which, for any given time period is defined by the formula:

$$\text{Incident rate} = \frac{(\text{Number of injuries} + \text{illnesses}) \times 200{,}000}{\text{Total hours worked by all employees}}$$

OSHA bases the formula on the assumption that 100 employees will work forty-hour weeks for a total of 200,000 hours annually. To report total recordable cases, the number within the parentheses is the sum of fatality cases; cases that result in lost workdays; and cases without lost workdays but which require termination of employment or transfer to another job, or those which require medical treatment by a physician. Not included are first-aid cases (minor scratches, cuts, burns, and splinters which do not ordinarily require medical care) even though treatment is provided by professional medical personnel. By substituting the appropriate numbers in the parentheses, the incident rate for lost workday cases only, or for nonfatal cases without lost workdays, can be calculated.

To measure the seriousness of accidents and illnesses that occur, the number of cases in the formula is replaced by the number of workdays lost:

$$\text{Incident rate for lost workdays} = \frac{\text{Total lost workdays} \times 200{,}000}{\text{Total hours worked by all employees}}$$

SAFETY DATA AND INFORMATION

Much of the effort needed to make plants safe today requires the application of specialized information. There are several sources of information to help you and those you work with in setting up your safety program:

■ The National Safety Council, a nonprofit, nongovernmental, privately supported organization, continually sponsors various programs to promote safety. This public service organization was chartered by the 83rd U.S. Congress to arouse and maintain interest in accident prevention. As such, the Council does not endorse commercial products nor does it lobby for specific legislation. Its policy is stated as follows:

> The National Safety Council, by virtue of its charter, its bylaws, and its traditional procedures, has established a wide field of competence. The overall function is to deal with the accident problem of America. The specific ranges of its field of activity are determined by the enormous toll of life, limb, and property taken each year by accidents on the highways, and in the workplaces, homes, farms, schools, public places, and transportation systems of our nation.
>
> In dealing with the whole problem, the National Safety Council concerns itself, through study of the record and through research, with the initial facts of accident occurrence, and seeks to establish the ascertainable cause and practical measure of prevention. The Council is also properly engaged in determining engineering requirements, in helping formulate model safety legislation where the force of law is required, in participation in planning and executing educational programs, in disseminating accurate information to the general public, and in encouraging the establishment of community and state safety organizations.

In addition to carrying out this policy, the organization publishes six safety periodicals, *Accident Facts,* an annual report of accident statistics, and several accident prevention manuals. It also conducts safety training courses at its Chicago headquarters and onsite at plants, and it sponsors the annual National Safety Congress.

■ Many other organizations and trade associations, created to meet the general interests of their respective industries and member companies, also promote safety and supply good safety information. The International Safety Academy, for example, operates a training center designed for conferences, consultations, and professional development of individuals. Another is the Chemical Manufacturer's Association (in Washington,

D.C.), which publishes a series of *Chemical Safety Data Sheets* covering the properties, hazards, and safe handling methods for specific chemicals.

■ Other educational societies and institutions concerned with safety include the Institute of Safety and Management at the University of Southern California, the National Safety Management Society, and the American Society of Safety Engineers.

■ U.S. government agencies publish information on safety subjects. The Superintendent of Documents, U.S. Government Printing Office (Washington, D.C.) prints subject bibliographies at no charge; these are lists of the various publications available. To get the bibliographies on industrial safety, write for SB-229, *Accidents and Accident Prevention,* and be familiar with your state's codes and regulations because they state the minimum legal standards for conditions in your plant.

■ Insurance groups and other associations offer plants a wide range of inspection, advisory, and educational services. For example, your company's fire insurance carrier probably furnishes inspection and fire protection assistance through the Factory Insurance Association (in Hartford, Connecticut) or the Factory Mutual System (in Norwood, Massachusetts). In addition, The American Insurance Association (New York), Underwriter's Laboratories (Northbrook, Illinois), and the National Fire Protection Association (Quincy, Massachusetts) all conduct research and issue publications on a wide variety of fire protection subjects.

CAUSES OF RECURRING SAFETY PROBLEMS

If your plant operates similarly to others, you probably experience recurring problems with safety in the workplaces. Possible reasons for this repetition could be failure to identify the real causes of problems, failure to follow up on corrective actions, or failure to communicate job requirements.[5] Most often, repeating problems occur because of inadequate identification of the basic causes. Usually, the search for causes stops when an accident, or near-miss, is reported and investigated.

However, the first or easiest answers may not be the only answers needed to keep this type of accident from happening again. You need to understand what allowed the obvious causes to exist. For better insight to solving these problems, you need to distinguish between immediate and basic causes.

Causes of problems that an investigator can see, hear, taste, smell, or feel are immediate causes and by themselves are not enough to prevent recurrence. Not all immediate causes can be readily identified by using one's senses. What is needed in any problem-solving process is the determination of why the immediate causes exist.

The immediate causes exist because of basic causes. An example of an immediate cause could be that maintenance was not performed on a machine at the prescribed interval. What investigators need to know is why the maintenance was not performed.

To be effective in solving recurring safety problems, you need to ask the all-important question, "Why?" After identifying multiple immediate and basic causes, you will be in a better position to develop effective controls to keep the problems from recurring.

ELECTRICAL SAFETY

Many of the electrical accidents that occur in plants today can be prevented by following safe practices and adopting good safety habits, particularly around high voltage or high current circuits.[6]

In order for you to experience an electrical shock, voltage across your body is necessary. But it is the resulting current that does the damage. According to experts on this subject, you respond to alternating current at three levels of its intensity:

1. *Perception or reaction level.* This current produces a slight tingling sensation.
2. *Let-go level.* This current is the maximum one at which you, when holding a conductor, can release it by using muscles directly affected by the current.
3. *Lethal level.* This current causes chest or heart muscles to contract and breathing to stop. If the current is maintained, you lose consciousness and eventually die.

Serious shock depends on the ratio of voltage to resistance, thus determining the current and the degree of danger. Voltage is the pressure required to send the energy that is necessary to do the work, while current is what does the work. Voltage is measured in volts and current in amps.

Resistance, measured in ohms, restricts the current and is determined by the physical size of the object through which the current flows—the larger the area, the less the resistance; the smaller, the greater. The current level is determined by the resistance to ground of your body and working conditions. If your hands or feet are wet, your skin resistance will be lower and the current higher. The effects of electrical shock depend upon the type of circuit, its voltage, resistance, pathway through your body, and contact duration.

Although there are several methods of protecting against electrical shock including double insulation, grounding and isolating transformers, these methods are not foolproof. Double insulating a tool does not protect you against cord, plug, or receptacle defects. Grounding a metal housing helps prevent shock caused when voltage-carrying parts inside contact the housing, but if you touch the housing, you'll get a shock unless the ground path offers no resistance to the current. The safety of isolation transformers can be voided by defective wiring and worn insulation.

Circuit breakers and fuses provide protection for equipment from receiving too much current but do not prevent shock. You can protect yourself against current that is too small to actuate fuses or circuit breakers by using a ground-fault interrupter (GFI). When a GFI is connected between a power source and a load, it monitors current in the hot wire and grounded neutral wire. As long as the current stays equal in both wires, there is no fault. But the instant there is a decrease in the amount of current in the neutral wire greater than a predetermined value (about 0.005 amps), the imbalance causes the GFI to disconnect the shock source, often in as little as 0.025 seconds.

With the exception of combined GFI-circuit breakers, ground-fault interrupters are not designed to replace fuses and circuit breakers because GFIs do not protect against shock caused by line-to-line contact. Instead, they are intended as a complement to other safety devices, providing an added measure of human safety. GFIs are effective only when the overall electrical circuit reflects good safety practices.

Emergency Lighting

Emergency lighting systems are required in all commercial, industrial, and institutional facilities by the National Fire Protection Association's National Electrical Code, Life Safety Code, and many state and local electrical, fire, and building codes. Such systems supply sufficient illumination and egress marking during a power outage, fire, or other emergency to enable persons in buildings to exit safely. While various methods for complying with the codes can be used, the most popular one is with the installation of battery-powered emergency lighting and exit signs.

The primary code covering the installation and maintenance of emergency lighting is the National Fire Protection Association's National Electrical Code. Article 700 of this code supplies guidelines that apply to the electrical safety of the design, installation, operation, and maintenance of emergency systems. Emergency systems are defined as: "Those legally required and classed as emergency by municipal, state, federal, or other codes, or by any governmental agency having jurisdiction. These systems are intended to supply illumination and power automatically to designated areas and equipment in the event of failure of the normal supply or in the event of accident to elements of a system intended to supply, distribute, and control power and illumination essential for safety to human life."

Article 700 also states that batteries should be suitably rated and sized to supply and maintain power at not less than 87 percent of the nominal battery voltage for the total lamp load associated with the unit for a period of at least ninety minutes; or the unit equipment shall supply and maintain not less than 60 percent of the initial emergency illumination for at least ninety minutes.

TOOL SAFETY

Through knowledge, common sense, and attention to environment, many injuries can be prevented by improving hand tool safety in the plant.[7] Following are some of the most common industrial hand tool safety issues.

- *Unintentionally using the wrong tool for a job.* Workers sometimes use the wrong tool to perform a given task. This can result in damage to the tool or product, injury to the worker, and loss of time. To solve this problem, make sure your workers know the intended use of each tool.

- *Modifying or misusing a tool.* Often, a tool will be intentionally used for something for which it was not intended. The best example of this is a screwdriver. You can use a screwdriver to open a can of paint, but a small pry bar will accomplish the same thing without compromising your safety. A screwdriver is not engineered for prying; it is designed to turn, not go up and down.

The reason employees modify or misuse a tool is usually because of convenience or economy. Either they don't want to take the time to get the correct tool, or the correct tool was not purchased in order to cut expenses. To correct this situation, make sure your employees have the right tools at their disposal.

- *Tool maintenance.* In addition to making sure your employees are using the proper tools, you also need to insist that the tools are properly maintained. Tools should be inspected on a regular basis to expose any defects or weaknesses. Look for cracks in hammer handles, chips in cast tools, and dullness in cutting tools. Make sure any problem is handled immediately and properly. Don't fix a crack in a hammer handle by wrapping it with tape. This will not prevent the handle from completely cracking and the head flying off. Hammer handles made of wood, fiberglass, or graphite should be replaced.

Get your employees into the habit of regularly inspecting, fixing, and cleaning their tools. This includes lubricating moving parts, tightening screws, and dressing striking surfaces.

■ *Personal protection.* Eye protection, gloves, and other protective devices are essential in the prevention of both minor and major injuries. Employees should be trained to anticipate potential dangers to their person, and then take proper precaution to prevent them from occurring.

■ *Working environment.* One of the best things you can do to prevent accidents is provide your employees with a workplace conducive to performing their jobs safely. You can begin by providing adequate lighting, good ventilation, and temperature control to suit the work being performed. Noise is another offender to paying attention to the job. Whenever possible, reduce the noise level and provide people with ear protection so they are able to concentrate and not be distracted.

Also, make sure everyone keeps their workbenches and walkways near their area free and clear; clutter makes for an unsafe environment. Instead of having one main tool area, have several tool stations each equipped with the proper tools for the jobs being performed in that area.

ELECTROSTATIC HAZARDS

Most electrostatic hazards in plants arise when uncontrolled handling of materials occurs.[8] When any two materials come into contact, one acquires an excess of electrons and is negatively charged while the other is deficient in electrons and is positively charged.

Although charge generation itself is not hazardous, charge accumulation can cause discharges capable of igniting certain flammable atmospheres. The major step in avoiding ignition is to test the electrostatic properties of the materials handled in the plant. These tests include:

1. *Powder sensitivity to ignition.* A minimum ignition energy test will determine the smallest amount of static energy that is required to initiate a dust cloud explosion.
2. *Powder volume resistivity.* The powder volume resistivity test provides an estimate of the time it takes for electrostatic charges to relax to ground once they become charged.
3. *Electrical conductivity of the liquid.* This test determines whether or not a liquid can become charged during transfer or processing. It also provides an estimate of the time it takes for electrostatic charges to relax to ground.
4. *Electrical resistance of the floor.* If resistance to the ground is greater than 10^8 ohms, it means the floor is insulating and can therefore

electrically isolate people and other conductive objects from the ground.

General precautions should be taken throughout the plant in environments where flammable dust cloud or vapor atmospheres may exist. These precautions concern:

- *Conductive (metal) items.* These items should have special grounding connections to ensure a resistance to ground below 10 ohm.
- *Footwear.* Where a person may come into contact with a flammable vapor or dust with a minimum ignition energy up to and including 100 milliJoules, it is recommended that he or she be grounded. Grounding can be achieved by the use of suitable antistatic footwear and floors.
- *Floor.* The flooring should not raise the total resistance between the person and earth above 10^8 ohms. Deposits of insulating contaminants on the floor should be removed.

PROTECTION AGAINST FALLS

More and more plants have invested in fall protection programs in recent years.[9] Creating a program involves purchasing safety and fall protection equipment, and training the workforce in the proper use of protective equipment. Although the program is an investment for an employer, the payback includes higher productivity, discounted insurance rates, compliance with OSHA regulations, and increased worker safety.

A fall hazard exists any time a worker is at a height greater than six feet. This distance is measured from the working surface to grade or a lower level. From this height, the free-fall velocity at impact is nearly 11 mph, enough to cause serious and permanent injury.

Hazards can be found on powered platforms, scaffolding, ladders, roofs, or elevated workstations. Construction sites pose a continually changing hazardous environment. Access holes for maintenance of underground sewers or tanks are particularly dangerous because rescue is complicated.

Once a fall hazard has been identified, a plan of action specifying how to eliminate it or how to work with it safely must be formulated. A thorough plan identifies the proper protection equipment, explains how to use it, and defines who should be trained, who is responsible for overall supervision and training, and who is responsible for rescue.

Fall protection equipment consists of three components: body gear, connecting device, and anchorage or tie-off point. Body gear may be a safety belt or a full-body harness. A safety belt is a strap secured about a worker's abdomen that can be attached to a lanyard, lifeline, or deceleration device. A full-body harness is a system of straps secured about the worker to distribute arresting forces over the thighs, shoulders, and pelvis. The harness, like the safety belt can be attached to a lanyard, lifeline, or deceleration device.

Harness styles include low-weight, subpelvic, adjustable-fit, construction, heavy-duty, and universal-fit. The low-weight harness provides maximum worker mobility. A universal harness fits sizes medium to extralarge and allows unrestricted movement during the workday. All full-body harnesses are designed to be attached to a connecting device such as a retractable lifeline, rope grab, or lanyard. Rope or webbing lanyards are the most common connecting devices.

Retractable lifelines automatically take up slack or release more line as a worker moves about. Designed to be mounted above the worker, usually from an I beam or the top of a fixed ladder, these units connect to the back D ring of the harness, providing unrestricted vertical movement. If the worker should fall, a centrifugal braking mechanism limits the free fall to two feet.

Fall protection is also required for climbing ladders and for ascending and descending poles, bridges, antennas, or any structure more than twenty feet high. Protection on these structures has traditionally been a protective cage surrounding the worker during a climb. For additional safety, many workers use a track system that runs vertically alongside the climbing structure. The worker attaches his harness to a trolley that runs on the track. The trolley moves with the worker and catches on the track if he or she slips or falls.

Fall protection is also necessary for confined spaces. A rescue and retrieval system should include built-in fall protection because these systems arrest falls quickly and can be used to raise and lower an incapacitated worker.

A suspension system supports the worker in a position that allows hands-free work. For example, bos'n chairs are widely used for washing windows or painting. Engineered to support a worker rather than arrest a fall, these systems should be used with fall arrest components.

HAZARDS OF COASTING EQUIPMENT

Most users of machines forget their safety concerns once they turn off the machine. They fail to realize that this is when machines harbor an insidious danger to the unsuspecting: silent and hazardous coast-down.[10] A typical example is a sawblade coasting down in a noisy shop environment, lurking as an unheard and unnoticed hazard to someone making a machine or workpiece adjustment, or even a passerby.

While it's impossible to say exactly how fast a given machine must stop to meet the code or make it safe, a little common sense goes a long way. If the moving parts or tooling are physically well-guarded, coasting may not be a problem. An exposed sawblade, however, offers only risks during coasting. It should be stopped in seconds rather than several minutes. Coast-to-stop times of five to fifteen minutes are common in industrial environments. Of course, the equipment must not be stopped so violently that parts or tools can loosen. A massive grinding wheel fastened with a left-hand threaded nut, for example, must not be stopped so quickly that the nut comes loose. In general, stopping at two to four times the start-up time is reasonable.

Good applications for eliminating coasting include woodworking machines such as radial arm saws, table saws, band saws, shapers, jointers, routers, tenoners, lathes, drills, sanders, and planers. The ANSI anticoasting safety codes apply here specifically. OSHA codes also apply on some specific equipment such as mills and calenders.

Fortunately, it is relatively easy to reduce coasting without affecting the equipment or operating procedures. Electronic motor brakes have been developed which uniquely meet the need. Unlike mechanical brakes which are difficult to install and maintain, electronic motor brakes install with just a few wires to the existing motor control system and operate without friction. By injecting direct current to create a stationary magnetic field between the rotor and stator of the motor, they drive the motor to zero speed quickly and automatically whenever the machine is turned off. An adjustable torque feature permits matching to any equipment. The compact electronic package can be remotely located and uses the same power that the machine runs on. They require no air, hydraulics, or separate power sources.

SAFETY CLOTHING AND EQUIPMENT

You can accomplish much toward increasing the safety of employees if you convince them of the importance of safety clothing and persuade them to wear it. When employees understand how clothing and equipment protects them, and when they've been trained how to use these things, they will more willingly participate in this part of the plant's safety program. Here are some ways you can promote and gain their cooperation:

1. Let employees make decisions relating to the model and style of protective clothing they're going to wear. As one manager aptly put it, "If allowing employees to choose fashionable safety eyewear will get them to wear it on the job, I'm all for it!"

2. Discuss with them the hazardous conditions and how the safety systems and equipment that the company provides them will give them the best protection. Point out the necessity of being familiar with and knowing how to use such devices.

3. Set an example. Wear safety glasses and other appropriate clothing such as a hard hat or safety shoes as circumstances and workplace conditions require them. Tell employees that you would not feel safe without these items.

4. Get the backing of the union or the informal leaders in the plant. If those people set the pattern for proper clothing on the job and the use of safety devices and equipment, others will follow.

5. Be firm and persistent that the safety clothing be worn, going so far that you take disciplinary action if it is not. Tell employees that some plants make the wearing of safety clothing a requirement for being on the payroll. Remember, you are responsible for the safety of your people.

LIFTING AND CARRYING LOADS

With improper lifting and carrying near the top of the list of industrial accident causes, it is evident that many plant workers either are careless when lifting and carrying or don't know how to properly lift and carry objects.[11] As for what load should be considered too heavy for an employee, there appears to be no simple answer. The U.S. Department of Labor's Bulletin 110, "Safety in Industry—Teach Them to Lift," contains this statement:

> There are no simple solutions to the setting of maximum permissible weights to be carried by any one worker. Due regard must be given to the physiological aspects of lifting and load carrying. Externally, we must give consideration to the climatic conditions, as well as the degree of training and experience each worker has had in lifting and carrying. The setting of manual lifting and carrying limits must be predicated upon, among other things, the size and type of load to be carried (compact or loose), distance of lift, height and position of lift, the working or walking level, the incline of the surface, and so on.

Although physical differences among individuals make it difficult to set safe lifting and carrying load limits for workers, training in these techniques can greatly reduce injuries caused by improper lifting and carrying habits. Here are some recommendations you can make to your workers on how to lift safely:

- Be sure you can handle the load. Never attempt to lift something if you doubt your ability to do so.
- Before lifting, inspect the item for sharp edges, splinters, exposed nails, weak bottom, or slipperiness.
- Make certain you have good footing. Do not try to lift something on a slippery, steeply sloped, or cluttered surface.
- Place feet close to base of item to be lifted to prevent back muscles from taking all of load. Feet should be eight to twelve inches apart to ensure good balance and stability.
- Bend knees and squat.
- Keep back, neck, and head straight and as nearly vertical as possible. Spine, back muscles, and internal organs will be in correct alignment, reducing compression of intestines and the possibility of hernia occurring.
- Grip item firmly. If lifting a box, grasp it at opposite top and bottom corners with full palms.
- Hold arms and elbows as close as possible to sides of body. Arms lose strength if held away from the body.
- Begin lifting. Use arm muscles while simultaneously pushing up with legs. Continue lifting steadily and smoothly, keeping load close to body, until item is in a secure and comfortable carrying position.

Carrying can be safer if your employees observe the following rules:

- Allow a load to fall if you should lose your grip, or, if possible, ride it to the floor by body pressure, keeping hands and feet out of its path. A quick bending motion when trying to catch an item can cause a back sprain.
- Turn your body with changes in foot position. Do not twist if it becomes necessary to change direction while carrying the load.
- Hold the load close to the body to better maintain balance.
- Keep front end of a long object such as a ladder slightly higher than rear end. Such loads are easier to carry if they are held a little toward the front end.
- Be sure you can see over and around the load, especially when walking up or down stairs.
- Use two or more workers to carry heavy loads and keep the load evenly balanced. When two people carry long sections of pipe or

boards, they should carry the items on the same shoulder and walk in step.

Workers who are lowering a load should follow these guidelines:

- Turn the feet and entire body to face location where the item is to be placed.
- Place the load that is to be lowered onto bench or table on edge of furniture, thus transferring a portion of its weight. Then push load to desired position using arms or body.
- Reverse the lifting procedure when lowering an object to the floor. Keep the object close to the body and bend the knees until the body is squatting. Keep the back straight, maintain balance, and allow leg and arm muscles to do the work.

WORK PLATFORMS

More and more plants today are using self-propelled elevated work platforms for overhead maintenance work involving piping, ducts, lighting, and electrical wiring. Maintenance managers have found that the quality and productivity of overhead work is much better when craftspersons operate from a stable platform. Efficiency is much greater when the platform holds tools and materials, and moves to the next elevated location without requiring the employees to return to the floor level.

Not only manufacturing plants, but also the construction industry has realized several benefits from work platforms of this type. Safety is enhanced and employees are more at ease when standing on a solid platform rather than a ladder. In addition, they are even more productive when working alone on platforms. Construction industry research shows that the productivity of two people working on separate work platforms is 40 percent greater than for two workers on a single platform.[12]

The safety benefits of elevated work platforms are even more important than productivity benefits. Work platform safety is equal to that of scaffolding; it also doesn't require the planning and labor needed to build scaffolds. Yet the maintenance manager and the craftsperson(s) using self-propelled work platforms are each responsible for inspecting the workplace for possible hazards. Among possible unsafe conditions are bumps, holes, and floor obstructions; overhead obstructions and high voltage conductors; inadequate surface and support to withstand loads; and the presence of unauthorized persons.

If you decide to invest in one or more work platforms for use in the plant, try one before you purchase it. Most work platforms are sold by dealers specializing in aerial work equipment. The dealers often rent and lease equipment, allowing your plant to test it before buying. In fact, more than half the units sold are first leased by a future buyer.

SAFETY ON THE NIGHT SHIFT

Night shift employees are more likely than day shift workers to be involved in accidents and injuries because many such incidents are fatigue-related. These employees are also prone to higher rates of illness and digestive problems, some of which undoubtedly are due to not getting enough rest and sleep when they are home.

The amount of sleep a person gets affects his or her mood, mental capability, memory, concentration, and judgment. A deficiency or weakness in these areas makes for a potentially dangerous situation on the job, especially if machinery and equipment are involved. Making matters worse, many night-shift people experience periods lasting from a few seconds to several minutes where they doze off and lose consciousness.

You can help employees with their rest and sleep problems by suggesting that they try to sleep in an environment that is quiet, dark, and cool. The time of day they sleep is also important. Morning persons working the night shift will probably sleep better late in the day before reporting to work. Night persons will probably sleep better during the morning hours after work. There are several other ways you can increase the alertness and improve the safety of your night shift workers. Following are a few recommendations:

- *Increase the lighting.* The brighter you can make the workplace, the better. Increased wattage is especially beneficial in control rooms containing gauges and instruments. It also helps in process and assembly areas where close observance of operating machines and equipment is necessary to be safe and avoid an injury.

- *Control the noise.* Recognize that some sounds are actually sleep inducers. To eliminate a constant hum or buzz, consider masking it with music. Be careful, however, with the volume—loud music may distract employees, preventing them from hearing safety alarms or sensing equipment malfunctions.

- *Provide color and contrast.* In addition to perking up work areas, color coding is great for identifying firefighting equipment, dangerous machine parts, physical hazards, and even simple piping systems. The use of accent colors on walls and floors also contributes toward making the environment more pleasing and less dulling to the senses.

THE OCCUPATIONAL SAFETY AND HEALTH ACT

National impetus on safety began with the 1970 Occupational Safety and Health Act (OHSA). In broad terms, three out of four civilian workers come under its jurisdiction. Standards were set under OSHA in a voluminous document that listed in detail various requirements of design and operation of equipment, machines, facilities, and structures, as well as specifying safety training and equipment for workers. In an effort to update the original standards and make them apply more directly to current workplace conditions, and administration continually makes many revisions each year.

This law requires all employees in the private sector of business to provide their employees with workplaces free from those recognized hazards likely to cause physical harm or death. It does this through the publishing of volumes of the Code of Federal Regulations. These documents are available from the Superintendent of Documents, U.S. Government Printing Office, Washington, D.C. 20402.

The two most pertinent publications for plants are the General Industry Standards and Interpretations, and the Construction Standards and Interpretations. The former publication is issued in two documents: 29 CFR Parts 1901.1 to 1910.441 and 29 CFR Parts 1910.442 to 1910.1000. The latter publication is issued in one document: 29 CFR Part 1926.

OSHA Functions and Achievements

Despite the fact that some companies are not entirely in agreement with how the administration conducts its business, OSHA can save some companies money. Savings can be realized from lower workers compensation costs because compliance with OSHA laws improves a company's accident record, thus reducing the cost of workers compensation. OSHA also has other influences on industrial organizations.

Before OSHA, the management of a company could deny an expense for safety because it would put the company at a competitive disadvantage if a competitor chose to forgo the same expense. With OSHA forcing all companies to spend money for safety, that argument no longer prevails. Better safety can result in other benefits. Changing a process to eliminate a hazard sometimes improves not only the safety but also the efficiency of the operation.

In addition, enactment of occupational health standards by OSHA has forced many managers to become involved in the evaluation and control of industrial hygiene problems in their facilities. For example, industrial hygiene factors must receive attention when operating and maintaining ventilation systems, makeup air, enclosure and/or isolation of processes using toxic chemicals, handling and storage of toxic materials, and cleanup of exhaust emissions.

Lastly, OSHA states that all employees must keep accurate records of work-related injuries, illnesses, and deaths. Any injury that involves medical treatment, loss of consciousness, restrictions of motion or work, or job transfer must be recorded. Required information must be logged and specific information regarding each case detailed. With this information readily available to management, there is no excuse for not knowing what has to be done to improve a plant's safety record.

HEALTH AND HUMAN SERVICES

The National Institute for Occupational Safety and Health (NIOSH) is part of the Department of Health and Human Services. It was established by Section 22 of the Occupational Safety and Health Act of 1970. NIOSH conducts research and experimental programs for the development of new and improved health standards.

The Secretary of Labor looks to NIOSH results when formulating standards under the Act. NIOSH also develops criteria for handling toxic materials and aids in determining safe exposure levels for physical conditions involving noise, illumination, vibration, radiation, temperature, and pressure.

In addition to its research and development activities, NIOSH inspects and investigates workplaces to evaluate and improve employee safety and health. Although it has no authority to enforce standards, its authority to inspect is established by Section 8 of the Act.

Thus, a NIOSH inspector may visit a plant for one of two reasons: Either a request for a Health Hazard Evaluation (HHE) has been received, or NIOSH wants to make an inspection as part of its general research responsibilities.

An HHE of a particular workplace may be requested by the employer or an individual employee. Whatever the reason, the HHE must give specific information about the plant, the process, and the substances or materials that are the basis for the request. Much of what happens after the request is similar to what takes place with an OSHA inspection.

HANDLING AN OSHA INSPECTION

Since an OSHA inspector may show up at your plant at any time to investigate a major accident, conduct a routine inspection, or investigate an employee complaint, you should be prepared to handle the visit properly. While representatives from the safety department will be primarily responsible for assisting OSHA during the inspection, you can, and should, play a vital role. Here are some recommendations to make the inspection come off as smoothly as possible:[13]

- *Accompany the inspector yourself if possible.* If not, arrange to have another exempt employee do it. Two people (you and a colleague, for example) are even better. One person can take notes, samples, and photos, while the other talks with the inspector and answers questions.

- *Pay close attention to what the inspector does.* If the inspector takes samples of something, you should do the same. Similarly, if the inspector takes photographs, you should take photos of the same items. In addition, take extensive notes on what he or she observes during the inspection. If the inspector reports a violation documented by a sample, photo, or visual observation, you want to have the *exact* information as the inspector does so that you can make necessary corrections or challenge the allegation of violations.

- *Listen carefully to the inspector's questions.* Failure to pay attention and give thought to your answers can cause confusion. If you answer a question so quickly that you don't give adequate thought to it, you may be incorrectly cited for a violation.

- *Don't worry about proprietary information.* If the inspector insists on visiting areas where proprietary technology is being used, don't be concerned. OSHA inspectors are trained to keep this information private.

- *Keep the tone professional.* Be cordial but businesslike in your conversations with the inspector. Resist temptations to show hostility or be overly friendly.

- *Respect employee-inspector conversations.* Allow the inspector access to employees, and do not eavesdrop on conversations between them.

- *Know where your OSHA-related records are kept.* You should be able to direct the inspector to required postings, notices, and advisories. You also should be able to show your MSDS sheets, OSHA injury logs, employee safety-training records, and equipment-inspection sheets.

- *Make corrections — now.* If the inspector notes any violations that can be corrected before the inspection is completed (for example, housekeeping improvements), attend to them while he or she is onsite.

- *Clarify misunderstandings.* During the exit interview, the inspector will provide a summary of the violations he or she noted. Pay close attention to this because it is another opportunity to correct any misunderstandings that may have taken place and to provide fuller, more supportive answers.

■ *Begin immediate work on abating any violations.* Don't wait until the deadline to fix safety faults. Make corrections and document them with work orders, receipts, other related paperwork, and photographs.

OSHA's Noise Standard

Lack of a written hearing-conservation program is among the most frequent workplace citations issued by OSHA each year. Hearing protection in the workplace is regulated by OSHA under its noise standard and its hearing conservation amendment.[14] The standard defines several types of noise and establishes maximum allowable workplace levels for each type.

Continuous noise's highest levels occur more often than once per second. Impulsive noise has peaks occurring less often than once per second. For example, noise from an engine would be continuous, while noise from a pile driver would be impulsive. There is no mathematical definition for intermittent noise, but an example would be periodic announcements broadcast from a public address system. Each of these types of noise can be hazardous to workers and must be considered in a hearing protection program.

OSHA measures noise exposure parameters in dB(A), which are sound intensity measurements recorded in decibels by an instrument that simulates the human ear.

OSHA's noise standard calls for a maximum noise exposure level of 90 dB(A) as an eight-hour, time-weighted average (TWA). As Exhibit 6-1 shows, higher levels of noise are permitted for shorter durations, up to a maximum exposure for continuous noise of fifteen minutes at 115 dB(A). Impulsive noise is allowed up to peak levels of 140 dB(A). Whenever the sound levels in Exhibit 6-1 are exceeded, engineering or administrative controls must be used to reduce noise exposures.

Protection Requirements

While hearing protection must be offered to all workers exposed to noise levels of 85 dB(A) and above, hearing protectors must be worn by workers exposed to a TWA of 90 dB(A) and above; workers exposed to 85 dB(A) and above, if they have waited six months or more for a baseline audiogram; and by all workers who have a standard hearing threshold shift, which is an average shift from baseline hearing levels of 10 dB(A) or more at the audiometric frequencies of 2,000 Hz, 3,000 Hz, and 4,000 Hz.

Employers must offer workers at least one type of earplug and one style of earmuff suitable for the specific noise environment. These hearing protectors must reduce noise to a TWA of 90 dB(A) or less, and to 85 dB(A) when employees have had a standard hearing threshold shift.

Exhibit 6-1. OSHA's permissible noise exposure.

Duration per Day (hr.)	Sound Level, dB(A) Slow Response
8	90
6	92
4	95
3	97
2	100
1$\frac{1}{2}$	102
1	105
$\frac{1}{2}$	110
$\frac{1}{4}$ or less	115

Hearing protectors can wear out. Earmuff seals can become inflexible and acoustical leaks will result; headbands can lose their tension; and malleable and premolded earplugs can lose their elasticity. Worn hearing protectors must be replaced; daily if necessary.

Monitoring Exposure

Workers exposed to noise levels of 85 dB(A) or greater as a TWA must have their noise exposures monitored at least once. If a change in equipment or a work process causes a significant increase in noise exposure, monitoring must be repeated. All continuous, intermittent, and impulsive noise between the levels of 80 and 130 dB(A) must be included in the assessment. Area monitoring is permitted, but personal monitoring must be used when there is considerable variation in noise level over time.

A baseline audiogram must be performed within the first six months of an employee's exposure to 85 dB(A) or above. If a mobile testing service is used, the baseline audiogram must be conducted within twelve months of the employee's first exposure to noise.

After this initial test, an audiogram must be provided annually. These tests must be conducted by trained personnel and supervised by an audiologist or physician. Workers who have standard hearing threshold shifts must be notified in writing, counseled about the use and fitting of hearing protection, and referred to a specialist if necessary.

Training Requirements

Training and education sessions must be given, at least annually, to workers exposed above 85 dB(A). These sessions must include information on the effects of noise on hearing, the purposes and procedures of audiometric tests, and the proper selection, initial fitting, use and care of hearing protectors. Records of noise measurements, audiograms, audiometer calibrations, and background levels in audiometric test rooms must be maintained and given to employees upon request.

OSHA's Requirement on Personal Protective Equipment

On April 6, 1994, the Occupational Safety and Health Administration (OSHA) finalized its rule on Personal Protective Equipment for General Industry (1910.132, 133, 135, 136, 138). The new standard contains provisions for performing a hazard assessment, training, retraining, and proper documentation.[15]

According to the standard, a hazard assessment of the workplace must be performed in order to determine what personal protective equipment should be worn. Based on the results of the assessment, appropriate equipment should then be selected and employees notified of this decision. The hazard assessment must be documented, which will help to certify that it was, in fact, performed.

Another aspect of the new standard is training. Employers are required to provide training on the proper uses of equipment for protection from workplace hazards. Retraining is required only when the employer has reason to believe the employee does not understand the previous training or when changes in the workplace occur that make previous training obsolete. If new or different personal protective equipment starts being used, once again retraining is necessary. The employer must document training in order to provide proof that every employee is in compliance.

Following is a synopsis of the requirements and guidelines for each area covered in the standard:

- *Eye and face protection (1910.133).* If employees are exposed to flying particles, molten metal, liquid chemicals, acids, caustic liquids, chemical gases, vapors, or potentially injurious light radiation, eye protection with front and side shields is required.

Employees who wear prescription lenses must wear eye protection that incorporates the prescription in its design or wear protection that can be worn over the prescription lenses without disturbing the proper position of the prescription lenses or protective eyewear. Protective eyewear must comply with ANSI Z87.1-1989.

■ *Head protection (1910.135).* If workers are exposed to falling objects or electrical hazards, hard hats are required. There are three types:

1. Class A hats protect from falling objects and 2,200 volts of electricity for one minute.
2. Class B hats protect against falling objects and 20,000 volts for three minutes.
3. Class C hats protect against falling objects but offer no electrical protection.

Protective helmets purchased must comply with ANSI Z89.1-1986.

■ *Foot protection (1910.136).* Whenever there is a chance of foot injuries due to impact, electrical hazards, falling or rolling objects, or objects piercing the sole, foot protection is required. Protective footwear purchased must comply with ANSI Z41-1991.

■ *Hand protection (1910.138).* Gloves are required for workers if there is potential for cuts or lacerations, skin absorption of harmful substances, severe abrasions, punctures, chemical or thermal burns, or temperature extremes.

There is no current ANSI standard to reference for the selection of hand protection equipment. It is suggested, however, that the selection be based upon an appropriate evaluation of the performance characteristics of the equipment relative to the task being performed, conditions present, duration of use, and the hazards identified.

AVOIDING AN OSHA INSPECTION

If plant employees believe unsafe or unhealthy conditions exist in the workplace, they or their representatives have the right to file a complaint with the nearest OSHA office. Since a complaint very likely will result in an official from OSHA visiting the plant for an inspection, or at least making an investigation, you must do everything you can to maintain safe and healthy conditions in the plant. Unquestionably, you need the help of the employees in this effort. Here are ways to get them to work with you:[16]

■ Create a safety committee whose responsibilities include making regular plant inspections, investigating accidents, and suggesting safety improvements in the plant, its machines, equipment, and tools. Ask the members to also help in developing and implementing safety rules. Rotate membership over time so that all employees have an opportunity to serve on the committee.

■ Promote safety contests and encourage all employees to participate. Give awards to employees who submit usable safety suggestions and to the department with the best safety record over a given period of time.

■ Hold safety meetings regularly, making attendance compulsory. Use films, videos, slides, and other visual aids that show how to deal with hazards in the plant. You can also use these meetings to train employees to work safely.

■ Point out to employees the necessity of wearing protective clothing and using safety equipment and devices in the performance of their jobs. Follow up, if necessary, to ensure they do so.

■ Instruct employees responsible for maintenance and repairs of safety devices to install or replace them only as designed. Make sure they understand that no change is to be made without approval of management.

■ Inform employees responsible for maintenance of instruments and controls to regularly check and adjust them to within their specified limits. Insist that these items also be tested after they have been serviced to confirm that they work properly.

■ Promote good housekeeping and a clean environment in the plant. Explain how such conditions contribute to the safety and health of everyone.

■ Ask employees to report the presence of a hazardous material or gas to supervision immediately after they detect it. Then see that steps are taken to correct the condition and do what is necessary to prevent a reoccurrence of the leak or spill.

■ Request that employees periodically check ventilation, lighting, and noise levels to make certain they are satisfactory and are not causing anyone to feel ill at ease, get headaches, or tire abnormally.

■ Tell employees to report any machine, equipment, or tool condition which could conceivably cause an accident or injury. Follow up to confirm that the condition was corrected and the area or item made safe.

EMPLOYEES' REFUSAL TO WORK BECAUSE OF "UNSAFE" CONDITIONS

The Occupational Safety and Health Act prohibits an employer from discharging or discriminating against any employee who exercises "any right afforded by" the Act. Among the rights that the Act so protects is the right of an employee to choose not to do an assigned job because of a reasonable fear of death or serious injury coupled with a reasonable belief that no less drastic alternative is available.

This OSHA regulation was challenged by an employer in a case that went to the U.S. Supreme Court for decision.[17] Two maintenance employees at a plant were ordered by their supervisor to perform a job that required that they step onto a steel-mesh net suspended 20 feet above the plant floor. Claiming that the net was unsafe, they refused to follow their supervisor's order. Two weeks before, another maintenance employee fell to his death through the net.

The supervisor sent them to the personnel office where they were ordered to clock out without working or being paid for the remaining six hours of their shift. The two maintenance men subsequently received written reprimands, which were placed in their employment files.

The Secretary of Labor sued the company, charging that its actions against the two employees constituted discrimination in violation of OSHA. However, the company contended that the Secretary's charge was invalid. While the U.S. Supreme Court upheld the validity of the charge, it pointed out that the rights given to workers under the regulation are restricted. The regulation does not give any right to walk off the job because of potential unsafe conditions at the workplace. Ordinarily, a worker is expected to use the procedures set out in the Act, including a request for an OSHA inspection.

But the Court added:

> As this case illustrates, however, circumstances may sometimes exist in which the employee justifiably believes that the express statutory arrangement does not sufficiently protect him from death or serious injury. Such circumstances will probably not often occur, but such a situation may arise when (1) the employee is ordered by his employer to work under conditions that the employee reasonably believes pose an imminent risk of death or serious bodily harm, and (2) the employee has reason to believe that there is not sufficient time or opportunity either to seek effective redress from his employer or to apprise OSHA of the danger.

The Court ruled that the two maintenance employees had been discriminated against when they were given written reprimands, but it also issued a general warning to employees by stating, "Any employee who acts in reliance of the regulation runs the risk of discharge or reprimand in the event a court subsequently finds that he acted unreasonably or in bad faith."

Although this case went to the U.S. Supreme Court about two decades ago, the problem occasionally arises in manufacturing plants today. You might have to contend with the problem in your plant. Note that while the Supreme Court upheld the validity of the charge, it pointed out that the rights given to workers under OSHA regulations are restricted. The regulation does not give any right to walk off the job because of potential unsafe conditions at the workplace. Here are some suggestions on what you can do:

1. Suspend without pay for the remainder of the shift any worker who refuses to perform a job that plant management considers safe. Also place a letter of the incident in the worker's employment file.

2. Recognize that the worker has the right to file a grievance on the matter if the plant operates under a union/management contract. (Whenever a member of a union disagrees with a work assignment, it is customary for the supervisor to try to persuade the worker to do the work first and then turn in a grievance for later retribution.) If there is no union, the worker has the right to request that an OSHA officer visit the plant to decide if the worker acted unreasonably. In neither case, however, should doing the work be postponed.

3. Call a local contractor to come to the plant to do the work as soon as possible. It is unlikely you will find a service organization that will turn down the job.

CHANGES IN OSHA

Since OSHA represents a series of comprehensive federal laws that have been and will continue to be initiated to cover plant operations, it is subject to many influences and will continue to experience change. For one, Congress can curtail or encourage specific activities through annual appropriation bills. For another, as political administrations change, there may be greater or lesser emphasis placed on various aspects of the program.

At one time, inspections were made in as many plants as possible in high-hazard industries; later it was decided to omit those plants with lower-than-average lost workday accidents. At another time, the agency exempted from routine inspections all plants with ten or fewer employees.

While plant management should keep up with the current status of OSHA through the news media and management journals, plants can best reach their objectives by implementing effective safety programs, regardless of any legal requirement to do so.

Much of what has been presented in this chapter is quoted directly from the Act or follows closely the wording in OSHA publications. Regardless, nothing stated here should be considered as a legal interpretation of these laws. You should get professional help when interpretation is needed.

NOTES

1. W. H. Weiss, *Plant Supervisor's Complete Desk Book* (Englewood Cliffs, N.J.: Prentice Hall, Inc., 1987), pp. 142–144, 152, 155.
2. Excerpts from the article titled "Safety Meetings That Work," published in the August 1995 issue of *The Safe Foreman*, pp. 18–22.
3. The material in this section is excerpted from "Don't Ignore Unsafe Acts," *The Safe Foreman*, October 1988, pp. 2–3.
4. Excerpts from "A Clean Workplace Can Mean a Safe Workplace," *The Safe Foreman*, September 1995, p. 22.
5. Jerry Baird, "Identifying Basic Causes of Recurring Safety Problems," *Chemical Processing*, November 1994, pp. 110, 112.
6. Excerpts from "Protecting Against the Shock of Electricity," *The Safe Foreman*, November 1982, pp. 18–20.
7. John Werner, "Improving Hand Tool Safety in Your Plant," *Plant Services*, December 1994, pp. 47–48.
8. Vahid Ebadat, "Guarding Against Electrostatic Hazards," *Chemical Processing*, August 1995, p. 92.
9. Miller Equipment, "Protecting Workers From Falls," *Maintenance Technology*, February 1995, pp. 74–76.
10. Al Nagler, "Recognizing the Hazards of Coasting Equipment," *Engineer's Digest*, February 1994, p. 16.
11. W. H. Weiss, *Plant Supervisor's Complete Desk Book* (Englewood Cliffs, N.J.: Prentice Hall, Inc., 1987), pp. 157–159, 200–201.
12. Mayville Engineering Co., Inc., Mayville, Wisc., "Work Platforms Increase Productivity," *Maintenance Technology*, July 1994, pp. 23–25.
13. William Atkinson, "How to 'Host' an OSHA Inspection," *First Line Supervisor*, September 5, 1995, p. 4.
14. James Kvikstad, "Complying With OSHA's Noise Standard," *Chemical Processing*, February 1995, pp. 107–108.
15. J. A. Hayman, "Personal Protective Equipment: What OSHA Is Requiring," *Plant Services*, December, 1994, pp. 52–53.
16. W. H. Weiss, *Plant Supervisor's Complete Desk Book* (Englewood Cliffs, N.J.: Prentice Hall, Inc., 1987), pp. 204–205.
17. Ibid., pp. 217–219.

7

Process and Quality Control

Process and quality control in plants today covers the disciplines, systems, and staff operations necessary to ensure error-free output of product without requiring excessive inspection. The function includes appropriately skilled and trained individuals serving as staff to assist line department workers.

Process control provides for the correlation of measurement results between the plant and its customers. This includes documentation from drawings and process specifications for the manufacturing and inspection procedures. In addition, process control includes all the data collection and analysis, and auditing procedures needed to ensure that a system or process continues to operate as planned.

Quality control systems based on process control differ considerably from systems based on final inspection. In many plants, however, inspection has been found to be both too costly and too inefficient a way to ensure quality. The abandonment of heavy final inspection can be tolerated only if it is replaced with stringent controls at every step of the process.

STATISTICAL PROCESS CONTROL

Statistical process control is one of the most important parts of a process control system.[1] The procedure guarantees that unfavorable trends on a manufacturing process are detected and corrected before any off-specification material is produced. Thus, it is a dependable way of determining that some factor is causing variations outside the normal variation of the process.

The technique is a way of evaluating a process to identify both desirable and undesirable changes. Each characteristic that is measured is evaluated to determine if statistical process control methods can be used. Preliminary limits are set for each characteristic based on technical judgment, past experience, and/or the specification limits. These are the limits within which natural variation is expected to occur. Control sample size and frequency are also set.

Measurements are best taken in the workplace or on the process line by an individual assigned to the job. This individual records the data and plots data points on control charts. It is critical that the person taking the samples or making measurements also do the analysis of the control charts since he or she needs to be continually up-to-date on the state of the process.

Once this system is underway, the process is monitored to determine if the process sample data stays within the control limits for at least twenty-five samples. If not, causes of the variation must be identified and eliminated until the test is passed. At this point, the process is stable enough to make a process capability study.

The purpose of the process capability study is to learn if the controlled characteristics falling outside the specification limits are below a predetermined limit. When a process capability study has been successfully completed, sufficient real process data will be available to replace the original preliminary control limits, with ongoing process monitoring limits statistically determined from the real data of the stable capability process.

In case a control chart sample point indicates that the process has gone out of control, the individual in charge of the process must immediately take two actions:

1. All output since the last in-control sample was taken must be examined to determine if it is in specification. Any deviant output must be either corrected or eliminated.
2. The person(s) running the process must be notified immediately so that it can be stopped before additional off-specification material is produced.

If there is a compelling reason to keep the process going, such as economic necessity or customer demand, all output must be screened until the process is back in control. In no case should the process be allowed to continue in the hope that a few more samples will indicate that the process has corrected itself.

Methods for Analyzing Processes

Most procedures for analyzing processes are based on observations and measurements. Much written material is available on how to improve a process, and many of our universities, training organizations, and consulting firms offer short courses and seminars on the subject of process control. To continually improve a process requires that you keep up with the latest technology in your industry and adopt the procedures that are appropriate for your particular application. First and last piece inspection using a gauge is a common technique for production of small lots, especially in job and machine shops. If you want to make a more complete study, you can use one or more of the following tools of process analysis other than the statistical process control procedure already described:

- *Pareto analysis.* To use this technique, plot upsets such as machine failures or stoppages and late deliveries every time they occur in the process flow. Then select the worst case, which is the longest bar on the Pareto chart, for further study.
- *Fishbone chart.* Here you make a major disruption the spine on a fishbone chart with secondary causes becoming branch bones connected to the spine. Tertiary causes are connected to secondary causes. Begin experiments on the bones at the extremities.
- *Histograms.* With this procedure, you measure a process characteristic and plot the measurement data on a histogram. The shape of the figure will suggest answers to causes.

CLASSES OF QUALITY

It is difficult to categorize quality in business and industry. Production, engineering, design, development, and marketing departments in a company often define it differently, and there is no reason to believe consumers are any more in agreement. This situation is likely to continue. Yet we must investigate and discuss the basic elements of quality to identify and analyze the situation and to come up with a strategy for managing and controlling it. A generally accepted approach is that quality should be defined from the customer's viewpoint. Following are the various terms associated with quality:

1. *Performance* is the primary operating characteristic of a product. Qualities inherent in the item are involved, and product lines can usually be rated on at least one magnitude of performance. Overall ratings, however, are more difficult to describe. For example, suppose that two lift trucks have identical capacities for handling loads up to one ton, but

achieve them differently: One can lift to a height of six feet, while the other can raise a load ten feet. While the capacities are the same, the capabilities are different. The truck with the higher lift capability could stack more pallets on top of others, while the truck with the lower lift would be limited in this respect. As to which of the two offers the best performance, that depends entirely on the pallet storage method a plant uses.

The relation between performance and quality is also dependent on conditions and circumstances. Consumers typically have many different needs. Each user of a product is likely to measure quality with high performance by the way the product satisfies a particular need.

The relation between performance and quality also has a language connection. The words that describe product performance include those frequently associated with quality along with those that don't.

2. *Options and special features of products* are those secondary characteristics that add to a product's basic function. An example is the automatic adjustment of a machine to its load along with a high temperature cutoff on its drive motor. In many cases, distinguishing between primary product characteristics (performance) and secondary characteristics (specials) is difficult to do. The distinction between the two is mainly a matter of degree of importance to the user.

3. *Reliability* concerns the probability of a product malfunctioning or failing prematurely. Other meanings of reliability include dependability and trustworthiness. Because these meanings define use of a product for some time, they are more appropriate for durable goods than for products and services that are used instantly.

Reliability of machines and equipment normally becomes an issue in a plant as downtime and maintenance become problems. Reliable equipment may mean the difference between a profitable year and a poor one for a manufacturing plant. For similar reasons, consumers in other markets have become increasingly aware of reliability. Both computers and telecommunications equipment are often advertised on this basis.

4. *Conformance* is considered the degree to which a product's design and operating characteristics meet established standards. In the United States, this is usually expressed as whether the product meets specifications. Since all products and services involve specifications to some degree, when new types or models are developed, dimensional standards must first be set for parts, and uniformity requirements set for materials. These specifications are seldom stated as a single figure or level, but as a permissible range of variation or tolerance.

Conformance is a critical matter with process control and sampling procedures. Specification limits are set for the variables in a manufacturing process, and the process is controlled to ensure that the majority of products will be within the specified limits.

5. *Durability* is normally thought of, both economically and technically, as the amount of use or life one gets from a product before it fails or physically deteriorates. But durability becomes more difficult to explain when a product can be repaired. Then the term takes on additional connotations because product life will vary with changing opinions and economic conditions. Durability becomes the amount of use one gets from a product before it breaks down and replacement is seen as preferable to continued repair. At that time, users must make a decision. Each time the product fails, they must weigh the likely cost, in both dollars and inconvenience, of future repairs against the investment and operating expenses of a newer, more reliable model. In such circumstances, a product's life is determined by repair costs, valuations of time and inconvenience, losses due to downtime, and relative prices as much as it is by the quality of components or materials.

6. *Maintainability* is the condition, preservability, and ease of repair of a product. Maintenance managers, for example, are concerned not only about a machine breaking down but also about the elapsed time before service is restored, and the frequency with which service calls or repairs fail to correct problems.

As you can see from the terms associated with quality, how a product is perceived is of utmost importance. Users do not always have complete information about a product or a service's attributes. Frequently, indirect and partial measures are the only basis for comparing brands. A product's durability, for example, can seldom be ascertained directly; it must usually be inferred from various tangible and intangible aspects of the product. Advertising and the use of brand names are perceptions of quality rather than the reality itself.

Reputation is one of the primary contributors to perceived quality. It is commonly believed that the quality of products manufactured by a company today is similar to the quality of products it manufactured in the past, or the quality of a company's more established products. Reputation is valued for exactly this reason. In the early years of a new product, especially a capital item whose reliability and durability may take years to demonstrate, users often have little other information on which to base their purchases.

TRAINING EMPLOYEES IN QUALITY CONTROL

Statistical process control (SPC) is concerned with the need for continual improvement. The technique of using statistical data on which to base decisions is a fundamental part of ongoing improvement. It starts with the premise that plantwide productivity levels, good enough in the past, will not be good enough tomorrow. In that respect, SPC is a tool that plants use to develop ways to implement efforts and then measure their results. Manager/employee cooperation and involvement are the keys.

While the technical aspects of quality control, and of SPC specifically, have been well developed and perfected, training of plant employees is sometimes inadequate. In many plants, the engineers who set up processes and the employees who run them need to receive more training in the concepts and techniques.

Your primary responsibility to employees is to furnish the right tools for the job and an environment conducive to doing the job right every time. Training cannot be left to chance or to another employee who may be doing the job but is not trained to instruct a new hire. Too often, plants do not have the in-house resources to provide the required training. However, training organizations, consultants, videotapes, films, and written instructional material are available on the subject.

In addition, it's helpful to review companies in your industry that have implemented statistical process control using a consultant or training materials. Ask for their experiences and recommendations. Don't be satisfied with advice from companies that have just sent a few employees to a class.

Quality Inputs

Acceptable quality of finished products depends on the level of quality in all the inputs to the process. Materials, equipment and tools, training, employee attitude, and supervision are among the major ones. They are interrelated to the extent that poor quality in one of them affects all the others. To get this information across to your employees, point out that:

- If the quality of materials is poor or low grade, defects will appear as the materials are being processed into a product. While these poor-quality products may be caught and removed, this runs up scrap or rework costs.

- If the equipment or tools used in the process are inferior or worn out, there is a very good chance that product quality will suffer regardless of the materials used.

- If the employees aren't trained in the correct methods of handling the material, the quality of workmanship will be poor, even if the tools and equipment are in good shape.

- If employees are faced continually with shoddy or defective material, and/or equipment that's difficult to use, and/or if employees have not received sufficient training, they will soon develop a "don't-care" attitude. This negative attitude invariably results in their turning out defective and inferior products because of the lack of attention and carelessness.

When you explain the importance of quality inputs, resist the temptation to talk about "improving quality." Product quality is determined by one or more of the inputs you talked about. A defect anywhere along the process will undo all the good quality inputs that precede or follow it. To ensure that the finished product meets quality standards, you have to maintain continual quality control on everything that goes into the product.

MEASURING QUALITY BY DEFECTS

While multiple measures typically are used to judge a plant's quality, most involve defect rates of some sort. They are defined as the proportion of parts, subassemblies, or finished units that fail to meet specifications. Such measures are often used to monitor the plant's processes. Little attention has been given, however, to the precise meaning of defect rates and the degree to which they are truly objective measures.

From a broad viewpoint, defective products are those that fail to meet preestablished standards. They may function improperly (if at all), show obvious deficiencies in workmanship, or perform poorly in safety tests. Both functional and cosmetic problems are involved: parts that have been attached incorrectly, loose screws, incomplete or uneven paint, misaligned labels, mechanical and electrical weaknesses. While these are mainly deficiencies in conformance, aspects of performance and aesthetics are involved as well.

Defect rates thus cover a wide range. Because problems vary in seriousness, various schemes have evolved for grouping defects into categories by their expected impact. Most schemes use some variant of an A-B-C system, distinguishing "critical" from "major" and "minor" defects. Such systems serve a valuable purpose by showing that not all defects are alike, but they fail on a more critical matter: Defect rates are seldom recorded with great accuracy.

Not all defects are equally apparent. Some, like wiring problems, are unmistakable: Units on the assembly line reach designated testing stations, are plugged in, but fail to function. Other defects, however, involve elements of discretion; for them, the dividing line between acceptable and unacceptable products is hazy and ill-defined. Noise levels are a good example, as are fits and finishes. In both cases, the inspector determines whether product imperfections are serious enough to be called defects. Particularly where subtle technical distinctions must be made, inspectors tend to see only what they have been trained to see. Parts misalignment, for example, is seldom obvious; unless inspectors know exactly what to look for and where their attention should be focused, problems will remain undetected. In the absence of clear direction, reported defects would be lower than actual defects.

Inspection accuracy might be related to other variables as well. For example, defects in hard-to-reach places are easily overlooked. In addition, inspections often are divided among several individuals, so that each sees units for only a brief period as they move by on the assembly line. The larger the number of inspectors, the greater the oversight provided, and the more likely that a defect missed by one inspector will be caught by another. Similarly, the more time devoted to inspection, the less cursory will be the investigation, and the more likely that defects will be found. The underlying principle here is simple but compelling: More careful inspection is likely to mean higher reported defect rates.

PRODUCT INSPECTION PROCEDURES

An effective way to ensure that employees have adhered to product inspection procedures is to set up a paperwork system in which documents accompany material to each assembly point or step in the process during the manufacture of the product.[2] Documentation is tangible proof of the operations that have been performed and verified on each part or subassembly. If there's no supporting inspection documentation, there's no alternative but to reinspect the entire output of the process. Documenting inspection throughout the process is well worth the effort and time to do it. Here are the steps for carrying it out:

1. See that the paperwork is developed and available. This is best handled by a staff group such as the Technical or Manufacturing Engineering Department.
2. Set up the procedure and rules covering it on what employees should do at an inspection point in the process.
3. Confirm that responsibility for carrying out the actual inspection belongs to the Quality Control Department.
4. Assign "check off" responsibilities for the inspectors. When they inspect and document each job in the process, they report that the job was done properly and according to specifications.
5. Route the paperwork to the Quality Assurance/Quality Control

Department when the process is complete. This group audits it to ensure that the specifications have been met.

6. Remind employees about the importance of adherence to product inspection procedures by posting signs at each workstation where paperwork is checked. State that employees who fail to inspect and document their work are subject to disciplinary measures.

IMPLEMENTING QUALITY STANDARDS

To ensure that employees' output is of high quality, management should provide written guidelines specifying the standard of quality required. In some industries, standards are set by local, state, or federal enforcement agencies, such as the Environmental Protection Agency. In others, standards are set by groups like the Food and Drug Administration or the various organizations that set standards for specific industries. Whatever, management must make sure that employees know and understand these guidelines. Managers must also see that the required quality control checks are being made and that the tests are verifiable. The first step toward reaching these objectives is to rewrite official and technical jargon into simple standard operating procedures. These documents should then be reviewed with employees and quality control analysts to ensure they understand and are able to follow them.

Once these standards are implemented into the plant processes, a manager must now regularly confirm that all the plant's analysts are tested. Although it's more expensive to interject performance evaluation samples into the system of real samples, it's the best way to ensure a quality product.

If an analyst fails the test, consider the possible reasons. An incorrect analysis could be due to an error in the system, such as a problem with the instrumentation. If the failure is due to an analyst's error, what you do is dictated by the experience level of the person:

- If it's a human error by an entry-level employee, additional training or coaching will help.
- If it's a human error by an experienced employee, it's probably due to a lack of concentration. Point out the problem in a nonaccusatory manner. Work with the person to determine the cause, and then do anything you can to improve the person's performance.

QUALITY AND COST RELATIONSHIP

It pays to convince employees that when the plant places a high priority on the quality of its products, operating and manufacturing costs are usually lower. But some employees may question that this actually occurs. You can sell the importance of the plant putting out high-quality products on an ongoing basis in a number of ways:

- Tell employees that the best and most immediate way to reduce the cost of a product is to make it right the first time. When you produce scrap, costs go up because you are paid for your time on the job, machine costs are incurred, and productive capacity is wasted on something the plant can't sell. All those costs are tacked onto the remaining good products.

- Confirm that it's to their advantage to do error-free work. Their chances to get ahead in the company are directly related to the high standards of work performance they set for themselves.

- Point out that when customers buy the plant's product, they expect it to be free of defects. If the plant ships some questionable or low-quality products, either inadvertently or to meet a customer deadline, and the customer detects the poor quality, the company has a real problem on its hands. The products may be returned collect—the company pays the freight costs. Then there's also the possibility that the customer may be lost and the company may never get another order. In such cases, poor quality can be very costly.

- Tell them that defects hurt the company's reputation in the marketplace. Customers won't buy the plant's product if they've heard it could be defective because other products the company has made have proved faulty.

- Emphasize that, if the products the plant makes bear a trademark, the symbol supposedly assures buyers of a certain level of quality. Advertising frequently mentions trademarks in telling and persuading customers that they can trust the product. But trademarks don't mean much if that trust is broken. The result is that the cost of advertising is for naught if the quality of the product is poor.

- Stress liability as a factor to be reckoned with. If the company is taken to court, subjected to government-mandated recalls, adjustments, or other settlements because of product defects or failure to perform as claimed, making matters right can be very costly.

- Talk about pride. A serious as well as costly effect of turning out poor-quality products is what such workmanship does to you. You have no pride in your work. If you are determined to build quality into the company's products, you usually like your work. When you like your work, your productivity is high. High productivity of employees means low operating costs for the company.

Balancing Cost and Quality Standards

High quality products plus good service are fine if cost is no object, but most manufacturing companies have to meet certain cost standards; these standards enable them to offer products or services at a price that attracts customers. Their quality standards are set on what it costs to meet them.

It's not always easy to meet standards, particularly when they conflict with one another. Time standards, material standards, dimensional standards, and others all add up to produce cost standards and quality standards. Therein lies the problem: If the benchmarks that set the cost standards are too rigid, it becomes hard to maintain the wanted quality standards.

Since customers will not accept inferior products or poor service, plant managers encounter a conflict. They must adhere to the standards for labor, material, and appearance to the point where they can ensure an acceptable level of quality. What this often amounts to is shortcutting the standards that contribute to cost reduction on one hand while maintaining acceptable quality on the other.

There's no question that a plant manager has a very tough job: that of satisfying both cost and quality demands. Each time you try to cut costs, you have to make sure you don't sacrifice quality. In addition, you have a "reverse" problem: If you find a way to improve quality, you must see if it can be done within your current cost standards.

Unfortunately, there's no simple answer. You are responsible for both quality and cost of your company's products and services. All you can do is keep in mind that cost changes affect quality standards, and quality changes affect cost standards. No good decision with respect to one can be made without considering the other.

QUALITY CIRCLES

In industrial plants, a quality circle is a small group of employees, usually six to twelve, who meet voluntarily to solve problems related to the workplace. In most cases, the employees select their own chairperson, rather than have you or some other manager lead them. However, in many plants, a manager or facilitator is assigned to coordinate the quality circle program for the company.

Quality circles work on problems that directly affect employees' productivity. With management approval, the group is formed to solve a specific problem that the employees have identified. The employees are responsible for defining the problem, agreeing on a meeting schedule, and obtaining your approval of the project. But if you see a problem that lends itself to quality circle treatment, ask one of your group leaders to volunteer to organize one. Point out the benefits and advantages of quality circles if you sense any reluctance to do so.

If you are asked to be a manager or facilitator for a circle, your responsibilities will be to:

1. Direct the entire program. Explain how a program functions and promote its advantages to employees.
2. Arrange for meetings to be held in a place that is free from noise and distraction. See that the meetings are limited to a maximum of one hour.
3. Prepare and give training programs on quality circle procedures.
4. Serve as the leader of a meeting until the chosen employee leader is ready to take over.

The first few meetings of quality circle groups are usually training sessions conducted by a manager or facilitator. Employees are trained in:

- How to conduct and participate in brainstorming sessions
- How to make cause-and-effect diagrams and analyses
- How to make histograms, graphs, and check sheets for solving problems

Following these introductory meetings, the next ones cover problem analysis that reinforces earlier training. In addition, the manager teaches: how to collect data, analyze it, and present it; how to use control charts and sampling for process control; and how to make unstructured cause-and-effect diagrams.

TOTAL QUALITY MANAGEMENT

In recent years, many plants have abandoned quality circles in favor of total quality management (TQM) programs along with employee empowerment. But only those companies who develop and implement effective programs will achieve good results from TQM. Effective programs include the establishment of performance standards and the installation of quality improvement goals. The following procedures enable you to carry out the programs:

- Learn the wants and needs of your company's customers. Prepare a checklist for meeting their requirements, and add some extras. Come up with ways to work more closely with customers and build their trust. Use customer feedback to improve your products and/or services.

■ Look into your company's present ways of improving total quality. Determine how to build on strengths and overcome weaknesses, the musts of a successful TQM program. Become aware of what it takes to create a TQM environment, and find out if your company is doing it. Act on what is necessary to upgrade employees' performance.

■ Empower employees to see themselves as internal customers who conduct endless buyer/supplier transactions inside your company's operation. Encourage individuals to participate in solving problems, especially when those problems directly affect the quality of their work.

■ Measure your company's total quality efforts. Take corrective steps if they are not producing superior employee performance, streamlined decision making, greater customer satisfaction, and better response from suppliers. Use measurements and benchmarking to motivate employees.

The differences between companies that practice TQM and those that don't are evident in the results the companies achieve. The former companies are driven by customer needs—management anticipates problems before they occur and accepts nothing less than 100 percent dedication from employees. The latter companies are driven by company wants— management detects problems after the fact, and establishes maximum acceptable levels of error or waste.

Those companies that practice TQM are committed to quality at the source; form cooperative, interdepartmental teams; and realize high employee participation from their empowered workforce. The companies that ignore TQM believe inspection is the key to quality, operate with autonomous, independent departments, and function with top-down, management-directed workforces.

Employee Involvement and Empowerment

One of the precepts of TQM is that employees must be involved and they must be empowered.[3] For employees to be involved, they must be considered as unique individuals (not just ordinary workers), and dedicated to helping their company reach its goals. Being involved also means that their input is solicited and valued by management. Although many managers today want their employees to be involved in improving the plant's operations, or at least to be active participants in helping the plant meet its objectives, in some plants this is not true for all employees. It's relatively easy to identify employees who try to raise standards, and others who are only interested in picking up their paychecks. It's also possible to identify people who are well suited for the work they are doing (and who enjoy their work), and others who seem to enjoy their work less, and maybe are not so well suited for it. Facilitating employee involvement requires recognizing the value of each individual, understanding human motivations, assigning people jobs they can handle, and listening to them.

Employee empowerment is different in meaning in regard to the role of employees in running the plant. It means that both employees and management recognize that many problems or roadblocks to reaching organizational goals can be identified and solved by employees. Employee empowerment means that management provides employees with the tools and authority required to continually improve their performance. It also means that management states its expectations about employees recognizing and solving problems, and empowers them to do so.

THE ISO 9000 STANDARDS

With each new trade agreement being made worldwide, more and more American companies anticipate doing business overseas. A prime requisite for participating successfully in such ventures is understanding the ISO 9000 registration or certification process and the quality standards it covers. The International Organization for Standardization (ISO) was founded in 1946 to promote the development of international standards and related activities, including conformity assessment. Its main objective is to facilitate the exchange of goods and services worldwide.

The ISO is composed of member bodies from more than ninety countries, and it continues to grow. The United States member body is the American National Standards Institute (ANSI). The ISO's work encompasses all areas except electrical and electronic engineering, which are covered by the International Electrotechnical Commission.

With the publication of the ISO 9000 series and the terminology standard (ISO 8402) in 1987, the organization promoted quality as a factor in international trade. The standards have been adopted by many countries, and in the United States they are rapidly supplanting prior national- and industry-based standards.

The purpose of ISO 9000 standards is to promote quality and consistency in production or service. The standards are a necessity for companies of any size wanting to do business worldwide. Every company wanting ISO 9000 registration must continually audit its systems in order to satisfy the requirements of the standard.

For companies not inclined to do business overseas, properly implemented standards may provide a number of benefits which include gaining a competitive edge, achieving a long-term marketing advantage, and improving the organization's profitability. Many companies may see ISO 9000 as the minimum effort that must be made to ensure quality of their products or services.

Components of ISO 9000

The components of ISO 9000 indicate that customers of companies and organizations play a key role in determining what these standards consist of and why they are necessary. ISO 9000 standards also illustrate that customer satisfaction can only be achieved when there is agreement among the components and they are mutually supportive. The components are:

■ *Management involvement and responsibility.* Management must be committed to promoting high quality in the company's products and/or services. This is accomplished by establishing a policy for quality and customer satisfaction. To be successful in implementation, a quality system must be developed and effectively operated. The procedure includes incorporating quality objectives, defining responsibilities, providing authority guidelines, and conducting periodic reviews.

■ *Human and material resources.* People are the most important asset a company has. Issues concerning them include motivation, education, training, and development; all of these are dependent on effective communication. Material resources are an essential ingredient in the operation of a business which makes a profit.

■ *Procedures to assure quality.* The quality system should be designed to focus on the output of the organization. Its structure should ensure adequate control of any process that affects quality. The system should also contain ways to avoid reoccurrence of problems without sacrificing the ability to respond to and correct failures, should they occur.

The ISO 9000 Registration Process

Management and employee commitment are required for effective implementation of ISO 9000. Although ISO 9000 is organized into four separate documents, 9001 through 9004, most companies try for certification of 9001 (production, installation, and maintenance of a product) or 9002 (production and installation) standards. A system consisting of eighteen quality elements needs to be met to achieve certification.

Depending on your company's business requirements, you may ask for certification for a division, department, plant location, or the entire company. The elements represent supplier-customer approaches to quality. For each quality element involved, there are relevant systems, procedures, personnel, and documentation to confirm that a viable quality system exists.

How your company handles certification depends on the quality systems and procedures the company already follows. Attaining certification usually means taking several important steps: forming a quality task force, conducting an internal audit, preparing a quality manual, visiting the assessing agency, and guiding the agency through your operation. The entire process may take twelve to eighteen months to finally gain certification.

The agency your company selects to do the certification depends on the country in which you want to do business. A few European countries may not accept foreign accreditation. Choose, if possible, an agency that specializes in your company's particular type of product, and make sure that your customer acknowledges the agency. Of course, you should also consider cost and the certifier's reputation.

Certification Costs

The ISO 9000 registration process may be quite costly. It will depend on the size of the company, the ISO 9000 series standard selected, the scope of the registration, and the location of the facility. Costs incurred outside the company involve the certifier's assessment fees, travel costs, document preparation, and review. Costs of $20,000 to $50,000 per site are not uncommon.

Costs incurred inside the company can be significant as well, particularly if a lot of staff training is required. To be cost-effective, company personnel must be involved and adequately trained. Without employee involvement, it may be prohibitively expensive to obtain and maintain certification. Similar to quality control efforts themselves, certification is an ongoing process, and a company's quality system must be periodically reviewed.

Benefits of ISO Registration

Although there are many benefits claimed for going through the ISO registration process, the true value of ISO 9000 can be expressed in a few pertinent words: providing satisfaction on the part of customers in their business relationship with suppliers. Yet some of the following benefits are significant when viewed in the proper context:

■ *Improved quality and consistency.* Over time, an ISO 9000 registration will result in improved quality through corrective action procedures. However, because registration does not affect absolute quality, there may still be wide differences in quality among companies which have been registered.

■ *Lower operating costs.* Adoption of quality control procedures, through simply documenting what is being done and taking corrective action when necessary, will result in reduced manufacturing and processing costs. But this will occur if the procedures are conscientiously applied, whether a company is registered or not.

■ *More effective advertising.* While having an excellent system on quality that has been verified by an outside organization is something to be proud of. The implication in advertising this fact is that your company's quality is better because you are registered. This may be far from the truth since the registration process only confirms that a quality system organized according to ISO 9000 standards is in place.

■ *Fewer audits.* When a company requires its suppliers to provide materials that meet ISO 9000 standards (the most common reason for specifying ISO 9000 quality), it's likely that the company will make fewer audits. However, the specified level of quality may be realized by using procedures and setting up systems much less stringent than those that might be required by a registrar. If the procedures and systems are rigidly controlled, there will be fewer audits whether a registrar is used or not.

■ *Better employee morale.* By implementing a quality system (using ISO 9000 standards because of their acceptance and reputation), a company may consider this a major step toward Total Quality Management (TQM). While TQM may be viewed as aiding employee morale, registration contributes little or nothing to this procedure.

■ *Less friction between departments.* Since the registrar polices the process, the friction that is normal between the quality and production/manufacturing departments is cut down. The registrar plays the role of a neutral party in making assessments rather than letting the departments make them. However, because this benefit may be attributed to a management deficiency, it is difficult to determine its actual value.

THE FUTURE OF ISO 9000

As a guide for companies doing business abroad or planning to, ISO 9000 is rapidly becoming the worldwide quality standard. Although considered cumbersome by some authorities, it is flexible enough to grow with technology and change in the marketplace while ensuring quality by design and enforcement.

The ISO 9000 standards were intended to be advisory in nature. They were developed principally for use in two-party contractual situations or for internal auditing. With recent revisions, however, the standards are currently being applied under a much broader range of conditions and circumstances. In some cases, compliance with one of the ISO 9000 standards (or their equivalent) has been or will be mandated by a United

States foreign national, or regional government body. Conformance to ISO 9000 standards is also being required in purchasing specifications with increasing frequency.

However, the future may not be bright for the registration process. Because it does not really contribute to the major benefits of having a quality system, and because there are differences in the degree of registrar severity, registration may actually be a barrier between customers.

CONNECTION BETWEEN ISO 9000 AND TOTAL QUALITY MANAGEMENT

To consider the connection between ISO 9000 and total quality management (TQM), it helps to consider the evolution of the four stages of quality-thinking as described by David Garvin of the Harvard Business School:[4]

1. *Inspection.* Quality management focused on the product. Inspectors who sorted out defects were responsible for quality.

2. *Quality control.* The focus remained on the product as well as the production process, but statistical techniques to control processes and reduce variability were introduced. In production, manufacturing and engineering departments assumed primary responsibility for quality.

3. *Quality assurance.* The entire production or service chain (from design to delivery of the product or service to the customer) became responsible for quality. Prevention, rather than detection, became the prevalent notion.

4. *Strategic quality (or TQM).* In this current era, the focus shifts from the product to the market and customers. Senior management has assumed responsibility for quality, which is concerned with the positioning of the organization and its product or service in the marketplace. Quality expands markets, increases market share, and, if market conditions permit, even influences pricing.

Inspection, quality control, quality assurance, and TQM each represent a philosophy that drives a company's quality system. The quality system (philosophy and procedures) guides how the organization conducts itself to satisfy customers.

TQM and ISO 9000 address similar aspects of quality management, but emphasize different things: TQM focuses more on human resources issues, while ISO 9000 emphasizes quality process issues. The choice is not between TQM and ISO 9000. A comprehensive quality process requires both.

An organization can be ISO-registered and very effectively produce and deliver the wrong products or services. TQM is essential to ensure that the "right" products and services are effectively delivered to the customer.

QUALITY EFFORTS APPLIED TO MAINTENANCE

Quality may well be a key factor in how United States plants succeed in the world marketplace. The problem is that most plants confine their quality efforts to production and manufacturing processes and vendor/supplier relationships. Not enough plants have recognized or taken the third step in the quality evolution—to ensure that their machines and equipment receive quality service.[5] The success of other quality programs will be limited unless the third step is taken. Machines and equipment running below design specifications will have a negative impact on the product.

To successfully implement quality programs, everyone in the organization must be involved, including upper management as the driving force behind the effort. Management must supply the plan and provide the direction. All other departments should be informed, should understand the project, and should willingly participate in the venture.

The management plan must cover the three principal areas of a quality strategy: organizational development, management development, and information systems development. The goal of organization strategy is to create a climate that will foster positive change. Understanding and commitment are the two essential elements in developing a positive climate. A maintenance organization cannot provide quality service if it does not have agreements on goals and strategies with its customers. Furthermore, the active support of other parts of the organization (stores, purchasing, and engineering) is imperative.

Quality strategy in maintenance requires the development of a new set of managerial and supervisory skills. Problem-solving groups, decision-making teams, reliability engineering, and self-managed work teams are excellent concepts. Participants must cultivate and practice good communication and work management skills to ensure success.

A maintenance work management system is a valuable organization tool that provides an effective method to identify, plan, schedule, and report maintenance activities. Training, however, is the key. Personnel trained to use the work management system must become information-based decision makers as opposed to experience-based ones. An automated information system is beneficial only if the users understand the benefits of the system and how to apply them.

NOTES

1. W. H. Weiss, *Plant Supervisor's Complete Desk Book* (Englewood Cliffs, N.J.: Prentice Hall, Inc., 1987), pp. 109–112, and 114–118.
2. Ibid., p. 122.
3. Joseph and Susan Berk, *Total Quality Management* (New York: Sterling Publishing Co., Inc., 1993), pp. 84–85.
4. Thomas C. Tuttle, "TQM and ISO 9000: The Quality Connection," *Successful Supervisor,* December 20, 1993.
5. Donald J. Deutsch, "Quality Strategy for Maintenance," *Maintenance Technology,* January 1993, pp. 30–31.

8

Plant and Facilities Design

All industrial activities require physical facilities for processing or manufacturing operations. The facilities are created and provided after design engineers plan, analyze, conceptualize, and implement systems for the making of products or the conductance of an operation. The design is identified as a layout, floor plan, or an arrangement of machines and equipment. Design or arrangement is critical in that it must optimize the performance of the machines and equipment while also making it easy for employees to operate and control them. In addition, provisions must be made for material and product flow and the process procedures required to achieve the plant's objectives safely, efficiently, and economically.

DESIGN OBJECTIVES

The primary design objective is to make possible the processing of material in, through, and out of the plant in the shortest time possible at the lowest cost. Additional objectives include:

1. *Make economical use of building space.* Only if each square foot is used to best advantage can the ever-present overhead costs per unit of product be minimized. Proper layout dictates suitable spacing between machines after the necessary allowances for the movement of labor and materials have been made.

2. *Arrange machines, equipment, and the workplace so that material moves smoothly along in as straight a line as possible.* Eliminate delays and plan the

flow so that the operation can be easily controlled. Most important, maintain conditions that are conducive to quality output.

3. *Reduce material handling wherever practicable.* Handling should be mechanical, and all movement should be planned to move the part or product toward the shipping area. Where possible, the part should be "in-process" while in transit.

4. *Reduce investment in equipment as much as possible.* Proper arrangement of machines and departments can aid considerably in reducing numbers. If it is found that only part of a machine's capacity is used, have some operations performed elsewhere.

5. *Promote flexibility.* An excellent way to facilitate the rearrangement of equipment is to install the utility systems in a way that connections can be easily made when equipment is relocated. Good examples are electrical and compressed air outlets. Such arrangements permit machines and equipment to be connected or disconnected, almost at will.

6. *Maintain high turnover of work-in-process.* If in-process storage of material is reduced to a minimum, the overall material turnover time is reduced, the amount of work-in-process is lowered, inventory is decreased, and a lower amount of working capital is required.

7. *Use labor effectively and efficiently.* You can most easily do this by limiting the mutual handling of materials. Also, minimize traveling by bringing materials closer to the employees with specially designed racks, hoppers, and conveyors. Balance machine cycles so that machines and employees are not unnecessarily idle.

8. *Ensure employee convenience, safety, and comfort.* Satisfying this objective requires attention to such matters as light, temperature, ventilation, and noise. Machines and equipment must be placed to prevent injury to personnel and damage to material. Incorporate safety and comfort into the layout by a careful study of the workplace for use of ergonomics in the design.

DESIGN STEPS

The design process for a major project should be handled in five steps, each of which terminates with a management decision approving the development of the project up to that point. Depending on the size of the project, its type (whether only construction work is involved or machines and equipment installations are to be made) and the contracting methods, certain design steps may be combined and others may be expanded. It's logical to expect that with time constraints, the various steps may sometimes overlap. With either new facilities or revisions and relocation projects involving building work or machines and equipment, the design steps to be performed are:

1. *Making a schematic and feasibility study.* A schematic design often includes rearrangement of activities, the addition of new equipment, and new building construction. Now is also the time to investigate designs that involve new techniques and technologies. As many alternative ideas or solutions as possible should be conceived and evaluated, though not all of the alternatives need be developed completely. Alternative design solutions may be ranked in several ways: from the least amount of cost to the most; from purely manual to highly automated; and from any logical sequence that fits the task to be done.

2. *Developing the design.* During this step, the schematic design is extended to specify the size, scope, and type of the project as well as the relationship of its parts. Major machines and equipment are selected, and the determination of structural, mechanical, electrical, and other building systems is made. The schematic design must be developed in such detail that all components are described by type and dimension, sufficient to permit the subsequent composition of construction documents.

3. *Preparing construction and installation documents.* This step, sometimes called the final design, begins with approval of the design development documents and considers any changes in size, scope, or character which came about as a result of the approval procedure. The schematic design is now further defined in detail by becoming the construction documents or drawings and specifications. These documents are then submitted to contractors for bids on contracts to construct and carry out the work.

4. *Bidding on and negotiating contracts.* There are several requisites on bidding for a contract to perform construction and installation work. The documents that serve as a basis for bidding must include procedure-type specifications and drawings; the bidders must be deemed equally qualified; and all bidders must comply completely with the bidding documents. When all these requisites are met, the contract award is usually made on the basis of price.

5. *Awarding of contracts.* The design procedure does not necessarily come to an end once a construction and installation contract has been awarded. Many activities are performed by the design staff, varying by the nature of the contract and the project. Invariably, construction and installation problems arise which, although minor, require additions and revisions of the design. Usually called follow-up work, designers, consultants, and field staff for onsite inspections may be involved throughout the construction period.

Layout and Design

Although industrial managers may infrequently participate in the original layout and design of a manufacturing plant, this being primarily an engineering staff function, they should be knowledgeable of the planning and design activities and the related details that are inherent in such functions. After a plant begins operations, the managers will certainly be required to make decisions and approve process equipment revisions, relocations of facilities, additions of new processes, and general plant expansions. It is for these reasons the subject of layout and design is included in this book.

Layout and design is a creative procedure. At the beginning, this activity may be originated by one individual, an architect or engineer who can envision a means to solve a problem. But design is also a technical process, and the design solution must be developed in all the detail necessary to obtain construction and installation proposals, and to execute the work. For a large project, this procedure will undoubtedly involve the efforts of many individuals including specialists. The particulars of a project dictate the makeup of the team and the extent of each individual's involvement.

No designer, whether a member of the plant staff or a consultant, can be expected to handle layout and design projects without following a prescribed procedure. While intuitive responses can be expected, it isn't good practice to react to all plant requirements with experience and intuition alone. Consequently, the venture should be viewed as a logical process and as a procedure that requires a systematic approach.

Getting Employees Involved

It pays to get the input of employees on a proposed layout or design, especially if they have been involved in a process or operation of the equipment in the area. Here is how you can gain from their direct experience and the information they can provide:

■ Continually keep employees informed on proposed expansions, additions, and relocations. You may be surprised at the number of individuals who may wish to make suggestions. This is especially true when their jobs or the work they do will be affected by the change.

■ Ask for their recommendations, particularly as to positions and locations of instrumentation and controls. Employees know better than anyone else how certain machines respond and what machines require close control.

▪ Show them how better design and layout can make their jobs easier. A good example of this is the need to service and maintain equipment. Oil and lubrication points on machines must be easily accessible when the machines are installed. In addition, maintenance personnel may need plenty of working room when making major repairs or when removing large machine components or motors.

The Role of the Computer

Technological advances in recent years have made the computer a powerful tool for use in layout and design. With computer-aided design, it is possible to analyze a greater number of available potential solutions to problems in detail that would require prohibitive time and cost if carried out manually.

The advances in computer graphic systems enable the development of three-dimensional models and the viewing and analysis of these models while varying many of the parameters or dimensions involved. Such systems are also used for building design, process layout development, and equipment design; they are also often used to produce finished drawings.

Another valuable use of the computer concerns its capability to prepare specifications, cost estimates, design and construction schedules, and to provide management assistance in the administration of contracts. Use of the computer within the design process can be expected to further expand as the technology becomes more versatile and less expensive.

Objectives of Plant Layout Procedures

Plant layout is concerned with the placing, location, and arrangement of facilities, machines and equipment.[1] It includes the spaces and areas needed for material storage and movement, supporting activities and services, and operating personnel. The primary objectives of making a layout plan are to: ensure safe and healthy working conditions for employees, make operations efficient, increase output of productive facilities, reduce operating costs, and provide better service to customers.

Each planning or rearrangement project has its own objectives; they will vary with management viewpoints, operating policies, and current considerations pertinent to each project. The general objectives of a layout should include the following:

▪ *Safety*—ensured for all employees in both day-to-day and periodic operations

- *Versatility*—readily adaptable to changes in process and product design
- *Flexibility*—easy to rearrange, modify, and update
- *Utilization*—effective and efficient use of machinery, space, and operating personnel
- *Orderliness*—a sequence of logical work flow with provisions for auxiliary activities
- *Closeness*—a practical minimum distance for moving materials, supporting services, and people
- *Convenience*—easy access for both line and staff employees

Types of Arrangements

Three types of layout are used in industrial plants, depending on the materials involved, the process or function performed, and the product made:

1. *Layout by fixed position or by fixed material location.* All tools, machinery, labor, and other pieces of material are brought to a fixed place. The job is completed or the product is made with the major component staying in the one location.

2. *Layout by process or by function.* Here all operations of the same process or type of process are grouped together. All machining is in one area, all welding in another, and all painting in a paint shop.

3. *Layout by line production or by product.* With this arrangement, one product or one type of product is made in one area, but unlike layout by fixed position, the material moves. This layout places one operation immediately adjacent to the next. Any equipment used to make the product, regardless of the process it performs, is arranged according to the sequence of operations.

The decision of which type of arrangement is most logical or practical should be based on the general objectives of a layout listed above. Thus, you should use layout by fixed position or by fixed material location when:

- Material treating operations require only hand tools or simple machines.
- Moving the major piece of material is costly.
- Making only one or a few pieces of an item.
- You want to fix responsibility for product quality on one employee.

Use layout by process or by function when:

- Machinery is very expensive and difficult to move.
- There are wide variations in time required for different operations.
- Making a variety of products.
- There is a small demand for the product.

Use layout by line production or by product when:

- There is a large quantity of pieces or products to make.
- The design of the product is more or less standardized.
- The demand for the product is fairly steady.
- Continuity of material flow can be maintained without difficulty.

In actual practice, most layouts are a combination of the above three types in order to gain the benefits and advantages of all three.

Phases of Layout Planning

As each layout project is carried out from its planned objective to its installation, the project passes through four phases:

1. *Phase one* involves deciding where to make the installation. This is simply a matter of determining whether the new layout or relayout will be in the same place as it is now, in a present storage area that can be freed for the purpose, in a recently acquired building, or in a similar type of potentially available area.

2. *Phase two* covers planning of the general overall layout. This establishes the basic flow pattern(s) for the area being laid out. It also indicates the size, relationship, and configuration of each major activity.

3. *Phase three* consists of the preparation of detailed layout plans and includes planning where each piece of machinery and equipment will be placed.

4. *Phase four* concerns the installation. This involves both planning the procedure to be followed and physically making the necessary moves.

Although these phases are listed in sequence, they should normally overlap each other for best results.

Management's Interest

Most industrial managers realize that processes and operations are constantly changing and that product improvement is essential to a plant's profitability, if not continued existence. These conditions often lead to projects involving new layouts or adjustments to current layouts. Thus, a layout planned and installed is not necessarily completed and can be considered complete only when it is entirely replaced by a new layout.

Because plant layout is a compromise of many factors, there will always be something about each layout that is imperfect. The most logical time for a layout change is when making improvements in procedures or machines. Layout changes and improvements in machines or equipment go hand in hand.

Since changes in other plant activities can be or will be made at the time when you are changing a layout, you should note the following relationships:

- A request for a layout change may be made to permit a change in another activity.
- A layout change gives you the opportunity to make other changes it may have been holding back.
- A proposed change in layout may not always solve the real problem; a bad situation may be the result of several factors of which layout is but a part.

Final Plant Layout Planning

Some specifics to include in final layout planning along with pertinent questions to ensure nothing has been overlooked are:[2]

- *Safety.* Is equipment using flammable material equipped with safety features, properly isolated, and proper fire protection provided? Are moving parts on machines guarded and the operators protected from accidents with safety devices? Are OSHA standards met?

- *Utilities.* Has adequate provision been made for all the utilities required in the area? Will any future moves of utilities be necessary? Are EPA standards met?

- *Space.* Are aisles wide enough for one- or two-way traffic? Is there enough room if a line forms? Has adequate space been provided for incoming materials and outgoing products?

- *Product quality.* Are there provisions for quality control operations and inspections? Are products protected from damage as they enter and leave the area?

- *Cleanliness and maintenance.* Is the layout designed for good housekeeping at low cost? Can machines and equipment be maintained easily and comfortably as well as safely?

- *Working conditions.* Do employees have enough working space? Has ergonomics been considered in the design and layout? Have adequate provisions been made for lighting, temperature, and ventilation?

- *Aesthetics.* Are the layout and surroundings attractive and motivating to employees? Will visitors be impressed with appearances?

PRODUCT AND PROCESS LAYOUTS

The primary objective in running a plant is to obtain the least possible movement of products and employees. The reasoning behind this is logical—productive machines and employee operators should not be idle and space should be used most efficiently.

Workplaces can be planned with a product or service layout or a process or function layout, or a combination of both. With a product layout, the machines are placed so that products or employees move along a line as they carry out the prescribed sequence of operations. An example of this type of layout is the assembly line in the manufacture of automobiles. The advantages of the product layout include (1) specialization of employees and machines; (2) low, if any, inventory; (3) few controls; (4) rapid movement; and (5) minimum space for aisles and storage.

With a process layout, machines perform the same type of work, and employees with similar skills are grouped together. This type of layout is based on keeping the machines and employees busy, reducing idle time, and concentrating similar skills in groups. Examples of this type of layout are drill presses and stamping machines. The advantages of the process layout include (1) flexibility to accommodate change and variety, (2) use of general-purpose machines and equipment, (3) efficient operations, (4) easy to locate, and (5) grouping employees with similar skills.

Most layout plans in manufacturing plants today consist of combinations of product and process layouts to gain the advantages of both. While a change from a product layout in the direction of a process layout increases inventory costs and decreases idle time costs, at some point there is a balance.

MAKING EFFECTIVE USE OF SPACE

With continued growth in business and industry, managers of many plants are looking for ways to do more with their existing facilities and space rather than face the cost and time constraints of new construction. One way to approach this problem is to eliminate some storage aisles or at least reduce their size.[3]

Typical storage areas in plants have rows of racks for pallets and rows of shelves for cartons and boxes, including items that are not packaged. Often the rack openings or shelves are back-to-back and face aisles. Such storage systems are classified as single-deep and selective in that no item is placed in front of another, and access to any item is easy.

But many plants don't need selective storage, especially if stored items include large quantities of the same item. If a plant can store these items behind one another without adversely affecting its operations, storage density increases and fewer aisles are required. With a lower aisle space percentage (ASP), space is available for other uses. Following are some storage configurations with lower ASPs than single-deep, selective rack, or shelving systems:

▪ With double-deep racks, you can place two pallets into storage in the same opening from the same aisle. A double-deep storage system with 14-foot aisles has an ASP of less than 50 percent.

▪ Push-back racks have carriages that allow pallets previously stored in a rack opening to be pushed back to accommodate a new pallet. Upon removal of a pallet, the pallets behind it move forward to the opening. In a system with 14-foot aisles, this system has an ASP of less than 40 percent.

▪ Drive-in racks allow trucks to drive into the rack and place pallets on various levels. The ASP for a drive-in system is about the same as for a push-back system with the same depth of storage.

▪ Drive-through racks are similar to drive-in systems except they provide truck access from both sides of the rack. For that reason, they have greater ASPs than systems using drive-in racks, but they allow both last-in and first-out and first-in and first-out operations.

▪ Flow racks are lanes of gravity (roller or wheel) conveyors installed in racks and sloped from the back or load area to the front or pick area. These are commonly used for pallets, cartons, totes, and other conveyable items of uniform size. The pallet flow racks have ASPs comparable to drive-through racks.

Two other strategies for gaining space are employed when a plant requires a selective system:

1. Although they require special trucks or machines, narrow-aisle systems as narrow as 4 feet may be used. Reducing the aisle from 14 feet to 4 feet reduces the ASP from 64 to 33 percent.

2. The most effective use of floor space available from any system employing an aisle for access to stored items can be realized from a single- or movable-aisle system; with this system, storage units move to provide

access to a selected storage location. At any time, there is only one aisle in the system and that aisle closes as storage units move, one at a time, to form an aisle at another point of required access.

Mezzanines

Many plants, at one time or another, wish they had more room for a job shop, a small production operation, or a place to store maintenance supplies. But most managements aren't in the position to undertake a costly enlargement of the existing plant or relocation of the entire facility to make this wish a reality.

If you happen to be in that situation, there is another option that costs generally about half of what new construction would—installation of a custom mezzanine.[4] A mezzanine is simply a second-story addition within an existing structure, frequently placed over existing space already in use. Such a choice enables management to use overhead space to advantage for production, miscellaneous storage, or an office.

In addition to its lower cost, a mezzanine installation can show other benefits:

- Since the space occupied by the mezzanine is already heated or cooled, added value is realized from the building's existing HVAC system.
- If bolted construction is the method of installation, the mezzanine may be later moved within the plant or to a new location.
- The productivity of employees will increase if they have shorter distances to travel to handle a project.
- Freestanding mezzanines may be depreciated faster than a building because they are classified as equipment in tax computations.

Design Characteristics

Mezzanines are always supported by their own columns and are not tied to the building's columns or walls. This design is a factor in safety and efficiency of plant traffic while also providing a high-load bearing, unitized upper level supported without cross bracing. Design flexibility is achieved with bolted construction—it can be added to or reconfigured to meet changing needs.

When installing a mezzanine in an existing plant, the size of the building compared to that of the mezzanine must be considered. Most of the building codes limit the mezzanine to one-third of the size of the building in which it will be installed. If the mezzanine size exceeds this, it is classified as a second story and is subject to different regulations. Design specifications; national, state, and local codes; design load; and span/column layout must be considered also in the planning of a mezzanine addition.

Design specifications from the American Institute for Steel Construction, the Steel Joist Institute, and the American Iron and Steel Institute are universally accepted. National, state, and local codes cover the design of stairs, handrail, and safety-related items; some model codes have specific design criteria; for example, seismic requirements (earthquakes).

PROCESS DESIGN

To meet competition and to satisfy consumer demand, manufacturing plants are continually examining their processes and operations for ways to increase production and decrease costs. Planning and implementing faster and more efficient manufacturing methods is also required when introducing new products, making product improvements, and changing models. Many procedures and techniques are involved, such as plant layout, value engineering, space utilization, and others, the culmination of which is process design. The three factors that affect the design of a manufacturing process are (1) the quantity of the product to be made, (2) the required quality of that product, and (3) the equipment that is used to make the product.

Quantity

The quantity of the product to be made must be stated in terms of time, or as the rate of production. It can then be correlated with the capacity of the manufacturing equipment being considered to determine the best design. The quantity should also be based on a sales forecast, especially when making a new product. Funds should be allocated for the improvement of processes only when the forecast predicts that the quantity of product being considered will bring about a satisfactory return on the investment.

The number of identical units to be produced determines the manufacturing method in that with a large number, the savings per unit can be applied to the purchase of more efficient equipment as well as new and better tools. Frequently, large quantities to be produced justify the acquisition of better auxiliary equipment such as jigs, dies, and molds; these, in turn, increase the productive capacity of the existing plant equipment.

Manufacturing methods vary greatly with the quantity of an item produced. The production of heavy and large machines is usually limited to a few units; requires skilled craftsmen using general-purpose machines and tools; and the assembly is by skilled individuals. In contrast, the mass production of home appliances, automobiles, and similar items is a matter of using a large proportion of automatic machinery and on an assembly line that requires a minimum of skill.

Quality

The desired quality of the product invariably dictates the design of the manufacturing process. To ensure the specified quality is attained, its level and scope are stipulated in the drawings and specifications covering the process design. Bills of materials, parts lists, and detailed drawings are also very specific on the quality requirements of assemblies and component parts. Now, it's simply a matter of selecting the manufacturing method and equipment to ensure the production of parts of the required quality at the lowest possible cost.

Dimensional requirements, strengths, durability, and other characteristics of parts and products to be manufactured must fit the capabilities of the available types of machines and methods of operation. In addition, the mechanical and electrical condition of machines and equipment should be checked to confirm that they will function properly to produce parts in accordance with their rated performance. By the use of statistics, it is possible to predetermine the quality level at which the machine that has been selected can operate. Generally, the higher the required quality of a product, the higher the cost to make it.

Equipment

Many factors must be considered when selecting equipment for a manufacturing plant. Process engineers generally are responsible for specifying the type of equipment to be used for each operation as they develop the manufacturing process and sequence of operations for a product. Although they may specify either a particular machine or only a generic type, greater flexibility in scheduling and routing the in-process product are achieved with the latter. Such flexibility also is an aid in plant layout design and the handling of materials.

The operator skill required on machines and equipment is a factor to be considered as are the safety features provided in the design. Machines should be fitted to the plant labor force as much as possible. The use of ergonomically designed equipment and tools will bring about greater safety, better productivity, and more comfort for employees.

Significant savings can result from standardizing equipment, provided, of course, that the standardization does not take from an operation the equipment best suited to meet quantity and quality requirements. Standardization cuts the cost of maintenance and reduces the inventory of repair parts.

Plants should always use their available equipment to the fullest extent before buying or leasing new equipment, as long as a new or different machine is not significantly better. When management wishes to add equipment, managers have three options: (1) Buy new or used, (2) rent or lease, or (3) fabricate the equipment within the plant. Leasing has become an increasingly popular way to procure equipment since no capital investment must be made. It's logical, however, that management should make a complete economic analysis of the situation before deciding whether to buy, lease, or make.

VALUE ENGINEERING

Value engineering is a decision tool. You use it to systematically analyze an engineering project with the objective of getting the maximum value or worth from the changes you're going to make and the money you're going to spend. It involves studying a function to see how the function can be performed most economically. It also means providing only the features that are required for the job. It concerns modification or elimination of a cost factor without reducing reliability, service, or capability of the basic system or equipment. Thus, value engineering is designing for optimum performance at least cost.

Many managers of industrial plants believe in operating their plant's equipment as long as possible, unless new designs are so far superior in performance and operating cost that there is no question about the wisdom of replacing old machines with new. Maintenance managers have seen there is little to be gained by replacing an old machine if it is still doing the job it was designed to do and it has minimal maintenance needs. This philosophy is especially true in the petrochemical and chemical industries where processes may change and equipment needs change accordingly. Another point in favor of continuing to use existing equipment is that delays and waiting time for delivery of new machines along with the time it takes to install them frequently more than overbalance costs of repairs to an existing machine.

There are many factors to be considered when you apply value engineering to plant equipment. Among the most important are: permanence of use, meeting government regulations, safety, maintenance requirements and ease of servicing, energy use, and spare parts availability. Following is a discussion of these factors:

■ *Permanence.* One of the first matters to be decided is the permanence of your engineering effort. Consider whether the process in which the equipment operates may soon change because of advancing technology. For example, in the chemical industry, depreciation of certain equipment is often set low. Processes are hard on the machines and corrosion is frequently severe. You do not design for twenty years of life if the odds are the equipment will be obsolete in only a few years.

If there is a question in your mind about the permanence of the plant's productive equipment, your best bet is to simply get a machine or piece of equipment in condition to run a few more years. All you need to do is to repair or replace worn parts. The only problem you might have is how to get those parts. With very old equipment, the manufacturer may have stopped stocking parts, or may have gone out of business. But even if parts are still available, or can be made by the manufacturer from old drawings, delivery time may be so long that too much production would be lost before you could get them.

You will probably find that it would be quicker and less expensive under such conditions to repair or rebuild the parts in the maintenance shop. The cost of repairs may be lower and considerable time can be saved. And you have the opportunity to improve the operation of the machine through innovation to adapt it more to your specific need.

If, for example, you could use more capacity, you can redesign and rebuild by changing gear ratios, speed of the drive, and/or the size of the equipment, and increase the motor horsepower accordingly. With today's improved motor insulation systems, many oversized motors can be redesigned and rebuilt for higher horsepower than their original rating. If you are working with a motor more than twenty years old and larger than 200 horsepower, it is likely that you can have it redesigned to a higher horsepower for considerably less than the cost of a new motor.

You may want to change the material of construction of some of the equipment components at the time you're doing this upgrading. You could go to nonmetallic gears, for example, and handle the noise problem when you do it.

It's a good idea to compare relative costs between in-plant and out-plant repairs. Too often, out-plant repairs are undertaken merely through habit without making a study or cost comparison. An investigation may show several advantages to doing the job in-plant.

■ *Meeting regulations.* When you take on a value engineering project, you've got to be conscious of whether the changes you make might result in a violation of environmental, safety, or health standards. In recent years, numerous governmental agencies have issued regulations on these matters. The OSHA and EPA regulations, for example, dictate construction and design standards that affect safety, health, and how the environment will be affected.

In addition to these government agency regulations, there are federal, state, and municipal codes to which you must conform. In some cases, you may have to obtain permits before you can proceed. An example of this is the altering or modifying of pressure vessels constructed under American Society for Testing and Materials (ASTM) codes. Only a certified welder can do this work and the change must be approved by an inspector before it is made.

■ *Safety.* When you consider modifying a machine, look into the safety aspect. You don't want to eliminate a safety feature that was part of the original design, nor do you want to introduce a new hazard. Make sure the modified equipment or system has fail-safe features if possible. You also should do your best to make the controls *idiot-proof* even though this may not be easy to do. Put yourself in the operator's shoes and design for human errors such as pushing the wrong buttons, performing operations in the wrong sequence, opening and closing the wrong valves, forgetting certain steps, and similar mistakes.

Then, there are always the standard matters of safety to be concerned with. For instance, you must provide guards for moving parts, speed governors, overload and overheat controls, relief systems, and vibration cutoffs, among other safety features. The matter of proper grounding is routine compared to some controls that make equipment safe to operate.

Good design is especially important when machines operate without human attention in an out-of-the-way part of the plant. Under such conditions, automatic protective devices are highly desirable. Remote indicators for warning and controls to shut equipment down when malfunctions occur are all part of designing and rebuilding for safety.

■ *Maintenance requirements.* Be sure you recognize the maintenance needs of machines and equipment when you make a value engineering study. Especially look at how you can limit maintenance labor costs. Consider, too, how much lost production time can be expected because of maintenance needs. The production department naturally wants equipment that can be maintained without numerous and lengthly shutdowns.

Determine how quickly maintenance can be handled, what tools or special equipment will be needed, and whether special skills will be required. With a little ingenuity, you may be able to find a way that routine maintenance can be handled by the operator instead of requiring the services of a more highly paid maintenance craftsman.

Good design pays off when you place lubrication fittings where they can be easily reached and make it easy to remove and replace access panels to machine components. Above all, when you install equipment, allow elbowroom for the people who'll do the maintenance work; you'll avoid a lot of frustration and irritation on the job. The craftspeople who do the work will be grateful and also more efficient.

■ *Energy use.* To ensure that your modified equipment uses a minimum of energy, see that the motors operate at full load ratings and with a favorable power factor. Other matters of energy use you should look at are optimum use of lighting, whether insulation is needed on piping and hot and cold equipment, what controls you should use on the utility supply lines, and ways of recovering energy. The operating costs of your machines and equipment are going to be lower if you design with the objective of using the least amount of energy.

Which form of energy you use for motive power is a decision you have to make. Should you operate equipment with air, steam, or electricity? Heat with steam or electricity? Your value analysis study will give you the answers to these and similar questions.

The energy factor is an important one because of high power costs, and you know that costs are going to rise in the future. You wouldn't be doing a good value engineering job if you overlooked ways to conserve energy.

■ *Spare parts availability.* A true value engineering analysis includes identification of critical machines and equipment; those which are vital to the production process. When you pinpoint such items, you can make sure that spare parts are available so that production downtime is minimized when failures occur or extensive maintenance is necessary. In addition, you should design so that standard components are used. Parts will be more readily available and will be lower in cost. Another matter to be considered here is that if you can standardize, such as by using the same part on different machines, you can reduce the number and investment of the spare parts you keep in the storeroom.

When applying value engineering, you must consider many factors and the interests of all departments of the company. If you design safety into the equipment, minimize maintenance requirements, make servicing easy, keep energy use low, and assure a ready supply of spare parts, you're going to experience minimum operating costs.

SELECTING MACHINES AND EQUIPMENT

The selection of proper machines, equipment, and process systems is a requisite for the availability, reliability, and maintainability of a plant. It is also a determinant of the operating costs of plant systems. Selecting capital items solely on the lowest obtainable cost, however, will not provide optimum plant performance.

To enable you to compete in the marketplace, you must select new and replacement items on the basis of maintenance-free design and low overall operating costs. What you should be concerned with is reliability, maintainability, and total operating cost.

Chronic maintenance problems that many of today's plants experience are due to poor design or misapplication including size and capability characteristics. Yet, a more critical issue are the managers and buyers of equipment who assume that all machine or system designs are equal and have the same operating and maintenance costs. These people feel that initial cost is the most important matter to be dealt with, and this is not true.

The selection of machines and equipment should include an evaluation of the factors that affect their total cost over their useful life. These costs include:

- *Capital costs:* purchase price, transportation, installation, start-up, and operator/maintenance labor training
- *Operating costs:* power, consumable items, adjustments, and manpower to operate
- *Maintenance costs:* preventive, repair, and spare parts
- *Out-of-use costs:* dismantling, removal, and expenses incurred in replacement

Requisites When Buying New Equipment

Whenever you decide to acquire a new machine or piece of equipment, you must make a decision on what make and model would be best for the plant. Several factors should be considered such as the reputation of the manufacturer, initial cost, operating expenses, warranty, service policy, and delivery date. If competing manufacturers are about equal in what they have to offer, your decision tends to become an economic one. However, you have the problem of deciding what costs to consider and how they can be determined.

The costs which will influence your decision are the initial cost of the machine and the costs of operating it such as: direct and indirect labor, materials, power, replacement parts, maintenance, insurance, and interest on the investment. You should also estimate the salvage value at the end of a machine's service life. With this information, two or more machines may be compared to learn which would be the best investment.

Regardless of the size of the investment, the equipment's acquisition, installation, and operation should be planned, monitored, and controlled. All these steps are necessary if you want to get the greatest return on your investment. Unfortunately, some managers fail to properly handle the monitoring step.

Monitoring requires being aware of and being specific about what characteristics of the equipment being installed should be measured and reported. Matters you need to be concerned with include: employee/operator satisfaction with the equipment, downtime experienced, maintenance requirements, and energy use. The data should be collected and reported in a format that enables you and others to compare the equipment's actual performance with what was expected of it. The frequency of the reporting should be such that problems can be corrected before they become serious.

DESIGN AND ANALYSIS OF PIPING SYSTEMS

A plant's piping system consists of interconnected piping, manual and control values, pumps, and heat exchangers. Knowing how these components operate together is the key to designing and installing a system that will accomplish its objective. To help an engineer design and analyze a system, a wide selection of computer software is available today. Most of this software can carry out hydraulic analysis and piping system design that was impossible to do on a personal computer just ten years ago. While the needs of someone designing a new system are different from those of an engineer troubleshooting an existing system, all the software covers how the piping and its auxiliary equipment work together.

For maximum efficiency, each section in a system should be sized to achieve the optimum performance for its purpose. But you must recognize that each section in a system affects the operation of the other sections. Once you have a layout of the individual sections, you can connect them in a hydraulic network model. With a hydraulic network analysis, you can then calculate the balanced pressures and flow rates throughout the system.

A completed hydraulic analysis supplies you the information needed to select and evaluate hydraulic equipment such as pumps and valves. Individual components can then be put into the model to see how the system will operate.

PIPING LAYOUTS

When making a piping layout, whether for a new installation, a revision, or an extension of an existing system, design engineers should be concerned with safety, functionality, and cost-effectiveness. Data and information from mechanical, civil, and electrical disciplines are required to achieve these ends. By combining these with plant operations know-how, current equipment maintenance procedures, and general piping principles, engineers can develop optimum designs to meet the plant's process requirements.

The starting point for producing a piping system for the plant is to first make a layout. This involves placing machines and equipment on a plot plan. You thus learn which equipment must be installed first to avoid conflicts and roadblocks of subsequent placements. The equipment layout determines nozzle and valve locations, and where utilities and instrumentation must be provided. The eventual piping layout will take into consideration the process unit as a whole, rather than only one line at a time.

There are many factors involved in designing piping layouts that are safe, require a minimum of maintenance, feature ergonomic principles, and are flexible. Following are some of the most critical matters in this respect:

■ Piping that must be periodically opened for maintenance or cleaning should be flanged with adequate space provided for connecting and disconnecting by maintenance personnel. Valves should be easily accessible or equipped with chain operators.

■ The piping design should be simple and contain a minimum of fittings to reduce friction loss. The elevations should not result in "head-bumpers," yet be near the floor to make support of the pipe easy.

■ It's good practice to include large loops for flexibility and thermal expansion on pump piping. Care should also be taken to prevent over-stressing pump nozzles when making the pipe connections.

■ The inlet piping on centrifugal compressors should contain at least three pipe diameters of straight run between the inlet nozzle and the first elbow. Strainers should be installed between block valves and inlet nozzles.

■ It pays to provide duplicate piping systems for pumps of the same size and similar service conditions, especially when the service is severe and the pumps frequently need maintenance. By arranging multiple pump piping, you may be able to minimize the support requirements.

■ The traps on steam piping to turbines should always be installed at the low point of a system. This avoids introducing condensate into the turbine case and causing blade damage.

Piping Supports and Restraints

The following definitions are helpful in clearly and completely understanding piping layouts as they pertain to supports and restraints:

- Supports are used to resist gravity loads.
- Restraints are used to resist thermal expansion.
- Anchors provide fixed supports in that no translation or rotation can occur in any direction.
- Stops prevent translation in one direction (single-acting) or in two directions (double-acting).
- Guides prevent rotation about one or more axes.
- Hangers suspend the piping from a structure.

The best way to minimize stress in a piping system is to install supports and restraints to control the direction of thermal expansion. By doing this, the support system can prevent leaks, excessive forces on connecting equipment, sag and distortion of the piping, resonance, and excessive vibration. If you need to better control a system that vibrates, you can divide a piping system into sections by using rigid anchors.

But support selection is often a matter of compromising because a proper support system must supply sufficient stiffness for operation under dynamic loading without restricting motion from thermal expansion. It's always better to support a piping system on the pipe instead of on fittings, valves, or expansion joints. The most common method of supporting pipe, without vibration loads, is to have it rest on the support or to use a hanging rod.

DESIGN AND SIZING OF DUCTS

Optimal sizing of duct systems is a major responsibility of heating, ventilating, and air-conditioning system designers. Duct system modifications are sometimes handled by plant engineers to get around obstructions and to eliminate unnecessary transitions and special fittings when making layout changes. Regardless, changes in duct design and location must be made carefully to ensure that the duct system will work as intended.

Layouts of duct systems are often dictated by the architecture of the building in which they are to be installed; also, small ceiling spaces, columns, and other obstacles may restrict duct sizes. Whether initially designing or making modifications, sizing a duct can be done today with simple, low-cost computer software. Similar to making a system layout, the proper sizing of ducts results in a balanced and cost-effective system.

Some sheet metal fabricators and HVAC contractors use a nomograph called a Ductulator (supplied by the Trane Company) for duct sizing. This device is based on equal friction theory for sizing and gives the user the recommended round duct diameters and equivalent rectangular sizes.

But as accurate as the Ductulator is, duct-sizing software is often preferred by designers for the following reasons:

1. The software allows the designer to consider other methods of sizing, including static regain, total pressure, and constant velocity. These methods may be more appropriate for special conditions and situations.
2. The software has the capability to print a bill of material with material and labor costs, carry out an acoustic analysis, and interface to a computer-aided drafting (CAD) system.
3. The software is easy to use. With hardware and software costs decreasing, anybody involved with the design and sizing of ducts can benefit from computerized duct analysis.

SECURITY LIGHTING

Well-planned security lighting in and around the plant is essential for the safety of employees and the protection of the plant's facilities.[5] Ensured good visibility in areas such as walkways, stairs, loading docks, and parking lots is critical to preventing accidents and reducing the risk of injury. Security lighting is necessary also to act as a deterrent against vandalism and crime. While closed-circuit television, guard patrols, and alarm systems are common used, security lighting has proved to be one of the least expensive anticrime devices.

Design

Although safety should be a top priority when designing a security lighting system, good visibility should be the intent of any design. Here are some suggestions on designing a lighting system that increases safety and reduces crime:

■ Lighting quantity, usually expressed in footcandles, is always a key part of a successful design. Following illuminating levels recommended by The Illuminating Engineering Society of North America is vital to the design of an effective system. Where visual work is performed, such as on a loading dock, a minimum horizontal illuminance of twenty footcandles is required.

■ Some workplace areas, including loading docks, may need more than lighting quantity. If color identification is required, the quality of light also becomes important. In such situations, a high color-rendering light source is needed. The color-rendering level of light sources is measured on an index of 100, with incandescent lighting as the point of reference. For color-critical applications, a minimum color-rendering index of 70 is usually recommended.

■ When proper vertical and horizontal illumination is provided, good visibility results. Effective vertical illumination ensures that people can be easily seen in a parking lot; horizontal illumination improves visibility in areas such as roads, walkways, and floor areas.

■ Glare-free visibility is another requisite for a successful security lighting system. To handle this problem, attention should be given to the selection of the fixture type and placement of the fixture itself. Special nonglare lenses are available for a variety of fixture types. Also, many lighting fixtures are engineered to control and prevent light beam patterns from generating excessive glare.

■ Good visibility is also achieved through uniform distribution of light. With uneven lighting, shadows appear. Since a light beam typically produces more footcandles in its center, overlapping light beams is one of the best ways to get uniformity. Fixture manufacturers usually supply spacing guidelines for each type of fixture model they produce to ensure uniform lighting.

■ One of the benefits of a security lighting system in fighting crime is that a light itself is highly visible. To keep it visible, a maintenance program should be implemented to prevent or limit the degradation of the system light output. The program should include regular fixture cleaning and immediate replacement of burned-out lamps including lamps that have significantly depreciated in light output.

ELECTRICAL AND INSTRUMENTATION DESIGN

Industry has begun to use computer technology in electrical and instrumentation design. Previously, most design work has been done by hand or with general-purpose, computer-aided drafting (CAD) software. Even though designers have had to learn both a new software package and new design methodology, they report a 50 percent time savings in completing projects with the new systems.

The success of the advanced software is attributed to personal-computer-based systems that are based on the AutoCAD graphics engine. These systems are capable of managing the very large amount of information required to describe a typical plant's wiring and instrumentation system.

GROUNDING SYSTEMS

The design and quality of the electrical wiring and grounding in a plant containing electronic machines and equipment is a critical matter to the plant's electrical power systems.[6] Properly designed and maintained systems are required to ensure the safety of operating personnel and the protection of data and telecommunications equipment. Correct and effective grounding provides a low level of electrical noise and prevents improper and faulty performance of sensitive electronic equipment.

The National Electrical Code defines *ground* as "a conducting connection, whether intentional or accidental, between an electrical circuit or equipment and earth, or some conducting body that serves in place of the earth." *Grounded* is defined as "connected to earth or to some conducting body that serves in place of the earth."

When applying the principles of grounding in a plant, you must distinguish between two types: *earth* grounding and *equipment* grounding. Failing to do so may result in a misapplication that is costly, ineffective, and even unsafe. Following are explanations and information about these two types:

- An earth-grounding system is used to protect a plant's electrical system and equipment from superimposed voltages caused by lightning and accidental contact with higher voltage systems. The connection also prevents the buildup of static charges on materials and equipment. Another reason for using an earth ground is to establish a zero-voltage reference point for the system. This purpose is the one that is important to ensure proper performance of sensitive electronic and communication equipment.

With an earth electrode system, there are three resistance components: (1) the resistance of the electrode and the connections to it; (2) the contact resistance of the electrode to the adjacent earth; and (3) the resistance of the earth surrounding the electrode. The majority of the resistance is from the earth surrounding the electrode. Thus, the resistivity of the soil around an electrode is the key factor determining the resistance of the system.

- An equipment grounding system is the primary way to protect personnel from electrocution. It is also the most critical common link to all electronic components of a data, telecommunications, or process-control system. When industrial process-control equipment experiences a sudden, inexplicable system halt, a grounding problem probably exists. The Electric Power Research Institute states that "better than 80 percent of all electronic system failures that are attributed to power anomalies are actually the result of electrical wiring or grounding errors or are generated by other loads within the customer's facility."

Equipment grounding systems are used to accomplish three objectives:

1. To minimize the presence of any voltages on equipment enclosures. This supplies protection from serious shock or electrocution of personnel in contact with the enclosure.
2. To provide an intentional path of sufficient current-carrying capacity and low impedance to ensure fast operation of a circuit's overcurrent protection under ground fault conditions.
3. To establish and maintain a zero-voltage reference point, at the location of sensitive electronic equipment, that will contribute to proper underground fault conditions.

BEARING RELIABILITY

Although bearing performance has improved considerably in recent years, many maintenance managers still feel they are replacing bearings on plant machines and equipment too often.[7] When you consider the number of factors that influence the operating performance of a bearing, this is understandable. They include: load magnitude and load direction, or a combination of both; shaft speed; bearing size; operating environment; lubrication type and method; type and condition of seals; shaft alignment; mounting and dismounting technique; shaft and housing fits; and running accuracy.

Because there are so many threats to bearing reliability, manufacturers and vendors of bearings have developed guidelines on the most common causes of bearing failure. If your machines and equipment are experiencing frequent bearing failures, the following troubleshooting tips should be helpful in diagnosing the problem. Here are the conditions which will result in bearing problems:

▪ *Using the wrong lubricant.* While bearings can be lubricated with an oil bath circulating system, oil mist, or grease, some applications, because of high speed, high temperature, or both, require oil lubrication systems. You can obtain greases with varying base oils, thickeners, additives, and consistencies, but because so many types are available, they are often misapplied. The most important property of oil is viscosity, a characteristic of the oil's strength or ability to develop a film that separates the working surfaces. For proper lubrication of rolling element bearings, adequate viscosity at operating temperature is required.

▪ *Mixing lubricants.* If two incompatible greases are mixed, lubrication failure is inevitable. Polyurea and lithium-based greases, for example, break down quickly when mixed. A soupy or runny grease, a grease that is much thicker than its original consistency, or a grease that has changed color are indications of incompatible mixing.

▪ *Using too much or too little lubricant.* It's commonly believed by maintenance personnel that it's better to over- rather than underlubricate bearings. Both procedures are poor practice. Underlubrication risks metal-to-metal contact and overlubrication causes heat buildup. This recommendation applies also to oil baths. When faulty seals allow oil to escape, the result is premature wear and frequent bearing replacement.

▪ *Presence of contaminants.* Dirt, sand, and water are the most common contaminants, although acid and other corrosives also can deteriorate the bearing lubricant. When contaminants dilute the oil film, they reduce its viscosity; they can also corrode the bearing surfaces and disrupt the oil film, thus creating abrasive particles.

▪ *Misalignment.* While some, but not all, bearings can tolerate minor misalignment, a serious misalignment such as one between the equipment shaft and the bearing housing bore introduces excessive vibration and load. Since overtightening the belts on belt-driven motors or equipment increases the load on the bearings, use just enough tension to prevent belt slippage.

▪ *Not enough internal clearance.* If the small clearance to accommodate thermal expansion of the bearing components is inadequate, excessive heat buildup results. Temperature affects viscosity, leading to a lubrication problem. Or worse, internal friction becomes so great that the bearing locks up.

▪ *Distorted housing.* Excessive loads and wear result when a housing bore is out-of-round or is not the right geometric shape. The problem arises when the housing is mounted to a pedestal that is not flat. If the housing is bolted to a crowned surface, for example, the housing will become distorted, which in turn elongates the bore.

▪ *Bearing arrangement.* This usually consists of a two-bearing system that furnishes radial support. One bearing has shoulders to axially locate or position the shaft assembly, and the other is unrestrained or axially free, to handle thermal shaft expansion. If the arrangement does not provide for adequate shaft expansion, thrust loads and high temperatures can result.

▪ *Damaged seals and shields.* If seals and shields are inadvertently damaged as bearings are mounted, they can interfere with the functioning of the bearing cage or rolling elements, thus permitting contaminants to enter the bearing. To prevent seal damage, always follow the prescribed mounting techniques when installing bearings.

■ *Incorrect shaft diameter.* The bearing needs to be fitted to an accurately sized shaft. If the shaft is oversized, the internal clearance is reduced. If the shaft is undersized, the bearing creeps on the shaft, promoting wear of the shaft and the bearing bore. With incorrect shaft diameter, friction and heat are created, increasing the operating temperature and generating particle debris that acts as a contaminant.

Motor Bearings

Bearing failures are one of the major causes of electric motor downtime and repair. Studies conducted by the Electrical Apparatus Service Association show also that bearing failures are by far the most common cause of motor failures. Yet only in recent years has it been recognized that steps can be taken to prevent most motor bearing failures. Here are some suggestions on how to handle this costly industrial problem.[8]

■ *Lubricate at correct intervals.* Even though bearing manufacturers have steadfastly warned against it, many maintenance personnel continue to overlubricate motor bearings. Too much grease can cause overheating of the bearings. Generally, two-pole motors should be greased twice a year, four-pole and slower motors only once a year.

■ *Use the best available grease.* The most commonly used bearing grease is polyurea-based, a low-cost, low-performance, highly compatible lubricant. However, it does not resist water, losing its ability to lubricate bearings. Industrial motor bearings should be lubricated with a synthetic-based aluminum complex grease, a high-quality product.

■ *Keep out moisture.* When a motor operating in a humid environment is shut down, moisture and condensation can collect on the surface of the bearing components. Eventually, this water breaks through the oil and grease barrier, contacts the metal parts of the bearing, and produces rust. Vapor-blocking bearing isolators can prevent this from happening. When the motor shaft is rotating, the isolator opens, eliminating the possibility of friction and wear. When the shaft is stationary, the isolator closes, preventing movement of air or water across its face.

■ *Keep out dirt.* Although lip seals, contact seals, and frequent grease replacement help minimize the amount of dirt and other airborne abrasives that can get into bearings, there is a better solution to this problem. Install a labyrinth-type noncontact seal over the bearing housing. These devices combine a tortuous labyrinth path with impingement and centrifugal forces to trap and remove airborne dirt and liquid. Virtually no contamination can reach the bearing.

While improved bearing protection and lubrication will reduce downtime and the maintenance costs of electric motors, these systems are not universally accepted as essential for long motor life. Specifying permanent bearing protection for new motors, or retrofitting isolators onto existing equipment usually requires iniative on the part of the user's maintenance or engineering staff.

PLANT DOORS

There are many ways that plant doors serve to separate environments, attenuate sound, and increase plant security. They also play a role in work throughput and traffic flow including conservation of energy. Well-designed doors can help plants with climate, dust, and noise control, while increasing productivity and safety.

Today's modern doors consist of a frame assembly, fabric curtain, a bottom bar system, and a motor with its drive system. While these doors are considered solutions to problems, there are no savings associated with buying and installing them if their annual maintenance costs exceed their original cost. Thus, careful design and construction are essential. Most high-speed doors rely on microprocessors to gain the advantage of adjustable speed, longevity, and reduced maintenance.

There are four important considerations to keep in mind when selecting a door for a specific opening:[9]

1. The most critical function of the door is its activation. Any door located in a high-traffic area cycles many times each day. Whether by pull cord, a floor loop, photo eye, or motion sensor, activation ensures the door operates every time and is cycled out of the way of approaching vehicle traffic.

2. The importance of door speed varies. If a door can be activated from thirty feet away and it is designed to move at two feet a second, it should be fully open before the driver of a lift truck reaches it. High operating speed is unnecessary if the door can be activated properly in a sufficient amount of time.

3. Visibility is a factor if employees need to see through a closed door. The more vision forklift drivers and pedestrians have, the safer the working environment. While increased vision can be obtained with transparent panels, the harsh environment in many plants along with abrasions from cycling, reduce the effectiveness of such panels over time. Another way to

increase vision is by selecting biparting roll doors that open sideways from the middle rather than from the bottom. This type of door enables forklift drivers to get full-height vision sooner. It also allows traffic to travel through faster, since there is no waiting for the bottom rail to cycle out of the way.

4. Impactability, the ability to "take a hit," is a key safety feature on a roll-up door. When a door is designed with an impactable, separating bottom rail, forklifts no longer are a maintenance threat to the door. With impact, the door's bottom rail releases and allows the forklift to pass through.

NOTES

1. H. B. Maynard, *Industrial Engineering Handbook* (New York: McGraw-Hill Book Company, 1971), pp. 11–31, 26–28.
2. Excerpts from *Successful Small Business Management*, Fifth Edition (Plano, Tex., Business Publications, Inc., 1988), p. 385.
3. Larry Beck, "Doing More in the Same Space," *Engineer's Digest*, April 1995, Copyright, Huebcore Communications, Inc., pp. 29–31.
4. Richard Kuchler, "Mezzanine Application Guidelines," *Maintenance Technology*, January 1991, pp. 46–48.
5. Tony Lucido, "Security Lighting: Safeguarding Your Site," *Plant Services*, December 1994, pp. 71–72.
6. Chris C. Kleronomos, "Effective Equipment Grounding," *Engineer's Digest*, February 1994, pp. 66–69.
7. Tom Jendzurski, "Ten Threats to Bearing Reliability," *Maintenance Technology*, February 1994, pp. 31–34.
8. Impro/Seal, Rock Island, Ill., "Extend Motor Life With Improved Bearing Care," *Maintenance Technology*, August 1993, pp. 28–31.
9. Kevin King and Lou Wiegand, "The Importance of Doors," *Plant Services*, June 1995, pp. 69–71.

Materials Handling and Flow

Proper handling of materials has always been an important requisite for efficient manufacturing of a product. Since it is most common to move the material through the manufacturing process rather than have plant employees move to the materials, large amounts of labor and equipment are involved in materials handling. This has resulted in a high ratio of materials handling costs to other costs of manufacturing.

Recognizing this problem, many managers in the last decade have changed their thinking on the subject. They no longer see it as the routine transfer of materials from place to place—it is now considered a *materials flow* function. This view evolved from the use of automatic handling and storage equipment combined with automatic processing and control systems. With the installation of such systems, managers have learned that they can benefit from space savings, better equipment layouts, more mechanization, increased automation, and better control of stores and inventory.

Manufacturing plants have much to gain by improving the methods and ways materials are handled. Here are how some benefits and cost advantages can be achieved:

- Overall materials handling costs can be reduced by reducing unit costs. Although this step requires that costs of handling be allocated or identified to the units of product or to its component parts that are moved, a unit-cost analysis can determine which handlings involve excessive cost.

■ The manufacturing-cycle time can be reduced by speeding up the movement of materials or shortening the distances they are moved. Reduction of cycle time will cut inventory costs and other production costs.

■ There is a tangible saving in reduced insurance rates and an intangible saving in improved employee morale that result from better working conditions in the plant and greater safety in the handling of materials.

■ Good materials handling practice can bring about savings by making the control of items easier. This is particularly true in continuous manufacturing where all materials handling operations are governed by planned procedures.

■ The moving and handling of materials in the fastest and most efficient manner possible will result in lower manufacturing costs for the plant and higher productivity of the employees.

■ Better handling and storing of materials will achieve more efficient use of space in the plant.

■ Greater attention to the care of materials and products will reduce waste, minimize rejects, and contribute to higher quality products.

■ Fewer injuries and accidents occur when workers use proper and well-maintained equipment for handling materials. Efficient equipment and work methods reduce worker fatigue and stress, thus preventing accidents.

■ Effective and efficient material handling cuts losses of material by minimizing spills, damage in transit or storage, and spoilage.

FACTORS AFFECTING FLOW OF MATERIALS

The faster, more efficiently you can handle materials in the plant, from receiving on through to shipping, the easier it is to get the plant's products to customers more effectively than your competition. Although many factors affect the flow of materials, all contribute to better productivity and greater efficiency when they are based on the latest technology in the industry. Following are some pertinent observations on the procedures and operations that are most critical to the smooth flow of materials in today's modern plants.

■ The use of pallets, slipsheets, and other methods of unitizing individual products so that they can be handled as a single load has greatly improved handling efficiency at the receiving dock. While lighter-weight corrugated slipsheets and pallets also help ergonomically, packaging that is too flimsy can be harmful by causing product damage or jamming automated equipment.

- Bar codes on the package streamline the receiving process. In some cases, plants use electronic data interchange to pre-receive a high percentage of bar-coded product. Plants are able to locate, control, and track stored items much more easily when containers and cartons are bar-coded. Bar coding and other automatic data collection methods also help to eliminate many of the human errors that lead to customer complaints.

- How a product is packaged can greatly facilitate the storing process; it can also make more efficient use of space. When products are stacked on pallets, they can be trucked directly to storage racks or block stacking areas to achieve high storage density. To further speedup the storing of palletized product, you can also set up reserve storage areas close to the receiving dock.

- Some manufacturing plants deliver fast-moving items directly to forward picking areas, bypassing storage completely. This procedure eliminates both a storage and a handling step. Selecting the right container helps matters. For example, plastic corrugated containers with handles help protect products during shipping; they can also be taken directly to flow racks or shelving units in the forward picking area. It is at order picking that the packaging process starts anew for individual items that are selected from one type of container and put together into another type of container.

- Packaging is a factor in affecting the flow of materials where just-in-time manufacturing requires that materials be delivered to the point of use. Bins on carts, or totes on flow racks provide a continual supply of small parts to process lines or assembly areas. More and more plants are adopting returnable container systems. Such containers coordinate the moving of materials through the process to final assembly. They also protect parts and reduce waste by replacing disposable materials.

- Since packing and sealing cartons is a labor-intensive procedure, semiautomated and automated dispensing equipment is increasingly being used. Systems are available that feed a predetermined amount of plastic loose fill into cartons as they pass by on a conveyor line. Equipment can also be installed for dispensing chemicals that form polyurethane cushioning in situ. These systems not only portion out the correct amount of material needed for a particular application, they also help to minimize waste.

- While employees once performed weighing and checking functions manually, now these operations are carried out by weighing devices without interrupting the flow of materials. Today's sophisticated electronic scales are programmed to supply piece counts, statistical data, and tracking information. The steady flow of data enables management to effectively control inventory and quality of the plant's output.

■ By applying identification information directly onto the product on-line, automatic data collection systems have been proven to be valuable components of a plant's packaging and materials handling activities. These systems eliminate manual operations, aid tracking, and help shippers comply with their customer's requests. Commonly, an in-line printer/ applicator system prints on blank, pressure-sensitive labels and applies them to cartons. Using information from a computer, a range of variable data can be designed into a label, including the company logo, address, and serial numbers in both bar code and human readable formats.

■ After packaging and identifying, the plant's products can now be conveyed, palletized, wrapped or banded, and loaded into trailers, every operation being performed automatically. Most of today's conveyor systems easily and efficiently handle container rotating, inverting, accumulating, inclining, declining, and palletizing. Palletizers can now handle many different products, including various carton sizes, bags, bundles, and even items not in cartons.

■ All unit loads on pallets need to be secured and protected before they are shipped. While manufacturers of stretch film and strapping equipment once pushed higher speed and greater capacity of their systems, the emphasis today is on economics, ergonomics, and the environment. Improvements in both stretch film and wrapping equipment have dramatically cut costs. Semiautomating or automating the process is accomplished ergonomically and there is a trend to offer films with recycled content.

■ To simplify and modernize the shipping process, some plants allocate extra space for staging palletized product at the dock. Multiple sortation lanes and flow racks can also speed shipments out of the plant. The use of telescopic loading systems, a type of conveyor that extends deeply into trailers for quick loading and unloading, is also rising in popularity. If shippers get together with their customers to carry out business transactions on a computer network, the customers know what products are being shipped even before the trailer leaves the dock.

BAR CODING

One of the most important advances in technology in business and industry is the use of bar codes for systematic data collection. It satisfies the need for accurate and timely data gathered from the manufacturing, inspection, transportation, and inventory cycles of a plant operation.

The black and white bars that you see on boxes, cartons, and packages in the marketplace represent a unique identification for that product. This symbol, called the *Universal Product Code* (UPC), is the standard for the industry and has been in existence since 1973. Bar codes have received overwhelming acceptance because they offer the simplest, most accurate, and most cost-effective approach for identifying objects by using reading machines (scanners).

One of the major advantages of bar codes over other technologies is its low susceptibility to errors in data input. Most bar codes have built-in safeguards (check digits) to prevent incorrect scans from being entered, thus minimizing the possibility of errors. Other advantages of bar coding are speed, timeliness, and cost efficiency. You can scan a bar code faster than manually record information or key data into a terminal. Bar-coded information is often immediately transferred to a host computer. Real-time data collection enables timely information to be accessed almost instantly, when the data are still current. Also, improved efficiency can be realized by substituting bar code systems in place of manual systems, resulting in increased productivity and lower labor costs.

Applications in Material Handling

There are many ways you can use bar codes, either with portable or stationary scanners. Portable units are powered by rechargeable or disposable batteries. Data is stored in memory for later transmissions by either direct link or phone line to a computer. The stationary contact scanners are often installed at workstations or assembly areas throughout the plant. They are usually connected directly to a master computer. Here are the most common bar code scanner applications involving the handling of materials in plants:

- *Inventory control.* A computer can download a portable scanner with operator directives to handle jobs such as order picking. The operator would go to the location displayed on the unit, use the bar code to scan the shelf tab item code, enter a quantity from a menu tablet, and proceed to the next picking location. At the end of the picking cycle, the data are transmitted to the main computer where inventory counts are updated and purchase orders to replenish stock are issued.

- *Material control.* Stationary scanners can be used to do work-in-process monitoring. A bar code label identifying each lot of material is attached to a container. As the material is processed through each workstation, the code is read and the process results are transmitted to a master computer. Real-time production information ensures that orders are delivered on time and that the product has been subjected to a thorough inspection operation.

- *Receiving/shipping.* Scanners located at receiving and shipping areas can be used to record product movement. In addition, captured information at the point of transaction permits invoices to be verified and bills of lading generated that are based on actual quantities shipped. Back orders can be immediately routed to the shipping dock.

MATERIAL HANDLING PROBLEMS

Despite advancements in methods of manufacturing and industrial production, material handling functions continually must contend with two major problems: the safety of employees involved in the functions and the productivity or costs of the operations. Many jobs in plants today still require some manual handling of materials. And whenever this occurs, the likelihood of back and overexertion injuries of employees increases. In addition, improper or inadequate materials-handling procedures and equipment result in inefficiencies and high operating costs.

Although industry has not dealt effectively with these problems until the last decade, the adoption of ergonomic principles has brought about welcome changes. But because injuries can be sustained through repeated awkward and unnecessary handling, it is necessary to review all material-handling tasks, regardless of their extent, in order to make improvements. Here are some suggestions on material handling and material flow to improve safety while at the same time increase productivity, which means cutting costs:[1]

- Recognize that manual material handling is more than just lifting. It includes lowering, pushing, pulling, holding, carrying, and transferring.
- Review plant design and layout to ensure there are no restrictions that may impede materials flow.
- Eliminate unnecessary materials handling by combining operations or shortening the distances that materials must be moved.
- Improve material flow by avoiding crossing paths, backtracking, and a general lack of direction from raw material to finished product.
- Repair floor cracks, depressions, holes, and damaged surfaces. The forces necessary for starting carts or trucks are very high on poor surfaces.
- Promote good housekeeping. Water, oil, and grease on floors reduce traction and are also slipping hazards. Poor housekeeping increases the number of materials-handling obstacles.
- Simplify, rearrange, or change the process to minimize material handling.

- Reduce work-in-process quantities by increasing controls and fore-casting for inventory, scheduling, and ordering of raw materials.
- Establish efficient disposition procedures for scrap, waste materials, and rework items.
- Ensure that aisleways for material flow are always free of obstructions. Avoid performing maintenance work in aisles.
- Plan for materials to arrive at the plant in suitable containers so that parts do not require unloading and reloading.
- Plan for materials to leave the plant in suitable containers to minimize product handling.
- Reduce the deadweight ratio of containers. Consider the weight of the container that must be repeatedly handled and transferred compared to the weight of the material inside. The weight of the container should be minimal.
- Avoid the use of large containers for low-flow volume materials in order to reduce the need for workers to reach to the bottom to get materials.
- Keep loads that are to be manually handled as small as possible. To avoid obstructing the vision of a carrier, load height should be thirty inches or less.
- Ensure that manually handled loads are easy to grip by using textured containers or containers with handle cutouts, handles, or lift straps.
- Stabilize contents in boxes and containers. Use vertical baffles or dividers, balancing the weight in a box, or use packing material to avoid the shifting of parts.
- Position the load center of gravity (or balancing point) of a manually handled load as close as possible to the person who is to handle it.
- Remove constraints that prevent materials from being positioned close to the body. Allow space for feet to get under tables and conveyor belts. Ensure clear access to shelves and adequate space to go around pallets.
- Arrange for workers to lower loads rather than lifting them. Encourage workers to slide loads instead of lifting and lowering them.
- Train workers in the use of mechanical-handling aids. Some employees may avoid the aids simply because they don't know how to use them.
- Study how material is fed into, processed in, and leaves equipment. Incorporate design and operational changes that fit the job to the worker.
- Consider maintenance and setup needs when planning, designing, and installing equipment.

- Review workplace and storage areas for proper illumination levels. Inadequate lighting can contribute to injuries and accidents as well as diminish the quality of products.
- Evaluate noise levels to ensure that mechanical handling warning signals can be heard and heeded.

RECEIVING RAW MATERIALS

Whether your receiving area serves as short-term storage for raw materials and discrete parts that are used in nearby manufacturing operations, or whether it is the first step in getting raw materials off the dock and moved to a longer-term storage area or warehouse, the goals are still the same. Incoming materials must be received as quickly, efficiently, and accurately as possible.[2]

Well-designed receiving areas have the right number of dock bays for fast and efficient trailer servicing and also as a means to receive railcar shipments. They should also be able to handle a variety of materials both palletized and unpalletized, and sometimes simultaneously at the same docks.

If your receiving operations are to be both safe and cost-effective, the industrial trucks used in the dock area must be in good condition. They should be able to handle the toughest and busiest trailer- and railcar-service demands with a high rate of utilization and minimal downtime. You should ensure, however, that there is enough space in the dock area to accommodate a safe traffic mix of trucks and dock worker pedestrians without congestion.

For accurate documentation of receiving operations, an automatic data collection system should be implemented, and the dock area is where it should start. Bar code scanners and radio-frequency data collection terminals, whether truck-mounted or handheld, are commonly used for this purpose. You should also determine how to put quality control/quality assurance activities in effect on receiving operations. Three equipment elements must be procured for receiving raw materials: dock levelers, seals or shelters, and lift trucks.

Dock Levelers

These devices are necessities for safe and efficient receiving operations at most plants in that they are the connecting link between the dock surfaces and trailer or truck beds. At most docks, the surfaces seldom line up because trailer beds vary in height. Besides, they float up and down with the vehicle's suspension during loading and unloading. In addition, the bed of an unevenly loaded vehicle may tilt. Dock levelers can compensate for all of these conditions.

Four types of dock levelers are on the market today: recessed, vertical, front-of-dock, and edge-of-dock. While each type has its own advantages and disadvantages, the recessed design is the most popular in manufacturing plants.

Recessed levelers are designed to provide the greatest operating range above and below the dock, low ramp grades, the highest load capacities, and long service lives. But because they are installed in concrete pits, they usually are difficult to retrofit.

Vertical levelers are installed in a continuous pit or stepdown that runs parallel to the building wall. This type of leveler makes a nearly perfect door seal on a flush dock because its ramp retracts to the inside of the building when the leveler is in its stored position.

No pit or other concrete work is required with front-of-dock levelers—they are bolted directly to the concrete wall that forms the front of the dock. Thus, they can be easily removed for reinstallation elsewhere.

The edge-of-dock type of leveler is generally the least expensive. It is permanently mounted on a steel channel that has been embedded in the front of the dock.

Loading Dock Seals and Shelters

If your receiving and shipping dock isn't equipped with seals or shelters, you may want to consider them to take advantage of the benefits that they give to dock operations. Here are the most important reasons for installing seals and shelters.[3]

1. The dock area will be cleaner for longer times, in that windblown dirt and debris will be mostly eliminated, as will wet floors. This results in safer working conditions and better morale for dock area employees.
2. Dock equipment such as conveyors, scales, and lift trucks will perform better in a cleaner operating environment.
3. Material and products being unloaded or loaded will stay dry and clean.
4. The loss of heated or cooled air from the dock area will be reduced.
5. Security and appearance of dock facilities will be improved.

A typical dock seal consists of a padded structure that is placed along the top and sides of the outside surface of the wall at a dock opening. Most dock seals use a high-density, polyurethane foam core bonded to a wood or metal backboard. The backboard is attached directly to the wall of the building. To protect the foam core from damage, it is enclosed in a tough cover fabric. Sealing is accomplished by compressing the foam core against the building as a trailer is backed into position at the dock.

Another seal design consists of inflatable pads in place of a foam core. After the trailer has been spotted at the dock, the pads are inflated against the outer wall of the trailer with compressed air from a small blower. While foam-core dock seals work well in many applications, inflatable seals can handle difficult sealing problems such as sloped driveways. They also work well on prefabricated metal buildings, which cannot withstand the compressive forces produced by backing trailers.

In its usual form, a dock shelter is a rigid-framed structure covered by fabric. The framework that supports the fabric can be wood, aluminum, or galvanized metal. The shelter may be permanently extended from the dock or it may be retractable. Unlike a dock seal, which contacts a trailer's rear edge, a dock shelter forms an enclosure around the outside wall of a trailer. As a trailer is backed up to the dock, curtains rub along the top and two sides of the vehicle. When the trailer is parked, the shelter forms a tent around it, sealing out dirt and weather.

Dock shelters can be used on almost any type of building wall because they do not require compression of a material to achieve a seal. Shelters also permit unrestricted access to the trailer opening, making it easier to handle tall or wide loads.

Lift Trucks

Although all lift trucks look very much alike, they certainly aren't when you consider their capabilities and performance. Lift trucks are specialized pieces of equipment that should be matched to their applications. Selecting a truck for the plant involves knowing and understanding the job the truck must perform so that operator productivity and truck efficiency will be at their optimums. Several factors should be considered when specifying truck design:[4]

■ *Safety.* For safe, efficient operation, lift truck operators must have a clear view of the area around the truck; this includes being able to see the fork tips or attachments through the mast.

■ *Ergonomics.* When operators are able to work efficiently and comfortably because of truck design, they are more productive. You design with ergonomics in mind when you consider the location of the controls and the ease of getting on and off the truck.

■ *Productivity.* Furnishing the right attachments for the truck improves productivity. Side shift attachments allow the operator to position the forks when handling pallets. For unpalletized loads, options include slipsheet attachments as well as carton and paper clamps.

Like other plant equipment, lift trucks must be specified correctly to maximize their efficiency and to achieve the lowest cost of operation. Specifying the right lift truck may compensate for the physical aspects of the environment such as aisle widths, ceiling and door heights, and inside dimensions of trailers where the trucks may be used.

You have two options when determining what the truck's power source should be: (1) electric (supplied by a battery), and (2) internal combustion (diesel fuel, liquid propane gas, gasoline, or compressed natural gas). A comparison of these two sources follows:

▪ *Electric.* When properly selected and maintained, electric trucks have several advantages over internal combustion (IC) units. Those advantages include:

1. Better fuel efficiency. The cost of electricity to charge batteries is almost always less than the fuel for IC engines. Depending on local energy costs, electric trucks are up to 60 percent less expensive to operate.
2. Longer lives. With fewer parts to wear out and operating at lower temperatures, electric trucks tend to last longer than IC units.
3. No emissions. Since electric trucks do not create combustion by-products, there is no problem with meeting environmental regulations.
4. Less maintenance. Electric trucks have fewer moving parts requiring service or replacement. Therefore, they require less preventive maintenance than IC units.

▪ *Internal combustion.* Along with electric trucks, gas-powered ones with IC engines are specified for many indoor applications, but liquid propane gas (LPG) doesn't offer the lower life-cycle costs of electric trucks. Users in plants often select LPG trucks when applications require more power than electric trucks are capable of providing and when they are needed for outdoor use part of the time.

Diesel-powered trucks are excellent choices for outdoor use, particularly where a powerful, economical unit is needed. Although diesel fuel costs about the same as LPG or gasoline, it furnishes about twice the work per volume as these other fuels. Diesel engines also tend to last longer than other kinds of engines. In addition, the maintenance costs of these engines are low—they do not have electrical ignition systems that require periodic tune-ups in order for them to run efficiently.

Pneumatic tires are good investments for absorbing the shocks caused by driving over rough terrain and railroad tracks. If an application requires further shock-absorbing protection, specify a hydraulic accumulator, which acts like a shock absorber.

JUST-IN-TIME STRATEGY

The management strategy know as just-in-time (JIT) implies prompt movement of materials to an operation or customer as they are required. Since materials are provided only as they are needed, it isn't necessary to build up inventory in anticipation of projected demand.

Many manufacturing plants today tie up a significant portion of their assets in excessive amounts of inventory. Management of these plants want to ensure that they never will run short of material or parts, and they apparently feel that materials can always be used sometime in the future. Unfortunately, this doesn't always prove to be the case. Occasionally, there may be a shortage of high volume items because all available storeroom and warehouse space is occupied by obsolete or overstocks of little used inventory.

Other pitfalls of excessive inventory include the following:

- *Administration and control.* A large inventory requires the involvement of people to manage and control it. Since such individuals are typically indirect labor, no value is added to the product. While some companies consider this to be a cost of doing business, it, without question, increases the manufacturing costs, thereby lowering the profits of the company.

- *Quality problems and damage of material.* With large amounts of inventory, quality of raw and in-process materials suffers. The longer material sits in a storeroom or warehouse, the more prone it is to damage especially if it is moved around to make room for new inventory. In addition, liabilities may be incurred with short shelf-life materials. If not carefully monitored, significant amounts of money may be lost on expired and obsolete material.

- *Inventory accuracy.* When physical inventories of massive amounts of material are taken, examination of the results invariably shows various mistakes: reconcilement errors, transaction errors, and inclusion of returned goods. Unfortunately, the inaccuracies often caused by the errors can't easily be resolved because the trail of information is cold. Additionally, it's likely that the same errors will occur again.

Just-in-Time Procedures

Arrangements and positioning of machines and equipment in JIT plants are different from conventional manufacturing layouts in several respects. Here are five of those ways:

1. *Less space required.* A JIT plant can operate with 40 to 60 percent less space than conventional plants because far less space is required for inventories and material handling. In most of today's plants, production equipment occupies only a small portion of the total space. The largest space user is that required to receive and store materials, hold work-in-process between operations, allow queues in front of machines, and aisles for transporting materials.

2. *Flow lines and cells.* JIT is characterized by flow lines and cellular processes patterned from Henry Ford's original assembly line. The work-piece moves from one operation to the next with little or no inventory between operations. Operations are balanced and synchronized along the line.

3. *Material handling.* While JIT plants require a constant flow of materials, the flow is steady in small units, and the intensity at any given time is low. This requires a different material-handling system from that of conventional plants. The JIT layout accommodates this with short travel distances and manual handling. When mechanized handling is required, it consists of fork trucks or trailers, which pick up and deliver small quantities on regular routes.

4. *Focused production.* A single JIT manufacturing plant cannot effectively make a wide variety of products in different quantities using many fundamentally different technologies. It is necessary for a plant to focus on a limited set of markets, products, and technologies when it operates on JIT procedures.

5. *Point-of-use delivery.* As a plant adopts more and more JIT principles, conventional receiving docks, inspection areas, and storerooms disappear. Deliveries are made where the material is needed, such as at assembly and fabrication areas throughout the plant. This means easy access at many points for small delivery trucks, and reduction in size with eventual elimination of the central storeroom.

INVENTORY CONTROL

Inventory control is a critical factor in a plant's need to reduce cycle time and maintain efficiency in material handling. To clarify just how important it is, note the implications of the dual aspects of the concept: real-time and control.

- The term *real-time* refers to immediacy and accuracy. You know right now exactly what you have in inventory. If you don't know whether you have an item, or where it is, you can't use it.
- When you have control, material input and output are entered in a reporting system without delay; there is no undocumented substitution, misplacement, or pilferage.

When material is stored in remote storerooms, on the floor in a process area, or in an unsecured rack, control is lost and soon your real-time data is of little value. The only good answer to this problem is to take complete control of inventory physically at the same time you are documenting the data and information about it. Material storage systems should be like perfect vending machines—compact, conveniently located, easily accessed, and secure.

Radio Frequency Data Communication

You can use radio frequency data communication (RFDC) technology to get and maintain real-time inventory control. A typical RFDC system handles the two-way exchange of inventory information between mobile terminals (handheld or vehicle mounted) and a host computer of any size. Inventory information is scanned into the mobile terminals from bar codes, manually key entered, or by voice.

There is no problem with information being collected and transmitted from any department and the most remote locations of a plant or warehouse. In addition, most RFDC systems are used in several departments simultaneously. Five benefits from the use of an RFDC are: real-time operations, increased database accuracy, reduced paperwork, shorter order response time, and higher productivity.

Before committing your plant to an installation of a RFDC system, however, you should discuss and check out a few technical points that will determine the effectiveness of a system in your facility. These items include: compatibility with current information systems, facility coverage, data throughput rates, response times, and narrow band/spread spectrum issues.

Since portable data terminals are lightweight, rugged, and easy to use, they save time as well as travel in the plant. Employees can perform inventory and testing jobs without needing to return to a central station for instructions or reporting. As process operations are carried out during the workday, data can be collected whenever inventory status changes.

With such timely collection of data, the database in each terminal always shows the current inventory, thus giving an employee knowledge of item availability to fill orders.

HIGH-USE STORES SYSTEMS

Efficient handling of materials and spare equipment parts is essential to any maintenance program in an industrial plant if the program is to be cost-efficient and reliable. You can improve efficiency by creating one or more stores areas separate and distinct from the main storeroom. Such stores areas have several advantages, particularly when they are stocked with items that are used by the craftspeople in relatively large quantities. By making such items handy to craftspeople in their work area, you can save them the time of going to the main storeroom. In addition to improving the productivity of employees, you can reduce the productive equipment downtime.

Although elimination of unproductive work time of the craftsmen is the most important benefit you can derive from creating these areas, there are other benefits to be realized. The system results in more space being available in the storeroom for handling and stocking items that do not have a high usage. It also reduces storeroom attendants' work in handing out items.

You can determine what to put in the high-use areas by reviewing several months' engineering stores withdrawals. Preferably select items that are used frequently by the craftsperson and can be manually handled rather than require chain hoists or rigging. Do not include items that have a high theft potential such as operating supplies; also, do not include insurance items, which are important enough to keep under control in the main storeroom.

CONTROLLING INVENTORIES OF MAINTENANCE MATERIALS

A plant can realize substantial savings by controlling inventories of maintenance material.[5] Two points should be made on instituting inventory controls:

1. Inventory control does not necessarily mean that inventories should be kept at the minimum. The lowest possible inventory is often not the best or least costly in terms of total cost.
2. Although the relative importance of various inventory control ob-

jectives may change with changes in business conditions, the need for effective control of inventories is constant.

Questions on inventory control can best be answered if specific information on each item stocked is available and various terms concerning acquisition and replacement are understood. Having information on all types of maintenance materials enables the stockkeeper to decide when they should be ordered. The stockkeeper or person who does the ordering should understand inventory terms and the reasoning as to why a formula should be used in deciding how much to order. In addition, the person should be familiar with what items are in the storeroom and which supplier will give the best terms. Following is a list of the most common inventory terms, with explanations of how they fit into an inventory control system. Many of the terms are shown in Exhibit 9-1, which is a theoretical and actual order diagram showing inventory levels for a typical item that periodically must be reordered.

■ *Annual usage.* The number of items withdrawn from stores over a period of one year. The person who orders the item needs to know the exact amount so he or she can decide when to reorder, allowing time to

Exhibit 9-1. Theoretical and actual order diagram showing inventory levels for a typical item that periodically must be reordered.

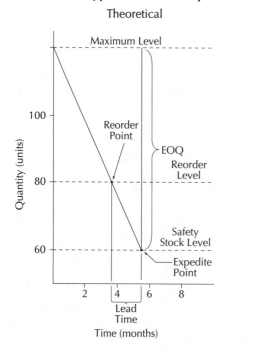
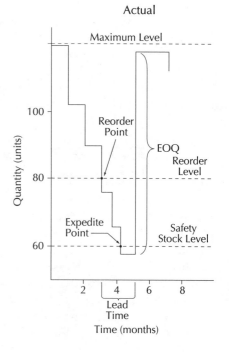

order, receive, and place in storeroom. Possible fluctuation in usage must also be analyzed. The more stable the use rate, the less likelihood of a stockout.

- *Unit cost.* The price of a particular item. A formula to decide how much should be ordered has to include the unit cost.

- *Lead time.* The time it takes to obtain an item. Lead time includes the time to process an order, the time to ship it, and the time to stock it. Lead time is not, as most commonly believed, the time from issuance of the purchase order to receipt of goods.

- *Order cost.* The cost of issuing a purchase order for a certain quantity. It includes the costs of labor and overhead, paper, office machines, and postage in all departments that go through the procedures of issuing the requisition, receiving the material, and delivering it to the storeroom.

- *Carrying cost.* The cost of storing an item in the storeroom. It includes the charge for floor space, depreciation, taxes, interest, and storeroom operating charges. The largest of these charges probably is the interest, or the cost of money. The next largest is the wages and fringe benefits of material-control people, matched by their overhead charges. Carrying cost is expressed as a percentage of the value of the average inventory on hand.

- *Safety stock level.* The stock of an item on hand for protection against running out when delivery is delayed or use is higher than normal. It can be thought of as insurance. To determine the quantity of safety stock to have, you must consider the cost of not having it in terms of lost production and lowered craft productivity versus the cost of carrying the added inventory. The amount of material depends on lead time for that item, its use rate, and its importance to the production effort.

If the lead time is very short, the material is readily available from several sources, and it is not critical to operations, you might opt for a zero safety stock level. If the lead time is longer, there are only a few alternative sources, and the material is of some degree of criticality, the level should be set at some minimum figure. If the lead time is relatively long, the material has a single source, and it is critical to plant operations, a maximum safety stock level should be established.

- *Expedite point.* The point in the inventory level at which the safety stock is used. At this point, it is important to follow up on an order to be sure it is received before zero inventory is reached. If the expedite point is zero, the item is not critical to the production effort and no safety stock is really needed.

- *Reorder level.* The low limit for the sum of the in-stock and on-order balances that is used to determine when to order another lot. The reorder level is determined from data on use and lead time. It is the lead time in months times the usage per month plus the safety stock level.

■ *Reorder point.* The point in the inventory level when, if an order were placed, the usage continued as expected, and the lead time were as predicted, the order would be received when the inventory reached the safety stock level.

■ *Economic order quantity.* The quantity that will result in the lowest total costs of ordering, making, or procuring the item, and carrying the resulting inventories. The theory of economical order quantity buying is that the cost of carrying inventory and the cost of buying are like balance scales: When one goes up, the other goes down.

■ *Maximum level.* The sum of the stock on hand at the safety level (expedite point) plus the order quantity.

Calculating the Economic Order Quantity

The following formula can be used to determine the quantity of an item that will result in the lowest total cost of reordering it and carrying an inventory:

$$Q_E = \sqrt{\frac{2SP}{IC}}$$

where:

Q_E = economic order quantity, units
S = annual usage, units
P = cost of issuing purchase order, dollars
I = inventory carrying cost, decimal
C = unit cost of item, dollars

To illustrate the formula, a $50 item that a plant uses at the rate of 75 a year can be considered. The cost of issuing a purchase order runs about $65 and the inventory carrying cost in industrial plants is about 30 percent of the value of storeroom inventory.

$$Q_E = \sqrt{\frac{2 \times 65 \times 75}{0.30 \times 50}} = 650 = 25.5$$

The economic order quantity would be 26.

Here is a purchasing problem to illustrate the value of the economic order quantity formula:

You are a buyer of maintenance materials. Periodically, you order additional solenoids to replace the storeroom stock. The local vendor has been supplying solenoids at $100 each when 26 are ordered. But today, when the order is placed, he offers them at $90 each if 50 are ordered. That is a 10 percent discount, but is it a good buy? How much would you actually save the company if the offer were accepted?

To solve this problem, see Exhibit 9-2, which shows the interrelationship of ordering cost and inventory carrying cost as variations are made in the quantity ordered. The equation that applies is:

$$T = \frac{Q}{2}IC + \frac{SP}{Q}$$

where:

T = total cost, collars

Q = quantity ordered, units

Records show that the plant uses 75 of the solenoids in a year. It costs $65 to process a purchase order, and the inventory carrying cost is 30 percent of the value of the storeroom inventory.

Exhibit 9-2. The interrelationship of ordering cost and inventory carrying cost as variations are made in the quantity ordered.

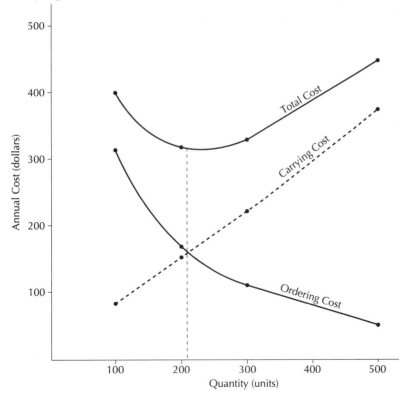

Let T_1 = total cost of usual order
Let T_2 = total cost of today's offer

$$T_1 = \frac{26}{2} \times 0.3 \times 100 + \frac{75 \times 65}{26} = \$577.5$$

$$T_2 = \frac{50}{2} \times 0.3 \times 90 + \frac{75 \times 65}{50} = \$772.5$$

Because T_2 is greater than T_1, the vendor's offer would cost the company more. It would not be a good investment.

Adding Material to Stock

How do you decide whether an item should be added to the storeroom? What is an insurance item, and should it be stocked in the storeroom? These are the types of questions that must be answered if your materials control program is to be cost-effective, efficient, and reliable. You need a comprehensive procedure.[6]

While the primary objective of your procedure should be to minimize inventories, the implementation of the procedure will create other benefits. A good procedure will minimize material acquisition costs, assure that optimum quantities of materials are purchased, eliminate duplication, and provide a reliable method of information retrieval.

Items are stocked in storerooms for two reasons: The item will be needed frequently for operation of the plant and equipment, or the item is critical to production and a spare must be on hand to ensure against a production loss if the item in place fails. Both of these situations should be addressed when a procedure for inventory control is developed.

If it can be documented that an item will be used in large quantities, a decision to stock the item immediately will pay off both operationally and economically. Decisions about adding to stock should not be handled by the materials control department alone, but should involve engineering, maintenance, and purchasing.

The responsibility of the materials control department should be to specify the factors that affect the procurement of inventory and the quantities maintained for all items on the stock list. These factors include the unit of measure, the unit cost, the economic order quantity, the reorder point, and the expedite point.

Perpetual Inventory Control

The inventory control system for storeroom items used in large quantities is commonly known as the perpetual system. This system, which can be run by a computer, uses a fixed order quantity and a variable re-view period. Item quantities are checked continually with each demand to determine if an order should be placed.

The system is based on the concepts of economic order quantity and reorder point. The reorder point and order quantity are fixed, the review period and demand rate are variable, and the lead time can be fixed or variable.

The perpetual system is completely defined by knowing the order size and the minimal stock level or reorder point. Control is achieved by learning as quickly as possible when the reorder point is reached. The review may consist of the computer printing a daily report of all store-room items that have reached their reorder point.

Requesting a Stock Addition

When it is anticipated that an item such as a spare part will be added to stock, it should be ordered direct several times first. These direct pur-chases will provide basic information about the item such as its cost and which vendors handle it. In addition, the user will be able to examine the received item and approve it or not approve it for acceptance.

The quantity ordered the first time should be the minimum that satis-fies the requirement of simply having one (or a set) of the items on hand. This policy is followed for several reasons:

1. There is no positive assurance that the item will be needed. New equipment may fail to operate as expected, processes may change, and a better design may be on the market tomorrow.
2. At the time the order is placed, there may be little history to sup-port a decision on annual use.
3. A high inventory of anything costs money in carrying costs.

The first requisition for the item should be sent to the materials con-trol department rather than to the purchasing department so the item can be coded (assigned an identification number). By coding an item now, it will be much easier to later retrieve purchasing data and historical use data from the computer database.

At this time, too, the item should be identified on the requisition form as potential stores material. A tentative date should be given for the time when the item will be added to stock. Noting this identification, materials control should initiate a tracking procedure to ensure that the item is not forgotten after it has been received but gets the attention necessary to determine whether it should be added to stores.

The tracking or follow-up should begin with making a copy of the requisition and putting it in a reminder file. The retrieval date would be the date on which the requisitioner estimated he or she would request the item be added to stock. The purchasing department should aid the tracking by sending materials control a copy of the purchase order. When the item is received, materials control should notify the requestor to verify whether the item is what was wanted.

Insurance Items

Items used infrequently are commonly called insurance items. They are critical to one or more of the plant's objectives, and stocking them ensures against a loss that could be incurred if the item were not immediately available.

Whether or not to stock an insurance item is a decision that should be based on economics. The very definition on the word "insurance" dictates that the item's annual use is not a factor. If stocking is a favorable move economically, the item should be put in the storeroom immediately.

The need to stock an insurance item becomes greater when it has a long lead time because the potential loss increases with time. When management chooses not to take the risk of a substantial loss, a decision to stock the item is likely.

Two alternative courses also may be considered. The most preferable course would be to ask the manufacturer or a vendor to stock the item. This practice could also be adopted with other than insurance items as a way of keeping inventories to a minimum. A second course available is to arrange for another company plant to stock the item. Reciprocal action can be suggested on different items.

EQUIPMENT SHORTAGES

Do you sometimes find you are short on machines or equipment but don't want to make a capital investment or buy the item at the time? Here are a few answers to this problem:

1. Many machines and other equipment can be rented, including lift trucks, maintenance tools, and even computer terminals. Although renting is in the long term more expensive than buying, in the short term it reduces the immediate outlay of cash. Looking at the problem another way, you may choose to write off a lease as an expense rather than spend capital money.

2. Occasionally an equipment manufacturer may finance your acquisition. The usual arrangement is that you pay the manufacturer a monthly

rent for a fixed period of time. Since the manufacturer has no further use for the equipment at the end of the lease, a clause is put in the contract that transfers ownership to you for a nominal amount at the end of the lease.

3. Dealers in used equipment may also be a source for a particular type of equipment you want to acquire. They buy up equipment at auctions or from companies that have surpluses and sell it at much lower prices than similar new equipment. Although used equipment is going to need more maintenance, with proper care it can be as useful as any new equipment.

4. You can ask new equipment vendors if they have any returned equipment or demonstrators available for sale. While you can expect the vendor's prices to be higher than those of used equipment dealers, the chances are good that this equipment will require less maintenance and may have a better warranty.

WORK POSITIONERS

Properly used positioning equipment can provide many benefits in the workplace.[7] With continual emphasis being placed today on safety and reducing worker fatigue, it is easy to justify the purchase of such equipment. The major benefits from using it include:

- Raising productivity by reducing manual handling of materials
- Eliminating accidents and worker injuries
- Improving product quality and minimizing damage to materials and equipment
- Reducing workers' compensation costs

As for which jobs are best handled by positioning equipment, mechanized methods of positioning offer advantages over manual labor when:

1. The item handled is heavy or awkward to hold.
2. The frequency of handling an item is high.
3. The environment is hazardous or inaccessible.
4. The likelihood of damage is great due to human error or inattention.

When positioning action involves only a lifting motion, a lift table can raise a part or load to the proper work height. Adding a rotating top to the equipment can further help. Tilting devices work similarly in limiting a person's reaching motions. The lifting or lowering of loads can also be easily accomplished by electric or air-powered hoists.

When both vertical and horizontal positioning along with rotational movements are wanted, manipulators are called on to do the job. Equipped with a mechanical "arm" and a "hand" for positioning, the power source can be electrical, hydraulic, or pneumatic. Since most industrial plants use compressed air in various process operations, many manipulators for manufacturing and assembly applications are pneumatically driven devices.

Vacuum manipulators work well on a variety of objects and surfaces; generally, the flatter the surface, the better the grip. Heavier duty lifting and manipulating jobs may require use of hydraulics. Electrically driven units may be the best choice when the grab consists of an electromagnet.

USE OF ROBOTS IN
MATERIAL HANDLING

Because of improvements in computer hardware and software, the use of robots in manufacturing plants now provides more capability for the investment and they are more reliable than ever before. There are now more than one million robotic installations worldwide.

Decisions about whether to install robots should be based in large part on the need for flexibility, along with dexterity and repeatability. Modern articulated robots are extremely dexterous, having at least five axes of motion. Fitted with the proper grippers, they can grab, hold, and transport many products and parts and manipulate them precisely.

In many applications, robotics is the most cost-effective way to automate processes. Robotic equipment is more capable than most alternatives and can be easily reprogrammed and reconfigured as required. This adaptability is vital when you realize that an all-electric robot can operate for an average of ten years before it must be rebuilt. But this does not mean that robots are cost-effective and efficient for all plant applications.

If a production run is complex with a low volume of finished products, manual labor is preferred to robots because it is usually most efficient, especially if working conditions are comfortable. However, if a large volume of products with easy-to-handle parts and high speed is essential, the robot is the answer.

Since electric robots can easily handle parts weighing up to 200 pounds, the decision of what size to install may be more a function of reach than of strength. Yet the need for repeatability and flexibility remains the primary consideration. This is especially true when a robot is not simply handling materials, but also transporting those materials to other machines; then, tolerances are measured in thousandths of inches. In applications such as spraying and dispensing, there is the added benefit of lower material costs through reduction of overspray and better process control. With robotics, there is also the potential for increased production because robots are designed for continuous operation. In fact, any job too boring or too dangerous for humans is a potential candidate for a robotic solution.

AUTOMATIC GUIDED VEHICLE SYSTEMS

Through the use of electronic technology, automatic guided vehicle systems (AGVS) have been of great help in material handling in many industrial plants. Today's AGVSs transport, lift, and transfer and position materials of all types. They also are designed with systems for communicating from one vehicle to another and from the vehicles to the dispatch station, local control, or central processor. Here are just a few of the ways AGVSs are used in manufacturing plants:

- To transport incoming materials to remote storage areas and to deliver picked orders to the shipping dock
- To pick up and deliver structural material, pipe, castings, and other items in yards and warehouses
- To transfer parts and product components between machining centers
- To supply kits and piece parts on assembly lines

Manufacturers of AGVs generally design their systems to put the controls at the decision locations. If the decision locations are static, the intelligence can be put in the floor; if they are mobile, the controls are put on the vehicle. One manufacturer, for instance, uses buried wire as both guide path and antenna for communications. The vehicles are in constant communication with each other, and thus don't run into each other at intersections or overtake one another on the same path. They also send a signal to the dispatcher or to a screen that shows their status on a path diagram.

There is also considerable sophistication in manufacturers' optical or chemical guidance systems in that much electronic know-how is put into the electronics that interpret the marks on the floor. Simple optical systems follow a white line on the floor that detects the difference between the white of the line and the dark of the floor. Other white marks are read as stops. Another optical method uses a chemical path or mark composed of a phosphorescent chemical. This is invisible under ordinary light but glows brightly when exposed to ultraviolet or black light.

The Litton Truckmobile's optical guidance system uses electronic proximity detection to avoid hitting obstacles instead of a bumper system used on most wire-guided vehicles. Its proximity detection system uses a limited radio field to detect objects. The antennas are sensitive up to eighteen inches ahead of the vehicle.

When automatic guided vehicle systems are properly designed, substantial improvements in materials handling operations can result. The major benefits include:

- Lower costs for unit material handling
- Reduced material-handling-related damage
- Increased flexibility in assembly operations
- Computerized control of the materials handling function
- Improved ergonomics for materials handlers and assembly workers

When the decision is made to install an AGVS, however, a plant may experience some problems. Here are a few of the most common:

1. The software for AGV systems may be complex and difficult to implement. Reprogramming may also not be easily accomplished.
2. Troubleshooting AGV systems can take a long time.
3. Getting help from the manufacturer or vendor with in-plant debugging of the system may be almost impossible to achieve.

CONVEYORS

Materials handling has usually been a human engineering problem in plants. But as technology developed, materials handling methods and equipment have kept pace, and mechanical means have been replacing human efforts in finding ways to move materials easily and safely. Modern production methods would be impossible without effective materials handling, which has been developed as part of our high-geared production system.

The conveyors used in plants are designed for a specific job: to move certain materials a certain distance under certain conditions. Although the components of a conveying system may be standardized, the conveyor itself is a piece of equipment that is designed and constructed to do a specific job. The same skill and effort should be put into its design and installation as would be used in any other plant equipment. Since each system is individually designed, no two are exactly alike; thus standard specifications are not practical.

Designing for Safety

Substitution of mechanical for manual handling usually results in faster and more efficient operations. However, increased safety can be an extra benefit if certain basic safety principles are adopted in the design. There are four basic reasons that safety should play a major role in designing and installing conveyors:[8]

1. *Ethical or humanitarian considerations.* The motivation to provide a safe place to work should be present.
2. *Legal implications.* You must comply with local, state, and federal regulations, and be knowledgeable about your responsibilities relating to insurance and liability.
3. *Worker morale.* A serious injury in the plant disrupts normal production routine, and the psychological effects may linger long afterward.
4. *Costs.* In addition to workers compensation charges, equipment damage and production losses often result from an accident.

Conveyor systems naturally involve many employees. So it's logical that a safety program concerning conveyors be addressed to everyone whose work brings them in proximity with a system. The best way to implement such a program is to install equipment that incorporates the best possible safety features. Guidance is available from the American National Standards Institute's publication "Safety Standards for Conveyors and Related Equipment" (ANSI B20.1-1976). Reputable suppliers of conveyor systems adhere to these standards in the design, manufacture, and installation of their systems.

Conveyor Safety Standards

There are many standards of safety that should be incorporated into the design and installation of a plant's conveyor system.[9] The important general features are as follows:

- Conveyors should be designed for the maximum load they will carry, and this load should never be exceeded.
- Where conveyors are elevated or operate in tunnels or restricted spaces, access platforms and sufficient clearance should be provided to facilitate repairs and maintenance.
- Where a conveyor passes over working areas or aisles, guards should be installed to protect against objects falling from the conveyor.

- All gears, sprockets, sheaves, or other moving parts that create pinch points should be guarded.
- When conveyors operate continually, means should be provided to lubricate and make adjustments safely during operation.
- The starting switch should be located so that the operator has an unobstructed view of the entire conveyor.
- An automatic time delay for starting a conveyor, during which time warning buzzers or bells are sounded, should be used. With such an arrangement, all personnel are alerted and can clear the equipment before a conveyor starts up.
- Drive equipment should be provided with overload protective devices as well as being designed to prevent the conveyor from running backward in case of a power failure.
- Automatic discharging conveyors should be designed to automatically stop when the bin, hopper, or chute into which they discharge becomes full.

AUTOMATED STORAGE AND RETRIEVAL SYSTEMS (AS/RS)

With the continual need to keep inventories at a minimum, more and more plants are adopting just-in-time operations. The objective of these is to receive material at the plant as frequently as possible to meet a day's or several hours' manufacturing needs. However, that doesn't mean there won't be a need to store materials in the plant. With few exceptions, plants simply can't operate without some spare or surge material to keep production running when one or more machines or processes are down for a short time.

As you reduce inventories, you must be able to move materials from storage to the workplace very quickly. However, you won't have any problem in finding a system that will do this job. To handle unit loads, there are automated storage/retrieval systems (AS/RS), car-in-lane systems, stacker cranes, and man-ride machines. To handle small parts, there are miniload AS/RS, small man-ride, orderpicking machines, and horizontal and vertical carousels.

The type of transfer equipment you select depends on several factors: the size and shape of the items to be handled, production rates, and the frequency of equipment changeover and setup to handle different products. Although the unit load AS/RS is usually associated with pallet load storage, these systems can store a wide variety of loads and large parts or products. They also can act on or communicate automatically with different types of conveyors and other transportation equipment. Additionally, they can operate with a minimum of human supervision.

Employees' only participation and control consists of entering load identification information to the system control computer through a keyboard or by using a portable scanner. Once that information is known, material can be routed from storage to production and back again, or to a different storage system, all automatically.

AS/RS systems are efficient and relatively safe methods of storing material. The labor cost per item handled is low, while the volume and weight capacity per square foot of floor area are high. Employee contact with moving material is limited, as are physical activities of system operators.

If your plant is in a position to benefit from the installation of an AS/RS, here are some recommendations on its selection and installation:[10]

- Learn what parts and material will be stored in the system so that all aspects of the AS/RS are sized correctly.
- Make sure that the throughput of the system is sufficient to support the requirements of your plant.
- Ascertain that the AS/RS software will interface and be compatible with other software already in place.
- Determine which vendors will best be able to supply your needs. You must be able to specify what you want from the vendor.
- Visit installations already completed by vendors. Select one after checking the company's ability to answer specific questions about how a particular design will meet your needs.
- Allow enough time for initial loading of the system. It will take longer than you expect.
- Look for ways to improve the system after the start-up. Work closely with the vendor to make these modifications.

MATERIAL SAFETY DATA SHEETS AND LABELS

Section 1910.1200 (g) of OSHA's hazard communication standard requires chemical manufacturers and importers to obtain or develop a material safety data sheet (MSDS) for each chemical they produce or import. In addition, employers are required to maintain an MSDS for every chemical that they use in their plant, and to make the MSDS available to employees. Violation of OSHA's hazard communication standards, exposure of employees to hazardous chemicals, and failure to provide safe procedures for handling chemicals are only a few of the problems a plant faces involving material safety data sheets and labels.

One of the problems is that MSDSs are not standardized. Suggested formats have been issued by OSHA, but no universal, easy-to-use format has been adopted. Usually, they contain the following data in this general order:

- *Product identification* lists product name, and manufacturer's address and phone number.
- *Hazardous ingredients* data tell what the product is comprised of, and what levels of material exposure might cause harm.
- *Physical data* explain product appearance, smell, and other unique characteristics.
- *Fire and explosion data* reveal the flash point and classification of the material and describe any appropriate firefighting procedure.
- *Health hazards* reveal the effects of overexposure to the product, and give emergency and first-aid information.
- *Spill or leak procedures* provide spill cleanup and disposal information, and the proper equipment and materials to use in such situations.
- *Special protection* covers personal protective equipment information.
- *Special precautions* detail any other precautions to use when handling the material.

OSHA also requires that hazard warning labels be put on all original and storage containers of hazardous materials and toxic substances. The label must state the name of the substance, and furnish an appropriate hazard warning. This warning should cover the hazard of both short- and long-term exposure, as well as the part or organ of the body that can be affected. Though not required by OSHA, effective labels will include the manufacturer, emergency procedures, an emergency telephone number, and safe use precautions.

Although plants are required to maintain an MSDS for every chemical on their sites and to make the information available to employees, several problems on consistency and clearness of MSDSs have arisen. For example, there currently is no requirement that the eight information categories be presented on the sheet in a specific order. This inconsistency in format from one manufacturer to another has led to confusion among users.

Another problem is that some manufacturers don't provide enough information, especially in the area of personal protective equipment. An example of this deficiency is that the user of a chemical is told to wear gloves but not exactly what kind.

A third problem concerns the language manufacturers use on the MSDSs. There is a need for simplification as well as uniformity. Examples are using the word "ingest" instead of "eat," and giving the chemical name of a material rather than its trade name.

The person who has the responsibility to provide employees with information on material safety data sheets should make sure they understand:

- The primary hazard of the material and when it is a hazard
- The proper means of protection
- The first-aid and emergency response procedures to be followed in the event of a spill or exposure to the chemical

Educating Employees About Hazardous Materials

Formerly, employees who wanted to know more about the hazardous materials in their plant had to depend on the cooperation of their industry and the willingness of management to provide that information. But if a company wasn't willing to share information about its operations with employees, there wasn't much a concerned employee could do about it.

All that has changed. In November of 1986, Congress passed a law designed to help communities and company employees deal safely and effectively with the many hazardous materials that are used in our society. The law is called the Emergency Planning and Community Right-to-Know Act. It has two main purposes:

1. To encourage and support emergency planning for responding to chemical accidents.
2. To provide local governments and the public, including plant employees, with information about possible chemical hazards in their communities.

Right-to-Know Laws

Right-to-know legislation at all levels of government—city, county, state, and federal—has been enacted into laws covering companies that produce or use hazardous materials. The laws, designed to protect all employees, embody legislation that requires corporate employers to inform their employees of any chemicals or conditions in the workplace that have potentially adverse effects if they are not dealt with properly.

Employees also have responsibilities under right-to-know laws. These include being acquainted with the materials they use, knowing how to protect themselves when handling these materials, and making sure they properly use the appropriate personal protection equipment.

There are several steps you should take to ensure that your employees comply with the laws:

1. Keep a list of chemicals and hazardous materials in the plant. Use the names keyed to those on the material data sheets (MSDSs). Compare this inventory with OSHA's list of applicable chemicals to find those covered.

2. Make sure that containers of the chemicals in the plant are labeled, tagged, or marked with the identity of the chemicals they contain. Placing suppliers' bags and cartons of the chemicals in sealed metal containers that are marked with the name of the chemical prevents spillage and also simplifies housekeeping in the plant.

3. Set up a training program for employees. The program must explain:

- How the hazard communication program is implemented
- How to read and interpret information on labels and MSDSs
- What chemicals in the plant are physical and health hazards
- How employees can learn the available hazard information

4. Observe employees on the job to confirm that they are handling the raw materials properly. Warn any person who is not, and discipline him or her if the individual still does not comply with the regulations.

WAREHOUSE FUNCTIONS

The functions of the warehouse and the employees who are responsible for its operation can have a major effect in four areas that are critical to plant operation: safety, product quality, operating costs, and customer service.[11] To get the most out of each part of the plant, you must be aware of how problems in the warehouse affect the four areas. Here are some solutions to problems the plant may be experiencing when carrying out warehouse functions:

- *Safety.* If employees' accidents and injuries are excessive, try the following: (1) Post safety guidelines throughout the warehouse; (2) set safety goals and measure performance against them; (3) conduct safety courses as a way of training employees; and (4) take automation/mechanization steps to reduce manual handling and operator risk.

- *Product quality.* If product quality is poor for any number of reasons, do the following: (1) Train employees on the importance of product quality; (2) improve handling procedures to avoid damaging packages; (3) measure quality control efforts by setting goals and posting the results; (4) consider contracting warehousing to professional organizations.

- *Operating costs.* If operating costs are high, try the following: (1) Make a study of product and item movement including cycle time to improve efficiency; (2) change the layout and arrangements; (3) use a different information system for better inventory recording, accuracy, and productivity; and (4) review staffing levels with an eye on downsizing by eliminating certain procedures.

- *Customer service.* If customer service needs to be upgraded and late shipments avoided, try the following: (1) Use a different layout to keep fast-moving products near the shipping dock; (2) change the storage method to achieve quicker turnover; and (3) revise the inventory policy to ensure products are on hand to meet varying and unexpected demands.

NOTES

1. Excerpts from "Moving Ahead," *The Safe Foreman*, January 1996, pp. 3–8.
2. Excerpts from "Raw Materials: Handle Them Quickly, Accurately!" *Modern Materials Handling*, mid-May 1994, pp. 8–11.
3. Les Gould, "Seals and Shelters: The Key to Safer, More Productive Docks," *Modern Materials Handling*, January 1994, pp. 48–49.
4. Michael E. Kelly, "Understanding Lift Trucks," *Engineer's Digest*, January 1994, pp. 22–27.
5. W. H. Weiss, "Controlling Maintenance Materials," *Plant Engineering*, July 8, 1982, pp. 59–61.
6. W. H. Weiss, "Adding Maintenance Materials to Stores," *Plant Engineering*, November 21, 1984, pp. 68–69.
7. Tom Feare, "Work Positioners," *Modern Materials Handling*, September 1993, pp. 44–45.
8. Stanley J. Curie, "Planning for Conveyor Safety," *Plant Engineering*, December 22, 1983, pp. 75–78.
9. Excerpts from "Conveyor Safety," *The Safe Foreman*, January 1977, pp. 2–4.
10. Gary Forger, "AS/RS Trims Errors, Conserves Floor Space," *Modern Materials Handling*, August 1993, p. 47.
11. Joseph Reilly, "Improving Warehouse Performance," *Chemical Processing*, October 1995, p. 90.

10

Cost Control and Reduction

All managers in a plant, including the plant manager, share a major responsibility: controlling costs. What you do about costs generally is not difficult because almost everything you control is a cost to the company in one way or another. While the ways by which costs can be controlled are many and varied, understanding them is a requisite to doing something about them. Following are the most common manufacturing costs incurred in operating a plant:

1. Labor

   - Production
   - Engineering and maintenance
   - Shipping and receiving
   - Material handling and stores
   - Quality control
   - Training
   - Supervisory and administrative

2. Utilities

   - Water
   - Steam
   - Air
   - Electricity

3. Depreciation

- Buildings
- Machines and equipment
- Vehicles

4. Raw Materials

5. Support Services

- Fire protection
- Guard service
- Lunch/cafeteria
- Medical and first aid
- Cleaning
- Waste disposal

6. Supplies

- Production
- Shipping
- Engineering
- Maintenance
- Office
- Janitorial

7. Taxes and Licenses

8. Insurance

Let's consider what you can do to control and minimize the four largest manufacturing costs: labor, materials, machines, and utilities:[1]

■ *Labor.* If you are not getting the fullest potential from employees, you are wasting one of the most costly items of running the plant. Here are six ways you can hold down your plant's labor costs:

1. Control absenteeism and overtime. These are the major reasons for excessive labor costs.
2. Prevent late starts and early quits, long breaks and lunch periods, and simple idleness.
3. See that clear instructions are given to all workers. They will be more efficient, work more safely, make fewer errors, and create less waste.
4. Assign only as many workers to a job as are actually needed.
5. Put skilled workers on skilled jobs and unskilled workers on unskilled jobs.
6. Provide enough labor to ensure that overtime work is limited.

■ *Material.* Positive ways to control material costs are to develop standards for their handling and use, followed by training workers to meet them. Although this will take time and cost money, the benefits will far exceed the costs. Here are six ways you can control material costs by instructing employees how to:

1. Avoid damaging containers, bags, and cartons in receiving and shipping operations.
2. Prevent loss in the warehouse and storerooms from poor stacking, inadequate protection, and failure of pallets, racks, and bins.
3. Keep spillage to a minimum in handling and dispensing.
4. Protect materials from spoilage by aging or contamination.
5. Avoid wasting material by not taking more than needed for a job.
6. Maintain the quality of finished products; cut waste and rejects.

■ *Machines and equipment.* Cost control of machines and equipment makes two demands on you: to keep these assets fully utilized, and to prevent malfunctions and breakdowns. The first is achieved by doing all you can to keep productive machines and equipment operating. The second is met by adopting a predictive and preventive maintenance program for the plant's machines and equipment. Here are four ways you can hold down machine and equipment costs:

1. When making acquisition decisions, recognize that the cost of energy to run machines depends on their design, the adjustments and control applied, and the condition of the machine's components.
2. Plan and schedule maintenance work to optimize running time of all productive equipment.
3. Adopt just-in-time procedures to minimize start-up and shutdown operations and smooth out processes.
4. Shut down machines, conveyors, and auxiliary equipment when they are not in productive use.

■ *Utilities.* The most accurate way of accounting for the consumption of utilities by various departments in the plant is to put meters on the steam, air, and water lines to them. Meters enable you to uncover usage and tell you also where leaks may be occurring. To control utility costs, you must be concerned and constantly checking to see that:

1. Steam, air, and water leaks are repaired.
2. Insulation is used in adequate amounts to prevent energy loss.
3. Lights are turned off when not in use.
4. Machines and auxiliary equipment are shut down when they are not in productive use.
5. Heating and air-conditioning systems are set appropriately for

working conditions and they are not running in areas with doors and windows open.

6. Engines are turned off when motor vehicles are not in motion.

Determining Plant Operating Costs

Managers have two responsibilities when plant operating costs are to be determined: to continually make an effort to control and reduce manufacturing costs, and to see that accurate cost reporting systems are being used and maintained.

The starting point for studying and controlling costs is to determine the types of expenditures with which the plant is involved. Any cost system is meaningless unless all the expenditures made by the plant, department, or other cost center are recorded and charged back to it on the company's cost report. This means that each of the manufacturing cost elements must be accounted for. It also requires the plant to use various techniques on those elements, such as the following:

■ *Labor.* Space should be provided on the hourly time card for the account number to which the employee's pay is charged; several spaces will be needed if the person works for different cost centers. When the hours worked by employees in one department must be balanced (often a requirement in a unionized plant), these hours are kept on a form designed for that purpose. Since salary employees ordinarily do not punch time cards, they may keep time sheets on which account numbers are listed.

■ *Raw materials.* Purchase price and freight charges may be obtained from suppliers' invoices and freight bills. Handling and production losses are determined by charging the quantities delivered to a department and comparing them to the amount in inventory and what went into the finished product within a fixed time period. Job tickets, shift logs, and intra-department/plant receipts are used to keep track of material used and transferred.

■ *Supplies.* Purchase orders, receiving slips, and suppliers' invoices are the key records. Company policy should dictate that nothing is to be bought without a written purchase order that is documented to show the account number to which the material is charged.

■ *Utilities.* If utility costs cannot be distributed accurately because of a lack of meters appropriately placed, staff people may be called upon to estimate the amounts of utilities used by each department and charge the costs out on that basis.

- *Support services.* When these services are furnished by plant employees, the methods of allocating labor and supplies already discussed will suffice. If the services are obtained outside the company, purchase orders or service contracts will be the basic documents used for cost distribution.

DEVELOPING COST AWARENESS IN EMPLOYEES

When an organization or company is well managed, it furnishes quality products or services, provides jobs and career opportunities for its employees, and contributes to community needs. To operate at a profit, however, management must develop a cost awareness in its employees. Moreover, this must be an ongoing procedure. Since success comes only if cost control/reduction is considered a way of life, a continuous effort to cut costs and improve earnings is just as important as maintaining quality and productivity.

Although it is essential that employees are aware of company costs, it is more important that they understand and accept how costs affect their jobs and the operations of their departments. The security of their jobs and amount of benefits they receive are related to and dependent on costs. Employees must see the connection between their success at reducing costs and the profitability of company operations.

If costs are to be effectively controlled, emphasis should be placed where it will be the most beneficial. As a manager, you are in an ideal position to provide the leadership that demonstrates your company's concern about costs. Your commitment to control costs can be facilitated by the implementation of an action plan. Here are the steps you must take to develop cost awareness in employees at all levels in the company.

- Show your personal concern and interest in how each employee can cut costs and save the company money. The efficiency of employees begins with their hiring, orientation, and first few days on the job. When hired, most individuals are not conscious of costs or profits. You must see that they are trained to meet the performance standards of their jobs. If their output is low, determine if it is due to lack of skills or job knowledge. Then take corrective action.

- Analyze your department or operation to locate the areas where inefficiency exists and waste is occurring. Once poor procedures are identified, develop ways to control and minimize such losses. Aim cost-control discussions with employees at an entire work area so individuals do not feel threatened or made to feel that they should have been carrying out a cost-saving operation. For example, point out how late starts, early quits, and extended breaks hurt productivity and increase the company's operating costs.

■ Discuss specific activities, procedures, and techniques that decrease costs and increase profits. Talk about how erratic or irregular workloads cause delays, equipment downtime, and worker idleness. Explain how planning and scheduling enables the assignment of an optimum number of workers to a job. Show how locating materials and supplies close to work areas minimizes travel time to storerooms and the warehouse. Point out that defective tools not only create unsafe working conditions, but also cause workers to be inefficient.

■ Furnish employees with costs of materials and supplies. Illustrate how fractional reductions in their use may add up to considerable savings, especially if the materials are expensive and used in quantity. Caution against using wrong materials or using materials when they are not required. Warn against using expensive supplies when cheaper ones would be equally satisfactory.

■ Promote quality, error-free work; state what quality standards are expected to be met. Tell employees individually what is wrong when the quality of the product or service is poor, and explain how they can improve their workmanship. Never allow employees to work unsafely—correct them in a positive constructive manner. When discussing performance, give specific examples of what work is acceptable and what is not.

■ Emphasize the objectives of the company, the results sought, and the savings that can be realized from cost awareness efforts. Keep employees knowledgeable about department expenses and what is being done to minimize them. Publicize company budgets and capital expenditures. State that money wisely spent will be returned many times over.

■ Perfect your management style to reflect your dedication to effectiveness and efficiency. Make sure you: plan and organize your work; make decisions based on facts; consider employees' needs when making assignments; and set a good example for others in how you spend your time.

COST CONTROL GUIDELINES

As a manager, you are in an ideal position to control plant costs and improve operating procedures. You have direct influence and control over the use of productive machines and equipment, the work methods employed, and the attitudes and performance of the employees. Here are some suggestions on what you can do to cut costs in the plant:

1. Ensure that cost control is one of your major responsibilities and you practice it daily, not only during periods of austerity.
2. Offer incentives to employees for successful suggestions on cost reduction, either with cash awards, time off, or providing other forms of recognition.
3. Attack wasteful practices such as: overuse of materials and supplies, scrapping of unused materials, underutilizing machines and equipment, and idleness on the job.
4. Promote employee training. Experienced, well-trained, and motivated employees are more productive and efficient than those who aren't.
5. Set objectives and goals on cost reduction for the plant. Make sure they are specific instead of general.
6. Insist on individual accountability. Hold employees accountable for the costs under their control.
7. Keep machines and equipment in excellent condition. Modernize, replace, or upgrade obsolete and worn equipment.
8. Set an example for others. Your attitude and action on cost reduction matters sets the tone for all the employees.

TRACKING COSTS

Too many managers today don't watch and keep close control of their department costs, relying entirely on the accounting department to provide information on expenditures. This is particularly true in larger plants, and many managers' careers have been ruined because they failed to keep track of costs in an effective manner.

Avoiding surprises is the key idea behind tracking costs,[2] and surprises come in many forms. A manager who fails to stay on top of his or her department's costs will sooner or later meet up with a budget overrun. Underrunning a budget can be just as serious because such budgets adversely affect the company's income tax strategy, billing plans, cash requirements, and credibility.

Credibility is affected because when you submit budgets or estimates in the future, people may think costs are inflated. Underruns are also serious because they usually suggest a project is behind schedule.

There's another point to be made for tracking costs. Many managers are surprised near project completion dates to learn that a project will require must more funding to complete. While this is often caused by poor planning, it can also be caused by poor cost tracking, even though costs were incurred at about the planned rate.

The reason is that costs can be incurred at the predicted rate, but if the jobs that are supposed to be accomplished as the costs are incurred are not completed, additional money will be required to complete the project.

The major pitfall to watch out for is, as mentioned earlier, relying on accounting reports to track your costs. Most companies' accounting reports are at least three to four weeks old by the time the manager sees them. Simply stated, managers can't afford to rely on information this old. In order to properly manage expenditures, you need to know about them either before they occur or as they occur. In order to do this, you must develop a system within your group to provide this visibility. Either require subordinates to track their own costs with you reviewing them on a regular basis, or delegate this task to a selected subordinate.

VALUE ANALYSIS

A plant can reduce its operating costs and realize significant savings in material and labor by applying value analysis to its production, engineering, and maintenance functions. Value analysis is the examination of systems, equipment, facilities, and supplies for the purpose of achieving the use of these things at the lowest total cost.

Just as there are many facets to value analysis, so are there many ways to go about implementing them. Prior to adopting a program, however, you should recognize and consider various contingencies. All company departments should be involved in order to realize the maximum benefits. The responsibilities of people must be clearly defined and objectives of the program established. Planning and scheduling play a part, and well-defined systems and procedures are vital.

The application of value analysis is a way of managing that is basic and continuous. People who participate in this function are constantly involved in analyzing operations and procedures, considering alternative courses of action and comparing costs. For example, if a company is manufacturing a product, management should be looking at the performance, reliability, and styling that makes the product competitive in the market. Value analysis must be promoted by managers if a company is to gain from its practice. Since value analysis can be applied to virtually every function of a business operation, its impact can be assessed only by totaling the contribution of each function. Here is how the various departments in a plant can participate in the program:

▪ *Design, maintenance and repair.* Engineers and supervisors should be constantly looking for ways to simplify and reduce maintenance and repair work. Design of equipment is one of the most significant factors to consider in this objective. Effective design involves making the replacement of parts on a machine a simple task. This can be done by providing easy access to parts and by using common connections.

Designing so that ordinary tools rather than special ones may be used for repair work is required. Fasteners should be limited, and they should be standard and readily available. Design of machines and layout in the plant should always provide for lubrication and oiling without dismantling and without interruption of operation, if possible.

A plant's maintenance and repair costs can often be minimized by contracting the labor for such services. Heating, ventilating, and air-conditioning repairs are typical examples of services where outside labor can be employed to good advantage.

Painting and roofing are other operations in which maintenance and repairs can often be accomplished at lower cost and faster than with company labor. The value of the contractor is realized in many of these cases because the pertinent skill is lacking in company employees or there is a lack of sufficient employees for such seasonal and infrequent type of work.

■ *Inspection.* Timing of the inspection of machines and equipment is critical to getting the most value out of them. While frequent inspection is costly and may not be justified, infrequent inspection will not reveal the need for maintenance before failure. Inspections must be made often enough to find problems and impending failures early. Repair costs can thus be minimized and major breakdowns avoided.

Special tools used by inspectors include pyrometers, leak detectors, potentiometers, vibration meters, and noise dosimeters among other non-destructive testing devices. Testing procedures are facilitated by keeping good records since the required frequency of testing is ascertained from them. If examination of the records shows that no problems are arising, it indicates testing is being overdone. But if testing always or usually reveals problems, more testing is advisable.

From an economical viewpoint, it may be best to let noncritical equipment run until breakdown rather than attempt any preventive maintenance. Inspecting and maintaining all equipment under a rigid schedule in trying to eliminate all breakdowns is not practical because labor costs would be excessive.

■ *Purchasing and stores.* The purchasing and stores departments of a company can contribute greatly to a value analysis program. Buyers can contract for the services of repair and maintenance specialists and schedule those services at opportune times. The purchasing department can contribute by working with designers and engineers on standardization of machines, parts, and supplies. By consolidating several departments' needs, a single specification may be established and an order of large quantity placed which, because of its size, will achieve significant savings.

The greatest benefit of standardization is that it enables the number of different parts and supplies carried in the storeroom to be much lower. Inventory control practiced by employing economic order quantity principles in purchasing can also result in large savings to the plant.

The purchasing department must recognize that there is a carrying cost for inventory, and that the company pays taxes on it. Buying in economical quantities also takes into account the cost to process an order.

Equipment performance records are of great help to the purchasing department. A history of trouble with a particular machine, piece of equipment, or tool would dictate that a different model or design be tried when repurchasing. The department should also retain documents that include statements referring to the performance of contractors. Other records should contain pertinent specifications, contracts, and documents covering agreements with vendors and suppliers.

▪ *Manufacturing operations.* There are many ways that value analysis can be practiced in the process and procedures of manufacturing. Beginning with the handling of raw materials and ending with the packaging of the finished product, you should look for process steps that can be simplified, combined, or preferably eliminated. The potential for improvement is particularly great with old equipment and processes where the "we've always done it this way" philosophy exists and change has been resisted.

If you want to carry out a value analysis of production operations, you should ask yourself questions such as:

- Why can't we use a lower cost raw material on this process?
- Is it possible to make the process continuous rather than batch?
- Can't we use a machine to perform this operation?
- Do we need such heavy material for packaging?
- Why not box the product in quantity instead of individually?

Value analysis properly applied can touch every department and operation in a plant. The most benefits are realized when every employee is involved. The benefits to be realized from value analysis are well worth the efforts made on its behalf.

DECISION TREES

Through the use of a model commonly known as the decision tree, managers can analyze problems and reach decisions that are most likely to accomplish an objective or take the least costly path on a plant project.

The decision tree groups the known alternatives for the decision at hand and presents them in pictorial form, thus clarifying the problem.

Exhibit 10-1 shows a decision tree for a problem on the cost of a construction project. In this example, a manager must decide what to do after learning that a construction project under way will cost more than budgeted.

Note that the decision tree presents all the alternatives at a glance. The manager can evaluate each of them methodically and thoroughly in order to decide whether to revise the budget, try to meet it as is, or cancel it.

Despite the fact that only a few companies have used decision trees extensively, growing interest in the technique suggests that it may become more popular with time. Regardless, the technique replaces judgment by focusing on the critical issues of a problem, bringing out the premises often hidden in judgment, and revealing the steps in reasoning by which decisions are made.

Deviations From Budgets

Despite all that you and others do to control costs, you eventually will receive a cost report that shows large unexpected deviations from the plant's budget. When this happens, take the following steps to learn the causes and decide what corrective action to take:

1. *Notify everyone concerned.* You will need their knowledge and opinions to uncover the causes. Also, ask for help from department heads who may be able to supply pertinent information. The more help you get on investigating the problem, the better your chances of success.
2. *Shorten the interval of the next cost report.* If, for instance, the problem is high material usage, take inventories weekly instead of monthly until you find the answer.
3. *Search for cost reporting errors.* If labor charges, material requisitions, or suppliers' and vendors' invoices are charged to the wrong accounts, the cost report will be unbalanced. You should be able to trace the postings in the accounting department to the original cost documents to find the error.

INVENTORY OPTIMIZATION

Inventory optimization is a continuous process to increase plant efficiency and minimize operating costs.[3] The procedure uses a number of ways to

Exhibit 10-1. The decision tree.

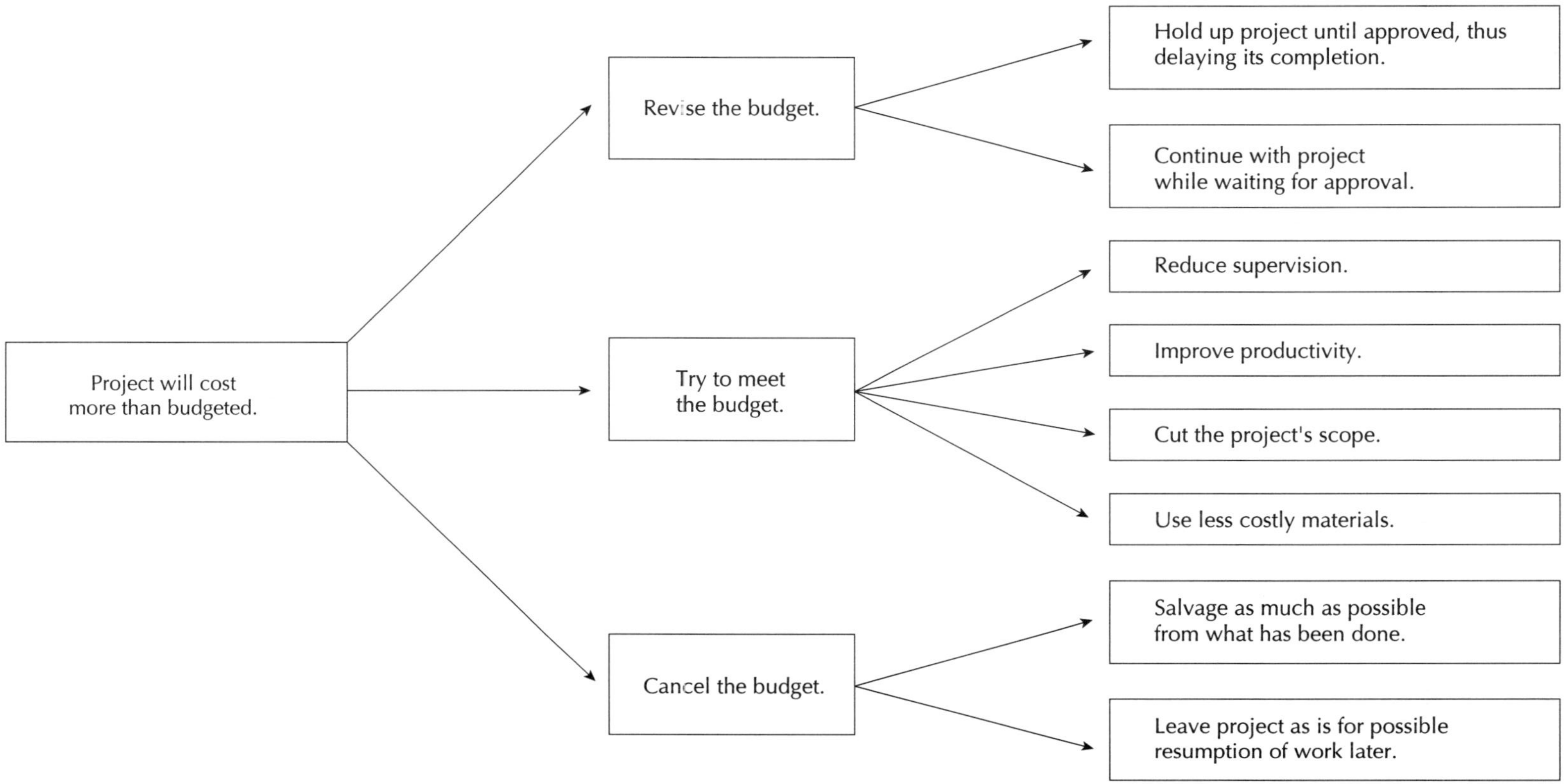

Project will cost more than budgeted.

Revise the budget.

- Hold up project until approved, thus delaying its completion.
- Continue with project while waiting for approval.

Try to meet the budget.

- Reduce supervision.
- Improve productivity.
- Cut the project's scope.
- Use less costly materials.

Cancel the budget.

- Salvage as much as possible from what has been done.
- Leave project as is for possible resumption of work later.

reduce inventory levels and improve service levels at the lowest possible cost. By balancing carrying costs with purchasing costs, and balancing stock-out costs with safety stock costs, both objectives can be achieved.

The first step in the inventory optimization process is to determine the fundamental costs. While you may calculate your company's internal costs or use the standards of your industry, it is vital that you understand and document how these costs were determined. The following costs are the ones with which you are concerned:

- Order costs involve the writing, reviewing, and tracking of purchase orders. These costs vary, depending on how the order is generated: manually, by computer, or electronic data interchange.
- Carrying costs are stated as a percentage of inventory value; they include all costs associated with maintaining stock, such as insurance, depreciation, security, and taxes. Typical carrying costs are between 25 and 35 percent of the total inventory value.
- Stock-out costs for parts in inventory depend on where the parts are used and on how critical they are to the operation. A stock-out on a critical item, for example, could slow or stop the production line, and costs could run into thousands of dollars an hour.
- Safety stock costs are based on statistical analysis of historical usage data and the desired service level required by the maintenance department. Add safety stock to demand during lead time to determine optimized reorder point.

Order controls can be put in place once the above costs have been determined. This is done by carrying out an ABC (Pareto) analysis, which is the classification of parts by number of issues. An analysis is performed by counting the number of parts with the same issue frequency or usage. The "A" parts have the highest usage value, usually the top 20 percent, while "B" parts have moderate usage and consist of 60 percent of all parts. The remaining 20 percent are assigned a "C" classification. You should concentrate your inventory optimization efforts on the "A" classification.

When the analysis is complete, the economic order quantity (EOQ) for a part can be calculated. The EOQ is the quantity that will result in the lowest total costs of ordering and carrying the resulting inventories. See Chapter 9—Materials Handling and Flow—for a more extensive discussion on inventory management techniques.

DISTRIBUTION RESOURCE PLANNING

Many companies use distribution centers for getting a plant's products to its customers. By stocking products close to markets, a company can provide faster, less costly deliveries. Controlling distribution, however, may be difficult at times.

The problem is to keep customer service up while keeping costs down. This requires good data and information along with close attention. Without these resources, the company may have plenty of inventory at a certain time and place, but not enough where it's needed.

With planning and control, however, you can conserve inventory and at the same time maintain good customer service. Here are the ways to do this without running up costs:

1. Keep inventory as far back in the distribution process as possible.
2. Prevent distribution centers from reordering until they have started using their safety stock.
3. Cut back reorder quantities and ship more frequently.
4. Evaluate faster methods of transportation to reduce replenishment lead times.
5. Request that salespeople determine which customers might be "back ordered."
6. Dole out inventory at the last possible moment.

Effective managing of inventory requires knowing more than just where it is. Other issues must be resolved such as: when more product will be available, how long it takes to ship an order, and what the weight and size is of planned shipments. Distribution Resource Planning provides this information using a bill of distribution to connect each stock-keeping unit in each distribution center with its source of supply. Competing demands can then be given to schedulers who, in turn, can plan the flow of products through the distribution network.

REENGINEERING

Plant process reengineering is being heralded today as a strong method of increasing a company's competitiveness in the marketplace. Cynics, however, dismiss it as a theoretical procedure for reducing the number of employees. To its advocates, reengineering is a productive process for reorganizing the company or "reevaluating" the business. This is done by examining every activity and function to find simpler, faster, and more economical ways to run the facility. Similar to upgrading a plant's products, reengineering redesigns the plant's operations.

Although there are different forms of reengineering, the most successful ones have at least one thing in common: They address horizontal cross-functional processes and activities throughout the company rather than the vertical functions such as finance, manufacturing, and marketing. Companies that have achieved more than small gains have concentrated their efforts in the following areas:

- *Managing customer relations.* A company must know its customers and communicate with them. The information they acquire should be used to point their product development and production in the right direction. To do otherwise would result in failing to meet their customer's needs.
- *Providing customer service.* The service should be supplied in a customer-focused, cost-effective manner; it should be more than just traditional production or customer service functions. Demand fulfillment includes logistics and demand/supply planning.
- *Developing new products.* To respond to customer needs and introduce new products to the marketplace, plants need to turn product and process development into a coordinated, cross-functional system.
- *Responding to change.* Plant management today must provide more capabilities than ever before. Reengineering of support functions will reduce costs and eliminate unnecessary activities. Reengineering is happening in business and industry for one simple reason: the need to change.

Prerequisites to Taking Action

The keys to selecting the processes to include in the reengineering effort are to clearly understand how your plant operates and recognize how a particular process will impact profitability. Before jumping into a program involving major changes, the entire venture needs to be carefully considered. Here are the prerequisites to taking action:[4]

- *Education.* Make sure that you and other decision makers in the plant understand what reengineering is all about. It's a good idea to talk with consultants and experienced practitioners.
- *Assessment.* You need to know what's currently working well in the plant. For what's not working, you need to identify the causes. Without this knowledge, your problem-solving techniques may be misapplied.
- *Objectives.* You must define the level of performance that will be required to reach your objectives, the primary one being to achieve a significant competitive advantage. This provides both the motivation and the target for the reengineering effort.
- *Resources.* If you anticipate making major changes, you need key

people to carry them out. Reengineering success depends on the skills of the people assigned to the job.

- *Analysis.* A cost/benefit analysis is needed to determine the return on investment. You should become involved only if the project will pay off.
- *Measurements.* Before starting, the objectives must be established and the means to measure them agreed upon.

Reengineering should neither be quickly rejected nor accepted. The misunderstanding about what it is comes about because the word "engineering" implies that better machines, equipment, or tools will achieve benefits. But making real gains depends on people who plan, prepare, and then do their jobs in different ways.

Pitfalls and Misdirections

Any plan to reengineer must recognize that there will be roadblocks to avoid or overcome. Entrenched habits and traditions are hard to change. So are people who are biased toward preferring the status quo. If you can get people to join a cross-functional team, you may be able to stimulate their thinking.

A weakness with some reengineering programs is that emphasis is misplaced. Instead of focusing on the core processes that are the backbones of the business, some companies attempt to reengineer many of the subprocesses. The result is a diluted reengineering effort and little cross-functional connection.

The use of obsolete ways of measuring performance is another stumbling block. Too high a percentage of what is measured by conventional methods is not relevant to a cross-functional process. Even traditional productivity data are related too much to worker output, and reveal little about other crucial business factors: product quality, customer satisfaction, and speed of delivery.

ENERGY EFFICIENCY AND CONSERVATION

According to David Farrell, president, General Energy Technologies Corporation, only three ways are available to you to reduce the electricity cost at your plant:[5]

1. Reduce the time something is *on.*
2. Reduce the load while it is *on.*
3. Change to more efficient machines and equipment.

Farrell came to this conclusion after analyzing the results of more than 2,000 energy audits conducted during the last ten years in facilities of all sizes. The audits indicated that most energy conservation measures with short payback periods and the greatest savings fall into relatively few categories. Although direct and concise, this conclusion sets the direction for most energy efficiency and conservation programs currently being carried out in plants today. Here are some suggestions and recommendations on what you might do to improve energy efficiency at your plant:

■ Expand your knowledge of the subject to enable you to take decisive action to cut energy costs. You can do this in several ways:

1. Establish a network of specialists (consultants, manufacturing representatives, and vendors) from whom you get help on energy problems.
2. Meet periodically with representatives of your utility company to be kept informed about their plans.
3. Benchmark your situation and position by visiting other facilities in your industry.
4. Maintain active membership in at least one professional society (for example: AEE, ASHRAE, AIPE, IEEE).
5. Meet with salespeople routinely to be kept abreast of new technology.

■ Install energy-efficient lighting when you can economically justify it. Lighting and HVAC systems account for 60 to 70 percent of building electric use. A 20 to 30 percent reduction in electric energy use is usually obtainable.

■ Run a heat balance on the HVAC systems to ensure that equipment is performing according to manufacturers' specifications. Adjust equipment, mechanical, and operating conditions to meet actual demand conditions, not design conditions.

■ Maximize energy savings of energy management systems by seeing that complex control functions, such as load shedding, duty cycling, totalization, weekend scheduling, and others, are being used.

■ Contract with a company whose business is energy conservation. Many such companies can also supply financing and, in some cases, finance the changes from the savings. Outsource maintenance and other operations if they are not part of your core business.

■ Distribute memos company-wide that remind departments of their part in energy conservation. Such communications typically include suggestions to: update HVAC operation scheduling, close doors and window shades, and turn off personal computers. Show corresponding dollar savings, if possible.

Obstacles and Roadblocks

Unfortunately, managers sometimes meet with resistance of one form or another when trying to sell energy conservation or improve energy efficiency in the plant. While everyone acknowledges its importance, few seem to like the remedies or procedures to make changes for the better, or are willing to spend many resources on it. Obstacles and objections include the following:

- Many plants require a year's payback, although some good energy conservation projects have two- or three-year paybacks.
- Programs to save energy lack priority over other plant programs.
- Energy conservation is not foremost on the minds of department managers. Production and maintenance operations are focused on keeping productive facilities operational and under control.
- Only during a major retrofit or equipment upgrade is it practical to do something about inefficient ventilation and lighting systems.

POWER FACTOR

One of the most effective ways to use electrical energy more efficiently is to control the power factor.[6] The power factor is the difference between apparent power (what the utility feeds the plant) and active power (that which can be used).

Inductive loads, such as motors and transformers, cause the current and voltage to be out of phase. In effect, the current lags behind the voltage and makes delivered power less effective. Therefore, more apparent power must be drawn to produce the required amount of active power.

The phase shift between voltage and current is measured by the phase angle ϕ, which can be a maximum of ninety degrees. Power factor, the ratio between apparent power and active power, becomes cos ϕ. Ideally, the power factor should equal one. This is achieved when the phase angle is zero degrees, there is no phase shift between voltage and current, and there is no reactive component to the power.

By measuring the power factor in your plant and compensating for it, you can make the plant much more energy efficient. Doing this will cut costs because the plant will be able to use smaller components in its electrical system. It will also cut the utility bill. And, depending on what your electric utility offers, the plant may now qualify for significant demand management rebates.

COMPRESSED AIR

Compressed air is often the most costly utility for manufacturing plants, the reason being that air compressors consume 10 to 15 percent of all the energy used. The procedure of converting electric energy into compressed, dried, and purified air, and distributing it in the plant, is usually inefficient, thus contributing to the cost. By practicing energy conservation, however, costs can be controlled and reduced substantially.[7]

Because of the wide range of compressor system design and operation, costs can vary considerably from plant to plant. There are two forms of system losses: power in pressure drop and discarded heat, and air that leaves the system before users have access to it.

Although air compressors and dryers have useful lives of at least ten years, initial equipment cost, which determines depreciation charges, becomes less important with time. The cost of energy, however, increases continuously. Energy conservation is best achieved by conserving compressed air and raising the low utilization of electric energy.

In general, electric energy is the major cost element and constitutes from one-third to two-thirds of the total cost of compressed air. This suggests that judicious use of compressors will result in the greatest amount of energy conservation. For example, it would be worthwhile to handle the baseload demand for air in a plant with one or more large compressors that run continually, with one or more small compressors (which can be shut down) to handle the trim and to supply standby spare capacity. Additionally, if the air is used at a varying rate, installing appropriate storage capacity could permit the trim air compressor to be periodically shut down.

Another energy conservation move is to recover the heat generated by the compressor system. If the plant has a need for heated water, quite a bit of this waste heat can be recovered, resulting in a savings of fuel. For example, about 80 percent of the input brake horsepower to a water-cooled screw compressor can be recovered as heat from the oil cooler.

Because of the continuing increase in the cost of cooling water, air-cooled compressors are becoming more popular. Even if the water is recycled and cooled (mechanical coolers, cooling towers, cooling ponds, and cooling tanks) rather than used on a once-through basis, cooling costs and maintenance requirements are still considerably higher than for air-cooled compressors.

Savings in electricity can be achieved also through optimum sizing of the air distribution system. Since pressure drop is inversely proportional to the 5th power of the internal pipe diameter, pressure drop falls off rapidly with increasing diameter. By using a larger pipe size, the design of the system will be more cost-effective. While the installed cost will not be much greater, other costs will be lower. Additionally, a larger pipe serves as a receiver. If you use the next larger pipe size over what would be adequate, the lower pressure drop would decrease the power loss, resulting in a decrease in electricity cost.

Contending With Air Leaks

Compressed air leaks in plants are an inexcusable waste of this costly utility, particularly when leakage at fittings, valves, hoses, and other components of a compressed air system can be as high as 20 to 40 percent of the supplied air. To make matters worse, in some plants this leakage occurs continually, even when productive equipment is not operating, if the system pressure is maintained.

Unfortunately, not everyone is aware that compressed air costs more than water, electricity, or steam. A plant that is experiencing excessive compressed air losses needs a program to educate the maintenance employees about testing procedures and technologies that would eliminate waste and allow the plant to run more efficiently.

Many of the leaks in air distribution systems consist of small holes through which pipe scale, iron oxide, and other dirt are blown. Abrasion from these contaminants causes the holes to grow larger as long as the system is pressurized. Contributing to the problem is the trend to operate systems at higher pressure. While standard pressures used to be 90 to 100 psig, today they are 125 psig for large compressors and 150 to 175 for small ones.

Air cylinders often leak around the rod seals or piston packing. Other leaks occur at pipe fittings that are loose because equipment has been improperly installed or because sealant was not correctly applied during installation. Then too, if a pipe connection is occasionally bumped, the fittings may become cracked.

Making an air-leak survey is simple, especially since you can use instrumentation to help you. There are a variety of ultrasonic leak detectors available which are relatively easy to use; they can pinpoint individual leaks that are ordinarily not detected by the unaided ear. When these detectors are used on a regular basis, payback on your investment is very short.

Any plant will benefit from a compressed air audit—an audit exposes all leaks. Typically, production demands account for only 50 percent of the total demand for compressed air; the remainder is lost.

STEAM TRAPS

Steam distribution and condensate collection systems in plants include numerous steam traps. When properly installed and maintained, these mechanical devices allow condensate drainage without wasting steam, thus saving a lot of energy.

When a trap leaks steam, the costs can be astronomical. For example, about 200,000 pounds of steam per month will be wasted with a leak the size of a quarter-inch orifice at 100 psig. If steam costs the plant $5 per 1,000 pounds, one such leak will cost $1,000 per month. Consider what the costs would be to the plant if 20 percent of the traps were leaking.

There are many different techniques and procedures for testing traps in service.[8] The most common ones are measuring temperatures, listening for sounds, and observing the discharges. Here is how these tests are made:

■ Measuring the temperature of the inlet and outlet pipes gives you information on the pressures upstream and downstream of a trap, based on saturated steam properties. Measuring the temperature differential across the trap will not tell you whether the trap is blowing steam because on a manifold with some failed traps, the back pressure may rise on all traps. If a trap is cold, this tells you that it has failed closed, that the steam is shut off, or that the system is plugged.

Other testing procedures involving temperature include: placing a pyrometer against the pipe to read temperatures; using heat-sensitive indicators such as wax crayons, paints, or stick-on strips, which change color above a predetermined temperature; and aiming an infrared gun at the trap to sense its temperature.

■ While sound is a more reliable indicator of trap performance, you must be a good listener to tell the difference between a trap discharging normally and one where live steam is escaping. Tools and instruments for testing traps by sound include a screwdriver with the blade touching the top of the trap and the handle held against the ear, sophisticated stethoscopes, and ultrasonic probes designed with read-out or print-out capabilities. But to get reliable data, background noises from other equipment should be eliminated. This may be difficult when several traps drain into one header, because sound travels through the pipe.

Listening instruments designed to filter out all but specific frequencies are available for such cases. Even if the listening device comes with an optical gauge or dial, it is recommended that this equipment also use earphones for more definitive analysis.

■ Until recently, observing a trap's discharge has proved to be the most reliable testing method. With systems that return the condensate to the boiler, all that is required is a three-way valve or a pair of valves. The piping must be arranged so that the condensate return line can be shut off and the trap permitted to discharge to atmosphere.

This method, however, requires training and experience. When the condensate discharges, part of it becomes flash steam, and the observer must be able to differentiate between this and live steam. Flash steam appears as a lazy white cloud.

A new testing technique involves inserting a special sensing probe into the bottom of an inverted bucket steam trap. The probe monitors two aspects of trap operation: the condensate level beneath the bucket and the temperature of that condensate. This instrument can determine whether the trap is closed or blowing through. Such units will also pinpoint a leaking trap faster than other testing methods. The completely automatic model can be operated with its own central processing unit and printer or with a user-applied programmable logic controller.

A comprehensive steam energy conservation program includes testing steam traps periodically and replacing those not operating properly. A consistent program of trap testing will pay for itself quickly in steam energy savings and better system performance.

LIGHTING SYSTEMS

Companies can save money as well as increase the lighting quality of the workplace if management properly maintains the plant's lighting systems. Effective lighting results in higher levels of worker productivity and safety while also reducing rejects and facilitating quality control. By introducing conservation measures, less energy is used to produce better quality lighting, saving money on electricity and helping the environment.

Installing new lighting systems, however, is not the only way to go. In most cases, proper maintenance extends the life of the lighting system, improves the lighting, and saves money immediately. While in some plants, maintenance consists only of changing burned-out lamps, true maintenance involves much more. You can realize savings on labor, electricity, storage, and other benefits that derive from better lighting.

Over time, dust and dirt accumulate on light fixtures, restricting their light output. It doesn't take very long before work areas become progressively darker and inadequate for safe operations. Cleaning the light fixtures is a simple answer to the problem—the cost is low, and the procedure can produce significant savings.

Scheduled replacement of lamps is another step in properly maintaining lighting systems. Although all lamps begin performing at their rated capacity, the capacity diminishes slowly until final burnout. Since different lamps fail at different rates, you should consider that fact when planning replacement.

There are two reasons why you should not wait until a lamp burns out before changing it: (1) The output of a lamp diminishes substantially as it approaches burnout; and (2) labor costs are higher for replacing individual lamps. The way to ensure proper light levels is to group relamp. With this plan, an entire section of lights is relamped after a prescribed number of hours.

While it may appear wasteful to discard lamps that are still functioning, the opposite is true. If a plant adopted a group relamping program, the money spent on electricity can be applied toward lamps working at peak output rather than ones working at 50 percent output or less. In addition, the plant will spend less for lamps because bulk purchases can be made, and more storage space is available for other inventory. Although group relamping will not completely eliminate spot relamping, it should be reduced to near zero.

Labor costs are higher for spot relamping. With group relamping, maintenance personnel can gather and set up all equipment and supplies at once, complete the job, and spend less time on each lighting fixture.

Lighting Provisions of the National Energy Policy Act

Elimination of the lamps outlawed by the recent National Energy Policy Act will reduce your plant's energy and maintenance costs.[9] Just as important, if your plant also changes to electronic ballasts, it can gain the benefits of greater productivity and better product quality. Here are a few of the most important lighting provisions of the Energy Policy Act:

- After April 30, 1994, the manufacturing and importing of certain eight-foot slimline and high-output fluorescent lamps commonly used in commercial and industrial applications were prohibited.

- After October 31, 1995, the same restrictions applied to popular four-foot linear and U-tube, 40-watt fluorescents as well as reflector and parabolic aluminized reflector incandescents.

- The act does not prohibit the use of these lamps. It simply makes them eventually unavailable. This means that when inventories of existing lamps are depleted, companies will be forced to buy and use more costly, government-approved lamps.

While the provisions of the National Energy Policy Act will reduce environmental pollution, other benefits are just as important if not more so. For example, according to Joseph Howley, manager of environmental marketing at GE Lighting, the one and one-half billion 40-watt fluorescents installed in the United States will eventually be replaced with more efficient, energy-saving fluorescents. Although the replacements are more expensive, they use less power (about 34 watts), are designed to fit into existing 40-watt lighting systems, and produce the same amount of light. If you do nothing more than change the lamps, the added initial cost will be worth the effort in energy savings.

Fluorescent Lighting

As we have learned, fluorescent lamps are an economical alternative to incandescent light bulbs in work areas. They provide energy savings as well as maintenance and labor savings besides emitting better light quality than incandescents. In addition, they can replace incandescent lamps in virtually every application where incandescent lighting is now used.

Compact fluorescent units are made up of several interchangeable parts: ballast adapter, which is good up to ten years; lamp, which is available in several sizes and wattages, and lasts for 10,000 hours; and reflector or diffuser. While the burned-out fluorescent lamp must be disposed of, the adapter and the reflector or diffuser can be reused.

The benefits you get from using compact fluorescent lighting are very much worthwhile:

- *Savings in energy.* In plant exit signs, for example, where one 9W compact fluorescent replaces two 20W incandescent lamps, the savings amount to more than $27/year.
- *Savings in maintenance.* Since longer life means less maintenance, replacing an incandescent lamp with a fluorescent one can reduce the cost of maintaining that fixture as much as 90 percent.
- *Savings in air conditioning.* Generally, 1W of air-conditioning energy can be saved for every 3W of lighting energy saved.
- *Longer life.* An incandescent lamp lasts an average of 750 to 1000 hours. Compact fluorescent lamps last 10,000 hours, or up to ten times longer.
- *Better light quality.* The quality of light is measured by how it reveals colors. Because of the use of triphosphor technology, compact fluorescent lamps rate higher than incandescent lamps in light quality.

But replacing incandescents with fluorescents isn't the only way to reduce your lighting costs. Following are some other ways to raise your plant's energy efficiency:

1. *Eliminate some fixtures.* If areas such as hallways are overlit, you can immediately cut costs by elimination of a few lamps.
2. *Use more natural light.* If the plant contains numerous windows or

even a few skylights, with lamp controls you can adjust inside lighting intensity according to the brightness of the light entering the building.

3. *Change to more task lights.* Task lights illuminate only specific areas rather than the entire workplace, thus saving energy.

4. *Install sensors based on occupancy in certain areas.* They will turn off lights when an area is vacant.

COGENERATION

Cogeneration is defined as the simultaneous production of power and other forms of useful energy such as heat or process steam. While government agencies restrict the definition of cogeneration to electric power generation only, various industrial associations extend it to include mechanical-drive power and electric power.

High-cost energy has made initial steam conditions for industrial plants economical up to 1,250 and even 1,800 psig. Higher boiler and turbine equipment prices are justified by the additional by-product power available from a given process heat load. Similarly, to further increase by-product power, steam should be expanded down to the lowest pressure consistent with the process heating temperature. For example, many industrial plants distribute steam with a single header of, say, 250 psig when most of the demand is at lower pressures. Two or three pressure levels of distribution can result in the production of many additional kilowatt hours of low-cost, by-product power.

Oil refineries are among the best candidates for cogeneration projects because they are large consumers of electric power and have a need for steam at multiple pressure levels. However, not to be overlooked is the use of cogeneration by process industries. New industrial plants or major expansions of existing facilities having process steam demands and continuous process operations offer ideal opportunities for cogeneration. Where process steam flow requirements are low in relation to the electric demand, diesel cogeneration systems should be considered.

DEMAND-SIDE MANAGEMENT TO CONSERVE ENERGY

Many utilities during the last decade have instituted demand-side management (DSM) programs in an effort to encourage their customers to save energy; the utilities offer rebates to industrial plants to take energy conservation steps that they would not otherwise do.[10] Early DSM programs involved energy-efficient lighting and ballast replacement. Once success was achieved, the utilities expanded their programs to include other technologies. Motors, which represent a major industrial load, soon followed, as did adjustable speed drives, chillers, and fuel switching.

However, energy savings achieved by the latter programs were frequently less than expected. It became evident that installing energy-efficient motors was not enough to realize savings. Decisions to install them must be based on actual use and loads, not just nameplate data and an assumption of full loading. A recent approach by utilities is to offer DSM programs based on *performance* improvements.

Under this procedure, a consultant makes an in-depth study of the energy-using system's performance by taking readings at full load and various partial-load conditions. The consultant then develops a load profile that represents the hours of full-load and partial-load operation of the system during the year.

To determine if a DSM program would provide savings for your plant, you should do the following:

1. Ascertain if your utility offers rebates for installing energy efficient lighting or a percentage of the difference between standard and high-efficiency motors.
2. Confirm that you know approximately what your actual loads and hours of operation are, that the economics are favorable, and that you are comfortable with the predicted energy savings.

NOTES

1. W. H. Weiss, *Plant Supervisor's Complete Desk Book* (Englewood Cliffs, N.J.: Prentice Hall, Inc., 1992), pp. 101–102.
2. Used with permission of Sterling Publishing Co., Inc., 387 Park Ave. S., New York, N.Y. 10016, from *Managing Effectively* by Joseph and Susan Berk, Copyright 1991 by Joseph and Susan Berk.
3. Paul M. Johnson, Steve Adams, and Eric Gutoski, "Optimizing Your Inventory," *Maintenance Technology*, June 1993, pp. 62–63.
4. Walter E. Goddard, "Rethink—In 6 Steps—Then Reengineer," *Modern Materials Handling*, November 1993, p. 37.
5. David Farrell, "Why Not Start an Energy Diet?" *Engineer's Digest*, November 1993, p. 100.
6. Bill Hansen, "Control Power Factor and Cut Costs," *Engineer's Digest*, May 1994, p. 14.
7. Victor Kevorkian, "Controlling Compressed Air Costs," *Maintenance Technology*, May 1992, pp. 31–34.

8. Thomas C. Rockwell and John McCallion, "Steam Trap Testing Yields Energy Savings," *Chemical Processing*, January 1995, pp. 87–90.
9. Larry Beck, "Good Reasons for Lighting," *Engineer's Digest*, September 1995, p. 34.
10. Keith J. Kempski, "Demand-Side Management Today," *Engineer's Digest*, June 1995, pp. 31–33.

11

Training

Managers of manufacturing plants are placing increasing emphasis today on training and retraining their employees. Employees must not only be trained in certain skills, they must also acquire a broad base of knowledge so that when conditions or situations require it, they can easily and quickly learn new skills and readily adapt to change. From an employee perspective, training helps to satisfy many different needs, among which are self-esteem, pride, security, and socialization.

OBJECTIVES OF TRAINING

To meet the objectives of training, you must recognize the need for training plant employees along with identifying the specific types of training that can be administered. The need usually arises from two situations: Either the employees' performance is not adequate or acceptable for the job requirements, or the employees are not capable of performing the future requirements of the job.

Among the many types of training programs currently in use are: induction training, new techniques, equipment and processes training, remedial training, technological displacement training, apprenticeship training, and rehabilitative training. In all of these programs, three interrelated objectives must be met:[1]

1. To develop within trainees pertinent technical skills such as machine and equipment operation, and motor skills so that trainees can safely perform jobs effectively and efficiently.
2. To embed in trainees the knowledge of ideas, concepts, methods,

and procedures to enable them to recognize and see what it is they must do and why it must be done.

3. To help trainees to develop proper work and interpersonal relationship attitudes. Proper attitudes are communicated not just by what is said, but by what is practiced.

TRAINING NEEDS ANALYSIS

Although you as a manager in a plant don't need to know the details of training design and development, unless you have to do some training yourself, you do need to know what an effective trainer does; you can then make sure the people who train your employees do it. Nothing they do is more important than making a needs analysis.[2] Training is always more effective when an analysis is done first.

Good analysis is just as critical for successful training as for any other successful corporate activity. In general, the more thorough the analysis and investigation, the briefer the training can be and still accomplish its objective. There's no question that time and effort put into a project in the beginning lead to far more efficient and effective performance later on. The reverse is also true—when preparatory work isn't done, problems invariably come up and hinder the procedure the rest of the way. If the objective of competent training is to improve performance, you can't expect it to work unless you first find out exactly *what* performance needs to be improved and *how* it can be improved.

While a good analysis paves the way for training that will result in the best performance improvement for the least expenditure, it will also do something more important: It will tell you whether training will help you at all. It's possible that changes in work flow, or compensation systems, or clarifying what's important in a job, can produce far more performance improvement than training. If you find this to be true, you don't want to waste money and effort on training.

Acceptance by Employees

Plant employees don't always welcome training. Some may fear it, especially those who have not been in school for many years or did poorly while there. Others may question its value. Since people work for self-serving purposes, if the benefits from training do not exceed the bother and time they must put in it, they are not going to want to participate voluntarily.

The risks of participating in any type of training is often a matter of concern to employees. Nobody wants to fail. If employees lose the right to return to their old jobs, or if they are unable to pick up a skill that is required for a new job, many may refuse to take the risk. For these and other reasons, you may have to do a good job of selling some employees on the advantages of being trained. Here are a few ways to do that:

- Tell them that trained people are more self-reliant and self-confident. They are more relaxed and at ease on the job. They also enjoy more what they are doing.
- Show them that training enables them to succeed in their current jobs and in their careers. Prove this by referring to one or more people holding high level jobs in the plant.
- Mention that trained employees take more pride in what they do. Insecure people and those who don't have confidence in their abilities often try to protect themselves by hiding their insecurities and inefficiencies. This is usually stressful.
- Play to their desire to be a success by stating that trained employees have more job security and opportunities for advancement and to receive pay increases.

FEEDBACK

Feedback is a critical factor in training functions in that when it is given to trainees, it enables them to continually improve their performance.[3] If trainers properly use feedback, improving their performance is easy for individuals because the information is:

- *Timely.* Trainees find out quickly how they performed, while they can remember what they've done and they're able to change it.
- *Direct.* Feedback comes from the trainer or system directly to the individual, not through a supervisor, inspector, or other intermediary.
- *Specific.* The message contains exactly what the trainee needs to evaluate and, if necessary, change his or her performance.
- *Reliable.* The information is accurate, trainees get it when they expect it, and it's in the form they expect.
- *Responsible.* It encourages shared responsibility to ensure that the program stays on track and the trainer and trainee work together for a successful program.
- *Valuable.* Trainees can understand and use the information once they get it. The information is best received when it's presented objectively and nonjudgmentally.

While you may not be able to recommend the number of times trainers should give feedback to individuals during training, you can still set a target you expect them to meet after completing the training. If, for example, supervisors participate in the training, it's not unreasonable for them to create at least several instances a week where they provide objective feedback to an employee who received training. It pays to make it a habit to give feedback to employees all year round.

JOB- AND NEED-DIRECTED TRAINING

Some companies have recently made changes in how they train employees. As a result of downsizing and the need to meet a budget, managers have decided that the training should be more focused as well as cost-effective. With this trend, training organizations, equipment vendors, and consultants are promoting more job-directed and customized training programs. Advanced technologies and training strategies are being used to save time and reduce the high cost of teaching people on the job. The major changes are as follows:

- Classroom instruction and off-the-job seminars are being augmented to include interactive, personal computer learning programs that enable workers to train at their own pace.
- Just-in-time training procedures and tools are replacing many costly "overtime" training programs.
- Customized training methods based on job performance and plant operation specifics are replacing general subject matter-based training that often lacks objectivity.

While it costs money to train people in today's computerized workplace, it can cost more not to provide it. You can measure the cost-effectiveness of a training program by looking at such data as uptime of productive equipment and the time required to repair or replace critical equipment. When courses are targeted to job responsibilities, you have an effective and efficient training program.

Personal computer software is now available that enables management and staff to supply just-in-time training to machine operators. Some of these software products, also called diagnostic aids, may run on the same computer that is running a process. If a machine fails, the operator presses a button and a screen prompt asks for the symptoms of the problem. When the operator punches them in, the software produces a list of possible solutions.

Other training innovations of benefit to industrial plants are organizations that provide a training need analysis. With this type of service, a certified instructional analyst goes through a plant, talks to employees, finds out how their operations of processes run, what the employees know, and what they don't know. The analyst then designs a training course to fill the gap.

Such training need analysts are invaluable in that they help organizations to focus on specialized needs. By directing the training to specific applications, the training time might take only two days instead of five or more that would be required with a standard course.

BENEFITS OF TRAINING

Employees, managers, and companies accrue many benefits from training. We live in a world of continuous change. As things change, people and companies must also change. The companies that can correctly forecast change and adapt through training will be those that will survive and prosper over the long run. Here are the ways people and the plants where they work benefit from training:

- Trained employees have a higher probability of not only being successful in their current jobs, but also in their careers. When employees develop a strong self-image, they become more pro-organization minded. This attitude is reflected in several ways: less absenteeism, more cooperativeness, and greater motivation, all of which lead to higher productivity.

- Managers who participate or are active in the development of employees interact with them and thereby get to know them better. They learn more about employees' needs, wants, concerns, and potential. This knowledge helps them to perform their jobs more effectively and efficiently, thus furthering their own careers as managers. Since trained employees usually are more conscientious, managers don't have to spend much time supervising them; managers have more time for making plans and decisions.

- Companies benefit greatly when employees are well-trained because they have fewer accidents and are more efficient. When productivity in the plant is high, operating costs are very likely to be lower than those of competitors' plants where workers are not trained as well. Profits, therefore, tend to be higher.

DEVELOPING A TRAINING PROGRAM

Before you start to develop a training program, you must define its objectives.[4] Similar to the reasons why employees in manufacturing plants need training, the objectives must involve and concern both employees and the company, and they should be both general and specific. Specific objectives could be to: (1) improve employees' existing skills; (2) teach employees how to operate new equipment; (3) increase the plant's output; (4) train individuals to be better leaders; and (5) reduce the number of accidents and injuries in the plant.

An important step in creating and developing a training program involves determining its content. This should include the information, knowledge, and experience that the trainee needs to get in order to do the job safely, correctly, and efficiently. For example, if the objective concerns changing the seal on a pump without an accident or injury, part of the program must cover how to disassemble the pump safely. Another part must cover how to install a new seal.

Putting together a program also includes deciding what instructional procedure should be used. While you may have a choice of several procedures, the one you select should clearly tell and show the employee what to do. It should also motivate him or her to adopt this procedure in doing the job.

Training Departments

In the early years of an organization or plant, training and developing people is carried out almost exclusively on the job. There is no training staff. When new people are hired, their immediate supervisors are required to train them in whatever skills they need on the job. In some organizations, this situation continues even as they grow much larger.

Yet, most companies of any size eventually reach the point where management recognizes that it would be an economical move to provide a staff to help line managers train and develop their people.[5] The limitations of on-the-job training are apparent when a company is growing rapidly or turnover is high; most line managers simply don't have the time to do it. Furthermore, many managers make poor instructors. Line managers become qualified for their positions for reasons other than their teaching ability. It may take a great deal longer for new employees to become proficient and productive on the job if you rely on line managers alone to train them.

Advantages

A well-organized training department can provide several advantages to the company. A formal training group can augment the on-the-job coaching of line managers while also contributing to the training function in the following ways:

■ The department can research the training needs of employees to establish a more certain basis for determining the type and scope of training that should be given. It can keep up-to-date with the latest techniques and what other companies are doing. Its research activities can include investigating the value of video training programs and the availability of consulting services.

■ The training staff can develop new programs and training techniques suitable to meet the training needs that have been identified through research. Members of the training department are undoubtedly in a better position than any outside training organization to relate training programs more directly to the work environment in the company. This program development applies especially to first-level managers. At that managerial level, where the largest supervisory population exists, the economics and advantages of in-house training are most favorable.

■ The teaching and instructing role is the primary function of the training department for most companies. When the department has its own group of seminar leaders, it can be very flexible in conducting training programs that bring about desired on-the-job behavior change. Special training sessions can be scheduled and presented on short notice; and ongoing training programs can be staffed much more economically with department people than by using outside consultants.

■ A training department is in an ideal position to constantly evaluate the effectiveness of its programs because results can be easily and quickly ascertained by observing and testing trainees. Thus, seminar leaders can try different ways to teach different subjects, and make changes and improvements as necessary.

■ Furnishing service and making recommendations to top- and middle-level managers on all aspects of training needs and methods is a further benefit provided by a training department. Generally accepted management theory makes line managers responsible for the training and development of their people. But this is with the understanding that the training department can be called upon for advice and assistance. In addition, managers may occasionally request advice and/or help in setting up development plans for individual employees or want to know how training can facilitate a major operational change.

TRAINING METHODS

The methods you use in your training program must relate directly to your training objectives and the content of a particular course. If, for example, you intend to train employees in the procedures of operating a computer, simulation or demonstration methods will be better than lectures. Here are some suggestions on selecting training methods:[6]

- Analyze the people to be trained to determine how to best do it. Assess their maturity level, skill level already attained, and their work experience. This analysis will help you decide what training approach would be most appropriate.

- Base the methods on the capabilities and strengths of your training staff, but also give the members additional training to expand their instructional skills.

- Consider time and cost factors. If you are to train a large group quickly, or have limited funds to work with, you will have to tailor your program accordingly.

- Allow for the physical limitations of the training environment. When planning and scheduling the program, take into account the availability of training rooms, the type of visual aids you can use, and the number of productive machines and equipment which may be freed for on-the-job training.

It pays to continually vary your training methods, if for no other reasons than to prevent them from becoming boring and to maintain the interest and attention of trainees. Switch your presentation style periodically and use different ways of getting trainees involved. If your training programs are not well-received, getting better results may be as simple as changing your training methods.

TRAINING WITH VIDEOS

Videotape technology has contributed much to training plant employees in recent years. Many high-quality videos are available; they have been made by professionals in several fields of industry and manufacturing, and they cover a wide range of subjects. What makes them so much in demand as training tools is that they are flexible and easy to use. A tape may be used with a group as large as twenty employees or on a one-on-one basis.

But all training videos are not equally useful. Here are some recommendations on selecting a training video from Connie Sasseen Bever, of American Media, Inc., a West Des Moines, Iowa, training-video producer.[7] She advises choosing videos that are:

- *Properly focused.* Check all videos you preview to see if they are directed to meeting the objectives of your training programs.

- *Appropriate and realistic.* The video should portray a work environment and situation that fits your employees; the characters should be diverse and the issues should be realistic.
- *Interesting and informative.* Any video you select should have a good balance of teaching and entertaining. It should also be interesting, well-paced, and command attention.
- *Logical.* The content of the video should be presented logically and be easy to follow. It should not last more than twenty to twenty-two minutes.
- *Current and modern.* Avoid videos that are out-of-date on language, clothing, and background scenes. These may be distracting to the extent that viewers will overlook the message.

Even the most effective videotapes, however, aren't complete in their training capabilities. For instance, a video can't depict each and every situation experienced by each employee. Nor can it answer every question that can come to the mind of a trainee. Thus, videotapes can't replace good instructors.

CROSS-TRAINING

Although cross-training plant employees to do one another's job requires your and your subordinate's time, in the long run, both you and the company will benefit. The ultimate ideal situation that can occur is that most hourly employees and many of the salary employees can do someone else's job as well as others can. The advantages of cross-training include:

- More employees become aware of the work flow and can anticipate problems or requirements in other areas.
- Some employees overcome the feeling that they are in dead-end jobs without improving their skills.
- Employees can be moved around to handle peak loads in busy areas, thus improving productivity of the department.
- New employees to a particular job may find productivity shortcuts.
- Greater output of the department can be obtained during high absence periods.
- Desirable skills that are latent in some employees may come to light.
- The more tedious jobs in the department can be spread around, thus improving morale and self-esteem.
- Overtime and weekend work can be handled by fewer employees.
- The best of the cross-trained employees could be a good skeleton force in the event of layoffs.

TRAINING FIRST-LINE MANAGERS

No job in management reflects changes in the industrial environment more vividly in recent years than that of the first-line manager (supervisor). Department managers now expect this person to understand the company's goals and how his or her work fits into them, and to be able to apply basic management principles. A first-line manager must recognize that today's plant employees want a greater say in how their work is performed, and are willing to assume more responsibility for the plant's performance. They are also less inclined toward blind obedience to authority.

If first-line managers are to perform as professional managers while keeping up with the demands of ever-changing technology, they must be given appropriate training. Two types of training are needed: technical and managerial.

1. Technical training is particularly needed by those managers holding positions in the engineering and maintenance departments. If your company is large enough to have a training department capable of giving technical instruction to its employees, you are indeed fortunate. The technical courses can be tailored to the technology, machines, and equipment the plant is using. Plants without training departments may recruit instructors from the engineering staff, line management, and data processing department; course material can come from suppliers' and manufacturers' manuals.

First-line managers can also get technical training at local colleges, technical institutes, and public high schools that offer training in the basic sciences, math, and computers. In addition, manufacturers of high-tech equipment such as electronic, pneumatic, and hydraulic systems often conduct training sessions on the operation and maintenance of their products.

2. The more managerial training a first-line manager can get, the better the person will be able to carry out the job responsibilities that are cost-related, especially when the plant operates in a highly competitive industry. Many private consulting firms today are conducting seminars, workshops, and training programs for supervisors and foremen. The programs usually last two to three days, covering such topics as principles of management, motivating and supervising hourly employees, administering a labor contract, disciplining, and human relations techniques. These courses offer well-designed programs taught by experienced instructors. The seminars and sessions also give first-line managers an opportunity to discuss common problems with peers from other companies.

Similar to technical training, many colleges and universities offer basic managerial training. If your plant is near such an institution, supervisors and foremen can attend evening courses while working at the plant during the day, thus not losing any time on the job.

SENSITIVITY TRAINING

A procedure has been developed to help individuals learn how others perceive their behavior.[8] Known as sensitivity, or T-group, training, it is based on the assumption that a number of individuals meeting in an unstructured situation will develop working relations with each other. From this, they will learn much about themselves, as perceived by the other group members.

Although the main objective of T-group training was originally personal growth or self-insight, the process has been used also to implement organizational improvement or change. However, it has some critics among organizations that have tried these techniques.

A central problem, according to some, is that sensitivity training is designed to change individuals, not necessarily to change the environment in which they work. When individuals attempt to use what they have learned, they often find their coworkers unwilling to accept it, or even worse, what they have learned may not be appropriate for their back-home situation.

TECHNOLOGICAL TRAINING

Increasing technology in processes, control systems, and industrial operations, combined with the aging of the technical workforce, have called attention to the need for training of technical employees in many manufacturing plants. Years ago, training was seen as the answer to a recurring problem on the plant floor, or an old-timer explaining to a new hire how to repair a machine. But with today's complex equipment and instrumentation, much of which is computerized, training has become a continuing and never-ending task.

Many companies are realizing the consequences of inadequately trained employees: poor quality products, machine and equipment downtime, and general inefficiency. As a result, training is playing a greater role and has become an important element in improving productivity and keeping manufacturing costs at a minimum.

There's probably nobody in your plant who knows how the processes and control systems should work better than the long-service technicians. These people have kept the equipment and controls up and running for years. They know where every sensor, actuator, and relay is located, what these controls and devices are designed to do, and how they should be operating. You cannot afford to let the mechanical skills these veterans possess be lost. You must not let these people become liabilities because of their possible resistance to or likely ignorance of new technology. Most of them, if not all, lack knowledge of new equipment that is computer-based.

Before you get involved in a training program, however, you should assess the employees' current skill levels and aptitudes. This helps determine how much training they need and how much they can swallow. You want to avoid training people on matters that aren't part of their jobs, or teaching them something they already know.

Technicians and maintenance people generally benefit from three types of training: basic skills, industry-specific, and job-specific. You have to decide what level of training to give them. For instance, when training them on maintenance and repair of new electronic equipment, they may first need some basic training in computer literacy and maybe even basic reading and math.

TRANSFERRING

The procedure of learning something in one situation and then applying what was learned to another situation is known as transferring. Thus, learning can transfer from the classroom to the job, or from one job to another. Transferring is most effective when trainers ensure that the following principles are considered basic in a training program:

■ *The training situation must be similar to the job.* When training employees to operate a machine, select a machine that is identical to the one the employees will use on the job. Do the same with the materials involved. But can you go any further? If you use off-grade or inferior materials in training (to cut costs), will the differences affect the ease of operating the machine or the precautions that should be taken in the operation? Obviously, you must avoid such possibilities.

As for nonphysical factors, recognize that the trainees will later be working under a certain management mode, under a certain organizational arrangement, and with varying conditions of temperature, lighting, ventilation, and noise. For maximum and realistic transfer, these conditions should be simulated.

■ *The rules must be explained before practice.* History has shown that the extent of transfer to the job is greater when the employees understand the rules, principles, and theory behind what is being taught. Employees who understand the basic safety rules that apply in the workplace are going to be more careful, especially if they know the rules that OSHA requires on the operation.

You can make a safety point more effectively, especially in a classroom session, if you have the trainees themselves develop and state the rules that apply to their operations. Teaching in this manner is much better in getting results than simply standing before trainees and lecturing.

■ *The basic operations must be well practiced.* When the trainee first starts the machine, he or she should be given time to practice all the operations thoroughly, particularly the various procedures and adjustments that are required in the operation. These are identified as the original tasks, compared to, for example, the complete cycle of tasks the machine performs in doing a job. The more complex the job, the more important mastery of the basic operations becomes.

What to be achieved here is the training of the body in the simpler tasks so that the mind needn't be concerned with them. When scientists talk about perceptual-motor skills, they are referring to training the senses and muscles so that they can act without conscious thought. This is important from a safety viewpoint because many accidents happen when employees are under stress. If an individual has not practiced a particular task enough, and gets into a situation where seconds count, he or she may accidentally make a wrong move.

RETRAINING EMPLOYEES

Today's advanced technology and complex production equipment have resulted in plant managers learning that many of their employees in both the production and maintenance departments have become obsolete. Management must therefore either hire new employees to operate, service, and maintain sophisticated machines and equipment, or retrain the employees to do this work. If you feel you are in a similar situation, you can cope with it in several ways:

1. Send the employees to trade schools and educational institutions to receive the training needed.
2. Take advantage of the training courses offered by the manufacturers of the new machines and equipment. Many instrument and computer manufacturers are currently active in offering this.
3. Arrange for in-plant demonstrations of operation, maintenance, and repair work by equipment vendors and manufacturers' representatives. If you do this, videotape the presentation. You will have

a valuable training tool on hand for off-shift employees or new hires.

According to a study[9] made by Work in American Institute, Inc., a New York research firm, it is more cost-effective for manufacturing plants to take employees in obsolete jobs and retrain them for new positions rather than hire skilled employees. This study confirms why it is common procedure today to retrain production workers to perform a different task or operate new machines and equipment.

"Retraining" is the word used to describe two procedures: (1) training in a different line of work, where a person's present job skills are of little or no use; (2) training in the modifications of a present procedure, where the job remains basically the same but the machines, equipment, or techniques are different.

Selling Retraining

Before you try to sell employees on the need for retraining, recognize that some individuals will resist it. Keep in mind also that it's more difficult to retrain employees than to train new hires, and the time you need to retrain may be longer than the time needed to train. You may have to persuade some of the older employees that they have much to gain and nothing to lose. The best way to carry out your selling and subsequent retraining is in steps:

1. Explain carefully why the retraining is necessary. Show how it will be of value and help the employee.
2. Point out what employees already know about the new job, and spell out what they will be learning. Often a person knows more than he or she realizes. This will come out in talking about the new job.
3. Beware of employees coming up with excuses that they can't do what is expected of them. Insist that they try. Such resistance can be overcome only by actually doing the new jobs.
4. Encourage employees frequently as you start the retraining. Letting them know that they are doing fine is a good way to motivate them and can spur them on to further learning.

TRAINING SEMINARS

Seminars are the most widely used of all the mediums for giving business and industrial employees training. American Management Association alone puts on 3,000 seminars each year, and there are literally thousands of other organizations and individuals sponsoring or conducting training seminars in the United States today.

The fundamental reasons for the popularity and acceptance of formal training are understandable.[10] There is a great need in business, industry, government, and organizations of all kinds to make people more productive and to make people in new jobs more quickly productive; and there is a limit to the natural talent of everyone. Besides, with the recent advancements in technology, there are few jobs in business and industry where natural talent will be of much help. The need for specialized knowledge and skills is present everywhere.

Although it is not universally recognized as is the need for technical training in manufacturing plants, training in management skills is seen as a special need. The instinctive approach most people take when they become managers is not going to be effective later on. Many of these managers will likely be indifferent to the needs of the individuals who report to them. They tend to be poor delegators, want to make all important decisions themselves, and not listen to the ideas of others. They often act intuitively without taking time to get and analyze facts, or time to consider alternatives.

All of these characteristics of new and inexperienced managers are likely to lead to an environment that represses individual creativity and prevents job satisfaction. Managers should receive training that will steer them away from such instinctive behavior and toward methods that are much more effective in raising the productivity of their subordinates. Training seminars are available that can bring this about.

Advantages

There are many practical as well as economical advantages to the use of seminars for training industrial employees at all job levels:

■ Seminars can handle large numbers of people with common needs and do it efficiently in terms of per capita cost. Through the use of standard audio/visuals, several different trainers can present essentially the same subject matter to groups in several localities. If groups break up into smaller subgroups, involvement and interaction can be greatly increased, thus adding to the seminar's effectiveness. While lectures can reach much larger audiences, as the audiences get larger, the opportunity for interaction between trainer and trainee, and among trainees lessens.

■ Almost any subject can be covered by a seminar. The subject can be very broad, such as a course on management procedures or policy; or it can be very narrow, such as how to operate a specific machine. But this isn't all. A seminar leader skilled in the same subject matter usually can respond to various needs and interests of different groups. In fact, this happens almost inevitably at many seminar presentations.

■ A training seminar has the potential to get quite a bit of motivation and commitment from a participant, primarily because it stresses involvement and interaction of the participant. This high impact potential is the seminar's principal advantage over lectures and self-instruction.

■ A wide range of high quality programs is available at training seminars. Some of these programs are conducted by the vendor, while others are run by in-house trainers trained by the vendor. The large number of good programs available can save training directors the time, cost, and effort required to develop their own programs.

■ An advantage of formalized training to the company is that you can make sure that the trainees really understand what they need to know. The most successful programs review and reinforce the lessons trainees have learned, making them understandable and something they can relate to.

Disadvantages

Although training seminars do have disadvantages or limitations, many can be alleviated or avoided. The limitations include the following:

■ Seminars are unable to build skills or form new behavior patterns. Time constraints and a high participant-to-trainer ratio make it difficult to train individuals in new skills. While participants will acquire knowledge and may attain better attitudes, skill-building is best achieved through on-the-job instruction.

■ The success of a seminar training program depends on the perceptivity, resourcefulness, and dedication of the leader to get participants involved and promote stimulating group discussions. While the importance of the leader diminishes as the structure of the seminar tightens, even then a poor leader can make the program ineffective.

■ There must be agreement between the needs and expectations of the participants and the subject matter of the program or else the seminar will not accomplish its objective.

■ The costs incurred in attending a seminar can be excessive; moreover, the full cost is almost always hidden. While the costs of consultants or leaders, educational materials, and the facility may be nominal, usually much larger are the transportation and subsistence expenses of the seminar participants; and still larger, the economic cost entailed in being away from the job.

RESPONSIBILITY FOR TRAINING

Some maintenance managers may not think of training as an essential part of their jobs. Some may insist that the training department handle all training. However, it is the responsibility of all managerial and supervisory personnel. It is essential that employees be trained in all aspects of their craft. Training should be an integral part of job enrichment within the department and company.

Training requires management to take a close look at the job and the employee. It is necessary to define what it is the employee should be doing and to determine whether he or she is doing it properly. It is equally important to find out why a particular employee is not performing as well as he or she can, so that the employee can be made aware of any deficiencies or problems.

The development and promotion of an effective plan for training is especially dependent on a managerial climate that encourages the employee to seek training. This climate can be created through sound managerial techniques. Management support must be effectively continued and not relegated to just lip service with no real support or follow-up.

CHARACTERISTICS OF SUCCESSFUL TRAINING PROGRAMS

If you decide to implement a training program, upgrade an existing one, or determine if your training department or individual trainers are doing a good as well as satisfactory job, you should know the requirements of effective programs. You should also be aware of how to design and develop them and how they are evaluated. Here are the most important characteristics of successful training programs:

- The training needs must be evident and clearly understood. If an employee problem arises because of insufficient knowledge or inadequate skills to do a job, then the problem concerns training.
- The objective of the training program must be agreed to by all concerned. In addition, it should be supported by statements of criteria.
- Learning, not teaching, should be the primary objective. The training should be designed to get results.
- The completion of training programs should make people creative, skilled, and productive rather than loyal, cooperative, and helpful.
- The training programs an organization conducts are based on and

relate to the situation, background, and environment of the organization.

- Training techniques and procedures are formulated to require action on the part of the trainee. While some learning may result without such behavior, if the trainee must perform in a certain manner, feedback will most likely result. Feedback can reinforce desired behavior.
- The training methods ensure feedback. The trainers receive feedback during the training sessions. This enables them to make adjustments in scope and style in order to reach desired objectives.
- The training program is evaluated by the degree to which it has achieved its goals. It is not rated on the opinions of the participants or the impressions of top management.

TRAINING ON SAFETY

Once employees have been isolated as the prime area of weakness in a company's effort to improve safety in the workplace, management now needs to learn what will lead them to work more safely. While motivation and incentives are important, employees must know the safe ways to do their jobs before you can motivate them to work safely. This can be achieved by seeing that they are trained specifically and thoroughly.

Training is based on two elements: (1) what you teach—the rules and procedures, and (2) how you teach—the principles and techniques that you use. Of the two, there's a wealth of courses and training material available for most of today's business and industrial operations. The information that can be obtained from machine and equipment manufacturers is usually of high quality, and technical societies can provide excellent materials. In addition, there are many sources of manuals, films, videos, brochures, programmed-instruction courses, and the like.

The problem often lies with the teaching—how the materials and instructions are given to the employees. Many trainers don't know what makes people learn, or what makes them remember what they have learned. At the same time, to the average industrial trainer, teaching new technology is a mystery, complicated by jargon, technical terminology, and trade lingo.

Although linking both safety and productivity in a training program contributes to a company's profitability and growth, the prime objective should be safety. Too few managers today are aware of the tremendous costs of accidents, and not enough managers see training as a way to overcome the hazards inherent in many employees' jobs.

Training Subjects

Deciding what subject to cover in a training program is just about as complicated as deciding which methods of communication to use. Here are a few options to consider:

■ Take a tour of your plant and observe the machines, equipment, and the surroundings. From what you see, determine what presents the most immediate danger to the employees. That can be the basis for beginning a safety program.

■ Note that OSHA offers free consultation services if your company has fewer than 250 employees. Ask an inspector to look at the plant and tell you what citations would have been issued had this been a real inspection. Or simply call OSHA and ask what things in plants similar to yours are most commonly cited. You'll quickly learn what safety subjects should be included in a plant's safety program.

■ Investigating and preventing "near-miss" accidents are essential parts of any plant safety program. But it is necessary that employees be made aware of their importance.

Regardless of what subjects you cover in a program, if the training is to be effective, employees must actively participate in their own training. A hands-on demonstration of a safety procedure is much more likely to get the employee's attention and much more likely to be remembered.

Safety and Health Programs

On-the-job safety and health training is as vital to the successful operation of a plant as it is for employees. Both the employees and management must be committed to adopting and implementing safety steps if a training program is to be effective. Efforts must be extensive and sustained, with little or no delay. Postponing safety and health training could prove to be costly.

Even before training is considered, safe practices, engineering controls, and ergonomic principles should be put in place to eliminate as many hazards as possible. Training can then be focused on the problem areas that remain. The programs that are undertaken should be continually evaluated and updated to ensure maximum employee protection as well as to keep current with industrial safety and health trends.

There is a strong need for training programs that not only give specific answers to safety and health concerns, but also stress constant safety and health awareness. If you can get employees to respond to the training, and supply them with the right tools, you will take a big step toward reducing the number of injuries and illnesses in the plant.

Employees in high-risk plants, where training would be an effective counter to injuries and illnesses, should receive more specialized training emphasis than those in low-risk plants where engineering controls have eliminated the hazards. However, basic safety and health training principles should always be stressed for all employees. Only when safety and health training becomes a constant reinforcement tool can companies reduce the number of work-related injuries and illnesses.

MAINTENANCE TRAINING

To help meet today's increasing demand for quality maintenance and the need for employees to work smarter, many companies have recognized the worth of maintenance training programs. Two of the most obvious benefits of maintenance training are:

1. *The reduction of unexpected downtime resulting from equipment failure.* When employees know and practice machine assembly, adjustment, and maintenance procedures, they help ensure equipment and system reliability while also extending the life of productive equipment.

2. *The accrual of substantial financial gains.* The payoff on money spent for training can be significant:

- Costly downtime of productive equipment is reduced.
- Operating equipment efficiently cuts energy costs.
- Electric utility rebates frequently result from optimum and timely use of electrical facilities.

One of the most effective and least costly answers to how to train maintenance employees is with programs put on by original equipment manufacturers. These companies are the best source of equipment and system knowledge. Product expertise and troubleshooting records in the database, trending, and failure analysis studies have furnished excellent resources from which manufacturers develop their training programs.

Original equipment manufacturers have an advantage over consultants in that they are capable of developing a training course for a specific machine without incurring additional costs. Consultants generate costs to ensure that training materials for a specific year, make, and model are accurate.

Ways to Train

You can conduct maintenance training in several ways, including class-room lectures, videos and films, and on-the-job sessions. The type or form of instruction depends on the characteristics of the trainees and the subject nature. Most craftspersons and technicians prefer to learn from example and practice rather than lecture. Thus, both show-and-tell and hands-on training methods are effective and well-received; yet they can be difficult to administer, especially in large classes. Also, when large, complex equipment is involved, the training can be tedious and time-consuming. It is for those reasons that the methods should be used only with very small groups. When possible, the training should be scheduled to coincide with a planned overhaul or redesign of the equipment at the work site.

The best type of training for large groups is with lectures given either at the plant or at the manufacturer's showroom. If the trainer is a manufacturer's representative or a technical salesperson, you can be assured that trainees will receive a professionally prepared presentation, usually supported with visual aids. The value of this type of training is enhanced when a comprehensive reference book is provided to each of the trainees for future reference.

Regardless of the training method, a program should cover a systematic description and explanation of the machine or equipment. Trainees should be thoroughly instructed on all of the components that are to be maintained: their operating principles, what each component does, how the machine is assembled, and what kinds of failure can occur. This training method, called a composite approach, identifies systems within the machine and explains how they work together as a unit. Since maintenance employees must be trained to find and correct the basic cause of a machine failure, the composite approach is important in troubleshooting.

Training Programs

If you decide to have the maintenance employees participate in a training program conducted by other than your own trainers, the first step is to study the qualifications and capabilities of various training sources to see if they can meet your needs. Here are the issues you should consider and evaluate:

- *The trainer's knowledge and ability.* He or she must be able to present the material in an interesting and skillful manner; one that gets and holds the attention of the trainees. While academic qualifications are of value and helpful, it is most important that the trainer understands what each trainee must know to identify and solve machine and equipment problems and to properly service and maintain the plant's facilities.

Instructors who have worked on installation projects and in customer service for large equipment manufacturers have the best and most in-depth experience. This experience has equipped them to answer wide-ranging questions and present examples of problems with which trainees are familiar.

■ *The training materials.* Handout material, manuals, and workbooks are critical to the success of a training program. They should be well-organized, appropriate, and easy to work with. In addition, such materials should be retained by the trainees for reference and review after they are back on the job. Copies should also be kept in the maintenance department's files.

■ *Trainee and program evaluations.* It's a good idea to incorporate a two-part written examination in the training program. The first part should be a pretest, given either before the training session or on the first day. It is used to help the trainer in adjusting the program to fit the level of trainee experience. The second part, or final exam, determines if the objectives of the program have been met.

After completing the program, the trainees should be asked to evaluate it. The evaluation enables the trainees to judge how the training benefitted them and the company. The questions in the evaluation form should be open-ended to bring forth answers that can be used to improve and update future programs.

■ *Trainer feedback.* If a trainer develops a well-constructed final exam, you will be able to determine if the training objectives were met. The exam will also reveal strengths and weaknesses within the trainee group. The information gained enables an experienced trainer to give you valuable advice. You should, therefore, request a trainer's summary report when you sign a contract for maintenance training.

■ *Follow-up sessions.* It's very worthwhile to schedule a follow-up session three or six months after a training program has been completed. Such a session serves not only as a review and a reinforcement aid, it allows trainees to share experiences since the original session. In addition, trainers can accomplish more in a shorter period of time after the trainees have applied the techniques and procedures that were previously taught.

COMPUTERIZED MAINTENANCE

More and more manufacturing companies are recognizing that their employees need to be trained in the use of the computer. Many jobs are being changed in the way they are performed and the computer is making inroads in almost every operation. There is no question today that plant employees, including those in the maintenance department, must learn to operate computers.

Use of the computer for controlling maintenance operations has greatly improved the effectiveness and efficiency of maintenance personnel in both line and staff positions. However, extensive and comprehensive training of all people involved with maintenance operations was required to achieve these advances.

But how should such training be conducted? Some companies have decided to use objective-based training methods because the principles of this type of training are appropriate and most training can be accomplished in a minimum of time. Objective-based training procedures are ideal for introducing people to the computer because training lessons can be written and administered that apply directly to particular job positions. When information and instruction is presented in this manner, the trainee is required to learn only those operations that come under his or her responsibility. Training thus can be accomplished quickly.

A common question in the plant is which employees should receive training in computerized maintenance. Every person in the company who is involved with maintenance operations or affected by them should receive the training. In an average industrial company, this would include all personnel in the engineering and maintenance departments from the managers to the craftspersons, including the staff people. Key line positions in the production department are also very much involved since today's maintenance management systems are based on their participation. In plants where the computer is being used to facilitate maintenance, supervisors and foremen of production operations request maintenance work through the computer rather than verbally in written orders given to maintenance personnel.

Planners and engineers are involved with computerized maintenance in several ways. To carry out their responsibilities, both groups must know how to make inquiries to the computer database on materials or equipment parts, such as the amount on hand in the storeroom. Planners and engineers need to know the characteristics of a machine or a machine component including its type, size, capacity, and cost. Storeroom material can be requisitioned as well as reserved for a future replacement or installation by putting that information into the database. This capability is especially useful in the performance of planned work.

Stores and material control employees must also be trained in computer operations. Materials and their control are vital to a maintenance system. For maintenance functions to be carried out promptly, efficiently, and at minimum cost, the computerized maintenance system must interface with the company's stores and material control systems. For example, terminals are used to initiate and speed up the withdrawal of parts or materials from the storeroom. When a craftsperson needs material or a machine part from the storeroom, he or she makes the request on a computer terminal. The request is printed in the storeroom, and the storekeeper has the material or part ready for the craftsman when he or she arrives. It follows that stores and material control people must be trained to add information to the database as well as adjust inventories when they make additions or withdrawals.

Task Analysis

The techniques used in objective-based training require that a task analysis be made of each job to ensure that all elements of the job are covered. A task analysis is a detailed list in logical order of all actions required to complete a job. The analysis is similar to a time study made by an industrial engineer in that every single job step, no matter how small, is detailed in writing, except that the length of time to complete each step is not required.

Instructional objectives are then designed for each element. Once these objectives are set, learning modules or lessons can be written for each of the tasks required in the performance of a job.

Learning Modules

A module states what the trainee must be able to do after instruction and training. This is identified as the trainee's objective. The module also lists how the instructor trains and teaches the trainee. This is identified as the instructional procedure. See Exhibit 11-1 for an example of a module designed for training on the subject of priorities.

The training program is arranged so that the material is presented in such a manner that a trainee accomplishes the objective of each module before proceeding to the next module. Objective-based training using a learning module requires the instructor to provide the training in steps.

The first step is to prepare the trainee to receive information and instruction by putting him or her at ease. At the same time, the instructor also finds out what the trainee already knows about the subject so that he or she can create interest in the learning objective.

In the second step, the instructor presents the instructional materials. Here, he or she explains or demonstrates the operation to be learned. The instructor makes sure to emphasize the key points.

Exhibit 11-1. Learning module used in objective-based training.

Module No.: ____18____

Date: __April 10, 1996__

Program Title: *Computerized Maintenance*	Subject: *Priorities*
Trainee's Objectives:	*Instructional Procedures:*
Trainee will be able to explain the subject of priority and why maintenance jobs must be given a priority rating.	Instructor will:
	A. Introduce the subject of priorities.
	B. Prompt for questions during the training.
Given a list of maintenance jobs, trainee will be able to classify them as deserving either high or low priority.	C. Explain that the person requesting the work to be done sets the priority for the job.
Given a work order, trainee will be able to show the instructor its priority.	D. Define and explain each of the several priority classifications.
	E. Have the trainee perform the objective.

Training Aids and Tools:

1. Descriptive material on the priority classifications that have been adopted for defining the urgency of maintenance work.
2. A list of common maintenance jobs.
3. A few work orders.

In step three, the trainee is encouraged to get involved. The instructor also provides the necessary guidance to ensure that the trainee will be able to explain or perform according to the objective.

In step four, the instructor asks the trainee to perform the objective.

Since the module is a major aid in training, it pays to know how to write one. You begin with stating the trainee's objective. The objective is a description of what a trainee should be able to do at the conclusion of the instruction or training. All objectives must include a performance. However, conditions and criteria are sometimes added to help clarify the objective. By adding the conditions and the criteria to the performance, the objective says *what, where,* and *how well* the trainee must perform. The performance called for in the objective statement should match as closely as possible the performance required on the job.

Next, write the instructional procedures which are the means for achieving instructional objectives. They are the methods, techniques, and strategies used by instructors to teach trainees to perform the objectives. Some instructional methods may be more effective than others, depending on the learning objective and other circumstances. Three considerations should be taken into account: (1) the instructional objective; (2) the trainee's needs; and (3) the training environment. Instructional procedures are always selected after instructional objectives have been determined.

To complete the module, list the training aids and tools that the instructor will use in the presentation of that lesson. These consist of forms, specifications, manuals, lists, and other types of descriptive literature. They include the computer hardware and software.

The more training aids provided, the better. Such aids make the trainer's job easier and they also help the trainee to understand the subject being taught. A course on computerized maintenance may contain only a few or many modules, depending on the involvement of the person being trained and the number of tasks performed by that person. A craftsperson, for instance, will have many more tasks involving the computer and its use than will a storeroom employee.

It's customary to include with the modules a check-off sheet to enable trainers to keep a record of who has received what training. This sheet is especially useful if the training is intermittent because of trainees being unable to attend a class. The records are of value also when the company sees that employees should be retrained or updated.

Training on computerized maintenance should not be carried out on a rush basis. Employees who are not familiar with computers tend to be nervous and hesitant. Many are afraid that they will not be able to learn the system. Time and understanding are vital parts of the objective-based training program.

TRAINING ON FEDERAL ENVIRONMENTAL LAWS

Under the Clean Water Act, the Environmental Protection Agency (EPA) has developed a set of regulations known as the Spill Prevention, Control and Countermeasures (SPCC) regulations. (See 40 C.F.R., Part 112.) The SPCC regulations cover the development and implementation of a detailed written plan on spill prevention procedures, methods, and equipment requirements. The plan must also contain a complete discussion of the issues covered by the regulations.

In the section covering SPCC training requirements, 40 C.F.R., Part 112.7(e)(10), the owner or operator of a facility is made responsible for properly instructing employees about applicable pollution control laws and regulations, as well as the operation and maintenance of equipment to prevent the discharge of oil. The regulations require that employees be briefed on spill prevention at intervals frequent enough to ensure an adequate understanding of the elements of the facility's SPCC plan.[11] These briefings should focus on and describe known spill cases, areas where implementation of the plan needs improvement, and recently developed precautionary measures.

One of the best ways to train employees on spill prevention and control is to focus on only one part of the SPCC plan at a time. For instance, if you want to cover railcar loading/unloading operations at your plant, you concentrate on the procedures and agreements you have put into your plan to prevent releases and spills with those operations. You instruct and teach employees what to do if a spill occurs. You also point out and discuss the steps that are taken to reduce the likelihood of a spill.

Employees should be told how to notify others of the spill and get help. They are also taken to the loading/unloading area to be shown the following: the equipment available for controlling and cleaning up a spill, and where released material can be expected to flow.

Plant managers need to be sure that employees are trained as soon as possible after they are hired. Further, the employee training should be documented. This can be done by use of an affidavit that is given to the employees after completing a training session. The affidavit should state that a particular individual received training on the SPCC plan on the date the training session was held.

Hazardous Waste Regulation

The Resource Conservation and Recovery Act (RCRA) governs the "cradle-to-grave" management of hazardous waste generated at a facility. Before you decide what training requirements apply to your plant, you must determine the quantity of hazardous waste generated from all your waste streams. This is necessary because the RCRA regulations that apply to your plant are dependent on the total quantity of waste generated.

Both small-quantity and large-quantity generators must comply with the training requirements set forth in 40 C.F.R., Part 265.16. See also 40 C.F.R., Part 262.34(a)(4). Within six months after the date of their employment, employees must complete training relevant to the positions in which they are employed. At a minimum, the training program must be designed to ensure that plant employees are capable of responding effectively to emergencies.

The training should cover emergency equipment and systems including:

1. Procedures for using, inspecting, repairing, and replacing plant emergency and monitoring equipment
2. Automatic waste feed cutoff systems
3. Communications or alarm systems
4. Response to fires or explosions
5. Response to groundwater contamination incidents
6. Shutdown of operations

Once they are trained, plant personnel should take part in an annual review of the initial training. The regulations also mandate that records documenting that the training has been given to the employees be maintained by the plant.

While the above programs make up the major training provisions applicable to most plants, there are, however, training requirements specified for various other environmental regulations. Although not all environmental programs require training, employees should be familiar with the laws and regulations that apply to the plant. Violation of environmental statutes and regulations can lead to significant civil and criminal penalties to the company and its employees as well.

TRAINING LIFT TRUCK OPERATORS

Since accidents involving powered industrial trucks are both numerous and severe, you must ensure that operators of lift trucks in the plant receive proper and adequate training before they are permitted to drive. Among other purposes, training is intended to:

1. Develop safe operating habits and reduce the risk of injury to pedestrians as well as themselves.

2. Clarify the differences in handling between a lift truck and a car. Point out characteristics and features of lift trucks.
3. Explain the consequences of taking certain kinds of chances.
4. Instruct on procedures for transporting loads.

Regardless of how much experience a potential lift truck operator has, all new drivers should go through an initial training course, followed by a refresher course every two years. Federal law requires you to train your lift truck operators, yet the law, which OSHA enforces, doesn't tell you how to do so. Here are the three main sources of lift truck operator training courses:

1. All of the major manufacturers of industrial trucks offer operator training courses. The courses are designed to be taught by one of your own employees who will act as the trainer, with the training materials supplied by the manufacturer's distributor. Large distributors may be able to supply a qualified trainer if you prefer to go that route.

2. Private training companies also sell courses that are meant to be taught by one of your employees. But with these there are more variations on the training arrangement. Some companies may not be able to provide an onsite trainer while others will only provide an onsite training program including a trainer.

3. Large companies that operate big lift truck fleets are another source of lift truck operator training courses. Coors Brewing, Dupont, and Kodak are three good examples of companies that have created programs tailored to their specific needs and trucks.

Program Content

Although most lift truck operator training courses are comprehensive in their coverage, before contracting for one, you should confirm that the training that operators receive includes:

- Inspecting the truck prior to use
- Procedure when truck defects are found
- Refueling and recharging operations
- Working in hazardous environments or with hazardous materials
- Precautions when leaving a truck unattended
- Traveling and cornering speeds
- Moving loads up and down ramps
- General truck loading practices
- How to load and unload railroad cars
- How to load and unload highway trucks and trailers

For maximum safety, trainees should also be instructed to keep safe distances, stop at blind corners, and not to pass at intersections.

TRAINING EMPLOYEES WHO WORK WITH ROBOTS

The key to developing an efficient and safe workplace where robots are used lies in learning what a robot is, how it works, how it is controlled, and how it interacts with its environment. Training employees who work with robots should start with identifying the hazards and assessing the risks. Three types of hazards exist:

1. An unexpected movement of the robot which results in being struck by it or the items carried by it. The hazard may be intensified by the robot's speed of operation.
2. Movements of the robot in relation to fixed objects such as posts or machines, or movements of auxiliary equipment such as pallets, transfer mechanisms, or work carriages which result in being trapped. If trapping points exist, they should be marked in an obvious way.
3. Exposure to electric shock, burns, radiation, arc flash, and toxic substances. These hazards develop both from the design, construction, and source of power for the robot, and the application or type of work performed.

Since the potential for creating hazards with robots always exists, training and instruction should focus on the safeguards: any guard, device, interlock, or procedure that protects employees from the hazards associated with robots. The application and type of robot determines which ones should be used. For example, safeguards for hydraulic robots differ from those for electric robots. The danger of fire and pressure leaks is greater with hydraulic robots.

All training programs should stress the following:

- Do not assume a robot is not going to move at any time.
- Do not assume a robot repeating a pattern will continue to do so.
- Maintain an awareness of the hazards of a moving robot system.

TRAINING ON SEXUAL HARASSMENT

More and more companies are recognizing the desirability of giving their employees training on sexual harassment. Liability continues to increase and penalties are meted out almost daily to companies, to employees guilty of harassment, and to employees who have wrongfully accused others. Many of these cases when resolved result in monetary losses, lost time on the job, and decreased morale.

Arranging an effective program on sexual harassment and adopting it involves many factors and requires that you treat all individuals equitably and with respect. Here are some suggestions on how to go about it.

Arranging the Program

Several steps are required to ensure that the program will be effective:

1. Match the training to your particular company by considering the following factors: type of work involved; gender distribution; allocation as to race, age, sexual orientation, and employment status; and existing knowledge about the personalities, habits, and values of the employees.

2. Approach the subject seriously and with a positive viewpoint. Employees should enjoy their work, the workplace, and the interaction with other employees. The training will be most effective if employees see it as an opportunity to learn about people by communicating with them in a productive work environment.

3. Ensure that adequate time is set apart for training. Group discussions, role-playing, and testing take time if they are to accomplish the objective and the trainees retain the information.

4. Select and prepare trainers appropriately and carefully. These people should be chosen for their knowledge of the current laws and your company's policies and procedures; they should also be rated on their instructional ability and their skill in serving as role models. Trainers should be alerted not to give their opinions when discussing cases because they may not have all the facts and information about a specific situation.

Adopting the Program

If handled correctly, sexual harassment training can not only reduce the possibility of company and individual liability, but can make the workplace a more pleasant place for all employees. This is why the procedures involved in implementing the training program are critical to its success. Here are the best ways to go about handling a training session:

▪ Start by creating a sense of mutual trust with the group—get the participants in a relaxed but serious frame of mind. Discourage any attempt to joke about the subject because if this feeling predominates, the effectiveness of the training can be impaired. Tell the group that the purpose of the program is not to eliminate workplace enjoyment, but to recognize that what is enjoyable for one employee may not be enjoyable for another. Point out the seriousness of the problem and communicate the company's policy, including giving a review of it.

■ Explain sexual harassment and what employees should know about it. While most employees are aware of what conditioning a job benefit on sexual favors means, many are unfamiliar with what constitutes a hostile environment—one that is intimidating and interferes with an employee's work performance. Tell the group that persons who are accused of sexual harassment may bring lawsuits against the company, against individuals involved in disciplinary actions, and against the accuser.

■ Discuss the importance of perception as opposed to intent, and the extent to which gender plays a role in whether or not specific conduct is seen as offensive. Emphasize that liability is determined by whether or not a reasonable person in the situation would be affected by the conduct, not by whether or not the accused intended to be offensive or even was aware that the conduct was offensive.

■ Talk about the needs of the group and get employees involved in how to handle a variety of hypothetical situations that cover the range of possible situations. Managers should be given information about how to handle specific problems that may arise. Nonsupervisory personnel may need guidance on the specific procedures available to effectively and assertively communicate a problem. Role-playing may be used to illustrate some situations.

After a training program has been presented, the participants should make anonymous evaluations of the program. Included should be comments on the program content and format along with suggestions for future programs. These can be useful to the company in planning the next training session.

Training on sexual harassment is most effective when it is periodically reinforced with other sessions. Additionally, management should see that information on sexual harassment is routed now and then to employees to serve as reminders.

ROADBLOCKS TO SUCCESSFUL TRAINING

Whether you, a supervisor, the company training department, or an outside organization is assigned to train employees, be aware there will be failures, misconceptions, and omissions that must be contended with if the training is to be successful. Among the many training mistakes that must be avoided are the following:

- Assuming that the trainer can teach employees how to do a job simply because he or she has the knowledge and skill to do it. Knowing all about the job doesn't guarantee the trainer will be effective.
- Failing to properly prepare for the training. An unorganized approach will create an image of inept management in the mind of the employee. Distraction and inhibition to learning occur when instruction is not given in a logical sequence.
- Permitting tension to exist. Putting the employee at ease is essential in job training. Clear thinking is a must during the learning process; tension inhibits learning.
- Not establishing definite training objectives. There's more to the job than just pushing the start button on a machine. Safety is more important than quality and quantity of output.
- Failing to provide a way to determine if objectives have been met. You must be able to ascertain if the employee can now perform the job safely and efficiently.
- Trying to do too much. Don't try to present too much information. Limit a training session to just one subject.
- Attempting to train too fast. Training too fast risks incomplete assimilation and misunderstanding.
- Believing that employees all learn the same way. Trainees learn at different rates for different reasons.
- Neglecting to follow up. You must get feedback from the trainee during and after instruction. Get it after instruction by having the trainee perform the job two or three times to demonstrate his or her understanding of it.

NOTES

1. Richard F. Chatfield-Taylor, "Employee Training Under the Major Federal Environmental Laws," *Engineer's Digest*, August 1995, pp. 13–15.
2. Clay Carr, *Smart Training* (New York: McGraw-Hill Book Company, 1992), pp. 37–38.
3. Ibid., p. 17.
4. Louis V. Imundo, *The Effective Supervisor's Handbook* (New York: American Management Association, 1980), pp. 65–66.
5. Lawrence Munson, *How to Conduct Training Seminars* (New York: McGraw-Hill Book Company, 1984), pp. 2, 5.

6. Marc A. Dorio, *Personnel Manager's Desk Book* (Englewood Cliffs, N.J.: Prentice Hall, Inc., 1989), pp. 138–139.
7. Excerpts from "What to Watch For in Training Videos," *Successful Supervisor,* August 14, 1995, p. 2.
8. Paul Hersey and Kenneth H. Blanchard, *Management of Organizational Behavior,* Fifth Edition (Englewood Cliffs, N.J.: Prentice Hall, Inc., 1988), pp. 164–165.
9. Reported in *Manufacturing Week,* April 6, 1987, p. 16.
10. Lawrence Munson, *How to Conduct Training Seminars* (New York: McGraw-Hill Book Company, 1984), pp. 31–33.
11. Robert Wenderlich and Ed Green, "The Importance of Maintenance Training," *Plant Services,* December, 1994, pp. 67–69.

12

The Maintenance Function

Today's industrial and manufacturing plants would be unable to operate, much less be profitable, without an effective maintenance program. And an absolute management commitment to carrying it out constantly, from the plant manager down to line supervisors, is essential. Companies must minimize machine and equipment failures if they are to be competitive and grow.

Yet in many plants, the maintenance function doesn't receive proper respect or get the attention it deserves. Management belief in some plants is that, since maintenance doesn't add value to its products, the less spent on it, the better. Because of this false and harmful thinking, nonprogressive plants have failed to adopt the requirements for successful maintenance.

ELEMENTS OF EFFECTIVE AND EFFICIENT MAINTENANCE

If your maintenance operation is committed to continuous improvement, you must endorse and conform to the principles of effective and efficient maintenance procedures. Here are generally accepted requirements for success:[1]

- *Priority*. Managers in successful companies see maintenance as a top priority operation, one that contributes to the bottom line. Priority areas for improvement are determined by an evaluation of the entire maintenance operation. Investments then will support the best maintenance practices.

- *Dedication and pride.* Tangible savings are realized and improvements occur when management is dedicated to perform maintenance. Dedicated leaders instill pride in maintenance through creating inspiration, enthusiasm, and cooperation within the company.

- *Professional viewpoint.* Progressive companies recognize the importance of maintenance. In these companies, every employee sees maintenance leaders as key assets to the success of the maintenance function. New technologies and advanced practices require a higher level of technical knowledge and skills. They are supplied by the maintenance function, which is a true profession.

- *Proficient maintenance personnel.* In order to keep pace with new technology, successful maintenance organizations require upgrading and retraining in the skill levels of their maintenance personnel. Managers achieve these upgrades through imposing higher standards in recruiting, and by adopting more effective craft training programs.

- *Adaptable and versatile craftspersons.* The development of more craftspersons with multicraft skills provides greater adaptability, versatility, and capability in the existing workforce. This achieves higher productivity and lower operating costs.

- *Planning and scheduling.* More coordination and better service to production are achieved with planning and scheduling. The production and maintenance departments must work together as supportive teams to reduce machine breakdowns, increase equipment effectiveness, and minimize overall maintenance costs.

- *Teamwork.* The strategy for efficient and cost-effective maintenance is based on a team approach that uses the knowledge, skills, and ideas of the entire maintenance group. In addition, cross-functional teams with representatives from production, engineering, and maintenance groups can address multidepartmental issues.

- *Pride in ownership.* Cost-effective maintenance requires machine and equipment operators to take on greater responsibilities for inspecting, cleaning, monitoring, lubricating, and making minor adjustments or repairs on their jobs. With this effort and participation, operators develop pride in ownership of their equipment.

- *Staff support.* In an ongoing organization, the engineering staff provides technical assistance on maintenance functions. Engineering personnel play a key support role in improving the effectiveness of existing equipment, and work closely with maintenance personnel in developing specifications for new equipment.

■ *Maintainability and reliability.* Equipment design focuses on maintainability and reliability, not primarily on performance. Thus, design for maintainability is the preferred course of action. That philosophy recognizes the cost of maintenance in the life-cycle cost of equipment. By applying the principles of maintainability and reliability at the design stage, life-cycle costs can be reduced.

■ *Standardization.* Designing machines and equipment with standardized units or dimensions makes for easy assembly and repair as well as flexible arrangement and use. This strategy is carried further by designing components for simple disassembly and assembly using the lowest skill levels possible.

■ *Uncertainty.* An efficient maintenance operation minimizes uncertainty. Preventive and predictive maintenance programs help maintenance managers anticipate problems in order to eliminate the uncertainty of breakdowns and high repair costs.

■ *Computerization.* A computerized maintenance management system (CMMS) makes maintenance operations more manageable. The CMMS covers the entire operation and furnishes the means to improve the overall quality of maintenance management. Large amounts of information associated with maintenance jobs are under computer control and available.

■ *Stores systems.* The maintenance storeroom is an integral part of a successful maintenance operation. Whether centralized or not, an effective storeroom system issues a catalog listing all maintenance supplies and includes a cross-reference of all storeroom items. The catalog serves as an ideal tool for identifying and locating items.

■ *Inventory control.* Management of maintenance inventory through use of a CMMS system ensures that the correct machine part is available at the right time without excessive inventory levels. Information from all available sources determines optimum stock levels and economical order quantities. A continuous review of stock levels eliminates excessive inventory and obsolete parts.

■ *Safety.* Management must create and support a working environment where safety is a top priority. Good housekeeping practices in maintenance foster safety awareness, thereby enabling the maintenance department to set an example for all other departments.

■ *Regulatory compliance.* Management must ensure that technical knowledge and experience are applied to environmental, health, and safety regulations. This means support and compliance with all state and federal regulations under OSHA, the EPA, the U.S. Department of Transportation, and the Americans with Disabilities Act.

■ *Performance.* Constant improvement of labor performance and utilization is inherent with successful maintenance. It is brought about by compliance with planned repair and preventive/predictive maintenance schedules, cost-effective labor practices, and managing maintenance as a business.

■ *Service.* Implementation of an effective planning and scheduling system is necessary for successful maintenance. When production and maintenance departments work closely to schedule repairs at the most convenient time, maintenance operations become more customer-oriented and focus on providing better service.

TYPES OF MAINTENANCE

Although there are a few traditional manufacturing plants that try to limit their maintenance practice to equipment failures and breakdowns, most of today's plants have progressed to better and more effective procedures. Successful plants have realized that "putting out fires" and adopting makeshift tactics are extremely costly. Besides, if you develop and implement other types of maintenance, you can avoid high costs. Here are the other types, along with a brief description of what each does:

1. *Preventive maintenance.* An effective preventive maintenance program anticipates the continuous wear and changes that equipment, machines, and systems undergo during operation. It calls for regular and appropriate action to minimize deterioration and breakdown. This involves periodic inspection and replacement of components.

2. *Predictive maintenance.* This practice foretells potential problems by sensing the operating characteristics of a machine or system. The procedure consists of monitoring operations, diagnosing undesirable trends, and pinpointing probable areas of failure.

3. *Proactive maintenance* responds to identified conditions that are known to cause failure. Emphasis is placed on changing adverse operating conditions before any symptoms actually occur. This makes it possible to extend the life of equipment, thus saving valuable time and money.

4. *Corrective maintenance.* By adjusting or calibrating a machine or system, corrective maintenance improves either its quality or performance. The need for corrective maintenance results from preventive or predictive maintenance or from statistical process control.

MAINTENANCE QUALITY

In recent years, more and more plants have used quality control strategies in carrying out the maintenance function. This has resulted in several worthwhile benefits to the plants. Through an effective quality control program, you can:

- Upgrade the maintenance function.
- Increase the efficiency of maintenance personnel.
- Serve the production department better.
- Reduce the costs of the maintenance department.

To operate efficiently and provide the service expected of it, a maintenance department must practice the principles of quality control. With higher standards of performance now expected of equipment and facilities plus more governmental regulation of design and operation, the quality of maintenance has had to improve.

Yet there is still a strong need for maintenance employees to do higher quality work as well as more of it. And there will always be a need for management to find ways to reduce and eliminate repetitive repairs. Controlling the quality of maintenance may be a big job, but it is not beyond the capability of plant personnel. The job should be approached in several ways because many factors must be considered. Here is how you and other managers should go about it:

- *Purchasing.* Controlling the quality of maintenance begins with purchasing. If the company buys top-grade material, the repairs made to equipment and facilities are more likely to also be first class. You can expect a paint job to look better and to hold up longer if you use good quality industrial paint. A wooden structure should last longer if your carpenters have high-grade lumber to work with.

The same logic applies to the tools you provide employees. A maintenance employee who has only makeshift tools won't be able to do a high-quality repair job, nor will he or she take pride in the work done. Special tools, such as ergonomically designed ones, which you purchase or rent for the department, will enable employees to handle tough jobs more safely and efficiently, and their workmanship will also be better.

- *Work performance.* One of the ways to determine the quality of maintenance in the plant is to analyze the performance of the maintenance employees. While this is logically your responsibility, it may be difficult for employees to be efficient and cost-effective when they are occupied principally with breakdown work because there is little if any time for planning. Since much of this work consists of troubleshooting, the skill of the craftsperson is critical. But the fact that breakdown work must be performed quickly should not be an excuse for you to accept poor quality workmanship. You can still control the quality of the work with close supervision.

■ *Variances of quality.* Perhaps the most crucial practice from a quality viewpoint is performance of maintenance work in an irresponsible and inept manner. The employee who damages equipment and machines when making repairs cannot be tolerated. Nor can the craftsperson who makes improper adjustments, fails to replace covers, caps, bolts, and nuts, and does work that results in stripped threads on connections. Other variances of quality workmanship concern how machines and work areas are left after the maintenance work is performed. Spills should be cleaned up, and worn-out parts as well as waste material should be properly disposed of.

Failure to do a thorough and complete job on an inspection or repair assignment is another example of poor-quality maintenance. If a work order calls for several operations to be performed such as determining motor load, testing for vibration, and making drive adjustments, then the work should not be considered complete or acceptable until all of these operations are handled.

You can control the quality of maintenance only if you set standards of performance and make employees aware of them. Establishing standards is especially appropriate when formulating a plant's preventive maintenance program. Standard procedures must be followed with inspections, oiling and lubrication, painting, winterizing, putting machines and equipment in standby condition, and other preventive procedures.

TOTAL PRODUCTIVE MAINTENANCE

Total productive maintenance (TPM) is not solely a type of maintenance nor is it production employees performing equipment maintenance. TPM is a total plant work culture that focuses on improving equipment maintenance. It's also a dynamic, profit-oriented approach to equipment management. It combines the best features of preventive and predictive maintenance with management strategies that increase participation and employee skills. An excellent definition of TPM is that of Robert Williamson, an independent consultant specializing in "Strategic Work Systems" for manufacturing.[2] He defines it as follows: "Changing the corporate culture to form a partnership with engineering, maintenance, and production focused on improving equipment effectiveness, improving quality, and reducing waste while continually refining teamwork among labor, management, and individual work groups."

Yet TPM is not entirely new. It includes many of the good manufacturing and maintenance practices already being used in many plants. Nor is TPM a single improvement program but rather a goal, that of improving equipment effectiveness. Process industries have a particularly urgent need for collaborative equipment management systems like TPM that can absolutely guarantee safe, stable operation. Process industry plants must operate continuously for long periods to be cost-effective. Accidents and breakdowns involving even one piece of equipment can shut down an entire plant and endanger life and the environment. In the past decade, many process industries in Japan and the United States have found it profitable to build TPM programs based on their existing preventive maintenance and quality improvement programs.

Perhaps the best way to accelerate TPM efforts in a plant is to add and augment the practices and procedures that are already in place. For success, the elements of TPM must coordinate with the following programs: maintenance and technology, safety, human resources, and high-performance work. Solidification of the elements is achieved through:

- Production, engineering, and maintenance working together to improve equipment effectiveness
- Complete management commitment to the objective of improving equipment effectiveness
- Integration of all related activities currently underway to result in the improvement
- Changing the corporate culture to maximize the effectiveness of production systems
- Pursuing the goals of zero accidents, zero defects, and zero equipment downtime

Benefits

Total productive maintenance may be considered the manufacturing ultimatum of the '90s if you add up its many benefits. To list them, it:

- Empowers operators to "own" their equipment.
- Helps teams develop simplified preventive maintenance standards and meet schedules.
- Frees up skilled employees to eliminate bottlenecks that hamper on-time delivery and product quality.
- Reduces the costs that maintenance adds to total manufacturing costs.

- Increases uptime of machines and equipment.
- Ensures less scrap and rework.
- Promotes cooperation of production, engineering, and maintenance in satisfying customers.
- Raises enthusiasm of employees for their work.
- Encourages craftspersons to use their skills to improve existing equipment and help design new machinery.

MAINTENANCE INFORMATION SYSTEMS

One of the reasons why a maintenance information system (MIS) is needed in plants is to supply data and information, which can be used to improve maintenance productivity. Typically, a system has at least two elements: (1) the information system itself, which covers the identification, control, and measurement of maintenance work; and (2) the work order subsystem, which feeds data into the information system for use in making decisions.

While developing a MIS to meet the needs of your plant may take considerable time and effort, a more important job is to successfully implement the system. When maintenance personnel are not properly trained to use it, an adequate system often fails to deliver. Here are the steps you should take to ensure that your system performs satisfactorily:[3]

1. Ensure the soundness of the maintenance management program. Most unsuccessful programs are due to inadequate program definition and lack of training. Because the MIS is the communications network of a maintenance program, the program must be properly defined before the network is selected or developed.

2. Confirm that key maintenance personnel are aware of their responsibilities in managing maintenance to make use of the information. An MIS has three objectives: identify required work, control the work, and measure the success of the work performed.

3. Load all files and modules, and ensure that a sensible numbering scheme is used for the equipment. Check that hardware and networking arrangements are in order.

4. Verify that historical data are complete, accurate, and up-to-date. The work order system provides data for the MIS. However, if the data are incomplete or incorrect, little worthwhile information will be created, fewer correct decisions will be made, and less action will be taken.

5. Assign skilled and/or experienced individuals to train employees on use of the MIS. The amount of training required depends on the knowl-

edge and background of the employees. The training of technicians who use a computer daily may require only a week. However, if the supervisor and the crew are unfamiliar with computers, training them may take several weeks.

6. Develop an implementation schedule with specific performance-related objectives. All employees must be trained. Because the MIS is the official communications system for the maintenance department, all personnel must be able to use it competently.

7. Follow up on MIS use and what is being accomplished. Realize that creating information is only the basic step in making the MIS pay off. The data and information must reach the proper employees who, in turn, must make decisions and take appropriate action. For example, if more preventive maintenance work is being done, confirm that fewer major breakdowns are occurring. If more work is being planned, see if worker productivity is increasing. If productivity improves, find out if fewer overtime hours are being worked.

KEY MAINTENANCE PERSONNEL

Several individuals play unique roles in today's maintenance organization. Technological advancements, computer systems, employee empowerment, and data and information proliferation have all contributed to the changing duties and responsibilities of these maintenance personnel. Here are descriptions of the duties and responsibilities of the planner, the supervisor, and the engineer:

▪ The primary function of a maintenance planner is to handle all the administrative duties required in the preparation of major repair jobs so that they can be carried out more effectively and efficiently. This function consists of checking out the work site, determining job details and materials needed, estimating labor requirements, confirming availability of tools, and coordinating equipment shutdown. Effective planners benefit the company because planned major maintenance jobs are completed with less labor and less productive equipment downtime.

There is generally a short period of time between the initial planning and the scheduling of maintenance jobs. During this period, the planner sets the best tentative timing of the shutdown of the equipment with the production scheduler. He or she then coordinates arrival of materials, equipment, tools, and other items to coincide with the shutdown. In some plants, a schedule meeting is arranged and attended by maintenance and production supervisors to discuss next week's maintenance jobs. With the concurrence of production personnel of the best timing for the various shutdowns, the planner allocates labor to approved jobs by priority, obtains approval of the schedule for execution of the work, and publishes the schedule.

Although small maintenance departments may need only a single planner, managers of plants that do not agree on the importance of the planner's job try to combine it with a supervisor's job. This practice is not recommended because the two jobs are different. A small maintenance department should use the planner to help the larger number of supervisors. With such an arrangement, the planner reports to the manager of the department and provides direct support to the supervisors as needed to help them carry out major jobs.

The number of planners needed in a plant should be based on the amount of planned work the maintenance department handles. Planning and scheduling 70 to 80 percent of the total work orders ensures that maintenance operations are controlled. In most industrial plants, there should be one planner for about every fifteen to twenty employees who maintain productive equipment. If each supervisor has a crew of ten to twelve persons, about eight crew members should do planned and scheduled work.

However, shop work (machining, fabricating, rebuilding, and refurbishing) is handled differently. In a shop environment, you can supervise more persons because work is concentrated in a smaller area. Although the managerial job may be more detailed, it is somewhat easier. Shop supervisors can manage more workers; eighteen to twenty is not an unusual number. Shops lend themselves more readily to the use of standards, and more work (85 to 90 percent) should be planned and scheduled. Operating under these conditions, a shop planner might support about thirty maintenance personnel, managed by two supervisors.

- No role in plants has changed more dramatically in recent years than that of the maintenance supervisor.[4] Instead of being based on the authority of supervisors, today's information-based organizations are flat in structure, built on the flow of information, and based on the responsible behavior of employees. This arrangement allows the span of control (how many employees a supervisor can control) to be replaced with span of communication (the number of employees reporting to a supervisor who can obtain their own information). Automation, technological advances, and management information systems also have eliminated much of the need for the supervisor's experience. The new role of the maintenance supervisor is to:

1. Represent management and safeguard company assets.
2. Assume responsibility for implementing company strategy.
3. Develop and appraise employees.

4. Participate in establishing performance goals.
5. Coach for performance.
6. Take responsibility for the health and safety of the workplace.
7. Make business decisions based on data.

Instead of monitoring employees and reacting to what is viewed as poor behavior, maintenance supervisors analyze data and talk to employees about specific instances of poor performance.

Because the use of knowledge and information has replaced the need for acquiring skill and experience, tasks are converted to processes. A process can be documented, learned, and measured for performance. The supervisor's past skill at performing a task is less important than his or her ability to document, communicate, and measure a process.

▪ The maintenance engineer advises and assists line maintenance personnel in establishing and perpetuating effective maintenance and planning and control procedures. He or she is involved not only in what maintenance is performed—when and how—but in the results as well. The duties and responsibilities of a maintenance engineer include:

1. Designing, assisting with the installation of, and modifying, as necessary, preventive and predictive maintenance programs
2. Providing a technical consulting service and coordinating the distribution of information developed on maintenance programs
3. Advising on engineering modifications that will improve the maintainability of equipment and facilities
4. Promoting the standardization of such widely used items as pumps, valves, motors, and similar industrial equipment
5. Assisting all maintenance personnel in analyzing plant maintenance operations or implementing planned maintenance programs
6. Monitoring ongoing work and projects to ensure that sound practices are followed
7. Maintaining control of plant equipment identification systems used to prepare management information reports, equipment histories, and maintenance material usage reports
8. Collecting and reporting comparative performance data to management
9. Monitoring the lubrication program to ensure proper lubrication, use of oil sampling, and proper replenishment

MULTISKILL MAINTENANCE

As today's plant maintenance departments try to improve their efficiency and cut costs, managers are closely examining the job roles and capabilities of their maintenance employees. Regardless of whether they are called craftspersons or technicians, maintenance employees of the future will have a variety of skills and abilities much different from the traditional skilled trades of the 1970s and '80s. Advances in technology have brought about significant changes in the skills requirement of maintenance employees as well as in the manner in which they perform their work. The trend today is to multiskilled maintenance employees.

Multiskill maintenance is defined as a blending of trade skills and duties in ways that are logical, and result in efficient and effective "whole job" completion.[5] Whole job completion means doing all (or most) of the tasks required to complete a routine job assignment. The reward and satisfaction of actually starting and completing a job is highly motivating to most craftspersons.

Benefits

Maintenance departments have much to gain with this practice when you consider the following benefits:

- Lower equipment downtime (both scheduled and unscheduled)
- Improved equipment performance (responsibility for workmanship is not divided)
- Reduced idle and waiting time of craftspersons
- More preventive maintenance routines completed quicker
- Reduced overtime work

Challenges and Barriers

Converting to multiskill maintenance may present a challenge to management in some plants, and barriers may slow the effort to implement it and minimize the overall results of the conversion. Whether these roadblocks are obstructive and/or cause unrest depends on the existing management and labor structure. The challenges and barriers of multiskill maintenance include:

- Failure to connect multiskill maintenance to plant performance improvements.
- Existence of multiple unions for skilled trades. Working with one union to blend skills is much easier.
- Middle and lower management not understanding the benefits and strategies for multiskill management.
- Maintenance planning and scheduling not realigning from craft/trade focus to support multiskill job assignments.

- Lack of formal training and qualification processes to ensure safe job performance.
- Adversarial relationships among all parties involved.
- No link to new or modified reward/compensation systems.

Commitments and Justification

Ensuring that the maintenance workforce understands and accepts multiskill maintenance is an educational procedure. You must first spell out what will be accomplished by the multiskill effort, and then show how the concept improves efficiency and makes the company more competitive. The commitments and justification for instituting a multiskill system include:

- There will be no layoffs or pay cuts.
- The primary skill or trade has a place in a multiskill system.
- Multiskill is not a jack-of-all-trades concept.
- Broadening of the primary trade or skill area is stressed.
- Most (if not all) maintenance craftspersons are multiskilled at home; why not on the job?
- Today's technological equipment and systems require a multiskill approach.

RELIABILITY ASSURANCE

The change from craft-based maintenance to a flexible, multiskill handling of maintenance is often a result of new technology and integrated systems. Related forces such as competition, customer expectations, and productivity improvement provoke the shift from a maintenance mindset to reliability assurance.[6]

In the future, there will be more and more people working together in cross-functional groups, applying their job skills with a common objective. That objective is to make machines, equipment, and systems reliable, efficient, and effective, to consistently produce quality products with no breakdowns. The reliability assurance roles envisioned for the future include the following:

- Operating technicians (formerly operators) trained and qualified to perform routine inspections, adjustments, lubrication, and repairs as well as operate the machines and equipment
- Reliability technicians (formerly maintenance) trained and qualified to perform fundamental operating tasks as well as planned and preventive maintenance, reliability, and equipment improvement tasks

- Engineers who work directly with operating technicians, reliability technicians, and process and quality leaders to improve equipment performance and develop next generation equipment
- Process and quality leaders who work directly with engineers, operating and reliability technicians, and customers to improve process and product quality.

PLANNING AND SCHEDULING MAINTENANCE

Although closely related, planning and scheduling maintenance work are two separate functions. Planning is the process of analyzing each job to:

1. Study the job as to its nature and what results are desired.
2. Specify the logical sequence of the work and estimate labor requirements for each sequential step.
3. List the material, tools, and equipment required to do the job.
4. Estimate the total cost to achieve the required results.

Scheduling is the efficient allocation of labor and equipment to jobs based on operational requirements as indicated by the priority system. It also includes the delivery of materials, tools, and equipment to the job site. While planning answers the questions "who," "what," "where," and "how" to do the job at the least overall cost, scheduling establishes "when" the job will be done to meet the requirements for all customers of maintenance services.

The basic objectives of a planned maintenance program are:

1. To attain maximum effectiveness in minimizing equipment downtime and in promoting peak equipment performance
2. To attain maximum control, coordination, and efficiency with respect to the internal operation of the Maintenance Department
3. To attain minimum maintenance cost consistent with maximum quality performance

The purpose of planning and scheduling is to ensure that the maintenance department is efficient and effective. Efficiency is defined as the optimum utilization of all resources (labor, material, tools, and equipment) to keep delays and nonproductive activities to a minimum. Effectiveness is the use of resources at their levels of proficiency to anticipate and correct problems and malfunctions before they require major repairs.

An efficient and effective maintenance organization can take on additional workload of maintenance activities without increasing labor. Similarly, a constant workload can be accomplished with fewer craftspersons.

Proper planning and scheduling enables craftspersons and first-line managers to concentrate on their responsibilities. For craftspersons, this means longer sustained time at the job site without interruption, because all predeterminable work requirements are supplied before the job is scheduled. For first-line managers, this means more time for supervising and for on-the-job training. Planning and scheduling, when properly done, will ensure that equipment receives required attention at the pre-scribed intervals. Increased maintenance service is reflected in greater equipment reliability, which, in turn, reduces overall equipment costs.

Requirements for Control

There are five basic requirements of planning and scheduling to facilitate control of the maintenance function:

1. A formal procedure for defining, approving, and authorizing maintenance work to be done. The procedure should be spelled out in a manual so both maintenance personnel and the receivers of maintenance service will know how the other is to operate re-garding maintenance work.
2. A work-order system that clearly communicates the need for work to be done so jobs are completed as requested. This includes a work-order form with sufficient spaces to identify the job and sup-ply control information such as work-order and cost accounting numbers.
3. A priority system that classifies the job as to urgency and need date.
4. A scheduling system that states when the job is to be done.
5. A control and follow-up procedure to determine whether or not the planning and scheduling process is reducing maintenance costs.

Computerized Planning and Scheduling

While a formal approach to planning and scheduling can be carried out manually, a computer system enables you to do the job more quickly, eas-ily, and accurately. A maintenance planner, familiar with the database, should have no problem in operating the computer if the system also has an up-to-date maintenance control manual.

Computerized maintenance management systems supporting planning and scheduling modules usually contain all the tools needed by a planner. A maintenance stores catalog inquiry screen gives the planner descriptive keywords, stock categories and item numbers, and manufacturer part numbers. An equipment parts catalog lists recommended spare parts for a given equipment item, equipment numbers, and serial numbers.

Since maintenance jobs often are repeated, a compilation of repair procedures and job plans can be searched and copied; documented job plans can sometimes be used in conjunction with other jobs. Additionally, the job procedure can be reviewed with the intention of eliminating or reducing downtime.

A planner can also access equipment repair history and examine completed work orders. A study should include retrieval of orders by a range of completion dates for a given equipment number, serial number, equipment type, work type, or area of the plant.

PRIORITIZING MAINTENANCE WORK

The primary reason for establishing a priority system on maintenance work is to enhance the scheduling of maintenance jobs. Therefore, the system selected should promote the scheduling of every work request so that use of all resources and equipment reliability is maximized.

Establishing priorities should involve all the plant departments concerned with the maintenance activity. When production and maintenance have equal authority for setting a priority, the chances for success improve greatly. However, the more involved that production becomes with the maintenance function, the better the overall plant operations become.

A priority system should be practical to apply and easy to use. Within these parameters it should then be clearly defined. Once defined, it must be approved in writing by both production and maintenance, and also by the plant manager. Before establishing priorities, a distinction must be made between classification and prioritization of work.

Classification is the categorizing of work requests with respect to work type. In most plants, work requests fall within four categories: safety, repair, preventive and predictive maintenance, and modifications. A work order involving any of these classifications can then be given a priority using the following criteria:

- *Priority 1* (emergency) work must be done as quickly as possible to prevent an accident or injury to employees, or an immediate loss of needed production. Overtime is authorized.
- *Priority 2* (urgent) work must be done to prevent disruption of pro-

duction schedules, a hazard to employees, or damage to operating equipment.

- *Priority 3* (essential) work must be done to prevent potential loss of plant equipment or production delays.
- *Priority 4* (routine) work includes other approved projects to be scheduled as backlog permits.
- *Priority 5* (shutdown) comprises modifications, turnarounds, and major repair work that is planned to be done during a scheduled shutdown.

Note that safety is not a priority, but a class of work. Many safety-related work orders fall in Priorities 2, 3, and 4. The priority system prevents a work order from being changed to "safety" to get it handled faster.

It's the responsibility of the maintenance planner to see that low priority work requests are carried out within a reasonable length of time. With patience and good communication, the priority system described above will work well in most environments.

WORK ORDERS

The work order is the basic instrument of a plant maintenance system. Job origination, identification, and authorization materialize with work orders. You make job assignments with work orders, and you get information on job costs, equipment history, and worker performance from the completed work order. Maintenance work orders are of two types:

1. Those suited for planning involve work that requires scheduled equipment downtime. Such orders must represent enough expenditure of manhours or dollars to justify estimating and scheduling the job. Another requirement of a planned work order is that the lead time must be sufficient to permit the time it takes to process an order.
2. Those not suited for planning involve jobs that are of such high priority that work must begin too soon for planning to be effective, or those that are of short duration and do not require scheduling of equipment downtime. Unplanned work orders are often referred to as verbal work orders, or as breakdown work orders.

An efficient system uses the computer to issue work orders to the maintenance employees, a work order being required and created for each maintenance job. Whenever a craftsperson starts or completes a job, the order is updated in the computer database. This enables you and others to make inquiries through the computer to get information.

Work order processing captures the very information needed to form a company maintenance strategy. The information can streamline operations, reduce labor costs, reduce inventory costs, and improve relations with the production department. Work orders also form an information database to show compliance with governmental agencies.

The work order system provides a way to report activity on a piece of equipment: the who, what, when, where, and why of work performed. It should be flexible enough so the maintenance staff can enter information easily. Thus, most work order forms furnish a space that identifies the equipment that needs maintenance, and a text area for describing the perceived problem. There is also space for other information such as accounting codes, locations, and approvals.

A good system enables you to plan and schedule any type of resource, whether it's craftspersons, contractors, rented equipment, materials, or tools. You want to capture costs so you can make cost-benefit analyses of using contractors vs. company labor; rented equipment vs. purchasing your own; and other procedures where options are available to you.

More advanced systems allow you to reserve parts and material needed for a job or project, whether in stock or on order. A delivery code and date can be entered so the material goes directly to the job site when needed. Your craftspersons can then spend more time working on equipment and less time traveling to the shop or storeroom. It's also less expensive to pay warehouse or storeroom employees to move parts than to pay craftspersons to do it.

Work orders are the means for minimizing inventory of material and cutting purchasing costs. Only through properly captured work history can slow-moving parts, obsolete parts, or critical materials be identified. This information enables you to forecast usage, take advantage of vendor price breaks, and establish verifiable budgets.

Computer Analyzation

Work orders stored in the computer can be analyzed using a software system programmed specifically for that purpose. One such package that has found a lot of use is called the Statistical Analysis System (SAS). In order to use SAS, you must know what information is available in the database. Also, when requesting information, you must be very specific and inclusive to avoid receiving a large amount of data, much of which may not be of value to you.

Requesting a report on equipment failure, for example, requires that you make the following inquiry: the time frame (beginning and ending date and time) of the activity you want analyzed, the equipment number, and the type of failure you want to analyze. With information on the type and number of failures occurring with the plant's cooling water pumps, for example, you can decide which type should be covered in a training program. If, for instance, you learn that impellor failures are frequently occurring, you may be able to remedy this by giving maintenance employees appropriate instructions.

The type of reports that you can generate by the computer using SAS software is almost endless. You can obtain reports that give such information as:

- The average time it takes for a craftsperson to begin repairs on a machine after it breaks down
- The average length of time it takes to fix a particular failure
- Which machines require the most repair labor or parts
- Which machines are the most costly to repair
- Which repair items have been withdrawn most frequently from stores
- What repair material is costing the company the most money

In addition to receiving such information, you can also request data and information on the computerized procedures of purchasing, receiving, shipping, and stores operations. Thus, you can have access to much information to help you in reaching your objectives of lower maintenance costs and better performance of employees.

CHARGING OF MAINTENANCE COSTS

Since the maintenance department is a service department, all of its expenses should be charged out to the plant departments that use its services. The costs of operating the shop itself are overhead costs that are included in the charges to the departments. Work order forms are the most convenient means for distributing maintenance costs. The originator of a work order must include the operating account expense number or the capital appropriation number to which the cost of the work is to be charged. When the job is completed, the total costs of labor and materials can be entered on the work order, which is forwarded to the cost department for posting to the proper accounts and put into the database.

Individual time records have a dual purpose: They record the amount of a craftsperson's time applied to each of the jobs worked on, and thereby provide a way of costing out all of the person's time. They are also used to compare the time expended on a particular job with established standards or previous executions of the same job.

Although there are several ways of keeping individual time records, one of the most common is to print a form on the back of the work order. Each craftsperson who works on the job enters his or her name or clock number, the time spent on the job, and any materials used. A maintenance department clerk or someone in the accounting department can total the hours listed to be sure each person's time is fully accounted for.

Another way is to have each craftsperson fill out a separate card for each day's work, showing the time spent on each job. Maintenance supervision collects these cards at the end of each day, checks to see that each person's time is fully accounted for, and forwards them to the cost department for posting to the appropriate account numbers and for entering them into the database.

Maintenance Budgeting

There is usually considerable pressure on maintenance managers to improve their plant's budget performance. However, traditional budgeting methods are not effective in the maintenance function because plant maintenance activities are a series of unrelated events. Under such conditions—having each expenditure or item justified as to need or cost—a zero-base approach to budgeting works best.[7]

A zero-based budget breaks overall demand for maintenance services into constituents; that is, assets or areas. Each asset must be studied to determine its requirement for maintenance. All maintenance activity can then be traced back to the following disciplines' need for hours and materials:

- *Preventive maintenance.*
- *Corrective maintenance,* also called scheduled repairs or planned maintenance.
- *User maintenance,* including breakdowns and routine service requests.
- *Seasonal maintenance,* including the entire grounds maintenance.
- *Replacement, rehabilitation, and remodeling maintenance.*
- *Social demands,* sometimes known as hidden demands because they do not always appear on work orders.
- *Expansion.* Any expansion in the size of the plant or the work force, or additions to the scope of your control, will add to the department's overall requirements.
- *Catastrophes.* The time to handle these problems must be included.

Preparing the Budget

Considerable time and effort are required with zero-based maintenance budgeting. Here are the many steps you must take to come up with an accurate and inclusive document:

1. Make a list of all the assets you maintain. Arrange the list by department or cost center to facilitate reporting at a later date. Group similar items to simplify the process.
2. Add areas and items to the list that require maintenance but are widely distributed rather than unitized. Typical areas include windows, doors, roofs, roadways, and utility distribution systems.
3. Collect maintenance data available by unit or area for the last year.
4. Enter all data into a computer spreadsheet, and create a template to duplicate the accompanying form. List the equipment, areas, and groups of units and areas in the template.
5. Add the global lines that apply to the whole site and social, expansion, and catastrophe categories.
6. Copy the filled-in template onto diskette or tape. Once assets have been put into the template, it becomes the basis for a zero-based budget.
7. Review each unit area or group and estimate preventive maintenance, corrective maintenance, user maintenance, replacement/remodeling maintenance, and seasonal maintenance costs and hours.
8. Total the amounts in the various columns. Materials required are the sum of all material columns; labor required is the sum of all hours columns.

When you decide to reduce the budget, the changes you make should be justified in terms of higher or lower levels of service on individual assets or areas. It's wise to explain which assets will be allowed to deteriorate and which departments will not be served as well.

MEASURING MAINTENANCE PERFORMANCE

One of the responsibilities of maintenance managers is to periodically report on the performance of the plant's maintenance operation. As the current trend of increased interest in maintenance continues, there is a need for performance measuring systems for managerial control as well.

Since the two major components of plant maintenance programs are labor and material, it's logical that a procedure be established to track both components monthly with the information being supplied by the accounting department. After a period of time, this becomes valuable information, particularly during austerity periods when managers may believe they must reduce labor costs—the real culprit may be material.

Two ratios are commonly used to analyze maintenance performance. The first is the ratio of monthly maintenance expenses to monthly sales dollars. This formula, expressed in terms of a percentage, is as follows:

$$\text{Maintenance Performance} = \frac{\text{Maintenance Costs}}{\text{Sales Dollars}}$$

By making this calculation every month, and graphing the figures, you can see how you are doing. You can then compare your performance to others in your industry, or determine the effects of any changes you made in the plant where maintenance was involved.

The second ratio deals with the number of finished products shipped. This formula is as follows:

$$\text{Maintenance Performance} = \frac{\text{Maintenance Costs}}{\text{Units Shipped}}$$

Experience has indicated that the lower the maintenance costs per unit shipped, the better the performance. This information, too, can easily be graphed and communicated to interested persons.

Another approach to measuring performance involves the value of the machines and equipment in the plant. By considering not only the maintenance costs, but also the direct labor and capitalization values, an effective measurement program can be developed. By design, a maintenance measurement program should be based on a factor of unity. This can be done in a simple and easily developed calculation, as follows:

$$\text{Maintenance Performance} =$$

$$1.00 - \frac{\text{Monthly Maintenance Costs (\$)}}{\frac{1}{12}\text{Gross Book Value (\$)} + \text{Standard Direct Labor (\$)}}$$

The inclusion of the gross book value factor represents a departure from the typical straight line relationship between maintenance costs and direct labor costs that interest most managers. The point to be made here, however, is that the higher the asset value within a plant, the more impact and importance the maintenance function should have.

REENGINEERING

There are several criteria to help managers decide what business processes need reengineering. One of these is to ask the question, "Which process most needs reengineering?" The most obvious processes that need to be reengineered are those that aren't functioning properly, or are characterized by low productivity.

When maintenance managers examine their operations, they need to ask themselves, "Are we doing a poor job of handling the maintenance function? Are we really making efforts to accomplish our goals and objectives?" Investigating the basics of the maintenance function means understanding the mission of the maintenance process at your plant.[8]

Determining the mission and reviewing the goals and objectives of the maintenance function forces you to examine your company's attitude toward maintenance. Companies that fix things if, and only if, they break will experience many equipment failures, inefficiently operate equipment, and fail to optimally use maintenance resources. Something at such companies needs reengineering, but it's not maintenance—it's maintenance management.

Managing maintenance includes developing a clear mission and setting goals and objectives. Maintenance managers should promote and adopt concepts such as: availability, reliability, maintainability, productivity, operational efficiency, technology, utilization, and continuous improvement.

In most companies, the maintenance function does not need reengineering; it needs definition and development. Maintenance is effective when management pays attention to engineering basics (equipment dynamics) and management basics (measurable objectives).

DETERRENTS TO GOOD MAINTENANCE

Maintenance excellence has been defined as that state of maintenance readiness and application essential to the support of a world class operation. Yet the function is poorly understood and much maligned according to Donald H. Nyman, The Nyman Consulting Group, Hilton Head Island, South Carolina.[9]

A few years ago, Nyman's company made a survey from forums conducted for more than 500 managers with line and staff responsibilities within the maintenance function. It was revealed in the seminars that many of the managers do not understand the significance of deterrents they themselves impose on the realization of maintenance excellence. During the seminars, the attendees ranked thirty-three major deterrents to maintenance excellence. The issues are summarized into six groupings as follows:

Foundation Issues

Rank

Rank	
1	Lack of a clear maintenance mission (proactive vs. reactive)
3	No master plan for how maintenance is to progress from its current state of wellness to its goal level of wellness
4	Insufficient maintenance understanding throughout the organization
5	Insufficient management support of and commitment to the maintenance function
6	Insufficient understanding of principles and concepts upon which the maintenance function should be managed
10	Insufficient participation from the internal maintenance customer toward realization of maintenance excellence

Operational Issues

Rank

Rank	
7	Insufficient planning, coordination, and scheduling of maintenance work
20	Inadequate, unreliable, or untimely materials support of maintenance effort

Scorekeeping Issues

Rank

Rank	
2	Lack of meaningful, yet realistic and formalized objectives, goals, and targets for the maintenance function
8	Poor management control of the maintenance function
17	Unawareness of the current status of maintenance effectiveness, adequacy, and wellness
21	Unrealistic maintenance budgets
24	Poor management reporting of maintenance-related information

Reliability Issues

Rank

9	Ineffective preventive/predictive maintenance programs
11	Insufficient engineering support of the maintenance function
13	Too much emphasis on downtime limitation to the detriment of root-cause analysis of equipment failure
15	Excessive deferred maintenance
16	Insufficient integration of maintenance effort with that of other reliability-oriented functions
27	No provision for prevention/predictive maintenance in determination of realistic equipment capacity

Infrastructure Issues

Rank

12	Unreliable equipment history and equipment records
14	Ineffective work-order systems with resultant shortfall in the maintenance information base
19	Inadequate system support for maintenance
22	Unavailable or out-of-date facility and equipment drawings and reference documents
26	Insufficient or ineffective computer systems to provide maintenance informational needs
28	Inadequate or ineffective accumulation and reporting of maintenance costs

Organizational Issues

Rank

18	Inadequate or ineffective maintenance organizational structure
23	Insufficient on-the-job supervision of maintenance work
25	Inadequate maintenance pride and commitment to quality workmanship—the maintenance ethic
29	Insufficient stature and recognition of maintenance professionals and a corresponding weakness in career path opportunities
30	Insufficient facilities, equipment, and tools to support maintenance excellence
31	Inadequate multiskill cross-training and structure
32	Inadequate enforcement of established work rules and practices
33	Inadequate craft skills

NOTES

1. "Requirements For Winning Maintenance," *Engineer's Digest,* April 1994, pp. 50–56.
2. Robert M. Williamson, "TPM: Building on What's Already in Place," *Maintenance Technology,* July 1993, pp. 37–39.
3. "Assuring Information System Performance," *Maintenance Technology,* September 1993, pp. 65–68.
4. Paul Smith, "Is the Maintenance Supervisor Still Relevant?" *Maintenance Technology,* February 1996, pp. 19–21.
5. Robert M. Williamson, "Making the Shift to Multiskill Maintenance," *Maintenance Technology,* September 1993, pp. 78–79.
6. Robert M. Williamson, "Overcoming the Maintenance Mindset," *Maintenance Technology,* October 1993, p. 40.
7. Joel Levitt, "Zero-Based Maintenance Budgeting," *Maintenance Technology,* February 1995, pp. 59–61.
8. Terry Wireman, "Don't Reengineer Maintenance When Management Is the Problem," *Engineer's Digest,* September 1994, pp. 19–20, Copyright Huebcore Communications, Inc.
9. Donald H. Nyman, "Deterrents to Good Maintenance," *Maintenance Technology,* October 1994, pp. 14–16.

13

Maintenance Procedures and Operations

When it comes to developing maintenance procedures and operations for the plant, the best policy is to ensure that the ones you put in effect accomplish the maintenance objectives and support management's philosophy. Philosophies of plants differ, depending on the types of production processes, operating conditions, equipment reliability experience, regulatory requirements, and other factors.

Defining specific criteria to indicate when a piece of equipment needs attention or a plant system should be improved is the usual way of determining how many maintenance procedures you need.[1] Organizing should also include expanding plant equipment files to contain manufacturers' drawings, recommendations on frequency of maintenance, and suggestions on the stocking of spare parts. Actions you should consider when making an analysis should include:

- Increasing the safety of employees
- Meeting regulatory requirements
- Reducing and eliminating equipment failures
- Improving machine and equipment reliability
- Timing and scheduling of maintenance activities

Some plants classify the criticality of equipment in terms of safety or product quality when deciding the maintenance procedure to be used.

Highly critical equipment, for example, would require a detailed procedure; critical equipment, a checklist procedure; and noncritical equipment, the vendor's recommendations. The analysis should include an evaluation of maintenance jobs and not just equipment lists. In addition, keep an eye out for similarities in maintenance jobs that give you the opportunity to develop only one procedure for adjusting, replacing, and repairing several models of the same machine or piece of equipment.

DOCUMENTING MAINTENANCE PROCEDURES

Maintenance procedures should be technically accurate and complete, easily understood, and contain an appropriate amount of detail. They should also be written with concise action statements organized chronologically. Here are the characteristics of an effective and comprehensive maintenance procedure:

- The procedure is errorless, reflecting the writer's ability to thoroughly research and analyze the maintenance job covered. This research must ensure that the procedure adheres to the best safety, engineering, and technical practices. A procedure may be considered complete and acceptable only after it has been validated through an actual field trial.

- It is presented in a friendly and accommodating manner. The writing style should be consistent in terminology, format, appropriate word choice, and sentence structure. It helps to use drawings and exploded views of parts to improve comprehension and understanding.

- Details are suitable and fitting. The level of detail included in a procedure should take into account the responsibilities, experience level, and training background of the person carrying out the procedure.

- It should be brief and compact. The writer should use the active rather than the passive voice and avoid excessive words (like adjectives) that do not contribute to the procedure. Information that does not directly pertain to performing the maintenance job is best put in a training manual.

Be sure you refer to the vendor's or manufacturer's manual or instructions when writing a maintenance procedure for a machine. You want to avoid overlooking an important recommendation.

Referring to another document is also an efficient way to reduce the quantity of procedures to be written. With this strategy, the plant maintenance procedure would include the pertinent instructions and safety information related to the equipment service conditions, and the actual maintenance instructions would refer to the information contained in the manufacturer's manual.

MAINTENANCE TECHNIQUES

One of the best maintenance techniques available for most plants is a simple visual inspection. An inspection does not require special equipment nor additional employees. Properly carried out, it is free and may be made any time machines and equipment are operating. With proper training and formal inspection guidelines, plant employees can identify problems before they affect plant performance. For visual inspection to be effective, however, plant employees should understand basic machine dynamics. Knowing how machines work improves their ability to operate and maintain them. This knowledge also enables them to be proficient inspectors.

Most machines have characteristics that indicate their operating condition. These include noise, temperature, and the various process variables such as pressure, fluid flow, speed, and others. By noting these, an inspector can readily identify a problem. An example is the noise emanating from a pump that is cavitating. Pumps cavitate for three reasons: lack of suction flow or pressure, entrained air, or a change in phase in the liquid.

To make a thorough and comprehensive inspection, you must do more than simply observe something in operation. You must use an inspection guide or form that spells out what to look for and defines the acceptable limits of the machine or system variables. For example, a pressure gauge should read 100 psi $+/-$ 5 psi. If the reading is outside those limits, you should report the deviation.

Inspection forms are easy to create, providing you use the operating and maintenance manuals for the machine or system to get the information needed. In some cases, the manuals will also recommend an inspection frequency. Viable inspection programs should include both production and maintenance employees. The production employees who operate machines and equipment should fill out daily inspection forms (sometimes called logs) that require the operators to record operating parameters and adjustments made to a machine. Maintenance personnel should have weekly and monthly inspection forms that verify the operating condition of plant systems, including utilities.

Since these inspections are worthless until corrective action is taken, an essential requirement of the plant's inspection program is a way to compile, store, and use the data acquired by the inspections. The procedure established to do this can be manual or the data can be added to a CMMS or predictive maintenance database.

BREAKDOWN MAINTENANCE

When a plant carries out the maintenance function with breakdown maintenance, little attention is given to the operating condition of the plant's productive equipment. Management's only concern is how quickly the machine or equipment can be put back in use. Furthermore, maintenance is judged to be effective as long as the machine functions at a minimum acceptable level.

Managing maintenance in this manner is both ineffective and very expensive for the following reasons:

1. Most equipment repairs are either planned poorly or not at all because there isn't enough time to do so. As a result, labor utilization is both ineffective and inefficient. Typically, breakdown maintenance costs three to four times more than when the repair work is planned.
2. With breakdown maintenance, symptoms of equipment failures rather than causes are repaired. For example, when a bearing failure occurs, the bearing is replaced as quickly as possible and the machine returned to service. There is no attempt to determine the cause of the failure or to prevent its recurrence. As a result, the reliability of the machine is downgraded.

Most manufacturing plants have long realized that the practice of breakdown maintenance is not an acceptable way of carrying out the maintenance function. Managers have learned that by developing and adopting other types of maintenance, they can avoid major breakdowns of productive equipment and considerably reduce equipment downtime. These goals can be accomplished through various procedures and techniques including preventive, corrective, and predictive maintenance.

PREVENTIVE MAINTENANCE

Implementing a preventive maintenance (PM) program involves carrying out a preplanned, periodic operation in which inspections and minor repairs are made on equipment to prevent its failure. Two characteristics of PM are:

1. The work usually requires the shutdown or interruption of the equipment being inspected and/or repaired.

2. Inspection intervals are specified by estimating the wear or deterioration rate of the equipment.

The timing of inspections is determined from historical information on the equipment. This history may come from several sources including:

- Equipment repair records
- Maintenance and production personnel
- Vendors or manufacturers of the equipment

The objective of an inspection is to ascertain how close a machine or one of its components is to failure. Ideally, an inspection interval should be established so that the machine or component is inspected just before it reaches a critical limit. When the interval is the greatest possible without risking failure, PM costs are minimized while sustaining good equipment surveillance. Best practice is to select an interval that assures failures do not occur between inspections.

When a machine or component is judged to be close to failure, maintenance is scheduled. If the inspection reveals that minor maintenance is required, or time to make a correction is available, such correction is made at the time of inspection. The correction usually involves work such as cleaning, lubricating, adjusting, tightening, and replacing.

Procedures

While maintenance personnel may know that preventive maintenance involves inspections and replacement of parts on equipment and machines, many may not know about the factors that must be considered in setting up a PM program. Plans for inspection and replacements are determined from the following:

- *Age and condition of machines and equipment.* If machines are old and worn, they should be inspected more frequently.
- *Severity of service.* If machines are operated twenty-four hours/day, or put under heavy load conditions, they need to be checked more frequently.
- *Exposure to the elements and chemicals.* If environmental conditions are poor or extreme, machines should be examined for corrosion and deterioration frequently.
- *Reliability.* If machines must operate without fail for safety or other reasons, inspections and parts replacements should be increased accordingly.

By considering such factors, maintenance experts can work out a program that maximizes system efficiency and prolongs equipment life while reducing the cost of maintenance itself. Initially, PM may cost more than breakdown maintenance because of additional time spent in planning, keeping records, and making periodic adjustments. However, in the long term, overall costs will be lower.

To decide how much the company should spend on preventive maintenance to prevent major and costly equipment breakdowns, see Exhibit 13-1. Note that the lowest point on the total maintenance cost curve corresponds to the optimum cost of preventive maintenance.

Where to Use Preventive Maintenance

Planned maintenance programs for plant equipment are a necessity because of the type of machines and equipment being used, their high cost, and the value placed on keeping productive machines operating. But not every machine should be included in a PM program, nor can all break-

Exhibit 13-1. Relationship of costs.

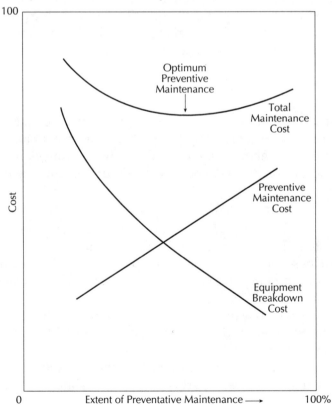

downs be eliminated. The variability of breakdowns is a factor, as is the time required to make repairs and the relative costs of each. Excessive repair work and high costs, however, can be minimized by concentrating inspections and repair on machines and equipment considered critical. A machine should be classified as critical if upon abnormal performance or failure it:

- Endangers the health or safety of employees.
- Affects the quality of the product.
- Slows or stops other productive operations.

By analyzing equipment and machines in this way, you can determine where PM should be applied—on those machines that will give the greatest return in production without sacrifice in product quality or safety of employees and the plant. Other machines may need only periodic or routine maintenance to perform satisfactorily within these critical concept limitations.

As for what machines should be included in PM programs, from an economic viewpoint it's best to let some noncritical equipment run until breakdown rather than attempt PM. For example, in many plants this policy is followed with fractional horsepower motors by considering their original cost and the cost of PM that would be required. Inspecting and maintaining *all* equipment under a rigid schedule to try to eliminate *all* breakdowns is not practical. Labor costs would be excessive and undoubtedly exceed the value of the benefits to be gained. A machine should be included in a PM program if the cost of the PM is less than the cost of production lost time, repairs, or replacement upon breakdown.

Critical Machine Parts

Since most equipment manufacturers supply a list of recommended spare parts for their machines, it's advisable that you follow these recommendations, at least during the beginning period of operation of the machine. To do this, you need to:

- Know what specific parts are critical.
- Keep a record or file system giving pertinent information on the parts.
- See that you have easy and fast accessibility to the parts.

The efficiency of a plant's PM program can be improved by setting up and using a good record system on equipment and parts. An illustration of the importance of such a system is the planning and scheduling of repairs to a critical machine. The work to be done on the machine should be carefully planned before the machine is shut down for the maintenance employees. If the diagnosis is to replace the machine's bearings, for example, then the correct type and size should be known before the machine is shut down. If they are not in the storeroom, they can be procured and be on hand. Nothing can be more discouraging to an embarrassed maintenance department and an anxious production department than to have production at a standstill waiting for a part that should have been available.

Benefits of Preventive Maintenance

Successful preventive maintenance (PM) programs can greatly benefit both the maintenance department and the production department. Following are the ways these programs contribute to a plant's profitability:

- *Fewer equipment failures.* An inspection program usually reveals problems before they become serious enough to cause equipment failure. As a result, routine adjustments and minor repairs prevent many failures, and breakdowns are considerably reduced.
- *More planned work.* The timeliness of PM inspections uncovers those major jobs that require planning. Sufficient lead time allows planning to be done.
- *Fewer emergencies.* An effective PM program puts every maintenance employee on the alert for impending equipment failures. Thus, fewer problems that would cause an emergency situation escape detection. Emergency work can be reduced drastically.
- *Reduced overtime labor.* One of the largest contributing factors to overtime is the need to do emergency work. A reduction in emergency work usually produces a corresponding decrease in overtime.
- *Extended equipment life.* PM invariably results in equipment lasting longer and running more dependably.
- *More efficient use of labor.* A job done under emergency conditions is always more costly in labor than a similar, well-planned job. PM inspections help in preventing emergencies and in increasing the amount of planned work.
- *Improved equipment operation.* Well-cared-for equipment is more energy-efficient and reliable.
- *Less downtime.* In the manufacturing environment, an investment in scheduled downtime for PM is better than unscheduled downtime for emergency work. Reduced downtime results in more production output.
- *Reduced maintenance cost.* Extra labor cost is attributable to emer-

gency work rather than planned work. An effective PM program can reduce this cost because employees tend to work more effectively with less lost motion in a planned job environment.

Effective PM programs are the result of a well-organized, carefully executed effort. Generally, the cost of implementing a comprehensive PM program will equal about 10 percent of the total savings realized by the program.

CORRECTIVE MAINTENANCE

The application of corrective maintenance enables machines and equipment to be kept in optimum operating condition. Corrective maintenance differs from preventive maintenance in that a problem must exist before corrective action can be taken. Preventive jobs are intended to preclude the occurrence of a fault. Corrective jobs solve existing faults.

A program's effectiveness is judged by the life-cycle costs of machines, not by how quickly a down machine can be returned to service. The objectives of corrective maintenance are to eliminate breakdowns, avoid deviations from optimum operating conditions, and avoid the making of unnecessary repairs. You also want to ensure that plant systems are as efficient as possible.

In the corrective maintenance process, engineering principles are used to study repetitive and costly faults in order to determine the cause of the fault. Once the reason for the fault is known, appropriate action may be taken to remove or "correct" the fault. Corrective action may involve one or more of the following:

- Redesign or replacement of the machine or component with one of more appropriate capacity or durability
- Control or reduction of the process factors causing the fault
- Training of the operator on proper operation of the machine
- Training of maintenance personnel on proper maintenance procedures

Prerequisites

There are several prerequisites for the successful implementation and practice of corrective maintenance in a plant:

1. You must be able to anticipate maintenance requirements before a breakdown occurs. A comprehensive predictive maintenance pro-

gram that can identify the cause of an equipment problem that is just beginning to exist is the primary requirement. Without this, you can't plan or schedule remedial action.

2. Corrective repairs or replacements must be efficiently planned and scheduled to minimize both costs and interruption of the production operation. Adequate time must be allocated to eliminate the cause of the problem and handle the damage caused.

3. Proper and complete repair of a fault is necessary. To meet this requirement, repairs must be made by craftspersons who have the necessary skills, material, parts, and tools to put the equipment in as-new condition.

4. Standard procedures that define the correct method of repair should be used for recurring maintenance jobs. The procedures should include information on safety, tools, and the repair parts required for the job, and a step-by-step sequence of making the repair.

5. Management must continuously train craftspersons in the skills required to properly repair and maintain the plant's machines, equipment, and systems. The training program should include ways to verify skills and periodically refresh skills.

6. Management must permit adequate downtime of productive equipment for maintenance purposes. Machines and equipment that are maintained in as-new condition and not permitted to degrade to a point where serious problems or breakdowns can occur will require less maintenance than those maintained in a breakdown state.

7. Repairs or replacements must be verified before a machine, equipment, or system subjected to corrective maintenance is returned to service. This verification ensures that the repair was properly made and that problems with performance have been corrected.

PREDICTIVE MAINTENANCE

Predictive maintenance (PdM) techniques are similar to those of preventive maintenance (PM) in that the objective is to prolong equipment life and prevent breakdowns. The applications and procedures, however, are significantly different. With PdM, the tracking of fault growth is accomplished by measuring a signal or parameter that grows in direct relation to the wear in the equipment or the component, whereas with PM, the fault is usually found by visual inspection or by direct measurement of the equipment or component exposed to wear.

PdM is often referred to as nondestructive testing because the technique does not require direct assess to the component being checked nor does it require shutdown of the equipment. In fact, it's generally better to measure the predictive parameter at normal machine load or speed to ensure that the reading is truly representative. In contrast, PM inspections frequently require shutdown of the equipment so that the component in question may be assessed and examined.

Because of the different analysis techniques, PdM has three advantages over PM:

1. The production department does not have to suffer machine downtime for an inspection unless a finding of impending failure dictates an immediate repair or replacement.
2. Maintenance labor for the inspection is minimal since a machine is not disassembled.
3. The advance warning of imminent failure provided by PdM enables maintenance management to plan the repair; collect parts, material, and tools; and to schedule personnel with the appropriate skills to make the repair efficiently and quickly.

Techniques

PdM techniques are generally different, one from another, in the instruments and procedures used to inspect and analyze equipment performance. Various techniques pinpoint specific components that are performing abnormally and are likely to fail. Most of the techniques can isolate those components that are performing normally and do not have to be replaced.

The particular types useful to a maintenance department depend on the kind of equipment being maintained, operating conditions, age and sophistication of the machine, and the cost of downtime. The most applicable techniques are:

- Vibration analysis
- Oil analysis
- Thermographic analysis
- Ultrasonic monitoring
- Shock pulse analysis
- Liquid penetrant analysis
- Acoustic analysis

Following are explanations and discussions of those that are most commonly used today in manufacturing plants worldwide.

VIBRATION ANALYSIS

This diagnostic tool involves the concept that all rotating machinery has some vibration and noise; thus, periodic checks for vibration reveal machine operating conditions. Vibration is the motion of a machine, or part of a machine, back and forth from its position of rest. The total distance of movements is the *peak-to-peak displacement* of the vibration. The number of cycles of this movement for a given period of time is the *frequency of the vibration,* and the position of the machine at any given instant with reference to some fixed point is the *phase of the vibration.*

A *spectrum* is a calculated data display of frequency versus amplitude. The frequency helps diagnose the *source* of the vibration, while the amplitude helps determine the *severity* of the problem.

Since the frequency of the vibration indicates its cause, this characteristic is the most important one measured. By comparing frequency of vibration with the rotating speed and multiples of rotating speeds, the point of vibration in a particular part of a machine and the cause of the vibration can be determined. Phase is used in balancing and is also helpful in identifying certain causes of vibration.

By using a vibration analyzer you can measure and indicate the amount, frequency, and phase of vibration of a rotating machine. When a vibration occurs at several frequencies, the analyzer separates one frequency from another to measure each vibration characteristic. To implement an effective vibration analysis program, you need to proceed as follows:

1. *Detect and record the vibration.* This is done by placing pads (pickups) at various points on a machine where the most useful vibration information can be obtained; and using handheld meters, automatic data collectors, on-line surveillance systems, or continuous monitoring instruments to make periodic vibration measurements.

2. *Analyze the data.* Vibration analysis quickly pinpoints a trouble spot. Because imbalance, misalignment, bent shafts, bad gears, defective bearings, and looseness cause vibration, each in a unique way, you can identify the problem without question.

3. *Correct the problem.* By identifying machine problems and impending failures early, you can plan the downtime and schedule the repairs before major breakdowns occur. If a problem is diagnosed as imbalance, it may be possible to correct it without disassembly. See Exhibit 13-2 for a troubleshooting guide for vibration analysis.

(*text continues on page 342*)

Exhibit 13-2. Troubleshooting guide for vibration analysis.

Machine Parts	Frequency Relative to Machine RPM	Other Symptoms	Probable Causes	Corrective Action
All machinery, foundations, and supports	Frequency determined by originating source	Excessive vibration amplitude. Slight changes in speed produce large changes in amplitude and phase angle. Slight corrections give large results	Resonance of machine part, foundation, or support	Raise or lower RPM or vibration frequency of source part, or make resonating part more rigid or less rigid relative to the weight it supports. Change length, position, or part, or rigidity of bearings.
All rotating machines with more than one vibrating source	Frequency not related to RPM usually very slow from several minutes apart to over 1000 cycles per minute	Thumping action or pulsating sound superimposed over a higher-frequency vibration	Two vibrations of nearly equal frequency (or multiples of) affecting the same structure, causing beats	Separate either the frequencies by changing RPM on one part or separate by keeping vibrations from adding to each other. Dampen. Balance to reduce.
Nonbolted down or nongrouted machinery	2 × RPM	Double image with strobe light	Poor mounting on foundation. Imbalance supplies action as machine base pivots about one line of contact, twice per revolution	Shim, bolt down, and grout in machine's base.
All rotating parts	1 × RPM		Unbalance or off-center rotor	Check centers and/or balance.

(continues)

Exhibit 13-2. (continued)

Machine Parts	Frequency Relative to Machine RPM	Other Symptoms	Probable Causes	Corrective Action
Armatures and electric rotors	1 × RPM	Looks like unbalance but immediately disappears when electric power is cut off	Eccentric armature	Correct eccentricities.
	7200 cycles/minute	Buzzing sound; immediately disappears when electric power is cut off	Loose iron affected by + or − of 60-cycle power input	Proper dipping or encapsulation, or correct looseness.
Couplings, shafts, and bearings	Often 1 or 2 × RPM; rarely 3 or 4 × RPM	High axial vibration, especially when reaches half or more of radial vibration. May also not produce high axial vibration	Misaligned coupling or shaft bearings. Occurs also in flexible couplings. Especially prominent in slender, long shafts to coupling position.	Align to tolerance required for smoothness.
Rotors and shafts	1 × RPM	High axial and radial vibration	Bent shaft	Prove with strobe before straightening.
Gears	1 × RPM	Looks like unbalance but motion is torsional vibration. Could well be resonant torsionally.	Eccentric gear pitch circle due to machining or mounting errors	Correct eccentricity. Try other line to line contact points: gear box to shaft.
	Number of teeth × RPM	Usually torsional vibration but not always. Could be in torsional resonance.	Bending due to unbalance causes side thrust between mating teeth. Eccentric gear pitch circle due to machining errors causing pulsating acceleration and deceleration of gear rotation	If resonant, change shaft or bearing stiffness, or RPM, or number of teeth.

Universal joints	1 × RPM	Looks like imbalance.	Too tight universal joint	Relieve tightness.
Universal joints and driveshaft	2 × RPM	Double image strobe picture	Unequal corresponding angles between input and output ends of driveshaft	Equalize corresponding angles through proper alignment.
Sleeve bearings	Slightly less than ½ × RPM	Oil whirl. Very rough amplitude; disappears suddenly with sufficient reduction in speed	Excessive clearance or bearing loads that are too light relative to its high rotational speed. Can also be caused by misaligned coupling.	Use pressure pad or pivoted shoe bearing or relieve sides of sleeve to decrease oil wedge pressure.
Anti-friction bearings	Usually relatively high frequency	Usually very low amplitude; noisy. Most often frequency is unsteady and many times rotor RPM	Excessive friction or rumble due to bad balls, rollers, rough races, poor lubrication, or too tight fit	Replace bearing. When applicable, relieve press fit.
V belts	1 × RPM	Very high axial vs. radial vibration	Mismatched multiple belt tensions	Replace with matched belts.
V belts and other drive belts	1 × RPM	High axial vibration (sometimes not too noticeable due to mass of structure but shows up in bearing wear)	Drive and driven sheaves not aligned so as to be in same plane of action	Align sheaves to act in same plane.

Source: Oil, Gas & Petrochem Equipment, June 1984, Penn Well Publishing Co., Tulsa, Oklahoma 74101.

OIL ANALYSIS

Another valuable predictive maintenance technique in manufacturing plants is the continuing analysis of the lubricants in the plant's machines. Oil analysis compares used lubricants to new lubricants to determine:

- The condition of the lubricant being used
- If contaminants, both liquid and solid, are present
- The condition of the wearing surfaces of the machine

What you want to learn from analyzing the oil dictates the scope of the testing and how often samples are to be taken. If preventive maintenance (PM) is your only concern, then you simply want to know when to change the oil or filters. With PM, you analyze the oil to determine oxidation levels, wear and contaminant levels, total acid number and water content. You might also make a spectrographic metal analysis, particle count, and ferrographic analysis. These analyses are mainly a report on the condition of the oil. To make the data meaningful, trend the wear levels as a function of time.

If you use predictive maintenance (PdM), you check the condition of both the oil and the machine more frequently. PdM reveals component wear, high operating temperatures, oil oxidation, and filter failure. Frequent sampling detects the beginning of wear and establishes trends more quickly. This gives you more time to schedule downtime for repairs, an advantage if production delays are costly.

Oil analysis serves as a complement to vibration analysis and is especially valuable with machines where the latter has limited application—reciprocating machines including internal combustion, slow rotating machines, and hydraulic systems. In addition, oil analysis may furnish confirming information that enables an analyst or technician to make a corrective action recommendation.

Implementing Oil Analysis

The following steps are required to implement an effective oil analysis program:

1. Select the machines for the program, categorizing them from a criticality point of view.
2. Document information about each machine, such as a description, identification number, type of bearing, and type of lubricant used. Information on the metallurgy of the wearing parts is also needed

to determine where the metal particles in the oil sample come from.

3. Determine how to get the oil samples: with a vacuum pump or from a valve. Retrofit the machine with sample valves, if necessary.
4. Make arrangements with the testing lab on the procedure to be followed for each machine. See that sample bottles are appropriately identified.
5. Take samples at scheduled times and from specified sampling points. See that they are delivered for analysis as soon as possible. Timeliness of testing is essential to an effective oil analysis program.

Sampling and Analyzing Techniques

Taking oil samples is a critical procedure, especially if the sample is to be analyzed for wear particles. While fine metal particles in the less than five micrometer size range tend to stay suspended, larger particles tend to settle out. When a sample is taken, it is usually warm or even hot; if volatiles are evident, that could mean fuel contamination. If water is present, it will produce a cloudy or milkly emulsion; but after a period of time, the water may separate out, depending on the additives in the oil.

When the lab has completed its tests, the data are trended and compared with norms. Trend analysis is a strong, statistics-based technique that works well with oil analysis, but it isn't simply graphing the test results. A comprehensive trend analysis requires use of complex math. Additionally, correcting the data for the time that the oil has been in use is an essential of trend analysis. Although interpretation of the data is partly based on calculated trends, many oil analysis labs report only raw test data to the customer.

Labs usually prepare a status report for an analyst who judges the results. If the data raise questions about lubricant condition, contamination, or machine wear, the analyst will probably call for additional testing to further diagnose the problem. If abnormalities are confirmed, the analyst will make a recommendation to the maintenance person responsible for the program.

ULTRASONIC MONITORING

All machines and their components emit identifiable sounds while operating. Because different components emit sound at different ultrasonic frequencies, you can zero in on specific components. For example, you can listen to bearings at 28–32 kilohertz and hear leaks at 40 kilohertz.

Ultrasonic inspection is used for mechanical analysis of pumps, motors, compressors, gear boxes, valves, and bearings; it is also commonly used for both liquid and gas leak detection.

A typical test system includes a sensor, signal conditioning and processing equipment, and data recording or data storage equipment. Most systems are also furnished with headphones and instrumentation to convert ultrasound to something that can be heard, so that you can hear what you are tracking.

To use ultrasound inspection, you hold the sensor against a machine as you would a stethoscope. Some sensors scan a machine or an area for abnormal readings, then tune in to and make contact with a machine or component in question. The procedure may be made easier by putting the machine under stress, so that a bad bearing or developing leak becomes noisier. Facilitating the inspection, a sound source can often be quickly located because the intensity of the signal falls off rapidly from its source of emission.

Although a trained operator can make assumptions based simply on immediate analog or even aural data, newer and more sophisticated systems store data for trend analysis. Using a computer, you can make a comparison of the latest readings with a "signature" of the ultrasound emitted under normal operating conditions.

Monitoring Bearings

Recent research by the National Aeronautics and Space Administration[2] has shown that using ultrasound technology to monitor bearing wear will locate incipient failure before it is detected by traditional heat and vibration methods. With an ultrasonic instrument, technicians can hear the sound quality of a bearing, and monitor amplitude changes on the built-in meter. Using the instrument's demodulated signal along with the vibration analysis, ultrasonic testing focuses on a worn bearing, enabling technicians to trend, troubleshoot, and confirm potential bearing problems.

In the case of extremely slow-speed bearings, a technician can use the instrument to listen to the heterodynad sound of the rollers or ball bearings, which are usually large and greased with high-viscosity lubricant. Usually, no sound is heard because the grease absorbs most of the acoustic energy. However, a crackling or grinding sound indicates some degree of deformity in the bearing.

Being light and durable, a portable ultrasonic instrument is easy to use. It is also so sensitive that the user can hear if a bearing is running dry, if there is too much lubrication, or if there is a small particle of dirt on the ball. The user can also record the meter readings monthly and use them to indicate when a bearing should be replaced.

THERMOGRAPHIC ANALYSIS

Infrared imaging is one of the most powerful of the predictive maintenance technologies. Valuable technical information can be obtained when this tool is properly used by trained people. The real power of thermography, however, is that it enables you to quickly locate and monitor an equipment problem. You can then present critical decision-making information in *visual* form. In the hands of qualified thermographers, thermographic analysis can save thousands of dollars in production and maintenance costs. There are two general classifications for these savings: equipment/component failures and energy losses.

Infrared imaging is a noncontact means of detecting heat radiating from an object or area and converting it to a visible image of thermal distribution. With cameras, maintenance technicians can examine the temperature distribution in plant equipment. When they detect abnormal temperatures, they can identify faults in electrical and mechanical components before they become serious and result in failure. A "hot spot" in a motor control center, for example, is a sure sign of a loose connection. The early detection of arcing across the contacts prevents ultimate destruction of a motor when the warning is heeded.

By noting trends, technicians are able to spot degradation as well as check the condition of refractory and insulation materials in boilers, insulated piping, dryers, furnaces, and other similar equipment. An improperly operating steam trap is easy to locate with an infrared camera. Other applications include locating underground water, steam, and sewer lines.

A number of factors should be considered when selecting an infrared imaging system, most of them being tempered by the environment where the equipment will be used. For example, portability and simplicity of operation are important features. The equipment's size, weight, battery life, and ergonomics should be evaluated. Some systems incorporate software for route storage and machine history, making it easier to perform periodic surveys as part of a predictive maintenance program.

Trained operators are necessary to get useful images. Some manufacturers offer training courses for their equipment; others provide overall thermographic training courses. While thermography is a valuable tool, it often is hard to justify the equipment and training costs involved in having "in-house" capability. Infrared equipment is generally expensive. For the camera and its associated equipment, the cost could run between $30,000 and $70,000.

PREDICTIVE MAINTENANCE INTEGRATION

The use of predictive maintenance (PdM) usually means adopting the practices of vibration monitoring and oil analysis. Both of these techniques are common and well-accepted in plants, and both are available at a reasonable cost. However, there are several other technologies that are appropriate for PdM programs. If a technology produces repeatable, reproducible, and accurate data that can be used to forecast equipment condition, it can fit into a PdM program.

A recent survey of industrial plants with more than 100 employees showed that 80.1 percent had a proactive or predictive maintenance program in effect.[3] These plants used the following programs: oil analysis (78.9 percent); vibration monitoring (78.3 percent); infrared thermography (65.2 percent); ultrasonic monitoring (54.3 percent); wear particle analysis (43.1 percent); and other technologies (1.2 percent).

With so many usable technologies available, the need for an effective way to integrate them can become important. While you may not want to use every technology available, several may be used to compare, reconcile, and interpret findings. One way to narrow down those that apply to a particular application is to consider how a machine operates and the most likely way it may fail. Then decide which technologies are best for that application by studying the characteristics of each technology and the cost of its application.

The most cost-effective, integrated PdM programs exhibit several characteristics in that they:

- Use several technologies for correlation and corroboration of equipment condition.
- Make full use of predictive analytical methods. Using various methods of analysis, diagnostics, and expert systems enhances the effectiveness of the program.
- Are capable of rapidly organizing, storing, and retrieving PdM data. A cumbersome system of data handling can result in the program being underutilized or completely ignored.
- Facilitate the display of data for comparison among technologies and for predictive analysis. Supplying the most effective means of data display and a way to manipulate the data promotes better analysis.
- Make data readily accessible and quickly dispense results. The results should be publicized so that other maintenance employees can

see what they accomplished and feel that they are contributing to the PdM program.

- Use the information obtained as a basis for maintenance action, and compare predictions with actual conditions to improve the accuracy of analysis. The maintenance technician and the data collector must record information on equipment condition with every maintenance action and see that the analyst receives it.

- Are flexible enough to be expanded, improve their displays, accept additional technologies, and document more results. An effective PdM program must also be capable to responding to various methods of analysis.

Software for Predictive Maintenance

Developers and vendors of software for predictive maintenance can supply industrial plants with a wide variety of their products. You may purchase software for just one technology such as vibration analysis, oil analysis, ultrasound, and infrared analysis, or a program that integrates many technologies and covers overall machine conditions. Software programs that are proprietary deal exclusively with one manufacturer's data collection. Other programs interface with a number of data collectors or other software.

All of the programs are universal in that they enable a maintenance department to manage a large amount of data, make sound decisions, keep productive machines running at an optimum level, and extend machine reliability. Faults and defects are more likely to be discovered early, before a failure occurs. Additionally, the software provides a means to verify that the maintenance performed solved the problem.

Safety Factors

Since many of the predictive maintenance (PdM) technologies require the acquisition of data from operating mechanical and electrical equipment, there is a need for management to ensure the safety of maintenance personnel doing this type of work. The close proximity of moving machinery parts increases the potential for accidents and injuries. Here are some recommendations on how to handle the problem:

- Implement a comprehensive training program for PdM personnel. In addition to training personnel on safe data acquisition practices, include courses on how the plant's machines and equipment operate.
- Hold frequent safety meetings, including daily meetings at the be-

ginning of each shift. Promote the philosophy of safety being more important than anything else.

- Design and arrange vibration monitoring routes to eliminate entry into hazardous areas, and minimize exposure to potentially dangerous machines.
- Directly connect dangerous measurement points by electrical wires or cables, thus relocating the points to a safe area.
- Provide additional labor for safety when PdM work is being performed in an isolated plant area and when the technology involves infrared scanning.
- Include good housekeeping practices in the plant's PdM program.

Selecting Predictive Maintenance Equipment

Implementing a predictive maintenance program can be a costly investment if you decide to purchase the best equipment and tools available. A more cost-effective decision would be to invest in an assortment of quality instruments and low-cost meters that will satisfy the level of condition monitoring your plant equipment requires.

While the critical equipment deserves the more sophisticated analytical capabilities that expensive microprocessor-based instruments give you, less critical equipment does not require the same level of analysis. Many of the average plant's machines do not require the latest state-of-the-art instrumentation to give you the information you need.

There are many low-cost instruments available today to supply analysis of noncritical plant equipment. Here is some information on such items:

- *Vibration meters.* Although most inexpensive vibration monitoring instruments do not furnish the type of data to enable you to pinpoint an impending equipment problem, they do give you a relative indication of their mechanical condition. These meters are ideal for small motors, pumps, and similar equipment that do not warrant full vibration analysis techniques. Most do not require computers or software, so they do not have trending or long-term data storage capacities.

- *Ultrasonic meters.* Similar to the vibration meters, this class of instrument gives you adequate information on a variety of equipment and systems. The main use of these low-cost meters is to detect air or gas leaks, various noises, and indications of impending bearing problems.

- *Infrared cameras.* You don't need full-color, computerized thermographic equipment for most of the noncritical electrical equipment and energy-loss problems you encounter in the plant. These applications can be served by low-cost, monochrome cameras that do not have diagnostic power or long-term data storage capabilities.

Implementing Predictive Maintenance

While some vendors of predictive maintenance (PdM) systems may say that implementing a program in the plant is easy and requires little effort, this is far from the truth. The time and labor required varies, of course, with the plant size and complexity of the process systems. With a small company, the time required to develop a viable program will be about three person-months.

Failures of PdM programs are usually due to a lack of planning and decision making by management concerning what the plant wants to accomplish. Here are the preparatory steps generally required to implement a total plant PdM program:[4]

1. *Determine the plant's current maintenance costs.* The best way to do this is to ask the accounting department for figures on labor and material. Then get their help on estimating and evaluating all maintenance-related costs such as downtime of productive equipment, safety of employees, environmental compliance, product quality, operating expenses, insurance, and the many other items that limit the plant's capacity and effectiveness.

The maintenance costs you come up with will be used to develop a cost-benefit analysis and justification for the PdM program. After you put the program in place, the costs will become the baseline for quantifying the benefits realized.

2. *Plan the activities of the program.* The plan should cover its scope, the goals and objectives, and the methods that will be used to implement, coordinate, and evaluate the program. The plan should also clarify how the success of the program will be measured.

3. *Select the technologies you intend to use.* To achieve maximum benefits, you should use several monitoring and diagnostic techniques. None of the individual technologies, such as vibration analysis or thermography, supply all the data and information required to evaluate critical plant equipment and systems. At a minimum, the program should include: visual inspection, vibration analysis, thermography, and process parameters. Oil analysis should be used only when the benefits derived equal or exceed the costs.

4. *Arrange for training of maintenance personnel.* Most plant maintenance personnel today are not knowledgeable or experienced with PdM technologies, so in-depth training is essential. Although vendors of PdM instruments and meters may offer a training course, many of these courses

cover only the vendors' equipment rather than comprehensive use of the technology. You should carefully evaluate the merit of their courses before deciding to use them.

5. *Ensure you have line and staff support for the PdM program.* An effective program cannot be implemented nor sustained with part-time personnel. Regardless of the PdM technologies used, regular, periodic inspection and monitoring of critical equipment is a necessity. Many PdM programs implemented with part-time personnel have failed because jobs required for the program have been delayed or ignored when those personnel are assigned other work.

6. *Develop a database for collecting and storing information.* The benefits derived from a program will depend on the accuracy and completeness of the database. Information must include descriptions of the equipment subjected to the PdM technologies along with the test data. The latter is used to facilitate trend analysis.

7. *Incorporate a plan for communicating results.* The corrective actions taken as outgrowths of analyses should be publicized along with feedback from the production department. Program justification is a never-ending procedure. Management and employees must be continually informed of the program's status and the benefits realized. Failure to communicate will reduce the potential for continuing success.

Benefits of Predictive Maintenance

The practice of predictive maintenance not only helps plant personnel to eliminate the possibility of catastrophic failure of productive equipment, but also gives management the opportunity to ensure that critical machine parts are on hand, schedule maintenance labor, and plan repairs during scheduled downtime.

Downtime in manufacturing plants can cost from $100 to $1,000 per minute. History proves that plants that establish and implement predictive maintenance programs can:

- Considerably increase the availability of productive equipment.
- Save $200,000 to $2,000,000 per year in maintenance costs.
- Virtually eliminate plant downtime due to unexpected machine failure.
- Substantially increase product quality through better equipment performance.
- Usually achieve payback on equipment and training costs within six months.

When a plant institutes a particular PdM program such as vibration analysis, the act often prompts the use of other predictive technologies such as oil analysis and thermography. A benefit of this is that oil analysis can often confirm the diagnosis made by vibration analysis and vice versa. In addition, PdM programs promote communication and cooperation between plant departments in using both condition and performance data to make decisions on plant equipment.

Payback

To determine the payback of predictive maintenance requires some work on your part. Basically, what you need to learn is the amount of unplanned downtime that *would have* occurred if a machine had been permitted to run to failure, resulting in a loss of production time.

When obtaining this information, use conservative estimates upon which production, engineering, maintenance, and other parties involved can agree. Search out and document increased component life, reduced average repair cost, and fewer number of repairs by looking at historical data from before the predictive maintenance program started. If you expect management to continue to fund the cost of a condition-monitoring program, you have to provide evidence of the program's success.

THE RELIABILITY ENGINEERING FUNCTION

It pays to add a reliability engineering function to the plant's PdM program.[5] This function can provide the means to get maximum output and continuous performance from the plant's production process systems. PdM programs may fail to achieve their full potential if reliability engineering is omitted.

A staff engineer is the best choice of personnel to take on these responsibilities. The duties of the engineer should include prevention, detection, and correction of design deficiencies, weak components, poor operating and maintenance procedures, and assembling and installation defects. The major responsibilities of the engineer are:

- *Estimating and predicting reliability.* The engineer should estimate the reliability that can be attained by using test and recorded information on production systems, machine and equipment components, and parts and material specified in the design. Tests will show if the estimated reliability has not been realized, thus making it necessary to predict what will happen if certain changes are made.

■ *Conducting reliability tests.* Reliability engineers should be specialists in designing test procedures and setting criteria for equipment and systems evaluations. They also should be familiar with predictive and preventive maintenance procedures. Reliability test equipment is often used for predictive maintenance testing.

■ *Identifying causes of reliability degradation.* Poorly designed parts, insufficient process control, inadequate attention, and other causes can contribute to reliability degradation. It behooves the reliability engineer to make judgments based on predictive maintenance data and reliability tests to recommend corrective action.

■ *Maintaining reliability data and information.* Reliability information should be collected and kept in the computer database of the maintenance department so that others can use it in the management of the plant. An engineer should periodically evaluate and analyze the information in order to make recommendations for changes in design, procedures, and systems.

Factors Affecting Equipment Reliability

Equipment reliability is a basic requirement of optimum plant performance. Product quality, plant output, and profitability of operations hinge on the performance level of the plant's machines and equipment. For a piece of equipment to be considered reliable, it must meet three requirements consistently:

1. Function at its rated capacity.
2. Carry out its function flawlessly.
3. Sustain its performance over time.

Most plants do not have a program or plan for addressing equipment reliability problems. While inadequate and improper maintenance may be blamed for limited production capacity, product quality, and profitability, many reliability problems cannot be attributed to poor maintenance practices. Here are some other functions that determine equipment reliability:

■ Equipment dependability originates with the specification and selection procedures. The design and engineering functions must focus on the appropriateness of equipment and systems for the application, and that are conducive to maximum utilization of these assets with life cycle costs in mind.
■ The purchasing function must use good judgment when procuring new equipment and replacing parts—price is not a true measure of equipment cost or how it affects overall performance.

- Employee skills affect equipment reliability. Training of both production operators and maintenance craftspersons are critical in this respect. Both must be knowledgeable about proper operational procedures and upkeep techniques to ensure equipment reliability.
- Poor planning is a source of reliability problems when equipment needs attention. Both production and maintenance personnel must recognize the importance of optimum timing for the shutdown and repair of critical equipment. Cooperation is essential to ensure future equipment reliability.
- Scheduling of production runs that involve constant stopping, setup changes, and restarts have an impact on equipment reliability. Coupled with the time lost to change of product, short-run orders are a major contributor to poor plant performance.

PROACTIVE MAINTENANCE

Proactive maintenance is a maintenance strategy that focuses on planning. In contrast, reactive maintenance receives minimal planning beyond a field inspection. The objective of proactive maintenance is to stay involved with the equipment to prevent decline or loss of capacity.

A good example of proactive maintenance is the controlling of contaminant levels in machines and equipment. When quality equipment is installed properly, lubricant contamination is the main cause of failure. Contamination is blamed for bearing damage more than any other cause.

To implement such a maintenance program in the plant requires that you take the following steps for each machine that uses lube oils, hydraulic fluids, transmission fluids, gear oils, and/or coolants:

1. Determine what level of cleanliness in terms of particle size, concentration, and corrosive content of the pertinent fluid is best for a particular machine.
2. Install proper filtration equipment to achieve the desired fluid cleanliness.
3. Monitor the fluid cleanliness at regular intervals to verify that the level of cleanliness is sustained.

MAINTENANCE LUBRICANTS

Determining which lubricants should be used in plant equipment can result in misspent dollars, wasted labor, and unnecessary equipment downtime if you make poor decisions on the ones you select. Because lubricants can be subjected to severe operating conditions, you must realize that, in most cases, the benefits of a superior lubricant outweigh its cost.

Lubricants that cost less are often made with lower-performing raw materials. The low quality of such products can lead to operating problems, parts failures, and ultimately, costly downtime. Even general purpose lubrication applications benefit from the use of a high quality lubricant. Performance is usually better and equipment life is extended. The resulting savings may well exceed the lubricant's higher cost.

To guarantee that a lubricant will perform satisfactorily, you must match it to the job it is expected to do. There are four operational variables in an application: load, environment, temperature, and speed.[6] Here is how these variables relate to lubricants:

• To select the proper lubricant, you must match its load-carrying capacity to the application. Lubricants that contain solids or surface-active additives generally do well in moderate-to-high load and speed applications. Some high-performance synthetic greases, for example, withstand high bearing loads. High viscosity fluid greases generally do not.

• The environment to which an application is exposed should be considered when specifying a lubricant. There are several lubricants that are formulated to withstand abrasive, dusty, humid, dry, or corrosive conditions. Dry-bonded films containing solids like molybdenum disulfide form a solid lubricant coating that adheres without dripping or running, and are excellent for such conditions.

• When specifying a lubricant, you should know if it will be exposed to high or low temperature extremes and heat generated by equipment. The highest temperature-rated grease is usually not the best choice for mid- to low-temperature ranges. Lower-rated greases are more stable at lower temperatures. However, low temperatures thicken grease, increase torque resistance in bearings, and decrease efficiency. Silicone-based greases are a reliable solution to these problems.

• Whether an application is high or low speed, lubricants are often called upon to operate under these extremes. While fluid oils have traditionally been used to lubricate extremely high-speed spindle bearings, some newer, high performance greases function well under high-speed conditions, even when high speed is combined with high temperature and high load.

Selecting the right lubricant for the plant's equipment is only one part of a successful plant maintenance program. By getting the facts about lubricants' capabilities, you can help decrease equipment downtime and extend service life without increasing labor and parts costs.

Maintenance Operations Involving Bar Coding

Most computerized maintenance management system developers have incorporated bar coding into their products. The simplest and most inexpensive devices for a maintenance crew include wedge-type bar code scanners that physically connect to a personal computer. Here's how maintenance personnel use the equipment:

- A technician or clerk in the maintenance department unplugs the keyboard, plugs the scanner cable into the keyboard socket, and plugs the keyboard into another socket on the scanner cable to get input capability from both the keyboard and the scanner. Computer programs can then take input from either the scanner or the keyboard.

With this arrangement, data from master sheets of bar coded data, such as an employee list, can be scanned instead of typed on the keyboard. While this improvement may seem minimal, if there are a large number of entries each day, the time saved is significant.

- Another application involves a craftsperson who uses a portable scanner when making inspections or repairs in the plant. At the start of a job, the person scans the bar-coded work-order identification code, punches a key to indicate work has begun, punches it again when the work is complete, and then moves on to the next work order. When this work requires parts, the person scans the bar-code label of the parts he or she needs in the storeroom, and punches the quantity taken.

At a job site, the person scans a bar-code label on the equipment being repaired to post the correct equipment identification onto the work order. These data refer to the work-order identification number and can be added to the computer database at the end of the day. The person doesn't have to use the keyboard to do this, and has accurate time measurements besides.

Scanning Devices

Laser scanners cost a little more than contact scanners but are worth it. Contact scanners require the operator to use the scanning device to make contact with the bar-code label, moving it across the label from left to right in one smooth motion. Holding the device at the proper angle, the operator must make sure it hits the whole label. But there may be a problem with the label. It may wear out and not be discovered until it is scanned in the field and it fails.

With a laser scanner, you can point to the label from a distance and aim the laser. This procedure is faster than contacting the label, and it saves wear and tear on the label since it is not being touched. Although contact and laser scanners can read the same kind of bar code, you should prefer to work with the laser device whenever possible.

Maintaining Steam Systems

The formation of condensate is the major problem with steam systems. Condensate can corrode metal pipes, erode fittings and valves, and cause water hammer that can crack pipe fittings and hangers. Maintaining steam systems is all about preventing and repairing damage caused by condensate.[7]

Condensate is usually removed by use of a steam trap, a self-actuated valve that opens when condensate collects in the trap, and closes when steam enters. The pressure of the steam forces the condensate out through its valve head and seat. There are several types of steam traps, each detecting steam and condensate differently, and containing various types of valves. While each trap design can operate under a wide range of conditions, reliability and service life depend on selecting the right trap for the service.

The damage that condensate causes can be reduced or even eliminated by following two simple procedures:

1. Minimize the amount of condensate formed in the steam lines.
2. Remove the condensate as quickly as possible wherever it forms.

Here's how you can most easily handle these problems:

- Condensate usually forms on the cold walls of pipe and equipment where it can drain away from the main steam flow. Thus, poorly insulated steam pipes contribute greatly to its formation. The amount of condensate produced depends on ambient conditions and the type and amount of insulation used. No amount of insulation prevents condensation—it only reduces its amount.

No matter what type of insulation is used, it must be protected. Insulation that has been crushed or soaked with water will not insulate. Outdoor insulation must be waterproofed, and both indoor and outdoor insulation should be inspected periodically to ensure that it stays dry and intact.

- To keep condensate from collecting and causing corrosion, erosion, or water hammer, it must be drained soon after it forms. The proper way to do this is as follows:

1. Slope steam lines downward in the direction of steam flow, at least one-half inch per ten feet of run, so that condensate flows toward collection legs.
2. Install collection legs at least every 100 to 150 feet of steam line.
3. Make sure collection legs are 8 to 28 inches long, depending on startup procedures used, and the same diameter as the steam line.
4. Install a steam trap at the bottom of each leg and test the trap frequently to make sure it is operating correctly. The thermodynamic disk trap is often recommended for steam pressures above 125 psi. For lower pressures, the float and thermostatic trap is usually recommended.
5. If a trap fails, replace it immediately. If you merely isolate the trap, condensate flowing to that collection leg will back up into the steam line and cause damage.

Steam Trap Maintenance

Because many steam traps fail in the open position, maintenance personnel often are unaware of trap failures until steam costs are determined. With proper attention, maintenance, and care, however, steam traps are capable of holding the plant's steam costs in line.[8]

In typical systems, traps wear out and must be replaced. But you can prolong trap life, as well as improve system efficiency, through regular trap surveys. Surveys can also help reduce the number of failures and improve efficiency by reducing operating costs. See the section in Chapter 10 (Cost Control and Reduction) for how to check for proper operation of steam traps.

Since the seat and valve area of a trap is subject to the most wear, it should be examined carefully. Pressure, temperature, and flow rate determine how fast the area wears out. Condensate is corrosive and also causes erosion. While regular maintenance programs help to prevent downtime, traps fail even in the best systems. Thus, you may be forced to decide whether to repair or replace a failed trap.

Although trap parts can be replaced, you may decide to replace an entire trap instead of rebuilding it. Repairing the bellows on a $100 trap may cost about $60 plus the labor cost, thus not making the repair economical. Yet when a $500 trap needs a part, it's common sense to make the repair.

It pays to investigate different types of traps when one must be replaced. The failed trap may not have been the most appropriate for the application—it may actually have contributed to the problem. Also, some of the plant's traps may have become obsolete after many years of service. Newer traps can be more efficient, smaller, and less expensive.

Techniques

Dirt, including rust, scale, and other contaminants, are the cause of many trap failures. Because traps are installed at the lowest point in a steam system, they naturally collect such debris. Float traps are more susceptible to this problem than other types of traps.

Contaminants generally can be controlled by using a strainer in the line ahead of the trap, but it must be kept clean. A clogged strainer can be as much of a problem as a clogged trap. Some strainers can be cleaned easily by removing them from the steam line and replacing them with little or no system downtime.

Checking the system regularly can ensure that the trap is clean and operating properly. Regular checkups will help ensure that the steam system runs efficiently and keeps costs down. Steam system equipment is simple and inexpensive. When you think you have a problem with your system or it is costing too much to maintain, call the supplier or vendor of your equipment and ask for help.

CORROSION

Corrosion has always been a major problem for manufacturing plants, particularly those in the chemical process industries. The use of more-aggressive chemicals and higher temperatures and pressures in recent years has accelerated corrosion rates in most process plants. The problem is acute because corrosion causes leaks, and increasingly-stringent environmental and safety laws have made almost any kind of leak unacceptable.

Although appropriate maintenance procedures can reduce the high cost of corrosion, implementing an effective control procedure may be difficult.[9] The problem can be approached in several ways:

1. Modify the conditions and environment under which the corrosion takes place.
2. Change the material that is subject to corrosion.
3. Separate the material from the corrosive environment.
4. Use a combination of these ways.

Separating an easily affected material from a corrosive environment with protective coatings is the most common way to control atmospheric corrosion. When the coating fails, the maintenance costs consist of removing the old coating, preparing the surface for the new coating, and applying it.

While preventive and predictive maintenance technologies are helpful for deterring corrosion, they are not popular because most maintenance engineers and technicians know little about the how and why of corrosion. Visual inspection is a critical step in controlling corrosion because corrosion rates tend to hold steady at low levels and suddenly accelerate to failure.

Priorities and scheduling are important when using protective coatings to control corrosion. For example, early touchup and repair prevent further corrosion and limit costs. On the other hand, correcting badly corroded surfaces that require complete cleaning, priming, and finishing can be delayed because additional corrosion will not significantly affect repair costs. The general rule is to touch up the surface when 15 to 20 percent of the surface has failed. If 30 percent or more has failed, it is usually more economic to completely repaint rather than to touch up.

Maintenance management can make significant strides toward cutting corrosion losses by acquiring some practical corrosion knowledge. A good way to start is to request information from the National Association of Corrosion Engineers (NACE) in Houston, Texas, and the Steel Structures Painting Council (SSPC) in Pittsburgh, Pennsylvania. Individual membership in NACE includes a subscription to *Materials Performance* and in SSPC, a subscription to *Journal of Protective Coatings & Linings*. Additional ways you can stem corrosion costs are:

- Promote corrosion control in the plant's quality-improvement programs so that the discipline receives more attention.
- Encourage maintenance staff people to keep up with trade literature and attend conferences and seminars to stay informed.
- Draw on the knowledge of contractors on how design and fabrication influence corrosion. Coating contractors have access to much information on corrosion and should be consulted when it comes to selecting protective coatings.

MAINTENANCE OF ELECTRICAL SYSTEMS

The importance of the plant's electrical systems depends on how critical electric power distribution is to the plant's processes and operations. For one plant, an unexpected outage may entail little risk to the business. For many, a major failure must be avoided at all costs; even a partial failure in one process area may have rippling effects on other processes or the entire production cycle.

To prevent crippling losses from fires and interruption of production processes, plant management must adopt a preventive maintenance program. This requires that all components of the electrical distribution system be periodically inspected. While some elements should be inspected frequently, others need to be checked annually.

A requisite to the implementation of a program is to locate and document all system components. As-built diagrams and construction drawings can be of much help as a starting point if the program is put into effect before the system is changed or modified. It is easy to overlook a remote switch or a panelboard in a locked or generally inaccessible area. Thus, the documentation should be comprehensive and thorough.

For an effective preventive maintenance program, testing of the plant's electrical system should be carried out in the following stages:

- Simple inspection by a trained maintenance electrician performed with no tools. This can be done daily or at least weekly.
- Hands-on operation of switches, circuit-breakers, and relays. These components need to be operated periodically to verify mechanical operation and to free up slightly corroded linkages and mechanical operators.
- Electrical tests of high-voltage cables and switches, transformers, protective relays, motor controls, buses, and circuit-breakers. These tests should be performed every few years by competent professionals equipped with the correct tools and instruments. The ground fault and and system ground should also be checked.

By keeping careful records of these tests, the maintenance manager can compare current values to previous checks in order to note trends or spot variations. Significant variations may indicate an incipient failure and should be thoroughly investigated. Using standardized forms for keeping records on major components helps to organize the program; it also ensures comparability and standardization of results. With check-off lists, you can ensure the completion of all visual and physical tests. Documents on tests should include a sheet on which discrepancies can be noted along with corrective action suggested by the inspector or tester.

NOTES

1. Sandee Baker and Bill Rieck, "How to Develop 'Good' Maintenance Procedures," *Plant Services,* July 1995, pp. 45–46.
2. UE Systems, Inc., Elmsford N.Y., "Using Ultrasound With Vibration Analysis to Monitor Bearings," *Maintenance Technology,* March 1996, p. 41.

3. Keith Young, "Integrating Predictive Maintenance," *Maintenance Technology*, June 1995, pp. 26–28.
4. Keith Mobley, "Setting Up a Predictive Maintenance Program," *Plant Services*, July 1994, pp. 59–62.
5. Keith Mobley, "Reliability Engineering," *Plant Services*, July 1995, pp. 53–54.
6. David M. Richard, "Dispelling Myths About Maintenance Lubricants," *Plant Services*, May 1995, pp. 64–67.
7. Art Hemming, "Steam System Maintenance Focuses on Condensate," *Maintenance Technology*, November 1993, pp. 22–23.
8. Dennis Drennen, "Steam Trap Maintenance Tips," *Maintenance Technology*, September 1994, pp. 29–30.
9. Robert C. Baldwin, "Controlling Corrosion," *Maintenance Technology*, April 1993, pp. 29–30.

14

Improving Plant and Employee Performance

Making an evaluation of the existing conditions and status is a requisite to implementing a program to improve plant and employee performance. The evaluation should include management's assessment of the plant's profitability, employee productivity, effectiveness of various plant functions, and operating efficiency of critical production systems.

Management must adopt a philosophy that is conducive to optimum plant performance. In some plants, too many decisions are based on short-term profitability rather than long-term. Not enough thought is given to the effect these decisions will have on the company next year or several years in the future.

Inadequate communication, both upward and downward, is a common problem today; constant efforts must be made to overcome this to enable the plant to operate effectively and efficiently. A serious problem for managers is a lack of accurate, timely information. Managers rarely have enough to plan, identify problems, or control operating costs unless the plant is making optimum use of the computer, such as with a CMMS.

To improve plant performance, employee involvement is necessary. Without their commitment and cooperation, management will not be able to make progress. While some group efforts are required for the success of an improvement program, they should be limited to: selection of critical process equipment, system design, problem solving, and participation where multidiscipline input is required.

Programs should be adopted to improve the reliability, maintainability, capacity, and life cycle costs of all process and production systems. Optimum performance of critical machines, equipment, and continuous process systems is dependent on design, selection, installation, operation, and maintenance. Unless these matters are addressed in the improvement program, it will be difficult to realize optimum performance and to control costs.

TRAINING EMPLOYEES

One of the most effective ways to improve a plant's performance is to raise the skill level of the employees. This can be accomplished through a comprehensive training program that ensures that each employee is knowledgeable and capable of efficiently performing his or her job. A continuous education program should be a major part of a program designed to improve the plant's performance.

To set up a program, you must first determine the existing knowledge and skill of each employee, and then identify their specific training needs. You should also develop a method for continual evaluation of skill levels along with establishing training standards. A standard lists the training requirements as behavioral or performance objectives for each position in the plant, such as production operator, maintenance craftsperson, and others.

The best training programs require both development of general and specific courses and are presented by qualified trainers. Training materials include texts, workbooks, manuals, reference materials, transparencies, and video or audio tapes. Usually, classroom training alone is not enough to ensure that plant employees acquire the usable skills needed on their jobs. Therefore, classroom training should be augmented with practical or hands-on training.

Practical training consists of workshop and on-the-job instruction conducted by the applicable department with assistance from the training department. Hands-on training, an extension of the classroom training, should be given by the training department; this training normally proceeds at the trainee's own rate of learning.

Training efforts must focus on mastery of the job. Beware of training courses that result in only short-term retention of information and procedures. What frequently happens with these programs is that many of the trainees will pass the course, but few will retain the new knowledge long enough to apply it on the job.

PRODUCTIVITY IMPROVEMENT

Productivity improvement techniques are essential in many plants if significant progress in profitability is to be realized. The techniques management adopts and the way the techniques are related to the business will be the keys to success. Effective techniques bring about a strong connection between the plant's performance and employee performance. To assure a successful productivity improvement program:

- The program should fit the work culture and the plant need.
- Employees should feel that the program is a challenge, and there is a sense of urgency about it.
- Management should demonstrate an ongoing commitment to provide leadership and continuing support.
- Changes in training and the reward system may be needed to start the program and sustain it.
- Employees should have an opportunity to modify the program to fit their needs.
- Union leadership should be involved and supportive early in the program.

PARTICIPATIVE MANAGEMENT

Because of the increasing complexity of decisions being made in many plants, and the rising desire for involvement and commitment on the part of subordinates, managers have been turning more and more to the practice of participative management. The theory rests on the assumptions that employees at all levels of an organization are capable of contributing usefully to the decision-making process, and that, in general, this willingness and capability have not been used. Supporting the theory is the thinking of many managers that when subordinates are more involved in decision making, superiors have greater influence in how decisions are carried out.

However, this is a difficult thing for some managers to accept, especially those who believe they have earned the privilege of making their own decisions because of the years of hard work, training, and sacrifices they have put in.[1] Such managers don't realize that management is not a privilege but rather a responsibility. Subordinates should participate in decisions concerning their work. Other managers see participation as a shifting of responsibility. It certainly isn't that, because no one knows a particular job better than the person doing that job day after day. Some of the best ideas and solutions to problems come from the very people doing the work.

In any business, the power to make decisions must be vested in managerial personnel. A higher-level manager or a supervisor must be in a position to take decisive action quickly, and the person must be given definite responsibility to do so. In numerous instances today, when people affected by a change become involved in making the decisions that determine how it is to be implemented, they tend to resist it. Yet this conclusion is not valid in all cases. The problem of how a supervisor can achieve participation can be complex because participation means different things to different supervisors. To some it is a way to manipulate people to share a viewpoint already held by the supervisor. To others, it is merely a routine to be followed to create an illusion that the employees have some voice in what is happening to them. Of course, such thinking diverges widely from the true meaning of participation.

True participation cannot be achieved simply by asking people for it, nor can a manager demand that employees join in. Real participation depends on the feelings and attitudes of the people involved. The act of asking people to attend a meeting to discuss a management problem is insufficient motivation to get them to participate.

Employees must *want* to participate, and they must believe that their manager is sincere and honest in his or her intention. They must believe, furthermore, that if their ideas have merit, there is a good likelihood that they will be accepted. For these beliefs to exist, there must be a good relationship between the manager and the employees based on mutual respect and trust. If these feelings are not present, then any request for participation would be viewed with suspicion and mistrust. In addition, a deterioration of the relationship could result.

Another prerequisite for successful participation is that the manager must feel safe and secure in his or her position. Some managers may be reluctant to try to get participation from their people because of how they perceive their managerial role. A manager might, for instance, believe that to ask for advice or opinion from employees would be a sign of his or her inadequacy to handle the managerial position. He or she might feel that any involvement of workers in making decisions that are considered the manager's responsibilities would risk his or her status as a manager. The truth of the matter, however, is that if employees are permitted and encouraged by their manager to participate, their respect for him or her often increases rather than decreases.

One more prerequisite for participation is absence of commitment on the manager's part to a certain course of action. The manager must be open to any and all alternatives. When employees are invited to participate in making decisions, their ideas will both agree and disagree with those of their manager. Some of their ideas may be superior. If the manager is convinced from the beginning that his or her way of handling a problem is best and is the only way of accomplishing a change, then it would be wise for the manager not to try to involve others as participants in making the decision. Any such attempt would soon be recognized as meaningless, a waste of time, and even dishonest.

A final condition necessary for effective participation is the employees' willingness to express themselves and to offer suggestions once they have been encouraged to do so. Participation fails with people who are passive or reticent. Such feelings are usually a result either of their experiences on the job or their cultural beliefs.

If all of these conditions don't exist in the manager/employee situation and relationship, a manager should be very careful in considering the participation of his or her people in decision making. If, on the other hand, all the conditions are positive, the use of participation can result in significant benefits.

Benefits

When employees participate in the decision-making process, both they and the company gain. Thus, it pays for managers to encourage participation at every opportunity. A few such benefits are:

- Participation often serves to prevent worthless ideas from being adopted and poorly conceived changes from being made.
- The procedure helps to increase employees' confidence in management's intentions.
- When employees are asked to express their opinion, they feel important and "in" on things.
- Participation helps to develop a better understanding of change.
- Because of participation, people become more committed to the decision in which they took part.
- When subordinates participate, their capabilities are developed and expanded.
- Participation helps employees to broaden their outlook.

ELIMINATING MEETINGS

Managers in plants often spend too much of their time in meetings. Since cutting back on the number of meetings you attend would give you more time for other management responsibilities, eliminating some meetings is a very worthwhile objective. Here are several ways to do this:

- *Avoid calling meetings.* You owe it to yourself (as well as others), to only call a meeting if it is absolutely necessary. If you need a meeting to facilitate reaching the plant's work objectives, then by all means go ahead with it. But if those objectives can be met faster and easier, such as with a few phone calls, then don't call a meeting.

- *Try to combine meetings.* By reviewing recently held meetings and noting those scheduled in the near future, you may find meetings similar enough to be combined.

- *Minimize serving on committees.* Recognize that by joining a committee, you are committing yourself to a seemingly unending number of meetings. If you can avoid serving on committees, you will reduce the number of meetings you'll be asked to attend.

- *Turn down invitations.* Don't go to meetings simply because you've been invited. Explain that you don't feel a need to be there, and ask to be excused. If the other person is unyielding, see if you can send a subordinate to sit in for you.

ORIENTING NEW EMPLOYEES

There are several good reasons for you to see that all new employees are given an orientation to the company. The orientation is an important management responsibility in that the first day on the job has a major impact on the new employee's future morale, safety, security, and productivity. Lasting impressions of the company, coworkers, and workplace environment are normal by-products of anyone's orientation period.

New employees are almost always enthusiastic. They've probably put a lot of effort and time into getting the job, and they've succeeded. Remember how you felt the first day on a new job. The new employee feels the same way and wants to make a good showing. You must want to turn the person on. By capturing that initial enthusiasm, what you'll gain in the days ahead is a happier, more productive employee.

According to the Bureau of Labor Statistics (BLS), 40 percent of employees injured are ones who have been on the job less than one year. BLS studies show that injured employees often lack the information they need to work safely. Plant personnel who don't understand safe work practices are a hazard to themselves and to others. No matter how much experience people have had on other jobs or in other departments, don't make the mistake of assuming that they have the safety information they need about the plant and your department.

After welcoming new employees, always wrap up your orientation with a couple of morale boosters. Tell them you're pleased that they decided to join the company, and indicate you will help them do well on the job. Encourage them to feel comfortable in asking questions and discussing problems with you and their immediate supervisor. Success on the job isn't just dependent on skill and diligence; employees who feel ill at ease never perform at their optimum ability. Act like you have confidence in their ability to succeed and succeed they will.

TEMPORARY EMPLOYEES

Many plants periodically need extra labor for short periods of time. For example, if your company occasionally gets some large orders that must be shipped quickly, you may decide to hire some people on a temporary basis. Fortunately, most temporary service organizations today are capable of filling temporary positions on a moment's notice. It's generally agreed, however, that you will get the best service if you take the time to be very specific in stating your needs. This means that you should put your requirements and pertinent information together to enable the service organization to assign the people that best suit your needs. Include an estimate of the length of time the temporary employee(s) will be needed.

Evaluate the temporary service organizations in your area by doing the following:

- Visit the organization's office to meet management and discuss qualifications and capabilities. Ask for references and follow up on them.
- Inquire if the organization interviews, tests, and checks references of all new employees it hires to ensure their qualifications. Find out if the organization guarantees their work.
- Assess the organization's training programs. The firm that is conscientious and careful in how it handles this is likely to have the best employees.
- Consider quality, reliability, and reputation when selecting the organization you want to work with, not just the price they charge.

When the temporary employee arrives at your company, make sure you have handled all the preliminaries to assure that the person feels welcome. By being friendly and courteous as well as treating the employee as a member of the company team, you will help him or her to work more efficiently and productively.

On the first day on the job, give the person a tour of your facility, pointing out the cafeteria, restrooms, storeroom, and departments that may be involved with the assignment. Outline work procedures including starting and quitting times; explain the times and places for breaks and lunch.

Introduce the person to coworkers and those employees with whom he or she will associate. Provide a list of executives and department heads including their titles and phone numbers; explain how to put a caller on hold and how to transfer a call.

Talk about what the company expects in performance from the employee; this will help you both in measuring the employee's efficiency and effectiveness. Include a temporary employee in appropriate meetings and company activities, especially if the person is a long-term assignment.

REQUIREMENTS FOR IMPROVED PERFORMANCE OF THE PLANT

An environment that encourages and promotes optimum performance of employees leads all other requirements for a plant to be rated world class. This trait must originate with management and be inherent throughout all departments and plant functions. Following are the responsibilities and contributions of pertinent groups for a plant to improve its performance:

▪ The sales and marketing group must ensure that there are customers for the plant's products. For equipment and machines to be efficiently utilized, there must be a demand that requires full use of the manufacturing, production, and processes. In addition, sales must contribute to the cause by providing:

1. A product mix that results in effective use of the production process
2. Order sizes that limit the number and frequency of setups
3. Delivery schedules that permit effective scheduling of the processes
4. A pricing system that enables the plant to realize a reasonable profit

▪ The production department must plan and schedule the processes to achieve maximum use of the plant's equipment and resources. This requires: knowledge of unit production capabilities; adequate material control; good equipment reliability; coordination with the procurement function; and cooperation with the maintenance function.

Equipment reliability along with standard operating procedures are essential for acceptable production performance. Operating practices and the skill level of production employees have an impact on equipment reliability. Therefore, human resources and/or the training department must conduct training programs that will ensure that employee skill levels remain at optimum levels.

▪ The procurement function must furnish raw materials, spare machines and equipment, and operating supplies at the proper times to ensure uninterruption of processes and production operations. This function is critical to efficient performance of both production and maintenance. In addition, the group must adopt procedures that ensure support for these functions on inventory and material control. Included should be the establishment of specifications based on life-cycle costs and incoming inspection.

▪ The asset care function must ensure that all productive machines and equipment are in optimum operating condition. This means that these facilities must reliably operate at or above nameplate capacity without causing quality problems or frequent operating interruptions. The objective should be prevention of such occurrences, not quick repair or correction of problems. Both preventive and corrective maintenance programs must be implemented to achieve maximum use of maintenance resources and the production capacity of plant systems.

▪ Efficient use of plant resources is dependent on effective communication among departments and sound management decisions; thus, information management is critical to plant performance. Plants must have systems and procedures that collect, compile, and interpret data that define the effectiveness of critical plant functions. Such systems must supply timely, accurate performance indices that can be used to plan, schedule, and control the plant's operations.

IMPROVING MAINTENANCE EMPLOYEES' PERFORMANCE

Your guidance, ability to evoke the competitive spirit in employees, and power to motivate them can prove to be effective ways to improve their work performance. Here are some ways to develop quality job habits in maintenance employees:

1. Start new employees off right by setting high performance standards for them. Make sure they understand what you expect of them, and see that they get the proper training for their jobs.
2. Get to know all the maintenance employees. Talk to them about how they are doing on the job. Tell them how they can improve and give them recognition when they do.
3. Don't accept less than the best from an employee. If a person's job performance is inferior, find out why. It may be that he or she needs additional training or individual coaching.
4. Encourage creativity and innovation. Give employees credit for suggestions; your recognition promotes pride, which is the key to quality performance.
5. Focus on good workmanship and attention to the job. Quality-

conscious employees realize they must effectively maintain the plant's equipment to give the company a competitive edge and to protect their own job security.

6. See that the plant's preventive maintenance program focuses on inspection. Careful inspection ensures high quality in machine and equipment maintenance and in employee performance, provided you can trace problems to their causes and correct them.

7. Promote quality performance of employees with top-notch leadership. As a manager, you set the pattern of attitudes in your department. Once employees get the quality habit, they take pride in being part of a team that efficiently handles the maintenance function.

COACHING

Coaching is an appropriate course to follow if you see that an employee is a slow learner. With this technique, you discuss the situation with the employee and give him or her personal instruction. Following are the positive steps to take when coaching:

1. Be honest with the employee, but don't destroy the person's self-image. What you say can bear on how effective your coaching will be in improving and speeding up the learning process.

2. Recognize that coaching a slow learner involves criticism. Use it sparingly and carefully. You do not want to cause the person to develop a negative work attitude. They key is to keep emotions out of your coaching.

3. Don't say, "Why is it taking so long for you to get this?" Instead, tell the employee that some individuals find this particular job skill difficult to learn. Ask if the person has any suggestions for possible answers. This approach cuts the potential for excuses from him or her. It also focuses on the problem, not the person.

4. Listen carefully to the employee's ideas and suggestions. Faster learning and better performance is more likely to occur if you can get the person involved. Further, you may discover that the cause of the slow learning is beyond the person's control.

5. Make sure that the employee accepts the training objectives. Repeat what they are before ending your conversation with him or her.

6. Follow up on what you and the employee agreed to do. This should include setting a deadline by which you expect the person to have corrected the problem.

EMPLOYEE MORALE

The employee who has low morale usually is an unhappy and dissatisfied person. What's worse, this employee often promotes a negative attitude and feeling among other employees. When viewed in this light, the problem of low morale deserves your immediate attention.[2]

Low morale is seldom hidden. You become aware of it by observing and listening to people on the job. Typically, employees with low morale do their work reluctantly, are overconcerned with their safety, are excessively critical of supervisors and management, and complain that they are underpaid.

Although treating the individual as an individual is basic, groups and group morale are equally important. However, groups are, in some ways, easier to understand. There are some things you can expect of them when you know their composition. In understanding the group, you will find that the seeming logic of the situation does not always reveal the meaning underneath—the one that counts. For example, if asked, most people would tell you that money is the most important factor in keeping people happy on the job. This is a reason people frequently give for leaving one job and taking another. But when you examine the reasons closely, you will find that few employees leave their jobs unless they are dissatisfied in a more personal way, not just with the income.

Good individual attitudes on the job, leading to high group morale are all important. If attitudes are poor, what you as the manager should understand are the emotional needs that lie beneath the reasons given. The way you look at things may not be the way your group does. It is your job to understand their viewpoint. This takes some application of the principles of behavior, and it takes some thinking on your part.

One of the basic psychological needs of an employee is the need to be accepted. When he or she comes into a job, the person is going to seek acceptance from the other employees. The person wants to be part of the group with which he or she is working. Part of being accepted is to go along with the ideas of the group, and to accept the attitudes that have already been formed in a working situation; the individual is no longer a separate entity. He or she is now part of a group or groups. The person has to accept those in the group in order to be accepted by the group. This is where the core of group feeling has its origins. If the group holds negative feelings, the attitudes of the new individual will be negative too, or he or she will not be part of the group for long. In working with groups, you will do well to permit the individual, where feasible, to choose his or her group. This can foster better morale.

Aspects of Good Morale

Good morale in a working situation such as in a plant has four key aspects. They are:

1. Satisfaction in the job itself
2. Pride in the other employees
3. Acceptance of pay scales and promotion opportunities
4. A feeling of "belonging" to the company

Basically, the group's morale is good when these four needs are being met and poor when they are not. Of course, in any particular department of the plant, or at any one time, one of these needs may be more important than the others. The different ways in which any one of them is satisfied will depend on education, previous experience, social relationships, age, and other factors.

For example, in terms of income-class groups, the lower and middle income groups place greater emphasis on security, whereas employees in high-income groups, by contrast, give more weight to social approval of their jobs.

Age of the employee also has its influence. Both at the very beginning of the vocational career and again toward the end, an employee tends to have better morale than during the middle of the career. This means that in terms either of economic class or age, wages tend to rank below the top place in affecting employee morale.

Financial incentives, in other words, are not enough for a sensible human relations program. Once an employee's basic need for adequate pay is satisfied, other nonmonetary aspects of the job take an ever-increasing significance. While employees often say that wages are the reason for poor morale, investigation shows that other, less obvious, less rational needs are often really the prime cause.

Employees' reactions can often be seen in terms of emotional needs. There is frustration when needs are not met, and morale goes down. If morale goes down far enough, there are company and department problems. It is also true that the varied groups in the plant—supervisors, hourly-rate employees, seasonal help, and other specific groups—do not have precisely the same needs.

Try to keep alert to symptoms that indicate low levels of morale. High employee turnover, absenteeism, grievances, complaints, and the like, tend to go with poor morale and the lack of a sensible human relations program. So do long faces, short tempers, hot arguments, and cold silences. Opposite conditions usually reflect good morale.

A preventive approach always works best. You should watch for "unimportant" and "illogical" matters that influence morale. Stay alert to the plant's working conditions. Complaints about them may be justified; on the other hand, they may be cover-ups for more important and serious underlying problems.

EMPLOYEE LOYALTY

It used to be that hard work and dedication to a company virtually guaranteed lifelong job security. Now, however, competitive stresses cause companies to continually reassess their employment needs.[3] As a result, many employees feel if a company is not going to retain them forever, they are not going to remain loyal—at least not in the old way. Thus, the job of showing employees they are valued and building loyalty is falling on supervisors and managers. If this seems to be a problem in your plant, here are several things you can do:

- Be sure you are honest when you are communicating. Say you don't know the answer to a question when you really don't. And admit when you know something but are not authorized to divulge it.
- Empower employees by allowing them to make decisions that affect the way they do their jobs. Empowerment builds trust.
- Treat employees fairly. If they give and give and get nothing in return, they will try to make the relationship more equal by doing only what is necessary to hold their jobs.
- Give employees feedback regularly on how they're doing on the job. Ask them to give you feedback on how you're doing as a manager.

EMPLOYEE BOREDOM

If some of the plant employees have begun to make more errors or fail to meet product quality standards, they may be bored with their jobs. This problem comes up in the best of organizations, especially if changes in the workplace, processes, or operating procedures haven't occurred for a long time. People simply get bored with doing the same thing day after day. However, there are answers to the problem. Here are a few options to consider:

- *Move people around.* Many employees are interested in what others are doing and why jobs are handled in certain ways. You can take advantage of the "want to know" and "how is it done" inquisitiveness that is natural to most employees. By training people to do their fellow workers' jobs, you help them to understand how the department operates. In addition, when everyone is familiar with most of the work procedures, you have protection in the case of unexpected absences or other emergencies.

■ *Promote special projects.* There's always a need for improved safety and a better organized, more attractive workplace. By rotating assignments to committees with responsibilities in those areas, and seeing that everyone gets his or her fair share of such work, you can minimize boredom and at the same time raise morale.

■ *Step up social activities.* Make the occasion of the plant getting a big order or gaining some new customers as a time to celebrate. It's easy to put on an informal party with very short notice. Getting away from a boring job for even an hour serves to rejuvenate many employees.

■ *Arrange visits and tours.* Recognize that some employees would like to see how other plants and organizations are operated. Set up exchange visits with other companies in your locality. Changes of scenery can be invigorating, spark new interests, and even lead to new and better ways of handling jobs.

EMPLOYEE EMPOWERMENT

Allowing your employees to make decisions that affect the way they do their jobs is one of the strongest ways you can gain their commitment. Most managers have learned, however, that empowerment works only if it is closely managed and nothing is taken for granted.

Especially during transition periods and periods of downsizing, it is essential that employees feel involved and empowered to act. This is fortunate because many employees want to get more involved in contributing to product quality and company profitability, which can make a significant difference just in terms of survival in restructuring periods.

The creation of teams is an excellent way to empower employees. In one company, teams have recently accomplished goals such as reclassifying and deleting jobs based on a division-wide position analysis. In others, the creativity, commitment, and camaraderie of empowered employees produce increased productivity results beyond what their managers had hoped for. The empowered employees of a General Electric plant in Fort Wayne, Indiana, are a good example of this. In the early '90s, the plant had a negative productivity rate; today, the employees have reduced rejects from 2,300 per million to only 150 per million. They also cut order-to-shipment time from 55 days to 16 days. The reason: Plant management reorganized work flow into cellular manufacturing and trained employees on teamwork and problem solving.

Empowerment Through Delegation

By entrusting your employees with work that builds them up and enables them to use their training and skills, you will have more time to manage, plan, and take on other jobs in the plant. Here are some suggestions on how to become an effective delegator and empower people at the same time:[4]

- Determine the tasks to delegate. Recurring tasks, detail work, attendance at some meetings, and activities that will be a part of an employee's future responsibilities are good examples. Don't make the mistake of delegating only unimportant tasks that insult employees and limit growth and advancement.
- Decide who will do each task. Consider the skills, interests, and current workloads of individuals when you make assignments.
- Explain your expectations and ask the employee to repeat your instructions to check for understanding.
- Grant authority to spend money, get help from others, or represent the department or company.
- Explain support available to the delegatee. This may include a budget, help from other departments, or your own assistance.
- Get agreement and understanding. Be sure you've handled all doubts, questions, and suggestions before work begins.
- Follow up and monitor progress. Don't overact if problems come up. Instead, give advice and the opportunity to correct any errors that may have occurred.

ASSIGNING EMPLOYEE RESPONSIBILITIES

One of the requisites for optimum plant performance is effective utilization of company resources through positive involvement of the work force. Management should achieve this objective by empowering employees, including assigning them responsibilities.

There's a difference of opinion of people on the job as to what responsibility means. One definition is that it means obligation. For instance, when an employee accepts a share of the responsibility for getting work done, it means that the person accepts an obligation to act or do a job. You are expecting him or her to satisfactorily carry out an assignment that he or she accepted.

While there are many employees who say they don't want to be responsible, and many who say they do, how many realize what they're saying either way? Accepting responsibility indicates that they have agreed to go beyond merely going through the motions required by their job or an assignment you have given them—they must produce acceptable results, which may be a little more than they bargained for. To them, sharing the responsibility may mean merely that you will keep off their back, to let them do their thing in their own way.

As for assigning responsibilities, major ones are more easily defined than minor ones. Manufacturing plants, for example, should never rely on verbal assignments on matters of this importance; they are too confusing, may be easily misinterpreted, and sometimes overlap. The most complete and reliable document for determining the responsibilities of individuals is a Plant Operations Manual or a compilation of Standard Practice sheets. Usually consisting of printed forms and notices, and distributed in a looseleaf binder, a manual contains all the responsibilities of both plant departments and individuals. Often, it also includes the procedures to be followed in the plant.

You should revise and update responsibilities as personnel are reassigned and as process methods, equipment, and operational procedures change. The reassignments should be as clear and formal as the original assignments and made prior to or at the same time as the changes requiring them.

COMMUNICATING WITH EMPLOYEES ABOUT PERFORMANCE

As a manager, you can directly affect the performance of your employees. What you say and don't say about their current performance, both good and bad, will determine their future performance. You should regard every discussion you have about performance as an opportunity to develop your people.[5]

It is your responsibility to direct your employees and maximize their work efforts. Your opinion means a lot to them; make the most of the opportunities you have to guide them. The managers rated highest by employees are those who help them become the best they can be.

Giving Feedback

You have three ways in which you can give employees feedback:

1. Coaching or counseling conversations
2. Performance reviews

3. Evaluations and recommendations about the readiness of an employee for advancement, a raise, a transfer, or new assignments

Providing feedback lets an employee know the results of his or her behavior. But you have to do some preparation to give feedback. You must be ready to describe the problem and talk about its importance. You should also have some ideas about how to actively involve the employee in the solution to this problem.

Have several objectives in mind when you give feedback. You want to:

- Bring about behavior change.
- Impress upon the employee the seriousness of the situation.
- Get from the employee whatever information he or she might have.
- Ensure that the employee clearly understands the nature of your concerns and your commitment to resolving those concerns.
- Arrive at a solution to the problem.

For the feedback to be effective, this discussion should have the following characteristics:

- Mutual trust
- Two-way listening
- Supportive behavior on your part to make it easier for the employee to talk

Guidelines on Feedback

Here are some guidelines to help you keep your feedback constructive:

1. Give feedback as soon as it is appropriate, not a month or two later after an incident or performance.
2. While it is important to get across how you feel about what has happened, after you have made your point, go on to something else.
3. Focus on a person's behavior, not his or her self-esteem.
4. Don't be judgmental. Report your observations of what has occurred and let the employee use the feedback as he or she sees fit.
5. Talk about the effect; do not try to imply what caused it.
6. Be specific, particularly about time and events.
7. Work with what can be controlled and changed. Wish comments are of no value.
8. Share ideas and information. Avoid giving advice.

9. Never demand change. You can't force people to do something they don't want to do.
10. Check for understanding. Even well-intentioned feedback can be misinterpreted.
11. Summarize frequently. Bring each point to a conclusion before you move on to something else.

RECOGNIZING AND REWARDING EMPLOYEES

Although some plant employees are given the opportunity to win awards for job accomplishments, if managers formally recognize their abilities and contributions in the presence of their peers, it can mean more to them than any awards or trophies. Unfortunately, not enough companies are aware of the value and significance of employee recognition. For something that costs very little and can be as simple as a "thank you" for doing an excellent job, the payback is much more than seems possible. Even acknowledging the efforts made by employees to reach an objective can result in a more motivated and productive work team.

What is being overlooked here is that more and more managers have gained worthwhile benefits from publicly noticing employees' increased productivity and achievements. These managers can point to more positive attitudes, greater job satisfaction, and increased communication within the company as evidence that recognizing employees pays off.

Some companies have implemented formal programs that show their interest in their employees' performance. These programs recognize employees for a variety of accomplishments, such as showing concern for the company's customers and trying to meet their needs. In addition, employees are noticed for routinely going above and beyond their job responsibilities and for everyday commitment to promote the company to friends and others.

Another way of recognizing employees goes beyond awards and positive feedback. It involves giving them additional responsibility, decision-making power, and a great deal of freedom on how they do their work. For employees who work primarily with their hands, this moral independence motivates them and also makes them feel important.

An excellent way of giving recognition while at the same time making a person feel important is to say, "You did an excellent job." You can say this or something similar whenever someone does an unusually good job or comes up with a worthwhile contribution to your work team or the company. Besides motivating employees, you can, to a greater extent, get them to cooperate as well as be creative when you make them feel important. Many times you'll find that a feeling of importance is their most dominant desire anyway. To give people such a feeling, try the following:

- Become genuinely interested in them and think in terms of what they need and want.
- Never take them for granted; learn to always listen to them.
- Be concerned about them and above all, be patient with them.
- Recognize that, from time to time, we all need recognition, a feeling of importance, and a good word from our superiors.

DOCUMENTING PERFORMANCE

With all the duties and responsibilities you have as a manager, you cannot expect to remember every incident and event, both good and bad, that occurs in the workplace. Even if you could recall most of them, there will be occasions where records, letters, and reports will provide the support you need to make good decisions and take appropriate action. To illustrate this reasoning, here are a few examples of instances when documents are invaluable to you:

- *When making performance appraisals.* When you prepare for a performance appraisal and are careful in implementing it, both the company and the employee benefit. You need to keep a log of incidents and performances of the employee to which you can refer. Before an appraisal, review the record and personal history of the person by collecting all the information including that from other people. Look into the person's background, service-time with the company, previous jobs held, and what progress the person has made since being hired. Also, study any notes made of previous appraisals with the person.
- *When disciplining.* A discipline program is effective only when it is documented to inform all employees of its content. It should also be characterized in three ways:
  1. *Uniform*—a spelled out, well-defined program prevents the imposition of different discipline for the same offense.
  2. *Corrective*—the program states proper conduct, thus telling the employee how to correct his or her improper conduct.
  3. *Progressive*—the procedure states how the severity of the discipline is increased with repeated offenses.
- *When handling personnel activities.* Hiring, transferring, promoting, and providing fringe benefits require that records be created and main-

tained. Although most of these activities are usually handled by the personnel department, you may frequently be involved. One of your responsibilities is to protect the privacy of such information. Records should be kept in closed folders, filed when not in use, and locked when unattended. You should permit an employee to have supervised access to his or her own file if there is a question about the accuracy of the information in it.

■ *When handling grievances and complaints.* Effective grievance handling requires a positive attitude toward employees. Learn where you can find the answer to a complaint. If it involves company policy, for example, the employee handbook may contain the information. If the complaint concerns interpretation of the union/management contract, study the wording in the applicable section. Always make a record of the grievance and your answer. The information will be valuable to management in future dealings with employees and/or the union.

PERFORMANCE APPRAISALS

Appraising or judging employee performance is one of the most difficult parts of managing.[6] While many organizations profess to use merit (job performance) as the primary criterion for rewarding employees, most merit systems do not work out that way. Because money is such an important influence on job-related behavior, employees adjust their behavior to acquire salary increases.

Employees should clearly understand that all forms of rewards—whether money, promotions, privileges, or status symbols—are directly related to their performance. If rewards are given for other than job performance, employees' time and energy will likely be directed accordingly in order to gain the desired rewards; thus, performance will suffer.

Managers usually consider a performance appraisal as the formal procedure of measuring how well an employee has handled responsibilities and assignments during a given period of time. Performance appraisals, however, are used for a variety of purposes, including compensation administration, promotional consideration, disciplinary consideration, transfer, layoff, and assessing training needs.

Preparing for an Appraisal Interview

Since managers frequently conduct appraisals of subordinates, you should know the most effective way to handle one. An interview will be easy for you and you'll do a more extensive job if you prepare for it. Here are some suggestions on how to do this:

■ Review the record and personal history of the person by collecting all the information you have, including that from other people. Look into the person's background, service-time with the company, previous positions held, and what progress the person has made since joining the company. Study any notes made of previous appraisals with the person.

■ Consider the work the person is doing. Become familiar with the standards and responsibilities of the position in order to judge how he or she is doing. Determine what a person in that position must do to be a success.

■ Pick a time for the interview. Avoid scheduling it for when you or the person might be very busy or could be interrupted. Plan to not start the interview unless you're fairly sure you can finish it.

Guidelines on Interviewing

The key to a good performance appraisal interview is to have the interviewee at ease, willing to discuss his or her job, and wanting to learn how to improve. To put the person in this frame of mind, you should begin by explaining the purpose of your meeting. Say that you are talking to all your people, and that your main purpose is to help each person. Tell the person that you want to talk about the work and how it is going, and that you also would like to talk about any problems the person may have.

When you counsel with your people, you let them know how they are doing and what they can do to improve their performance. Since an appraisal interview is like a progress report, most people consider it important and will take it quite seriously.

The interview is equally important to you because it presents an opportunity to learn more about the person and to motivate him or her through encouragement and praise. Because both of you have a lot to gain from an interview, it's essential for you to do the best you can with it. Here are some guidelines:

1. Listen carefully when the person talks. This may be difficult for two reasons: First, you may already think you know what the person is going to say, and second, while the person is talking, you may be thinking about how you will respond. Remember, however, that if you don't listen carefully, you may not understand completely what the person is saying. Consequently, you'll be unable to supply the right motivation for better performance.

2. Allocate equal time to praise and criticism. Resist the inclination to spend a lot of time discussing a person's weakness or area of below average achievement. Recognize that too much finding fault can cause resentment.

3. Be friendly and sincere. You are trying to help the person, not tear him or her down. Be encouraging and positive when suggesting how performance can be improved.

4. Limit the goals and objectives you set for the person both in number and degree. Recognize a person's capabilities in anticipating what can be accomplished. Don't expect a complete change of behavior during or immediately after a single interview.

HUMAN RESOURCES MANAGEMENT

With today's shift from an industrial to a service-based economy, a change in the nature of social values, and continuing technological advancement, a role change is required for managers in plants. They must place more emphasis on information management, planning, and coordinating. In addition, they must expand recruitment and training functions. All of these efforts are required if managers are to be effective in improving plant and employee performance. Getting the best from employees will depend upon managers' skills and abilities in the following areas;

■ *Workforce diversity.* Companies must be able to meet a variety of individual needs because the workforce is changing in gender, life-style, age, and ethnic background. Changes in the current methods of compensation and benefits are expected. Both male and female workers will look for different forms of compensation, and the greater number of women in the workforce will necessitate more emphasis be placed on flexible schedules and child care.

The more diverse age range of the workforce will require changes in how management satisfies the needs and expectations of employees. For example, younger employees tend to be more satisfied with good pay, greater responsibilities, and time off, while medical and retirement benefits along with job security are generally more important to older people.

■ *Different work allocation and matching job skills with requirements.* With the changing nature of the workforce and continual technological advancements, managers have found that work must be allocated and designed differently. Other changes, such as social values and faster economic cycles in the business environment, require that allocation of work be more flexible. Solutions to these problems include part-time work, job sharing, flextime, and on-call schedules.

Most of the newer technologies: automation, bar-coding, video teleconferencing, computer-assisted design, and others, demand that new equipment and instrumentation be furnished. These advancements have brought on autonomous work groups, many of which are highly specialized.

But matching job skills with requirements continues to be a problem for companies engaged in new technologies. Rapid changes in technology have created needs for skills that many companies' existing workforces do not currently have. At the same time, these changes are making other skills obsolete.

■ *Extended recruitment and training efforts.* Today's companies must be concerned with doing more recruiting, developing screening procedures, and training new hires. Managers must also recognize when existing employees need to be retrained to help them adapt to change and to take on new jobs. With both efforts, the company must provide appropriate and sufficient educational programs.

The change in human resources accounting requires that ways be designed to account for investments in people's capabilities. Through the use of systems, companies will be better able to decide if recruiting or retraining is more cost-effective. Companies can limit training costs by carefully screening for those skills they anticipate needing in the future. In general, people should be recruited who have a high learning capacity, adapt easily to change, and tolerate uncertainty.

■ *Employee personal growth and participation in management.* More and more companies are becoming involved with redesigning jobs in order to meet employee needs for personal growth, autonomy, and recognition. This is the way to respond to job seekers who increasingly are looking for work where they can be recognized for their individual talents, skill, and knowledge.

When managers adopt the principles of participative management, they encourage and promote the taking part in decision-making of employees on matters relative to how the company should be operated. True participation means more than just physical involvement in a work situation. It is involvement of the employees' minds in their thinking and opinions of the work and how it should be performed. Managers should realize that true participation isn't achieved easily. Besides, there are limits to how far management can go with it. For one thing, it is more difficult to get the participation of a large group than a small one. For another, the procedures of attaining participation are not always clear-cut and straightforward.

DIVERSITY

Learning to manage effectively and get along harmoniously with employees of all races, backgrounds, and abilities is an unfamiliar experience for many new managers in plants. What is happening is that the makeup of the United States workforce is rapidly changing as earlier minorities become majorities and organizations become increasingly multicultured. This diversity brings you face-to-face with a lot of new problems. With the nature of the work group clearly different, you are required to communicate fully and clearly with diverse cultures, across the generation gap, between genders and classes, and among races. In addition, each employee is working for and expecting acceptance by others. Since many managers have never been put in this position before, it's understandable that some of them are frequently not at ease.

Yet, now more than ever, you need to understand and take advantage of the human resources available to you by delving deep into the capabilities of *all* members of the workforce to do their best. With the predicted workforce shortage becoming reality in the future, you must be prepared to accept and put to work more and more immigrants and employees with disabilities.

Realize that everyone you work with is as complex, talented, and has distinct characteristics and qualities as you; however, they appear in different colors and speak different languages. As a manager, you can create an environment of sensitivity and acceptance, model inclusive behavior, and foster expectations for respect and civility among all employees. You can also help to promote relationships where all people are valued, respected, and appreciated by dealing with diversity in a positive and friendly manner. The ways to do this are as follows:

- Become comfortable with not acting like you are in charge, in control, or always right. Value the strengths of others and empower them to do their best.
- See every worker as a human being with worth. There is more than one way to be human, productive, and get the job done.
- Recognize that others have different needs and preferences. Respect other points of view and include those who are different from you in discussions.
- Insist that intolerant behavior among fellow workers is unacceptable. Emphasize that everyone should work together to achieve mutual goals.

IMPROVING EMPLOYEES' PRODUCTIVITY

To achieve higher productivity from plant employees, you need to get them involved in the decision-making process.[7] Experience has shown that employees who understand why they are performing certain functions, and how those functions contribute to the company's objectives, are more proficient and productive on the job.

Once involved in the process, employees' productivity can be further increased by measuring both individual and team performance against several objectives on a regular basis. Objectives are the day-to-day tasks that must be accomplished in order to achieve the company's goals. Many objectives are stated as ratios, thus establishing tough but achievable numerical targets.

For example, in a manufacturing plant, typical employee objectives are finished product out versus raw materials in; pounds packaged per shift versus the nameplate capacity of the packaging line; and machines and equipment inspected or serviced versus total plant equipment. Objectives should be stated in realistic terms over which the employees have control. Stating objectives in a variety of different terms such as labor cost per hour or dollars per pound packaged creates confusion and delays results.

Once objectives are discussed, established, and understood, they must be continually measured. Constant feedback is necessary to achieve high levels of productivity, and may be provided in several ways. Meetings, charts, graphs, and other ways of getting across the information are effective as long as they are frequent, the objective is understood, and a clear pattern toward the objective is shown.

WORK SAMPLING

Work sampling, or the random observation of people on the job, is a technique whereby you can effectively determine how much time employees actually spend working. From a work sampling study, you can discover how productive they are and how they spend their unproductive time. It is possible to determine whether employees are as efficient or inefficient as they appear.

The laws of probability provide the basis for work sampling. These state that a large number of observations made at random intervals and classified into distinct activities will provide a fairly reliable account of how often specific activities occur. A requisite of a work sample study is that observations must be made randomly if unbiased results are to be obtained.

When work-sampling individuals in a plant, you should measure the following:

- *Direct work.* Performing specific work duties at the work site such as operating machines or equipment, repairing or servicing them, and handling materials.

- *Receiving instructions.* Conversation with first-line manager with specific work papers or tools on hand indicating that more than a casual conversation is taking place.
- *Traveling.* Walking or traveling to a work area such as a machine *without* carrying work materials or tools.
- *Transportation.* Moving materials, instruments, or equipment within the work environment.
- *Preparing.* Getting ready to begin specific work or a job, getting out or putting away tools or papers, and cleaning up after work.
- *Idle-off-job.* Performing nonjob-related activities *away* from the job site which cannot be classified in one of the other categories.
- *Idle-on-job.* Performing nonjob-related activities *on* the job site which cannot be classified in one of the other categories.

To ensure success with a study, get the cooperation and participation of the employees to be studied. Knowing that work is to be investigated creates uneasiness and concern. You should fully explain the purpose of the study while also assuring employees that their jobs are not in jeopardy.

After finishing the study, announce the results and thank participants for their cooperation. Later, if changes are made in procedures or work areas, employees will be more willing to accept them because they will realize that it was a result of their own actions.

MAINTENANCE FUNCTIONS

When you consider the seemingly endless list of functions performed by the plant's maintenance department, you can see why optimizing the productivity of maintenance employees is critical to the plant's financial success. The way you handle maintenance responsibilities affects overall plant performance in five prime areas—production, quality, safety, cost, and housekeeping.[8]

Management control is essential to operating a cost-effective and efficient maintenance department. The major step in achieving control is the planning and scheduling of maintenance activities. To implement planning and scheduling, you need to:

1. Plan and schedule all maintenance work that requires two or more workhours to complete.
2. Establish a priority system for all work orders.
3. Get agreement between the production and maintenance departments on which of the highest priority work orders should be put on a daily schedule.
4. Have the schedule duplicated, posted, and distributed to supervisors and managers of interested or affected departments.

ERGONOMICS

Ergonomics, sometimes called biomechanics and human engineering, is defined as a multidisciplinary science that combines engineering, medicine, and psychology to optimize human performance, safety, and health. When ergonomic applications become part of a plant's safety program, the design of the workplace and the procedures and tools used not only increase employees' skills and productivity, but safeguard them from overexertion and stress.

Ergonomic solutions to plant safety problems can be as simple as adding a footrest to a work bench or elevating the work surface to a comfortable height; they can be as extensive and complicated as providing ergonomically designed, adjustable workstations, altering material handling operations, redesigning hand tools, and modifying the environment. The results are that the employees can see and feel the difference, and this benefits safety, labor relations, productivity, and product quality.

The practice of ergonomics more than pays for itself in all types of plants. Here are a few specific areas where ergonomic efforts have proved to be worthwhile:

- *Layout and design.* Many plant employees need more room than they have to move around as they do their work. Confined and tight work areas limit their freedom to shift their weight and relax their muscles. These situations cause tenseness and strain, conditions that lead to painful cramping and muscle spasms.

As women continue to work on jobs previously held only by men, the challenge for management is to design the workplace and furnish equipment safe for everyone. For instance, most equipment and machine design favors male physical attributes, such as strength, size, endurance, and body structure. Although much of the need for size and strength in plant employees has been reduced by more efficiently and effectively designed procedures, many of these adaptations have not yet been fully applied to tools, equipment, and machines used by women.

Making allowances for differences in employee heights can eliminate the need to stretch or reach unnecessarily. This may help alleviate sore muscles and back injuries. Workers who need to bend over often during a shift may tire quickly and be more prone to accidents. When workers have to devise their own methods of adjusting to awkward work positions, like standing on pallets or boxes to reach controls or material, the chance of accidents also increases.

- *Work procedures.* Although instructing and training plant employees on how to lift prevents injuries, a better answer to this problem is to install machines to perform lifting operations. Fortunately, many equipment and machine manufacturers have long produced various types of these machines. Additionally, manufacturers of material handling equipment are supplying industry with pallet positioners, tilters, turntables, and containers sized to eliminate heavy handling.

When tools are ergonomically designed and easy to handle, craftspersons and production operators are less likely to have accidents involving them. Using the proper tool for a job also lessens physical and mental stress. Studies have shown, however, that many traditional tools are not compatible with the body dimensions and performance characteristics of humans.

The traditional design of pliers, for example, requires a bent wrist with a grasping force at some angle of the arm. This fault has been remedied with a bent nose or pistol grip design, so the tool can be used without bending the wrist. Another point to be made here is that tool handles should be extended through the hand because the center of the palm does not bear stress well.

■ *Computer operations.* By applying ergonomics to the design of computer workstations, you can considerably improve the comfort and well-being of computer operators.[9] Furniture construction and placement, along with recognition of human body, wrist, and hand weaknesses, are the primary bases on which to build improvement programs. Following are the major functions and factors that are involved in the effective use of ergonomics in computer operations.

1. *Seating and sitting position.* Because almost all sustained terminal operation is performed from a seated position, seating posture deserves particular attention. Proper posture assures both comfort and accessibility to the keyboard. For operator comfort and a minimum of stress, ergonomic features of the furniture should include:
    a) A chair with an adjustable backrest and seat to provide low-back support and to control the amount of pressure on the back and thighs. The chair should have five legs for stability and wheels to enable the operator to easily change position at the work desk.
    b) A foot rest for operators with shorter legs. The rest will relieve thigh pressure or furnish support when the seat height is adjusted for a fixed-height work surface.
2. *Work desks and surfaces.* While the average work desk is thirty inches high, that's too high for the placing and operating of a keyboard. If separate surfaces are provided for the screen and the keyboard, an operator has a choice of a wide range of adjustments to position the keyboard and screen to suit his or her

needs. The best ergonomic design of desks and work surfaces requires:

a) A desk that is between twenty-three and twenty-eight inches high, depending on the operator's height. The desk should allow for knee clearance over the full range of body movement required to operate all accessories.

b) A work surface that holds all work materials and also permits efficient work flow. The operator should not have to stretch or get out of the chair to pick up or place material.

3. *Keyboard and screen.* Operating a computer requires frequent wrist and hand motion. Thus, measures should be taken to prevent strain and injury. When screens are mounted on arms and stands, valuable work space is created. Effective keyboard and screen design includes:

a) A detachable keyboard that can be positioned for efficient keying. The top surface of the front row of keys should be no higher than two to three inches above the work surface. With the operator's elbows at ninety degrees and his or her forearms parallel to the floor, the keyboard should be at the level of the person's thumb joints. Wrists should not be bent up, down, or sideways.

b) An elevated, cushioned support to help align wrists to the keyboard. This device relaxes muscle tension in the operator's wrists, arms, shoulders, and neck to ease the discomforts of repetitive motions.

c) A screen stand with an arm that extends, retracts, rotates, and lifts the screen, allowing it to be positioned to eliminate glare and reduce neck pain or backache. The screen should be located eighteen to twenty-four inches distant from the operator's eyes for easiest focusing.

■ *Noise control.* This means keeping sound in ranges that are comfortable for humans in plants and offices; it does not mean eliminating all noise and sound. A complete absence of sound is undesirable because of its psychological effects. Many employees are unable to work under such conditions.

High noise levels can cause an accelerated heart rate, a rise in blood pressure, increased muscular tensions, and even poor digestion. In addition, noise can be responsible for other psychological effects including mental stress, irritability, nervousness, and a reduction in the ability to think and work efficiently.

Acoustic problems in the plant are mainly due to heavy equipment and machines running at high speeds. Noise in the office includes that from machines and from the much higher density of people. Management can use similar methods of sound control for both areas, primarily through the use of acoustic materials and proper construction and placement of these materials.

▪ *The environment.* There is more to ergonomics, however, than the installation of a man/machine system. Redesign of refurbishing of workstations should include consideration of such factors as color, room temperature, and ventilation. Management can very easily change the color of facilities or the walls of a room to suit employees. People in a room decorated in warm colors will tend to feel comfortable at a lower temperature than those in a room that is decorated in a cool color.

Cost Justification

Ergonomics contributes to productivity in three ways:

1. By applying ergonomic principles in the plant, you improve employees' ability to perform service, manufacturing, or material handling tasks.
2. Ergonomics can be a major factor in controlling employees' claims for injuries that are primarily musculoskeletal in nature. Most of these injuries occur in manual material-handling operations.
3. When you increase the safety, protect the health, and improve the comfort of employees, they are usually more productive.

Because the motivators for adopting ergonomics are strong, by focusing on them, you, as a manager, can change the viewpoint of ergonomics from being something you would *like to do* to something you *must do.* Most companies have more money invested in their employees than all other budgetary factors combined. Since employees are expensive, you should do as much as you can to protect that investment.

If you see ergonomic changes as costly and not worth the expense, consider that you could spend as little as $500 for equipment such as a work positioner that would make a material handling job safer and easier; or $200 for a pushcart to help a disabled worker; or $400 for an adjustable chair for an employee who spends the entire day at a computer. Compare these investments with the average cost of $10,000 or more of a lost-time injury of an employee; or thousands of dollars in legal fees for a Disabilities Act Compliance lawsuit.

PROMOTING A TEAM SPIRIT

Making employees feel that they're part of the team is a major undertaking for many managers in plants. Pressures such as the push to achieve greater productivity, the introduction of new technology, and the constant need to train and retrain affect the desire and ability of people to work together efficiently and with a common goal in mind.

Yet knowledgeable and astute managers have found ways to overcome these problems. Here is how you should go about it:

- Be aware that many of the employees know little about the technical aspects of the department's operations; they may occasionally have problems because of this. Encourage them to ask questions when they don't understand something.
- Promote enthusiasm and creativity. By having the team and a leader collaborate in developing a project plan, team members will see it as *their* project and *their* plan. They will be more likely to do what it takes to meet goals, including doing more than is expected of them.
- Recognize that tension and stress often result when people make errors. Refrain from faultfinding and be positive with your remarks. Focus on commitment, cooperation, and pride in a job well done.
- Encourage interdependence among team members by defining roles and responsibilities. When members have mutual respect for capabilities and differences, they work better as a team. They trust other team members and they help one another. They also become adept at managing conflicts to achieve a win-win result for everyone.

Self-Directed Teams

As more and more companies empower their employees as a means of staying competitive, managers are looking for all the elements of productivity to improve—quality, cost, decision making, and scheduling. Self-directed teams, the highest degree of employee participation, usually consist of five to fifteen skilled individuals with decision-making power. They are responsible for completing a product, carrying out a project, or providing a service; they work without supervision.

But not all companies should go to this level of employee participation. In an organization where the existing management structure runs counter to giving up command and control, it would be doomed to failure. Organizations need to examine their strategic plan, technology base, and employees' skills and capabilities to decide whether self-directed teams, or another form of participative management is appropriate.

If a plant does decide to implement autonomous teams, the transition period can be a critical time. To achieve efficient self-directed teams may take more than a year unless the plant is already practicing some form of participative management at the beginning of the transition. Management should slowly relinquish control, yet continue to provide support.

There may be a time when turmoil exists, but that doesn't have to last long if management is prepared for it. The companies that have good results are those where the existing managers and teams get together and discuss specific tasks that will be changing hands, and the proper training and skills to do this are provided. Also, it helps if a recognized leader emerges on the team.

FLEXIBLE SCHEDULING

Flexible scheduling—working variable hours during the day or week—has been a blessing to those plant employees who need to accommodate the demands of family or other personal needs. It also offers an advantage to management in that when employees work without the stress of personal problems resulting from time demands, they are more focused and productive.[10]

Despite these pluses, flexible hours for employees often aren't easily accepted by everyone. Some managers operate by the long-outdated concept of face time: That is, the amount of time spent at work determines dedication to the job. Other managers are afraid they will lose control and that traditional workers will resent any "special privileges" granted the flexibles.

Nevertheless, many companies are moving toward flexible scheduling. Some plants that have tried it have seen productivity rise. Those that have the best solutions to helping their employees address the needs of their lives outside the plant are going to be able to attract the younger people to their organizations.

Some employees may also want to work a certain number of hours at home. If their managers grant them this option, the employees must reciprocate in several ways including:

- They must be reachable, keep their managers up-to-date on their projects, maintain contacts with other employees, and be flexible themselves.
- They have to be willing to change their schedules to accommodate the needs of the company. For example, if there's a meeting called for a day or time they're normally at home, they must adjust their schedules to attend the meeting.
- They must call their managers at least once on the days they are working from home to pick up messages as well as to keep posted on breaking events.

Reducing Equipment Downtime

Downtime of machines and equipment is costly to a plant. With no production there can be no sales, no income, and no profit. Worse, overhead costs continue. However, depending on your authority and responsibility, you can help keep your plant's equipment uptime high. Here are the ways to go about it:[11]

■ Ensure that employees who operate equipment and maintain it receive adequate training—they will make fewer mistakes on the job. As a result, there will be fewer malfunctions, plug-ups, and shutdowns for adjustments. Maintenance work can be performed faster and more efficiently when craftspersons are familiar with the equipment.

■ Plan and schedule maintenance and repair work. Repairs can be made faster since people will be available to do the job, and they will have the required tools, material, and parts when they need them. Delays due to failure to satisfy any of these needs can be avoided. Planning and scheduling results in another benefit: The work may often be undertaken when the production line is down for cleaning or a product change.

■ Promote cooperation between production and maintenance departments. When these two groups work together, they can significantly reduce equipment downtime. Replacement or repair of equipment is accomplished in three steps:

1. The production people alert the maintenance people when equipment failure appears likely, or a machine is not performing up to standards. They also point out the nature of the problem and what is wrong. This enables the maintenance people to acquire the replacement machine or the parts which will be needed.
2. The departments agree on a scheduled time for the equipment to be shut down and made available for replacement or repair.
3. Both departments keep each other informed on progress of the work, anticipated time of completion, and releasing of the equipment for resumption of operation.

■ Use value analysis when procuring equipment, materials, and tools. Check to see that more items are purchased for reasons other than lowest price. A value analysis study of proposed equipment purchases can be very revealing in answering questions on corrosion resistance, ease of dismantling, maintenance requirements, and the availability and cost of spare parts—all factors that determine or affect downtime of equipment. By paying a bit more for durability and better design, a plant can acquire machinery and equipment that will undergo a minimum of downtime over its useful life.

▪ Spend more time developing and debugging new equipment before putting it into production use. The petrochemical and chemical industries practice this principle by operating pilot plants where equipment and processes are studied on small-scale levels. Problems of equipment performance are worked out before the large-scale production line goes into operation.

When a plant doesn't have such resources or when it doesn't have time to use them, management should make a preliminary run of the new equipment with staff and development people as operators. Operating characteristics should be charted, capacities tested, and reliability determined. Design changes can then be made, if required, before beginning production operations.

A side advantage of such practice is that the equipment capability and performance constants can be recorded. The information is valuable later when questions of "performing up to standards" arise.

▪ Practice preventive maintenance by arranging for inspection and testing of machines and controls, particularly of critical equipment. The use of preventive maintenance enables management to reduce the number of equipment failures as well as their severity. Frequent inspection can reveal impending failure, permitting repairs to be made during a scheduled shutdown rather than during a production run. Preventive maintenance also reduces and eliminates major breakdowns, whose occurrence results in long downtimes for equipment replacement or repairs.

▪ Take time to correct a problem rather than accept a quick fix. The philosophy of management on how machines should be maintained is a factor in determining how much total downtime the machines experience over a production period. When a breakdown occurs, the machine can be completely overhauled or just the faulty component repaired.

If you are not alert, you can be caught in the current of making repetitive repairs of the same nature rather than taking time to upgrade or redesign the machine. Taking time to correct a problem rather than making a quick fix will reduce downtime in the long run.

▪ Keep good records. Note causes of failures, their frequency, and the downtime incurred. You can more easily apply corrective maintenance when you keep records of performance variables and breakdowns. You can upgrade machines in areas where failures have occurred and thus bring about a reduction in the number of such failures in the future.

In addition, prior knowledge of the downtime that will be needed to make repairs enables you to more efficiently schedule and carry out related process operations so that the effects of the failure are minimized.

Cutting Maintenance Downtime

Productive equipment in most plants is arranged and installed to reduce wasted motion and to aid material flow. With effective and efficient layouts, quick changes in setups and process equipment can be made when necessary as can other steps to ensure continuity of manufacturing and just-in-time inventories.

Since maintenance operations are an integral part of manufacturing, steps should be taken to carry them out similarly to production operations. When productive equipment breaks down, it must be brought back on line as soon as possible. Here are some suggestions on how you can cut maintenance downtime of machines and equipment in your plant:[12]

1. Install cabinets for storage of maintenance parts and supplies near major concentrations of production machines. Too much time is lost when maintenance employees must go to a distant part of the plant to get parts or material to repair a machine.
2. Follow the same procedure for special tooling and supplies required to maintain a specific machine. Store wrenches, clamps, setup and adjustment tools, shims, and other supplies nearby. Include the operating and maintenance manuals for the machines with the tools.
3. Ensure that parts stored in the cabinets are exact replacements for those in use. Also, attach all necessary fittings and hardware to parts so that they are ready to install.
4. Label and organize parts so that they can be retrieved quickly. Replace parts as they are used to ensure the cabinet's usefulness.
5. Install electrical and pneumatic outlets on major production machines. They will eliminate the need to run long power lines and hoses to operate repair tools needed to make repairs to those machines.
6. Use quick-disconnect fittings on hydraulic, pneumatic, and electrical lines that feed wear-sensitive parts such as cylinders, strainers, filters, solenoids, and similar items. Such fittings can cut part replacement times significantly.

Using Checklists

The use of checklists in both production and maintenance operations helps greatly in coordinating repairs, cleaning machines and equipment, and performing preventive maintenance. Whenever a process line or a major machine is shut down for one or more of these operations, make a list of the work to be done and the jobs to be handled. Leave space on the sheet for initialing each item when it has been handled. Here is what you gain by using checklists:

- You can readily determine at any time during the shutdown period what still needs to be done. Depending on the resources available, you can do what is necessary to satisfy those needs.
- Use of the list aids in coordinating cleaning and maintenance activities because labor can be assigned to different areas so that workers do not interfere with each other. Safety and efficiency are better with such arrangements.
- Multishift operations are better coordinated because status of the downtime work can be kept current from shift to shift. Whenever a job is completed, it is initialed by the supervisor whose workers accomplished it.
- No job or activity is overlooked; every job and procedure should be initialed before plans are made to resume production.

OPERATOR PERFORMANCE OF EQUIPMENT MAINTENANCE

Getting production operators involved in the maintenance of their equipment can result in considerable savings to the plant, but conditions must be right. There may be a problem of convincing maintenance personnel that operators can and should perform much of the routine maintenance and inspection. Nevertheless, it is generally agreed by everyone that repairs requiring high skills and jobs of an electrical nature should always be performed by skilled maintenance personnel.

While craftspersons perform many routine jobs that are considered low-skill by the craftspersons, much of such work may be considered high-skill by production operators. If management decides to introduce operator-performed maintenance, all involved personnel must participate in this thinking and sorting process; they must also cooperate and avoid confrontations.

Good reasons for adopting the procedure include: a shortage of skilled maintenance people in the area, improving equipment availability and uptime, improving product quality, and reducing waste. However, reducing the number of operators and maintenance craftspersons is not an acceptable reason to implement operator-performed maintenance.

To create a sense of equipment ownership, operators should be with their equipment not only when it is running, but also when it is not. Equipment downtime usually gives operators the opportunity to perform routine maintenance and inspections. Thus they can do many jobs that are not considered skilled maintenance work. For example, most operators can:

- Clean equipment and perform basic housekeeping.
- Conduct superficial equipment inspections.
- Identify potential upcoming repair needs.
- Lock out and prepare equipment in advance of scheduled repairs.

However, training and qualification of operators is essential for other tasks. Without it, operator maintenance could quickly turn into a disaster. Managers should carefully select tasks that will be assigned to the operators; the job of training and qualifying the operators should be assigned to the best maintenance craftspersons.

SLOW PERIODS OF PLANT OPERATIONS

Plant managers should be prepared to deal with a number of conditions affecting plant output which are beyond their control. Events such as a protracted sales decline, disabling fire in all or part of the plant, a shortage of essential raw material, or a major change in a product line could require temporary layoffs to cut costs. Such layoffs can offset their achievements in building a capable organization, especially when employees can find permanent jobs in other companies in the area. There are several steps you can take, however, to lessen the impact of such a temporary slow period on your organization:[13]

- *Start by predicting the length of the slow period.* You will need an accurate estimate to make sound decisions on the cost break-even point between retaining and laying off employees and to plan interim programs. Get help on this estimate from planners, engineers, the sales and purchasing departments, and other appropriate groups.
- *Compare the cost of layoff with the cost of retention.* It will be simple to calculate the cost of keeping any given number of employees for the duration of the slow period, but don't overlook the direct dollar costs incurred by laying off. Unemployment insurance rates go up, severance pay may be involved, and you will have the cost of hiring and training the replacements for the predicted number of laid-off employees who will be lost to the company for good. After you calculate these costs, you should be able to establish a break-even point in time; how long you retain people beyond that point depends on the dollar amount you feel should be spent as an investment in the plant.
- *Find other work for the employees.* During periods of high production some incidental work and a number of other jobs may have to be post-

poned because of the press of business. Handling these jobs during slow periods can supply the economic justification needed to keep the organization intact. Here are some suggestions on what can be done:

1. Take inventory of finished goods, raw materials, capital equipment, fixtures and furnishings. Decide what facilities should be sold as used equipment and what should be scrapped.
2. Use production employees to assist with equipment repairs and preventive maintenance activities.
3. Paint equipment and buildings. Clean machines and floors. Reorganize stores areas.
4. Train or retrain employees in plant procedures, equipment care, safety, quality procedures, new technical developments, and general background of the company and its products.
5. Try to find substitute operations using the plant's equipment and facilities.
6. Suggest employees take vacations or leaves of absence rather than go on layoff.

If layoffs are inevitable, adopt the "key person" concept. This requires setting up a procedure for protecting a proportion of the employees in the top classification of any department from being laid off. You want to keep the more qualified and ambitious employees from being pushed out by less able employees who happen to have more seniority. If you operate a nonunion plant, you should carefully establish and announce this provision well ahead of time; if the plant is unionized, get a contract clause covering this at the next collective bargaining meeting with the union.

WORKPLACE NEGATIVISM

There is too much workplace negativism in American business and industry today, according to Cherie Carter-Scott, a human-resources consultant and expert on the subject.[14] Negativism is defined as a habitual attitude of skepticism or resistance to the suggestions, orders, and instructions of others.

Carter-Scott believes that negativism may be "a root cause of compulsive-addictive behavior patterns that lead to use of drugs and alcohol and violence in the workplace." Cutbacks, downsizing, and workplace change create stress and a climate of fear, doubt, and uncertainty that causes negativity, explains Carter-Scott. Here are some guidelines on what to do to stop negative attitudes from developing in the plant:

- Notice, appreciate, and stop taking for granted what employees are doing *right*.

- Realize that if employees don't get the positive attention they want, they will resort to poor or uncharacteristic behavior to get *some* type of attention.
- Keep employees working toward goals, and tell them when they have met or exceeded those goals.
- Ensure employees get feedback through periodic performance appraisals. Point out how they are contributing to reaching the company's objectives.

If you find that some employees are showing signs of negativism, take the following steps:

1. Learn the source or origin of the negativism—from an individual, a group, or another department.
2. Confront the offenders. State your expectations for workplace behavior that are acceptable and satisfactory.
3. Present a remedial plan, including consequences for undesired behavior along with disciplinary action if required.
4. Follow up with appropriate discipline if the attitudes and behaviors do not change.

WORKPLACE VIOLENCE

Although most people feel safe in the workplace, potentially violent situations occur frequently in business and industry today. Violent acts, often carried out by frustrated and disgruntled employees, have greatly increased in numbers to the point where it is estimated that more than one million violent workplace crimes occur each year. In addition to understanding the theories and reasons behind such behaviors, there is a strong need for action you and the company can take to help reduce your risks.[15]

With job losses, layoffs, downsizing, and reengineering occurring, many employees must work harder for longer hours; frequently they experience a sense of hopelessness. Some of them blame the company for their problems and resort to violence to show their displeasure and frustration. Even a minor setback can cause an unstable employee to lose control completely.

To understand why an employee might act aggressively, managers must view the violence in terms of the individual's attitudes, values, and perceptions toward violence. Management must realize that most employees have beliefs about what is right and wrong, beliefs that have been developed over a lifetime and cannot easily be changed. There are a number of theories on why employees who are unable to handle stress look to violence as an acceptable way to gain personal control. One of the most popular theories concerns how exposure to frustrating events initiates an emotional reaction that violence-prone people simply cannot control.

In addition to becoming familiar with the theories and behaviors associated with workplace violence, there are several steps your company can take to reduce if not prevent workplace violence. Here are explanations of what they involve:

- *Using preemployment screening procedures.* An effective program includes tests that serve as a baseline for measuring future changes in an employee's behavior. In addition, reference checks, criminal record checks, drug testing, and structured interviews should be carried out. Interviewers should be trained to ask questions that may elicit responses indicating a candidate's tendencies to violent outbursts.

- *Communicating the company's commitment to workplace safety.* This will make employees feel more secure about reporting statements or behaviors that they see as threatening. To encourage such reports, employees should be required to read and sign a policy form concerning violence that prohibits the use of weapons, harassment, and verbal or physical threats while on the job. After signing, employees usually feel obligated to notify the human resource or security department regarding any threats or violent encounters.

- *Training and educating supervisors and employees to recognize early warning signs or symptoms of impending violence and respond using nonconfrontational techniques to defuse problems.* Management can help frustrated employees by giving them an outlet to air their grievances without fear of reprisal; listening and giving positive encouragement should be part of the training program.

- *Forming a threat management team.* The team should set criteria for convening and reporting incidents to law enforcement and the news media. Threat management teams plan escape routes, coordinate medical and psychological care of injured victims, train employees to administer emergency aid to victims, and keep employees and families informed during and after a crisis.

- *Implementing security measures to protect against violence from individuals outside the company.* Arrangements can be made for regular police checkups. Other steps should be taken to limit and control access to the plant and to install surveillance cameras and silent alarms. Ensuring that high-risk areas are visible to more people and installing adequate external lighting make it difficult for anyone to engage in an act of violence.

NOTES

1. W. H. Weiss, *Decision Making for First-Time Managers* (New York: American Management Association, 1985), pp. 127–130.
2. Excerpts from "Worker Morale," *The Safe Foreman*, January 1996, pp. 20–22.
3. Reprinted with permission of Dartnell Corporation, 4660 N. Ravenswood Avenue, Chicago, Ill. 60640; (800) 621–5463.
4. Jenny Hart Danowski, "How to Empower Through Delegation," *Successful Supervisor*, October 11, 1993, p. 1.
5. Brad Thompson, *The New Manager's Handbook* (Burr Ridge, Ill.: Richard D. Irwin, Inc., 1985) pp. 125, 127, 128–130.
6. W. H. Weiss, *Supervisor's Standard Reference Handbook* (Englewood Cliffs, N.J.: Prentice Hall, Inc., 1988), pp. 161–163.
7. Excerpted from "Measuring Productivity," by Joseph M. Reilly, *Chemical Processing*, May 1996, p. 83.
8. W. H. Weiss, *Plant Supervisor's Complete Desk Book* (Englewood Cliffs, N.J.: Prentice Hall, Inc., 1987), pp. 86–87.
9. W. H. Weiss, "Ergonomically Designed Computer Workstations Pay Off." This material first appeared in *TeleProfessional*, November/December 1993, pp. 64–65.
10. Reprinted with permission of Dartnell Corporation, 4660 N. Ravenswood Ave., Chicago, Ill. 60640; (800) 621–5463.
11. W. H. Weiss, *Plant Supervisor's Complete Desk Book* (Englewood Cliffs, N.J.: Prentice Hall, Inc., 1987), pp. 93–95.
12. Ibid., pp. 380–381.
13. Charles H. Becker, *Plant Manager's Manual and Guide* (Englewood Cliffs, N.J.: Prentice Hall, Inc., 1987), pp. 51–52.
14. Alan L. Applebaum, "Nullifying Workplace Negativism," *Successful Supervisor*, May 8, 1995, p. 1.
15. Susan M. Burroughs and John W. Jones, "Strategies for Creating a Non-Violent Workplace," *Plant Services*, July 1995, pp. 37, 42–43.

15

Contractors and Service Organizations

One of the major responsibilities of every plant manager is knowing how and deciding when to use contractors and service organizations to perform part of the company's operations. Because there are advantages and disadvantages to outsourcing and contracting, the choice is usually not either to contract or to do as much in-house as possible, but rather one of making a cost-effective and convenient division of the options available.

The problem is not a minor one when you consider the number of factors involved. It is a kind of "make or buy" decision with a few more considerations thrown in. But the economics of most contract versus in-house decisions are largely determined by three factors:

1. *The type of work to be done.* This determines the skills required. When the skills are highly and mainly technical, and especially when they are needed only infrequently, contracting may be the only rational option. Economics favors contracting also when lack of demand does not warrant having such skills available continually.

2. *The amount of work to be done.* If it is beyond the ability of the existing workforce to accomplish in a reasonable time (or in the time required), then contracting is an attractive option. Examples are a turnaround project, a major process equipment overhaul, or the installation of a new system.

3. *The amount of time available to do the work.* When the work peaks, adding to the in-house workforce by contracting is an economical way to meet schedules, commitments, and production quotas without incurring

the penalty of having an oversized and underutilized permanent work-force on hand at off-peak times.

Outsourcing Labor

Using outsourcing to manage labor costs has expanded rapidly in recent years. Some personnel authorities believe that in the not too distant future, one in three workers will be employed on a contingent basis. Equipment maintenance and janitorial operations are typical functions that outside companies can easily perform without affecting or disrupting a company's primary business.

The contracting of labor is popular with companies in highly volatile industries. Defense contractors, for example, have long used it in carrying out government contracts. This practice is the answer to a perplexing problem—how to soften the effects of frequent business expansions and contractions.

Outsourcing labor is also an attractive option in rapidly changing in-dustries in that it limits the amount of recruiting, hiring, and training costs that a company must incur. When these functions are outsourced, the con-tractor is responsible for supplying appropriate personnel to meet the contracting company's needs.

Nevertheless, outsourcing labor does have its drawbacks. When a company frees its management from direct attention to an area, it also transfers some control to an outsider. Avoiding this trap requires making sure the contractor completely understands your business objectives and your operational needs.

Then too, managers of a blended group of contracted personnel and permanent personnel must supervise the group somewhat differently from a staff composed completely of permanent personnel. You must carefully integrate the contract personnel into the flow and continuity of the work to avoid ending up with a two-tiered workforce that could lead to dissension, disagreement, and other labor problems.

Risks of Outsourcing

For a plant to grow and remain profitable, it must continually allocate capital for rebuilding and modernizing and to reward its owners for the risks of ownership. This usually means controlling both long- and short-term costs. The company must also guard against taking unnecessary risks.

Eliminating maintenance capabilities and outsourcing the work usu-ally is a risk with a short-term gain. In recent years, however, more and more plants appear willing to take this risk by reducing employee training, cutting investments in tools and equipment, and outsourcing the maintenance function to others. But when a plant makes such decisions, it also makes certain potentially dangerous assumptions such as:[1]

- *The technology and labor skills needed can easily be obtained.* For unskilled activities such as janitorial services, there is probably little risk in outsourcing.
- *Outsourced services are more effective than internal services.* Some maintenance services such as those required for computers and sophisticated electronic equipment might be outsourced to those who specialize in and have tools to service that equipment.
- *Quality of production can be maintained.* The care of temperamental equipment may not be realistically addressed by outside contractors; any action that jeopardizes quality production should be considered an unacceptable risk.
- *Outside labor will be committed to excellent performance.* Managers often find it difficult to motivate craftspersons whose loyalties are elsewhere. Without commitment, the craftspersons may not supply the maintenance required for top quality production.
- *Outsourced services are less costly.* Although both the company and the contractor incur costs for employee training, tool replacement, and administrative expenses, the contractor also needs to make a profit; thus, the contractor often cannot perform at the same cost level as the company employees.
- *Business risks are lower with outsourced services.* When a company experiences diminishing maintenance requirements, it may save money by contracting because it does not have to invest in training or sophisticated instruments or tools. However, the company must always guard against unexpected work interruptions and downtime.

CONSULTANTS

Consultants can be of great help to a plant, and they offer their services in practically every field of endeavor. Management consultants can specialize in organizational arrangements, organizational development, finance, compensation, union negotiations, and many other areas. There are design consultants, statistical consultants, warranty consultants, computer programming consultants, and many more. Although finding the right consultant can be a challenge, you must first decide whether you really need a consultant.

Bringing in a consultant is not a decision to be taken lightly. Consultants can be expensive, and if you don't have a strong need for one, both your company and you can suffer. Consultants are usually retained for one of three reasons:[2]

1. To solve a problem that cannot be solved with the skills available in the plant. If your group is facing a problem it cannot solve (or is having difficulty defining the problem), calling on outside help may be the wisest course of action. But carefully consider this step before you take it. If the problem is one your group ought to be able to solve but cannot, hiring a consultant may be seen as a threat by some of the people in your organization. You need to consider if the problems this perceived threat could cause are worth the expediency of consultant assistance.

2. To provide the answer to an overload situation. Overload situations can be brought on by seasonal increases in work requirements, a hiring rate that cannot keep pace with business growth, or other specific business needs. For example, the plant may receive a large contract that requires temporary engineering, manufacturing direction, or quality assurance help until it can hire the people it needs.

3. To supply a third party for reasons of objectivity, or to propose a distasteful solution. For example, the plant manager would probably not want to ask the personnel manager to determine if the plant manager and other department managers are being paid appropriately. A consultant specializing in compensation would be more objective.

As for proposing a distasteful solution, there may be a plant reorganizational problem, one to which the manager hiring the consultant does not wish to be tied. If, for example, the solution calls for a reorganization that would decrease another manager's responsibility, the other manager will probably be upset, but at least the recommendation didn't come from a manager in the plant. An added advantage is that such a recommendation may be better accepted by other managers from a neutral third party.

Selecting Consulting Engineers

The selection of a consulting engineer for an industrial project in the plant is usually the most important and difficult decision made by plant personnel during the period of completing the project. It is the most difficult because subsequent decisions are usually made easier with assistance provided by the consultant. It is the most important because the engineering firm's performance determines the entire course of the project—feasibility, design, plans and specifications, construction and operation, and maintenance costs during the project's lifetime.

The most successful plant projects generally are those for which three or four consultants have been interviewed. Interviewing more than this makes selection more difficult, requires too much time, and is the result of inadequate preliminary screening of the consultant's qualifications for the project. A recognized procedure for finding and selecting a consulting engineer is as follows:

1. Select three or four firms that appear to be best qualified for the project. Call each, describing the project and inquiring as to their interest.
2. Request that the interested firms come to the plant to inspect the site and operations, and to discuss the qualifications including past experience on similar projects.
3. Select the two or three firms most qualified for the project, and request written statements of qualification and proposals from each.
4. Review the proposals and contact the references. Since engineers deal in creativity, not commodities, the lowest bid isn't always the best from a financial viewpoint.
5. Discuss the fee with the firm considered to be best for the job. If a mutually acceptable understanding is reached, request the purchasing department to give the firm a contract.

EVALUATING CONSULTANTS

Although evaluating a consultant prior to signing a contract is similar to hiring a full-time employee, in many other ways it is much different. This is particularly true for the independent problem-solvers. For both categories, it's prudent to check references.

When interviewing a prospective consultant, you should search for several qualities that characterize successful consultants. Technical expertise is most important. The consultant must be proficient in his or her area of specialization, and must be able to solve the problems or do the kind of temporary work you have available. Evidence of professional competence may be obtained through conversations with previous clients, by reviewing papers or other documents the consultant has published, and by interviewing.

You will probably discuss the assignment with the consultant and assess his or her answers. Be aware that consultants are in business to sell advice, however, and won't solve the problem for you during the interview. Judging a consultant in this situation requires a careful evaluation of the answers to your questions. An astute and knowledgeable consultant should be able to quickly outline an approach to solve the problem without necessarily divulging the solution. You need to be wary of consultants, though, who have never worked on the type of problem you have but are willing to give it a try. Unfortunately, some consultants are more than happy to accept assignments in which they have no particular expertise.

PARTNERING

While downsizing an organization probably is here to stay, there are right ways and wrong ways of doing it. One of the right ways to downsize is partnering. When partnering, an engineering firm acts as a team member and is paid on a predetermined rate schedule or negotiated agreement for carrying out a particular assignment.

Partnering is especially effective when engineering services are involved. If your plant decides to implement partnering, it should incorporate a new approach to setting priorities in scheduling work, and rely on long-term planning. The benefits of partnering for both the plant and the engineering firm include the following:[3]

- The plant receives quick knowledgeable responses to its requests for service. A costly learning curve is avoided because the engineering firm is familiar with the facilities.
- Plant managers work with compatible people who understand the plant's particular requirements and operating procedures. The engineering firm becomes a valuable resource for immediate short-term projects and for participating in the master planning process.
- The plant avoids costly staffing of its engineering and maintenance departments by taking advantage of its partner's existing personnel. As needs arise, the engineering firm has staff available for meeting project requirements.
- The plant keeps up with industry trends. The various disciplines covered by the engineering firm supply a constant source of knowledge for the plant. While managing projects, the plant's staff learns from its engineering partner.

If downsizing continues to be practiced into the next century, the partnering of engineering services is one of the most effective and efficient ways to make certain that plant projects get addressed in the most appropriate and cost-effective way.

LEASING VERSUS PURCHASING

If you are concerned about how to finance new machines or equipment for the plant, consider that leasing by industrial plants has been increasing in recent years. The Equipment Leasing Association of America estimates that leasing represents about 32 percent of all industrial purchases of durable equipment.[4]

When interest rates are low and prices on new equipment are holding steady or increasing, leasing is economically justified. Leasing tends to pick up also when the economy is slow, because of the cash situation. Many companies want to maximize the use of what capital they do have by investing in plant equipment, facilities, or inventory.

But even when the economy is "up," leasing offers several advantages to industrial plants:

- Companies gain increased productivity when they lease new equipment because, under a leasing arrangement, managers are more likely to replace equipment when they need to.
- Leasing not only provides the advantages of the newest technology, but there's less temptation to hang onto obsolete equipment too long.
- There aren't any expenditures for maintenance when machines or equipment are leased. Plants with limited maintenance labor and facilities prefer such arrangements.
- Tax laws sometimes favor leasing over buying.

EVALUATING VENDORS

An essential ingredient for good control of stores and inventory in a manufacturing plant is a system for evaluating vendors and suppliers. Such a system will provide several benefits for the plant's purchasing department in that buyers will be able to:

1. Keep up-to-date on vendor performance.
2. Compare one vendor with another.
3. Confront vendors with a record of their performance, thus having a lever to bring about improvement if it is needed.

Vendor evaluation systems should be nonsubjective and unbiased in that they must be based on facts rather than opinions. This can be reality only if the data accumulated on vendors is based on documented purchase orders and receiving slips. In addition, the information from those records must be duly and promptly entered in the computer database so that it is current. An effective system defines which areas of vendor performance are of most importance to the user.

Quality, price, and delivery are the primary indicators of a supplier's performance. Quality can be interpreted to include service, cooperativeness, technical assistance, accuracy, action on complaints, and similar factors. A company's policy may dictate that purchase orders be given to the lowest price bidders when all other criteria are equal. Consequently, delivery performance serves as an important means for evaluation.

Programming the System

An effective evaluation of vendors' performance on delivery can be achieved with the use of two forms. One can provide data and information on all vendors who supply material to the plant. The other can compare the performance of two or more vendors on a specific item ordered by the plant. Headings on data and information should include the following:

- Number and quantity of items on a purchase order
- Total dollar value of a purchase order
- Discount offered, if any
- Requested delivery time
- Number of requests by vendor for extension of delivery time
- Percentage of items delivered early
- Percentage of items delivered late
- Percentage of lateness on the requested delivery time

Since the information appearing on purchase orders resides in the database, and the information on receiving slips is input by receiving and stores personnel, only the times the delivery date has been modified must be input by the buyer. The program for the vendor rating screen should be written so that the computer makes all the calculations necessary to fill in the columns under the headings. Whenever data is missing from a form, this indicates that the pertinent purchase order is an outstanding one; no delivery has been made.

Although how a vendor handles delivery is a good indicator of the vendor's performance, buyers will find that delivery has several facets in itself. Because of this, the computer should not be programmed to decide which vendor of several should be given a particular order. Buyers must make each purchasing decision. They will be aided in deciding where to place an order by comparing one vendor's performance with another's.

RELATIONSHIPS BETWEEN SUPPLIERS AND CUSTOMERS

Although there is a traditional adversarial relationship between suppliers and customers, the objective should be to develop mutually profitable situations that provide benefits to both parties. This recognizes that every business or manufacturing plant is both a customer and a supplier. The same philosophy of how the plant can best relate to its customers applies to how the plant can best relate to its suppliers. Attention to the following factors can help you improve relationships with the plant's customers:

- Knowing who your customer's customers are
- Being aware of the competitive forces your customers face
- Making suggestions that will help your customers to lower costs and raise quality
- Offering service and training to your customers
- Making it easy for your customers to do business with you

Similarly, your suppliers should be made aware of how they can develop better win-win relationships with the plant. Here are some steps they can take in this direction:

- Becoming truly interested in the plant and not always trying to "make a deal"
- Keeping up with new technology and ensuring you are aware of the latest products the supplier has
- Understanding total procurement costs
- Treating you as a partner in new undertakings

CONTRACTING MAINTENANCE

The trend in American industry today is to contract more of the maintenance function. Plants are doing more contracting for a variety of reasons, two of the most important being:

1. Management believes that savings result because the plant doesn't need to have a full force of maintenance personnel when most of the time only a few are needed.
2. Many contractors can supply craftspersons who are more skilled than the plant employees.

Once management has decided to use contractors, a policy should be established to determine when it is appropriate to take the step. Here are some suggestions on how you should proceed:[5]

1. Form a committee of key plant personnel to develop criteria to be considered when the need for maintenance has the potential to be contracted. Members should be drafted from the production, engineering, maintenance, service, and employee relations departments.
2. Develop guidelines for decision making on cost, labor relations, flexibility, workload variations, priorities, and urgencies. Organize the guidelines in a Contract Maintenance Policy for easy reference and retrieval.
3. Publicize the policy. While not everyone may fully agree with the policy, pointing out its existence and what it covers is better than rumor and speculation.
4. Implement the policy, following the guidelines, when conditions and situations justify it.
5. Review and revise the policy periodically when business conditions change or influential factors arise.

Predictive Maintenance Contracting

Because of the growing demand for contract predictive maintenance services in plants today, many organizations now are active in this field. Many contractors are very capable and do a good job, but for every excellent one, there are a few that are not qualified to furnish adequate support to a comprehensive predictive maintenance program. Here are some guidelines on selecting a competent contractor:[6]

■ While size does not indicate expertise, you must consider the contractor's ability to carry out your program. To learn this, you should get the following information about the firm: organizational structure; length of time in business; financial status; and a list of current clients you can contact.

■ A competent contractor must have the proper technical expertise to meet your requirements. The firm should have proven expertise in:

1. *All predictive technologies.* Since most programs require the use of vibration monitoring, thermography, and other diagnostic technologies, the contractor must demonstrate the ability to furnish these services.
2. *Machine design.* If the contractor's knowledge is limited to pre-

dictive maintenance, the firm will not be able to furnish cost-effective solutions to incipient problems.

3. *Process dynamics.* The contractor should know as much if not more about the plant's process or manufacturing systems as you do.

4. *Maintenance and repair practices.* A contractor must know how preventive and corrective maintenance is performed.

■ The pricing strategy of contractors varies in that some charge by the number of measurements taken, while others by the machine classification. You must be careful to ensure comparisons are valid.

■ A problem associated with contract predictive maintenance programs is the constant rotation of technicians and analysts. A dedicated team is a requirement if the program is to be effective and efficient.

MEASURING CONTRACTOR PERFORMANCE

To ensure optimum performance of a maintenance contractor, management of the plant should periodically assess and measure the firm's methods and procedures for handling the maintenance function.[7] This should be done particularly in the following two situations:

1. In a situation where a contractor furnishes supplemental maintenance capabilities, the contractor should be expected to benchmark and monitor appropriate performance measures. Here are some examples of frequently used measures:

- Percentage of planned work = planned hours worked/total hours worked
- Schedule compliance = hours worked scheduled jobs/total hours scheduled
- Percentage of preventive maintenance (PM) completion = PM hours completed/PM hours scheduled
- Percentage of material furnished through computerized maintenance management system (CMMS) from plant storeroom or through supplier by means of a CMMS

2. In situations where a contractor furnishes primary maintenance manpower, the following additional performance measures should be considered:

- Preventive and predictive maintenance hours as percentage of hours worked

- Maintenance cost as percentage of equipment replacement value (ERV)
- Uptime (scheduled and unscheduled maintenance downtime components)
- Investment (ERV) per craftsperson

One approach by management is to establish site baseline levels for these measures. The contractor and management can then meet quarterly to review the performance data, discuss problems and trends, and set goals for the following quarter.

REMEDIATION CONTRACTORS

Plant managers sometimes find they need the services of a remediation contractor. Environmental remediation projects present specialized problems such as the purchasing of property without knowing of the hazardous waste buried there, or being liable for disposal facilities where the plant's waste was sent.

To determine the type of remedial action your plant may be faced with, make a list of the most important factors for achieving your objectives.[8] These should take into account the:

- Type of contamination
- Risk to neighboring areas
- Input from state and federal agencies
- Site climate and geological profile
- Possibility of substances at the site being reused or recycled
- Extent to which existing natural barriers currently contain the substances
- Extent to which substances have migrated, or may migrate, from the original release area

Since selecting a cleanup method affects the overall remediation cost, you should investigate as many types of appropriate remediation technologies as possible. Recognize also that the contractor you select to carry out the remediation work often determines how the surrounding communities perceive your company. In addition, consider the candidates' work history with the Environmental Protection Agency (EPA), the Occupational Safety and Health Administration (OSHA), and other regulatory agencies. If the contractor has experienced difficulty in the past, you may experience difficulty in the future.

While a qualified remediation contractor will defend your best interests, membership in industrial associations and involvement with professional organizations may strengthen your ability to influence and negotiate with regulatory agencies. While no single set of selection criteria applies to all remediation projects, the better you explore your options, the more likely it is you'll make prudent choices, control your costs, and avoid operating according to terms dictated by others.

CONTRACTOR SAFETY PROGRAMS

Since an effective safety program is the best method contractors can use to cut the costs of accidental losses, such programs are becoming increasingly important. They are important not only from a compliance perspective, but because a safe working environment contributes to improved production and quality. The financial and legal implications of not having a safety program must also be considered. Under some state workers compensation and tort statutes, owners and managers in a contractor work environment can be held responsible for safety violations and accidents on a job site, even if the occurrence is caused by and affects only contractor employees.

The most important elements of a contractor safety program are as follows:[9]

1. The program must have a clear and definitive objective. A safety policy written by management informs the contractor what the plant expects from contractors working in the plant. A well-written policy:

- Establishes standards.
- Frees management from repetitive decisions on common problems.
- Makes more time available to focus on exceptional or unusual conditions.

2. An individual must be appointed and given the specific responsibility to lead and promote the safety effort. This "safety representative" must have the authority to manage the implementation of the safety program and to stop work when serious hazards are discovered. Typical duties assigned to safety representatives include:

- Identification of potential hazards
- Evaluation of the risk of harm from hazards present
- Investigation of incidents
- Coordination of company and OSHA regulations

3. The safety program should include a job hazard analysis. This is a procedure whereby each step of work is studied to identify hazards that

potentially could cause an injury. Job related injuries may occur when contractor employees do not recognize hazards, have not been advised of potential hazards, or are not trained in proper job procedures to deal with those hazards.

An initial analysis should be made during the tour of the work site by management and contractors bidding on the projects, and subsequently, by the contractor selected to perform the work before a "work release" is issued by management to begin work. With this procedure, both parties can identify and advise each other of potential hazards existing on the work site.

Successful safety programs invariably involve rules for orderliness in project work areas and good housekeeping procedures. Slips, trips, and falls are the leading cause of accidents on work sites; litter and debris often are the cause of injuries in addition to creating extra work as they need to be relocated.

4. Site orientations and safety awareness training must be included in the safety program. Orientations enable plant management to make known its commitment to furnish a safe working environment for its employees and those of contractors. Orientations also remind people of their responsibility to consider safety when planning and doing their work. Topics and subjects that should be covered in orientations include:

- Unusual hazards on the work site
- Personal protective equipment requirements
- Work site rules and regulations
- Procedures for reporting accidents
- Emergency evacuation procedures

5. Work site inspections are necessary and should be conducted on a regularly scheduled basis by representatives of both management and the contractor(s). Management participation in site inspections infers and confirms interest and commitment to the safety program. The return on the time spent by management on inspection is well worth the investment. Safety inspections are an excellent way for management to validate the program's effectiveness.

An immediate benefit of inspections and observations is the opportunity they provide for prompt feedback to contractor employees who might be working unsafely. Imminent danger conditions should be corrected as soon as possible. It is not unreasonable to suspend operations until proper safety steps are taken.

6. All injuries and major equipment damage, including near misses, must be reported and investigated immediately. These analyses serve to

avoid recurrences. Details of such incidents should be communicated to both plant and contractor employees through daily work briefings and frequent safety talks.

Investigations protect all employees as well as management, especially when they are documented. Records might protect both management and the contractor against claims for incidents that may not have occurred on the job, or serve to support an injured employee who experiences complications in the future. In addition, if all injuries are diligently reported and investigated, a legal claim for an occurrence that was not reported would have little support.

Since management ultimately pays for losses on work sites, it's good practice to oversee contractor activities to ensure that the firms are applying good management and safe working procedures. Fear of incurring liability by becoming involved should not be a reason for not defining the requirements of a contractor safety program. Management may well incur greater liability if they do not become involved. A proactive approach to the development and implementation of a sound contractor safety program, along with documenting incidents and events, is far better than taking a defensive stand.

CONTRACT MAINTENANCE COSTS

In order to decide whether to use contractors or in-house labor for maintenance, you should review each type on performance and cost. This procedure requires you to keep good records covering the functions both groups perform and to periodically compare them. Here are the factors that should be used in comparing the cost of contract services with in-house services:

■ In addition to the estimated or actual contractor's bid that includes the company's labor, materials, profit, and overhead, you must determine the cost of:

1. Writing specifications and preparing drawings, preparing bid documents, soliciting and evaluating bids, negotiating and awarding the contract, and managing the contract
2. Equipment, utilities, and material you will supply the contractor
3. Incentive or premium provisions in the contract
4. Maintaining facilities or equipment that will be used by the contractor or that will become inactive because of the contract, unless they will be used for some other function or eliminated

   5. Overhead other than that for contract management
   6. Other events or transactions including terminating of employees, security checks and additional security measures, and losses incurred in the sale of organization-owned equipment

■ In addition to the costs of labor and fringe benefits of plant employees, you must determine the costs of:

   1. Materials and supplies
   2. Storage, handling, and custody of materials and supplies
   3. Equipment and facilities maintenance
   4. Utilities and the protection of property
   5. Direct and indirect overhead
   6. Depreciation of facilities and equipment

SERVICE CONTRACTS

Whether your plant is small or large, it cannot run profitably and competitively today without modern, sophisticated equipment. Just as important, it takes more than average technical knowledge today to repair the electronic programmers, controllers, and other instrumentation on processes and on the production line, not to overlook the computers and their peripherals. In addition to well-trained craftspersons and technicians, you should have service or protection plans, say the manufacturers that supply them. Without taking such steps, even the most carefully prepared plant budgets can easily be overrun.

Since idle productive machines and equipment threaten profits, it's easy to see why service plans, extended warranty plans, or protection plans, as they are called, are becoming more and more popular. Not only do they make it easier for you to have repairs completed or equipment replaced if necessary, they also help you to prepare your budgets accurately. When managers begin to learn that keeping track of repairs for each piece of equipment in the plant is time-consuming, they will find service plans convenient and cost-effective.

Because it soon became too costly to make repairs, manufacturers of electronic equipment, who traditionally serviced the products they sold, have withdrawn from the repair business. Instead, they offer customers extended service warranty contracts supplied to them by protection plan companies. Extended contracts give you peace of mind. Today's plant equipment and control systems are too sophisticated and too valuable to be left to just anyone for repairs. By contracting for service, you'll get guaranteed repairs, whether they are done in the plant or at service companies' facilities.

Types of Agreements

With labor being the greatest portion of a plant's operating expense, machines and processes are becoming more and more automated in manufacturing plants. The automation is primarily accomplished by installing the latest generation of electric, hydraulic, and pneumatic driven data processing systems that control the plant's product output.

But only large plants can afford the large number of skilled maintenance personnel that are required to keep such equipment operating efficiently and productively. It is difficult to hire qualified technicians or train present employees to service such equipment with a prescheduled, step-by-step inspection/preventive maintenance program. The only alternative is contracting the service from a special equipment supplier, an area service dealer, or a contract maintenance service firm. Following are the different types of service agreements available from service companies:

- With *inspection only,* the service technician inspects the equipment using a printed inspection guide and check sheets. If there are any necessary adjustments, fine tuning, cleaning, repairs, or parts/materials replaced, an extra purchase order is obtained to cover these costs.

- With *inspection with labor coverage,* the technician performs all of the required inspections, preventive maintenance, and repairs for all equipment malfunctions covered by the service agreement. The service company must determine the necessary number of inspections because it absorbs all emergency service labor hours. Parts and materials are not covered by this type of agreement. These items generally are invoiced to the customer on an extended discounted invoice.

- *Complete parts coverage with reduced labor coverage* types automatically reduce and sometimes eliminate customer nuisance calls. The service company forecasts the minimum number of service calls to be scheduled during the contract coverage period. The agreement is attractive also to customers who only want protection from purchasing parts during the agreement coverage period, yet still want to be assured of priority service response time.

- *Time and material* types are agreement contracts. The agreement compels the customer to pay for all labor, parts, and material used by the service firm to restore and/or maintain the customer's equipment to efficient operation to meet production requirements.

- With *complete parts coverage only, no labor included,* the service firm assumes all cost of parts for the equipment during the agreement period, while the customer pays all labor costs. The agreement appeals to customers who are willing to gamble on future labor costs but not on the cost of parts.

■ With *labor coverage only, no parts included,* the service firm assumes all labor costs during the agreement period, while the customer pays all parts costs. Some customers would rather gamble on future parts costs, but are afraid to gamble with future labor costs.

■ A *full coverage* type of service agreement includes necessary labor, parts, and materials for all prescheduled inspections and preventive maintenance periods, together with cleaning, checking, testing, adjusting, and tuning for the agreement time coverage. This is the ultimate of service agreements in that the customer pays the service firm for all service including labor, parts, and materials used to maintain the equipment.

Evaluating the Options

Inexperienced managers buy service contracts offering maximum coverage on every purchase or lease, without giving any thought to cost-effectiveness, or to whether they are getting the most efficient service. You should take the same care when you buy repair and maintenance contracts as you take in selecting the equipment to be covered. Considerable time and money are at stake. While several factors are applicable to all decisions involving service contracts, others are peculiar to the equipment itself.

Service contracts on computers and peripherals, for example, are offered by small repair shops, including area chains, authorized dealers, and so-called third-party national maintenance organizations. The levels of service supplied by contract, however, vary from mail-in, carry-in, 48-hour on-site response, and the services of one or more resident technicians.

You must determine the best service company, as well as the level of service, by assessing your needs. Expect that tradeoffs may be involved. In addition, needed parts and current maintenance manuals for your particular brand or model may not be readily available, and service from some firms may not be as fast as you'd like. Authorized dealers, at the same time, are likely to employ factory-trained technicians, use the latest fault analyzers and maintenance guides, have direct contact with the factory, be well stocked with parts, and offer quick, efficient service. But a particular dealer may not offer onsite service, pickup or delivery, and the dealer's expertise may be limited to the brand or models sold.

The large, third-party maintenance organizations probably furnish the best service when a wide array of equipment is involved and many brands are represented. These companies usually hire the best trained personnel, maintain large inventories of both new and reconditioned parts, pretest parts prior to installation, and supply fast onsite response.

USING A REPAIR SERVICE VERSUS BUYING NEW EQUIPMENT

Many factors are involved when you must decide whether to use a repair service to rebuild/repair equipment or buy new. While immediate costs are important, you should be concerned about them only after you study and analyze the following factors:

1. Consider the time constraints:

   - The lead time required to obtain and install new equipment
   - The time required to rebuild the equipment onsite
   - The time required to remove, rebuild, and reinstall the equipment

Realize that idle equipment means lost production. In addition to lost profits, customers may also be lost if the equipment is down for a long time.

2. Decide if the equipment is wholly or in part obsolete, causing parts and/or service to be very expensive and difficult or impossible to obtain.

3. Find out if the plant has similar equipment in service, making spare parts or maintenance techniques interchangeable.

4. Check to see if improvements could be made in rebuilding the equipment.

5. Determine if modernization of the equipment would be beneficial and provide advantages.

6. Look into differences in maintaining the rebuilt equipment and new equipment.

7. Investigate if additional training or higher skill levels would be required to operate or maintain new equipment.

The knowledge and information you acquire from analyzing these factors will help you to decide between rebuilding or replacing plant equipment. However, if a significant capital expenditure seems inevitable, get the help of the accounting or financial department in making a cost justification study of the project. Simple payback time is often used, but other methods may be more cost-effective, especially for large expenditures. These include depreciation, taxes, and/or the present cost of money.

IN-HOUSE REPAIR OF MACHINE AND EQUIPMENT COMPONENTS

Even though you may use contractors and service organizations in the plant and gain the benefits and advantages of doing so, the maintenance department can sometimes achieve significant savings by performing operations that manufacturing plants normally don't handle. An example is the in-house repair of machine and equipment components. There are three requisites for success with such a venture:

1. The program or operation must have the backing and support of management.
2. The employees involved should be highly skilled in this type of work.
3. There must be a strong interest and desire on the part of the employees to do high quality work—they must take pride in what they accomplish.

If you decide to implement an in-house repair program in the plant, here are the steps you should follow:

1. *Determine if an item can be repaired.* The program begins when a maintenance craftsperson withdraws from the storeroom an item that will replace a similar item that has failed in service. If the stores records identify the item as one that is repairable, the storeroom attendant asks for the defective item so that it may be considered for repair.

2. *Tag the item for repair.* The tag should state the item's plant code number and also say what is wrong with the item.

3. *Issue a work order.* The storeroom attendant lists the item on a form with other repairable parts and equipment, and makes out a work order for its repair. The item is placed on a pallet or shelf with other items needing repair, and the work order is given to the supervisor of the repair crew.

4. *Log the work order.* To ensure that the repair procedure is organized, that no items are lost, and that costs are properly allocated, all work orders are logged in a book by the code number of the item. In addition, a folder with that number is created for the files. The folder will contain a copy of the work order, copies of requisitions and purchase orders for repair material, and repair procedures if they are complex.

5. *Obtain necessary parts for repairs.* Since many items need new parts, the first job of the supervisor is to determine if such parts are available in stores. If they are not on hand, a requisition is immediately issued for what is needed.

Repair job priorities are established by the storeroom attendant. Priorities are dictated by both the inventory levels in the storeroom and demand for an item in the plant. When parts are available, a crew member completes a repair, tests the item's performance, and returns the rebuilt item to the storeroom. Labor and repair material used are charged against the code number of the item in determining the cost or value of the returned item.

Benefits of Repair Programs

There are several benefits that result from a well-conducted program:

1. Repairing storeroom items is more economical than purchasing new ones. Making in-house repairs is a more economical procedure than contracting such work.
2. Management attention to equipment malfunctions results when defective or inoperative items are turned into the storeroom for repair rather than set aside or scrapped.
3. Better design and longer life of machine parts are an outgrowth of the repair function, provided the repair crew are highly skilled.
4. The program results in a parts quality improvement because obsolete, high-maintenance models and weak designs are scrapped rather than repaired.
5. A repair program promotes standardization. This results in lower inventory of spare parts.
6. The company can assign a lower cost to the repaired items in stores, thus reducing taxes on inventory.

NOTES

1. John J. Tracy, Jr., "Sensible Outsourcing for Maintenance," *Engineer's Digest*, July 1995, pp. 20–21.
2. Joseph and Susan Berk, *Managing Effectively* (New York: Barron's Educational Series, Inc., 1987), pp. 150–151, 153–154.
3. James W. Ohlheiser, "Using Partnering to Downsize," *Engineer's Digest*, February 1995, pp. 24–25.
4. "Equipment Leasing on the Increase," *Modern Materials Handling*, September 1993, p. 12.
5. Edwin K. Jones, "Contract Maintenance Strategies," *Maintenance Technology*, February 1996, pp. 11–13.
6. Keith Mobley, "Selecting a Predictive Maintenance Contractor," *Plant Services*, April 1995, pp. 93–96.

7. Edwin K. Jones, "Contract Maintenance Strategies—Part II," *Maintenance Technology,* pp. 8–11.
8. Bruce Wiebusch, "Choosing the Right Remediation Contractor," *Engineer's Digest,* October 1994, pp. 62–65.
9. The elements of an effective contractor safety program were discussed by Richard D. Hislop, Argonne National Laboratory, at a National Plant Engineering and Maintenance Conference in Chicago, Ill., on March 16, 1994.

16

Environmental Control

Because environmental control and improvement is required by the government, plant managers sometimes overlook the potential side benefits. Many companies, however, are finding there are significant savings associated with environmental improvement, including the benefits of increased safety and health of the employees.

Waste minimization, for example, usually generates tangible benefits such as increased product yield and reduced waste management and disposal costs. But the intangible benefits, including reduced risks of violations and liability, better employee morale and participation, and enhanced company image and community relations, may be even more important.

Air and emissions monitoring, as mandated by the 1990 Clean Air Act Amendments, is usually regarded as another hassle that some plant managers have to put up with. But other managers see this as an opportunity. They feel that regular checking for volatile organic compounds and for leaks of hazardous materials helps keep equipment, valves, joints, and systems in good repair. That pays off in a number of ways—some related to costs and profits, and others with control of the environment.

Plants using hazardous materials have much to gain from monitoring employees who handle these materials. Although the training of employees in correct and safe procedures along with spill prevention and control helps to avoid accidents and injuries, you should periodically check their work habits. Observe whether they wear their protective clothing, use the equipment and tools recommended for the operation they are performing, and are careful when they are handling the materials.

A good way to promote environmental control is to make short presentations to employees on what the plant has done and is doing environmentally. Point out the many governmental regulations dealing with the environment, and explain how the plant is complying with them. Spill prevention and control is just one example in this area. To expand and make your point, you can give them a handout letter afterward that tells them the ways they can avoid spills on their jobs.

PRODUCT STEWARDSHIP PROGRAMS

Many plant managers today are under pressure to manufacture and process materials faster, more efficiently, and with higher quality than ever before. They are also expected to control costs at every opportunity in order to meet the competition. At the same time, plant managers must also contend with increasingly stringent environmental, health, and safety requirements under federal, state, and local regulations.

Although these regulations often seem to conflict with improving the plant's efficiency, environmental compliance and operational productivity are now going more hand in hand. The improved relationship is due in part to managers learning how to minimize the amount of wastes their plants generate. By working closely with materials manufacturers and hazardous substances suppliers, managers have been able to substitute safer chemicals in the plants' processes, to reduce wastes by recycling, and to modify other methods of handling by-products.

Complementing these efforts, more environmental assistance has become available to plants from a variety of product stewardship programs offered by product and service vendors. Production efficiency has benefited and administrative problems reduced through these programs.

Product stewardship programs promote the safe handling of chemicals from their development and manufacture through their distribution, use, and eventual recycling or disposal. These programs ensure that chemicals can be safely managed throughout their product life cycle. In addition, some product and service vendors provide assistance with compliance and right-to-know training programs. A number of environmental contractors also will be responsible for ensuring proper documentation of activities related to managing hazardous wastes.

COMPLYING WITH ENVIRONMENTAL LAWS

Your plant could get in serious trouble if you ignore environmental issues today. Yet it is very difficult to justify an investment in proactive management programs and process improvements when it is all you can do to keep up with the regulations. There are, however, a number of arguments to justify why an environmental project is necessary.[1] Negative arguments include:

1. *To avoid criminal enforcement actions.* The lesson here is learning from other people's mistakes. Employees at some plants are being penalized for what you might consider minor reporting violations.
2. *To avoid contractor-listing sanctions.* Under the Clean Air and Clean water Acts, the Environmental Protection Authority (EPA) is authorized to bar facilities that are guilty of criminal or civil violations from being awarded federal contracts, entering into federal assistance agreements, or receiving federal loans.

While negative arguments are persuasive, positive arguments are more beneficial. They include the following:

1. Recognizing that your plant's public image on environmental issues directly affects the company's profits and growth. Plants can improve their public image by using and producing environmentally conscious products and processes, promoting pollution prevention activities, and participating in voluntary federal government programs.
2. Adopting ways to incorporate environmental goals into the plant's total quality management program. A few examples are: substituting less-toxic raw materials for very toxic ones, installing solvent-recovery systems, and modifying processes to create less waste water.

Regulatory Agencies

Plant managers should be knowledgeable about the governmental agencies under which plants are regulated, the primary ones being the Department of Transportation (DOT), the EPA, and the Occupational Safety and Health Administration (OSHA). Perhaps the best way to learn about each agency and what it covers is to participate in a seminar or attend a training course.

Many universities currently offer such courses. For example, the University of Florida's curriculum consists of more than 250 professional development courses in the environmental, health, and safety areas of air quality, asbestos abatement, groundwater, hazardous materials, health and safety, landfill design, lead abatement, solid waste, water and wastewater. Over 5,000 students attend courses annually in a facility in Gainesville and at other locations in Florida and the United States. In addition to the public subscription programs, the university also provides site-specific training on a contractual basis.

COST ANALYSIS OF
ENVIRONMENTAL PROJECTS

Many of the problems plant managers face when justifying environmental projects are concerned with cost. Traditional cost analysis is heavily weighted on the cost of direct labor. But such cost analyses are proving to be inadequate in today's more technologically advanced industrial plants. Environmental liabilities, including regulatory issues, testing procedures, and occupational health and safety concerns, demand new approaches to costing.

By using a more accurate analysis, activity-based costing, for example, you allow for the hidden costs in complying with environmental laws such as technology modification costs for process improvements and new equipment, expanding recordkeeping, and similar matters. When you include these and other environmental considerations in the programs and systems you want to implement, you will have a more clear picture of the real costs involved in running the plant.

Activity-based costing considers many factors that are easy to overlook. These include:

- Permitting costs and the time associated with the application processes
- Compliance costs related to meeting federal, state, and local regulations
- Environmental auditing costs of current operations, and research costs to ensure the plant is not in violation environmentally in any respect
- Costs associated with any proactive environmental management programs the company initiates as a result of the auditing process

Avoiding Environmental Compliance Fines

With the current trend of the EPA to issue more fines than in the past, and the threat of the agency to continue the pace, be forewarned to keep up-to-date on this agency's regulations. Be aware also that a small violation in one area of your plant can lead inspectors to other areas and larger fines. Here are a few steps you can take to avoid or reduce fines:

1. Since inspectors can't check on every plant's operations, they look for companies that are most likely to be violating the regulations. Asking the EPA for their help and advice is an excellent way to show that your plant is sincere in complying with the regulations.
2. With some regulations, the EPA may doubt that you'll comply until they see you've done it. If your plant has been cited for a violation, quickly correct the problem and document your action. This documentation will give your plant credibility and, as a result, the regulators may reduce the fine.
3. Compliance violations sometimes occur not because *you* aren't aware of the regulations, but because your subordinates are lacking in that knowledge. Informing all employees of the rules and involving them in compliance procedures can increase their understanding and reduce the risk of the plant being fined.

PREPARING FOR DISASTERS

Plant managers must accept the responsibility of protecting the plant's employees and the nearby community in the event of an emergency or disaster involving the plant. With floods, earthquakes, tornadoes, hurricanes, and fires as possible occurrences, the job of preparing for any or all of these is anything but easy. According to Ed Pedranti, principal educational consultant for Factory Mutual, the problem is best resolved in five stages:[2]

1. The first stage in disaster preparedness involves assembling a planning team that is made up of executive-level managers from all of the various departments of the company. The team must meet to discuss the plant's vulnerabilities and prioritize those that are most important. Communications systems obviously have to be kept up and running. The establishing of priorities will then enable the team to develop a plan that allows people in any type of disaster to respond appropriately. The best course of action is to plan for the most likely disaster, keeping in mind that no two disasters are ever the same.

2. The next stage in emergency response covers methods of prevention and control. Handling a few basics such as good housekeeping and maintaining a clean workplace can minimize and even prevent disasters in plants. Other preventive steps include the installation of alarms and automatic sprinkler systems, ensuring there is an adequate water supply, and fastening the roof in tornado- and hurricane-prone areas.

3. Preparations make up the third stage. All employees should be trained and capable of carrying out specified functions if a disaster occurs.

This preparation includes notifying the employees anytime a change is made to the plan and reviewing the plan periodically. Materials that would be needed should be on hand at all times, and everyone should know where all the emergency-response materials are kept. Another important preparation step includes having all current emergency phone numbers on hand such as police, fire, and ambulance services. These numbers must be posted around the plant in easy-to-reach locations.

4. If a disaster occurs, the well-prepared company immediately takes action, first accounting for all employees, providing medical attention to those requiring it, and contacting all of the necessary emergency personnel—police, fire department, whomever. Next, if at all possible, employees should be allowed to get in touch with their families. Keep in mind that the response stage takes place only if the disaster is manageable. Some disasters are too serious to attempt control. Know which valves to shut off, which machines to shut down, and then evacuate.

5. Regardless of the severity or the nature of the disaster, the last stage is always recovery. Once the plant is declared safe to reenter, the extent of the damage can be assessed. Begin cleaning up and getting ready to resume operations, but see that this is done safely. Don't let an employee be injured by attempting to do something he or she is not trained to do.

SYSTEMS FOR MANAGING HAZARDOUS MATERIALS

Regulations specified by laws of governmental agencies are designed to protect the environment and to minimize risks to the community.[3] They do this in several ways by:

1. Specifying that full disclosure of hazards be made to employees and the community
2. Mandating procedures to ensure that the materials are used properly and the risk is minimized
3. Requiring that emergency response plans be developed to deal with accidents that may involve hazardous materials

While the laws have been in effect for some time, the amount of compliance paperwork continues to grow. Final responsibility under the law rests with the plant manager who delegates the hazardous materials tracking job to others, usually the maintenance department. This is a logical move because the department frequently deals with such materials more than other departments; and it may already have implemented an inventory management and reporting system as a part of its computerized maintenance management system (CMMS).

Although compliance records and reports for various laws differ, they often use common data. However, the job of getting the information together, organizing it so that it can be quickly retrieved, and putting it in the form required by the regulating agencies is almost impossible without help from the computer. The computerized information system or systems selected for managing hazardous materials must be capable of handling several functions. Here are the most critical ones:

- *Document management.* This involves the need to search and retrieve, create and update documents, and perform file management jobs such as copy, delete, and move. Additional considerations include the need for auditing, archiving, security, and access control. There are a variety of commercial systems available.

- *Materials data retrieval.* Hazardous materials management programs require extensive information such as the quantities of various materials that trigger reporting requirements and tables for learning the chemical construction of trade-named materials. Hazardous materials data are often put in material safety data sheets for on-line review or printing.

- *Materials management.* A tracking system must cover manual maintenance of a hazardous materials inventory and the associated transactions. Ideally, the system would have or interface with a fully functioning purchasing/inventory control system so that all materials that enter the plant would be covered. The system could also be set up to include hazardous material information with the work order and to track which employees were exposed to certain materials.

- *Regulatory compliance.* Companies are required to submit toxic chemical release forms if they conduct manufacturing operations, employ ten or more people, and manufacture, process, or use any of the toxic chemicals listed under the Emergency Planning and Community Response Act Section 313 in quantities above designated threshold levels. One form must be filed for each chemical.

Storing Hazardous Materials

It's commonly known that regulatory agencies, specifically the EPA and OSHA, increasingly levy heavy fines and even jail terms for the release of hazardous materials. The failure to store any amount of a hazardous material in a way that protects workers, the community, and the environment might lead to a citation. Furthermore, the burden of proof is on companies, not the EPA or OSHA, to demonstrate compliance.

However, there are ways your company can demonstrate its intent to comply with environmental and safety regulations. Among those are the isolation and secondary containment of stored hazardous materials. If your company stores hazardous materials in relatively small containers such as 55-gallon drums and gas cylinders, you should consider isolating those materials.

The minimum security step for the storage of harmful organic compounds, paints, solvents, strong acids and alkalies, flammable liquids and gases, and other hazardous material is a separate, secured storage area within the plant. To prevent tampering and vandalism, the area should be accessible only to authorized personnel. Also, if the nature of the stored materials warrants, some materials should be isolated from others by fire walls and doors to increase the safety of employees, firefighters, and the community in the event of a fire.

Another approach is to use a predesigned and preengineered building for the "outside" storage of hazardous materials. While OSHA officials and insurance underwriters often suggest this strategy, the EPA is given credit for these "hazmat buildings" in 1981 (40 CFR, Subpart I, Paragraph 264.175). The advantage to going this route is that manufacturers of these units obtain the relevant approvals from Factory Mutual, UL, NEC, and others. Their structures also conform to other standards such as the Uniform Building Code and the standards set by the Building Officials Code Administrators. In addition, some of these manufacturers continually review environmental laws and building codes, thus putting them in a position to recommend and, if necessary, design and engineer units specifically for your plant and the materials you store.

SPILLS OF HAZARDOUS MATERIALS

Hazardous material spill regulations were enacted by the EPA in 1979 and were published in the *Federal Register* shortly thereafter. These regulations apply to all facilities that might have chemical spills including industrial plants, storage depots, and transportation vehicles such as trucks, railroad tank cars, and tanker vessels.

Under these regulations, plants are responsible for immediately notifying federal authorities, as well as state and local authorities, when a spill or other illegal discharge occurs. Failure to report a spill or discharge of a harmful quantity could result in criminal penalties of up to $10,000, a year in jail, or both. The regulations also require those who are responsible for a spill to pay the costs of cleanup.

The hazardous material spill regulations do not apply to oil. Spill prevention regulations to stop oil pollution became law in 1974, at which time the EPA required that every company that handles oil or "oil-type" materials prepare and implement a Spill Prevention Control and Countermeasure (SPCC) plan.

The Clean Water Act also contains amendments covering spill prevention and control. These amendments to the act resulted in federal regulations requiring secondary containment of hazardous liquids. Secondary containment means that equipment must be designed and installations made to prevent materials leaking from storage tanks, processing units, piping, and liquid transport equipment from leaving the plant buildings, grounds, or premises.

The EPA has stated that about 75 percent of the liquids spilled end up in rivers, streams, lakes, and coastal waters. In other words, three out of four spills that occur in plants affect people outside those plants.

When a spill gets beyond a company's property, it affects the health and well-being of people in the community and beyond. A large spill, for example, can affect the community's drinking water; result in a fishing, swimming, and boating ban; contaminate beaches and shorelines; not to mention kill fish and wildlife. The government has and will continue to levy fines on the persons or companies responsible for spills when they affect society.

Don't overlook the danger to the plant employees when a spill occurs. In most cases, these people must contain the spills as well as clean up and dispose of them. When hydrocarbons are involved, there is always the risk of fire or explosion. Hazardous chemicals are a danger to people's health. Even small spills are a problem because they create slipping and falling hazards, delay production operations, and cause housekeeping problems. Accidents often occur in a situation where a spill has taken place. In addition, there are always the costs of the material lost and the cleanup operations.

Preventing and Controlling Spills

Plants are violating the law if they store more than 1,320 gallons of oil or oil-type material without having a Spill Prevention Control and Countermeasure (SPCC) plan. They are also subject to a penalty if they discharge harmful quantities of one or more of the hundreds of hazardous chemicals specified by the EPA in the *Federal Register.* Having a plan and carrying it out can save a company a lot of grief and money.

The SPCC plan can be developed and written by anyone but must be certified by a registered professional engineer. While the plan must be available at the facility for review by the EPA at any time, it is not submitted unless the facility experiences certain spills.

A facility is required by law to notify the EPA and submit its plan if a single spill of over 1,000 gallons occurs or if two spills of harmful quantity occur within consecutive months. When the EPA regional administrator reviews a facility's plan, he or she may rule that it is not adequate and that a better, more comprehensive plan must be made.

Spill Kits

Laws enforced by the EPA and OSHA encourage managers and operators of plants to have spill kits. Properly designed spill kits provide everything needed to control and clean up a spill. They contain the specific type of absorbent materials, patch and seal equipment, and anything else that would be needed for a particular type of spill. Some of the kits are portable so they can be quickly and easily moved from a central location to the spill site. Others are stationary or permanently fixed in an area where there is a high potential for a spill.

The stationary kits should be strategically located at key points throughout the plant and each one should be clearly marked. These locations should be specified in the written spill response plan and identified as follows:[4]

■ Risk points are locations where spills have not occurred but might in the future. Examples are: (1) hydraulic line gasket or joint locations, (2) industrial liquid line joints, and (3) hazardous liquid storage areas.

■ Source points are locations that have experienced spills in the past and where the probability exists for future occurrences. These points can be identified by examining the plant's records of spills. Likely points include: (1) horizontal drum dispensing stations, (2) fuel transport and fill pipe locations, and (3) collection ponds.

■ Flow points are critical drainage paths that a spill is likely to follow. Drain paths can be determined by observing the contours and slopes of floors, ditches, culverts, and other pathways. It is critical that the flow be secured in order to contain the spill within the least area possible and reduce further exposure or damage. Flow points include: (1) floor ducts, (2) drain pits, and (3) aisle gutters.

■ Exit points include places where a spill might leave the confines of the plant. Fines and penalties may be levied if a spill enters sewer systems, reaches groundwater, or contaminates neighboring property. Sealing the drains and berming or sandbagging perimeters are typical containment strategies. Exit points may include: (1) indoor and outdoor sewer drains, (2) plant doors and docks, and (3) property line culverts.

Selecting and Assembling Kits

Many types of spill kits are available from manufacturers and their distributors. Some have wheels and some have brackets to hang on a wall. Large kits are usually made of a durable material like metal or plastic which enables them to have a long service life. Where space is at a premium and spills of only five to ten gallons are likely, wall-mountable cabinets are appropriate because kits are off the floor and out of the way. Small kits are excellent for tight places such as behind truck seats, in vehicle trunks, or at individual workstations. Kits packaged in DOT-approved shipping containers, such as 55-gallon drums and corrugated boxes, serve a dual purpose. They can be used to dispose of spent absorbents after a spill is cleaned up.

The first step in assembling kits is analyzing what types of liquids might be spilled.[5] The characteristics of the liquids determine the type of response equipment that is contained in a kit.

Acids or bases require absorbent materials that will not react or break down upon contact with the liquid. A petroleum-based liquid spilled on water requires different response equipment than the same liquid spilled inside a plant. Oil-on-water spills require barriers or absorbents that float on the water surface and absorb the oil but not the water. Inplant spills may require a different type of barrier that conforms to a floor surface for good diking.

Other equipment in properly assembled kits includes types of required protective clothing such as suits, gloves, boots, goggles, and respirators. Miscellaneous items include patch and repair material for punctured drums or leaking piping, shovels, scoops, and other requirements for site-specific needs.

Maintaining Kits

It is essential that a kit inspection and maintenance plan be developed to ensure kits are always ready when needed. The plan can be implemented in conjunction with periodic inspections of hazardous material storage and hazardous waste accumulation areas, or it can be done separately. Periodically, management should check to see that all kits are located where they were placed and they are clearly marked. Additionally, an inventory of their contents should be taken to make sure they were resupplied after a spill. It is easy to verify the contents if inventory sheets are placed in the kits.

To maximize the security of kits' contents, limit access to them with tamperproof seals. Seals such as tape or locking ties that must be broken to open the container alert everyone that a kit has been opened and needs to be checked. Instructions on whom to notify if a kit needs attention should be posted on the outside of every kit.

SPILL RESPONSE TRAINING

Although spill kits are indispensable in contending with spills, training of responders is important and, in fact, required. Besides, the presence of a spill kit at a site does not mean that it should always be used. The conditions of the spill must be considered first.

A plant's response plan must specify the expected response action according to the conditions of the spill. With accidental spills, the regulations give first responders three choices: evacuate, contain, or abate. Thus plant employees must be aware of the nature of the spill as to its character, volume, and risk. Legislation requires two types of training:[6]

1. Normal operations training is mandated by the Clean Water Act, the Oil Pollution Act, Resource Conservation and Recovery Act, Superfund Amendments and Reauthorization Act, and other regulations. This type requires training of handlers of hazardous liquids as part of a total prevention strategy. It includes:

- Training on the awareness of the nature of the hazardous liquids in an operational environment. This awareness is generally communicated by Material Safety Data Sheets, which are distributed and reviewed with employees in the area.
- Training on the proper handling of liquids and equipment to ensure that a spill is not caused by operator error. When plant equipment is designed with safety features to maximize spill prevention, the training covers procedures that guard against employees inadvertently overriding these features.
- Training on the inspection and maintenance of the equipment to ensure that equipment failure does not cause a spill. Preventive maintenance can identify and minimize spill risks such as worn gaskets, weakened supports, severed hoses, ruptured drums, and the like.

2. Emergency response training is mandated by OSHA regulations (CFR 29, 1910) which require training to comply with Hazardous Waste

Operations and Emergency Responce standards. These standards require the creation of emergency response plans and the presence of HazMat teams at industrial plants that use hazardous liquids. The plan should be reviewed and certified by a registered environmental engineer and then implemented through a continual training program. While this training can be either formal or informal, it covers several disciplines as follows:

- Employees learn to recognize and report a hazardous spill at this training step. They become aware, also, of the location and characteristics of the hazardous liquids in the work environment.
- With this step, teams of employees receive training in controlling and containing spills. They are introduced to the proper personal-protection equipment to use, to the containment and control equipment, and to spill-stoppage procedures.
- In recovery training, teams of employees learn how to clean up spills and restore the environment to a safe place to work. They also get training in the use of instruments to measure hazard and impact levels of various spills.
- With this step, individuals with specific responsibilities are trained on ensuring that response actions are in compliance with regulations. These specialists will know, through the use of technical instruments, whether a response is proceeding effectively, whether responders are safe, and which outside authorities must be notified.
- Direction training covers the know-how required to direct the activities of employees responding to a spill. The individuals receiving this training have full authority and responsibility over activities until outside authorities arrive at the spill site.

WASTE MANAGEMENT

Current EPA regulatory standards have fostered a strategy of waste minimization as a first important step in waste management. The following sequence of procedural steps is recommended for waste management:

1. Promote activities that reduce or eliminate the hazardous waste generated by processes.
2. Consider the use, reuse, or reclamation of a waste, either onsite or offsite, after it is generated by a process.
3. Look into the possibility of using waste as a source of energy. Some wastes can be beneficially used for fuel under carefully controlled conditions.

4. Investigate treatments as ways to reduce the toxicity of hazardous waste.
5. Adopt land disposal, but only as a last resort.

In the last decade, the EPA has stressed the importance of effectively treating hazardous waste before disposing of it in a landfill. The 1984 Hazardous and Solid Waste Amendments to the Resource Conservation and Recovery Act of 1976 apply to companies that generate large and small quantities of hazardous waste. These include chemical and paper manufacturers, petroleum refineries, transportation equipment and machinery manufacturers, vehicle maintenance companies, metal manufacturers and finishers, and printing companies.

Using Sorbents

Treatment alone is not the answer to all hazardous waste problems. The EPA has always encouraged waste minimization through the reclaiming, recycling, and reuse of hazardous wastes, such as organic and chlorinated solvents, alcohols, water- and oil-based cutting fluids, petroleum products, paint thinners, and machine coolants.

Since many recycling and reuse techniques are complex and expensive, a simpler way is needed. One, often overlooked, is to use industrial sorbents. Sorbents are organic, inorganic, or synthetic materials used to recover and retain manufacturing or chemical liquids. Their high absorbency minimizes the amount of waste generated, significantly reducing transportation and disposal costs.

The effectiveness of absorbents is dependent upon their characteristics, the time required for them to become saturated, the amount of liquid they can hold, and the amount of liquid by weight that can be absorbed in relation to the weight of the sorbent. Early types of sorbents for use in plants were natural organics (corn cobs, wood pulp, and cotton) and inorganics (clay granules and silicates). Although these materials are low-cost and lightweight, they disintegrate in the presence of harsh chemicals and exhibit low sorption rates. Using them is labor-intensive and they are bulky.

With the advent of synthetic sorbent materials, these inadequacies no longer exist. Manufactured from polyolefins, they are inert and have high sorbency. Moreover, they are available in a variety of configurations including pads, rolls, booms, and pillows. Synthetic sorbents come in two categories, depending on whether they attract or repel water- or oil-based fluids. These properties dictate their appropriate use in cleanup applications.

AIR MONITORING

Air monitoring concerns the study of industrial and commercial sources of environmental contamination. A source can be the exhaust from a chemical hood, a coal-fired process, or a piping or duct system. Under EPA regulations called "Enhanced Monitoring," an untight cover on a 55-gallon drum of a solvent could be called a source and would be subject to inventory documentation and control.

Most of the air monitoring in plants involves studying pollution control devices such as scrubbers, baghouses, and oxidizers. The plant's air permit or EPA documentation, such as the Code of Federal Regulations, discusses the factors of duration, load, and testing routines. At one time, industry was allowed to meet the regulations by having the air monitoring tests conducted by others. Within the past fifteen years, however, federal mandates required plants to install permanent systems that either replace these tests or operate in conjunction with them. Such systems run continuously with daily calibration and they record system parameters.

These systems involve many engineering disciplines in their design, integration, installation, and use. A continual emission monitoring system monitors industrial smokestack emissions whenever it is operating. Some processes, like a boiler, may require monitoring twenty-four hours a day, and every day of the year. The particular variable to be monitored depends upon the source as well as air permit and pollution concerns.

Monitoring Fugitive Emissions

Environmental and safety considerations are requiring refineries and petrochemical plants to monitor fugitive emissions of several gases. Volatile organic compounds (VOC) are a class of gases that are released from industrial processes. Some are toxic, and all react in the atmosphere to form smog. The 1990 Clean Air Act Amendments place strict limitations on VOC air emissions levels, and impose large penalties for companies that do not comply. If your plant uses solvents or organic liquids such as xylene, toluene, ketones, or chloroethylene, then you are probably affected under these regulations. Your company needs to be familiar with the air emissions regulations and with methods to attain compliance. Your capital and maintenance planning must take these emission rules into account to be competitive.

Fugitive emissions often indicate a nonoptimized process or equipment failure (pumps, valves, flanges, and control systems). To be effective, emission monitors must be capable of notifying operating personnel of an emission and its concentration. By using laser spectroscopy, monitors continuously measure and report trace concentrations of selected gases. The laser's wavelength identifies the specific gas monitored. Changing the laser to a different output wavelength allows other gases to be monitored. These units should have a response time and sufficient sensitivity to alert maintenance crews or automatically initiate emergency mitigation procedures.

Handling Fugitive Emissions

Fugitive emissions can be handled in two ways:

1. Open path monitors are capable of sensing a selected gas over a line-of-sight path that may extend up to 600 feet. Multiple open path units can be set up to form a perimeter or fenceline monitor around an area where potentially hazardous materials are produced, stored, or handled. An open path monitor can also be used to measure across a stack or duct.
2. Process control monitors continuously sample gas from a process stream. The unit reports the target gas's concentration within the sample to the operator of the process.

CARBON MONOXIDE

Carbon monoxide is the most toxic of the common air pollutants. Because it is a by-product of energy use, it is potentially present at excess levels. Exhaust gases of gasoline-fueled engines are a common source of carbon monoxide. If engines are not operating properly either because they are overloaded or poorly maintained, carbon monoxide production is increased. Other sources are forklift trucks, combustion-engine-powered tools, and heating systems.

Plant employees who may be exposed to high levels of carbon monoxide should be taught about its serious health effects. Unlike the smell of auto exhaust, it is an odorless, tasteless, and invisible gas with cumulative effects. At high levels, it can kill rapidly or cause irreversible damage. Employees should be trained in emergency response for leaks or breaks in gas lines or exhaust lines and know how to use appropriate respiratory protection.

Governmental agencies and other organizations have established standards or levels for carbon monoxide that they consider safe for workers and the community. However, each bases its standard on the population it wishes to protect; thus their "safe" levels differ. EPA's ambient air standard is 9 parts per million averaged over 8 hours and 35 parts per million for 1 hour. Workplace standards set by OSHA are 50 parts per million for 8 hours with a ceiling (15-minute average) of 200 parts per million.

Because of the extreme toxicity of carbon monoxide and its poor warning properties, preventing exposure to the gas is the best way to contend with it. Preventive steps that can be taken without incurring great expense include:

- Determining if there is a problem
- Assessing the seriousness of the problem
- Deciding if individuals have the ability, from a health standpoint, to work at carbon monoxide levels at or higher than the standard
- Training and educating individuals who work in areas where elevated levels are potentially present

Carbon monoxide can be detected readily with meters that use electrochemical sensors. While these meters are able to measure it in the very low parts per million range, you must realize that the instruments do not respond instantly to carbon monoxide. Since it takes time for the air to be moved from the probe tip to the sensor, the longer the connecting hose, the longer it will take to respond. Meters may require almost a minute to respond to the existing carbon monoxide concentration.

When sources of carbon monoxide are identified, you should immediately set up a maintenance program to improve combustion efficiency to reduce the amount of gas emitted from fuel-powered appliances and other sources. Where the output cannot be reduced because of intrinsic processes, continuous exhaust ventilation may be necessary and periodically increased for those processes that intermittently produce very high levels of carbon monoxide.

SECONDARY CONTAINMENT OF PIPING

Since a leak in a pipe carrying a caustic, acid, toxic, or flammable material can have a catastrophic impact on a plant and the community, there is a need for a secondary containment piping system. Concerns for plant employee safety, liability issues, and the environment are strong and relentless. That's why more and more companies have decided to install a means of secondary containment of both above- and belowground plant piping.

To select the best system for your plant, you have choices ranging from a simple ditch to a complete double-wall piping system. The former uses an open trench lined with concrete or some type of liner material to carry by gravity any fluid leaking from pipes to a common collection pool. But aside from not being conducive to modern leak detection instrumentation, this method of containment presents other problems.

For most plant applications, the best secondary containment piping system consists of a supply pipe surrounded by a conduit or jacket. This is generally known as a double-wall or dual-containment piping system. Depending on the nature of the chemicals involved, the primary pipe can be any of the common piping materials used today. When liquid or vapor sensors are installed in the annular space between the inner and outer pipes, the double-wall system will be compatible with automatic leak detection and monitoring instrumentation. These devices can be connected to a remote monitor that can activate alarms or shut down equipment automatically if a leak occurs.

In designing a double-wall piping system, consider the primary purpose of the secondary pipe. If it is meant to provide structural integrity to protect the supply pipe as well as to protect against leakage, avoid thin-wall polyethylenes and choose a schedule 80 PVC or steel jacket, one that is not subject to degradation or corrosion.

STORM WATER REGULATIONS

While there have been no new storm water discharge regulations from the EPA in the past few years, if there is any question in your mind about the need to have a permit, you should apply for one. Operational changes and stronger-than-federal state regulations aside, companies requiring permits are:

- Those conducting "heavy" industrial operations including manufacturing, recycling, transportation, publishing and printing, construction and demolition, grading, and excavation.

- Those conducting "light" industrial operations including those covered by Standard Industrial Codes to which storm water regulations apply, those that expose potentially polluting raw materials, intermediate or finished products, material handling equipment, or other significant materials to storms.[7]

Here are the general requirements of these permits:

1. Issuance of a mandate to certify that no nonstorm-water discharge is leaving a site by way of a route that conveys storm water.
2. Implementation of a storm-water pollution prevention plan to ensure that a company identifies potential sources of storm-water pollution.

3. Adoption of the monitoring of storm-water discharges. Although frequency and reporting requirements vary from permit to permit, once-a-year sampling is a minimal requirement.

AVOIDING PROPERTY LOSS FROM FIRE

In business and industry, where property losses can be catastrophic, astute managers actively work to prevent and control the elements of property loss from fire. Since statistics show that the average fire loss can be significantly reduced with an effective emergency response, managers should focus on getting employees to participate in a loss prevention program. Empowered employees are the key to a successful program because they understand that their actions protect the plant and their jobs.

Factory Mutual Engineering and Research has conducted comprehensive studies that identify the frequency and severity of losses. The results show that the leading causes of industrial fires are as follows:[8]

- *Electrical ignition.* This usually occurs from overheating or arcing in electrical equipment. To avoid such losses, train employees to operate equipment properly, know the kinds of electrical problems that result in fires, and understand what action to take when an electrical malfunction occurs. Employees should also be empowered to shut equipment down in the event of trouble.

- *Arson.* The most common arson scenario involves a disgruntled employee setting a fire in an unsprinklered storage area between the hours of 6 p.m. and 6 a.m. Effective arson safeguards include: well-designed plant security; proper screening of new and potential employees; and encouraging employees to challenge visitors in nonpublic areas of the plant.

- *Hazardous processes.* Many industries are vulnerable to fire and explosion hazards involving combustible dusts. Depending on the type of operations in a plant, employees must be committed to the safe handling of hazardous processes. They also need training on operating equipment safely.

- *Hot work.* Brazing, cutting, grinding, welding, soldering, and using torches for miscellaneous operations are considered hot work. Responsibility for fire safety begins with managers who must adopt a policy that clearly states when, where, and under what conditions hot work may be performed. A hot-work permit system is necessary to ensure that both employees and contractors follow safe procedures.

- *Flammable liquids.* The vapors of most flammable liquids easily ignite, burn fast and hot, and create intense fires that can spread quickly, often becoming uncontrollable. Spill fires of flammable liquids are most commonly the result of human error.

▪ *Smoking and inadequate housekeeping.* These are major causes of fires, particularly in high-hazard locations that store or process combustible materials. The best preventive action against smoking-related fires is employee support in the plant's smoking policy. Employee participation in good housekeeping practices is essential in preventing combustible conditions.

The potential for loss continues, however, despite much loss prevention activity by plant managers. Even though automatic sprinkler protection, fire detection, alarm systems, and the assistance of a local fire department complement your loss prevention efforts, the importance of an emergency response plan designed specifically for your plant cannot be overemphasized. An effective emergency response team, including a trained fire squad, consists of employees who can handle various fire fighting roles on a 24-hour availability.

COMPLIANCE WITH THE EPA

Because we are dealing with federal law, much of what has been presented in this chapter is quoted from the Code of Federal Regulations published by the EPA, or closely follows the wording in EPA publications.

The information and data given here are only a small part of that contained in the many pages of laws and regulations. Any legal interpretation of this information should come from qualified professionals.

NOTES

1. Philip L. Brooks, "Justifying Environmental Projects," *Engineer's Digest,* April 1993, pp. 40–41.
2. Larry Beck, "Preparing for the Worst," *Engineer's Digest,* September 1995, pp. 42–48.
3. Excerpts from "Managing Hazardous Materials Information" by Robert C. Baldwin, *Maintenance Technology,* July 1993, pp. 23–24.
4. Excerpts from "Spill Kits Are Key to EPA, OSHA Compliance" by Thomas Lutzow, *Chemical Processing,* May 1994, pp. 80–82.
5. Douglas Rhodes, "Using Kits as Effective Spill Response Tools," *Maintenance Technology,* August 1994, pp. 17–19.

6. Thomas Lutzow, "Specifying Kits for Spill Responses," *Engineer's Digest*, December 1993, pp. 89–90.
7. Excerpts from "An Update on Storm Water Regulations" by Larry Beck, *Engineer's Digest*, May 1995, pp. 29–33.
8. Jeffrey Mattern, "The Human Factor in Property Loss," *Plant Services*, November 1995, pp. 62–63.

Index

About the Author

W. H. Weiss holds a BS degree in Chemical Engineering from the University of Illinois and an MBA degree from Kent State University. A Certified Plant Engineer and a Professional Engineer in the State of Ohio, he became well known as a speaker and chairman at National Plant Engineering and Maintenance Conferences over a twenty-five year period.

Mr. Weiss's industrial career consists of forty-four years' experience in five different manufacturing plants in various management positions. Job titles included: Plant Operating Engineer, Maintenance Engineer, Development Manager, and Manager of Engineering. As a Corporate Engineer for Goodyear Tire & Rubber Company, he helped implement the use of computers in several engineering and maintenance departments in the company's tire plants. Presently, he is a consultant in the field of industrial management.

Mr. Weiss has written more than 1,000 articles on human relations, engineering, maintenance, and management for a wide range of management journals and trade magazines. In recent years, he has served as Editor-Midwest for *Plant Services* magazine and has written numerous articles for many of Dartnell's publications. He is also the author of several books: *The Art and Skill of Managing People*, *The Supervisor's Problem Solver*, *Decision Making for First-Time Managers*, *Supervisor's Standard Reference Handbook*, *Manager's Script Book*, and *Plant Supervisor's Complete Desk Book*.